The Share

Shepherd's Guide for End Users: 2016

Robert L. Bogue

AVAILTEK

www.SharePointShepherd.com

(This page was intentionally blank before we decided to put this message on it about it being intentionally blank. Now it's just mostly blank, except for this message. Carry on - there is nothing to see here.)

The SharePoint Shepherd's Guide for End Users: 2016

By Robert L. Bogue

Cover Design: Arnel Reynon

ISBN-13:

978-0-9824198-2-3

Printed in the United States of America

For more information about this book, including frequently asked questions and corporate licensing, please visit us at http://www.sharepointshepherd.com/2016.

Get the SharePoint Shepherd's Guide for End Users

Corporate Edition

Make the book more accessible to you and your users. The Corporate Edition of *The SharePoint Shepherd's Guide for End Users: 2016* is a searchable productivity aid for all of the users in your organization. Get answers when you need them without carrying another book.

Visit www.SharePointShepherd.com/2016 for more information.

About the Author

Robert Bogue is a thought leader on all things SharePoint and an engaging presenter who speaks at events around the world. Rob has been awarded the Microsoft MVP designation fourteen times, and earned recognition as a Microsoft Patterns and Practices Champion. Rob holds certifications from Microsoft: MCPD, MCITP, MCTS, MCSA: Security, MCSE as well as CompTia: A+, Network+, Server+, I-Net+, IT Project+, E-Biz+, CDIA+. Rob also served as a team member for the Microsoft SharePoint Guidance (http://www.microsoft.com/spg).

He is the author of 25 books, including *The SharePoint Shepherd's Guide for End Users* series which is also available as a Corporate Version. Rob is committed to "making the complicated, simple." Find out more about SharePoint made simple at http://www.SharePointShepherd.com or follow Rob's blog at http://www.ThorProjects.com/blog/. You can also email Rob at Shepherd@SharePointShepherd.com.

Dedication

For my lovely wife, Terri.

Acknowledgements

The problem with acknowledgements is they're not long enough. There's no way to spare the space to thank everyone individually for the ways that they've enriched my life or have helped me to grow. If you're in this group, I appreciate your friendship, guidance, and patience.

Contents

(This is the second page that was intentionally blank before we decided to put this message on it about it being intentionally blank. Now it's just mostly blank, except for this message. Carry on - there is nothing to see here.)

What is The SharePoint Shepherd's Guide for End Users: 2016?

In the old days, being a shepherd meant having the responsibility for the care and guidance of a flock of sheep. Sheep need a relatively large area to graze to sustain the flock. Protecting a flock might mean the difference between life and death for the family or social unit who depended upon them. Shepherds guided the sheep into safe meadows and protected them from predators.

The book you hold in your hands (or read on your screen) is designed to provide the same sort of protection that a shepherd of old would provide. It's designed to help guide you to green pastures. You'll not only learn some of the tasks that you can do with SharePoint, but also exactly how to accomplish those tasks. You'll get the core skills needed to be successful with the immensely powerful platform that is SharePoint.

The book will also guide you away from bad practices or simple problems that can be inadvertently created by missing a simple step, accidentally including a space in a name, or generally just making a mistake.

Information in this book is presented in a simple, step-by-step style. Need to do something in SharePoint? Find the specific task to guide you and follow the easy to understand, illustrated steps. We'll walk through the process of doing nearly everything that an end user might want to do in SharePoint. We'll point out along the way how different fields are used and what might go wrong if you try the process.

To a new user, SharePoint may seem daunting and confusing. With this book to guide you, you will see that the way to a greener pasture of SharePoint knowledge is not as difficult as you think.

Introduction and Decision Trees

Although the *SharePoint Shepherd's Guide for End Users* is specifically designed to deliver direct how-tos for accomplishing many things in SharePoint 2016, it is also recognized that there are times when background information is needed to better plan your SharePoint deployment. What are SharePoint's capabilities, and more importantly, what are the decisions you need to make when working with SharePoint resources?

In this section, you will learn about:

- What is SharePoint?: Fully understanding what SharePoint is can be challenging, but there are many things that are easy to understand about SharePoint and how it can be a part of how you work.
- What is a Content Type?: The real magic of content types isn't in the ability to define fields and processes. The real magic is in the idea that you can put multiple content types in the same document library (or list).
- How Do I Manage Versions?: SharePoint supports versioning for both list items and for files. You don't have to rename the file to know which version is which.
- How Do I Get Notified of Changes?: There are three basic ways that SharePoint can notify you of changes.
- Content Containers: SharePoint provides a variety of content containers, from the larger (such as Site Collections) to the smaller (like folders), to organize your content and manage your site. Each container has different benefits and drawbacks, so deciding which container to use can be a challenge in itself.
- Choosing the Right Site Template: SharePoint Server 2016 Enterprise Edition offers 18 site templates out of the box. Trying to figure out which template is the right template to create is more than a bit challenging, particularly if you've not seen the templates in use.
- Create a List or Library App: With SharePoint's document libraries having so many features that are similar to lists – particularly the ability to store additional metadata with the file – it can be confusing to decide whether you should be creating a list or a library.
- Organize with Folders or Metadata: The decision of whether to organize data with folders or with metadata is a classic problem that's been with SharePoint for many versions.
- Managing Permissions with Active Directory Groups or SharePoint Groups: A common question about managing security in SharePoint is how to control the users who have – or do not have – access to the system.

- **Creating Forms**: There are various different ways to create a form out of the box between SharePoint and Office. This provides a wide variety of options for you to capture data; but there are other considerations that you should factor into the overall decision.

What is SharePoint?

SharePoint may be a teenager now, having been released more than 15 years ago. However, many people are still having trouble understanding it and describing it. An old skit from *Saturday Night Live* (Season 1, Episode 5) talks about a fake product called Shimmer that is both a floor wax and a dessert topping. This idea, that a product can be more than one thing, has often been used to talk about SharePoint. Because SharePoint is such a versatile tool, it's often quite hard to describe. Consider for a moment how you might explain a Swiss Army knife to someone who's only ever seen a regular three-blade pocket knife. How would you explain eating utensils on a pocket knife? The situation with SharePoint is much the same – it's pretty hard to describe until you're using it.

Let me offer another analogy before we get into the meat of what SharePoint is and does. When you were very young, you didn't know how to ride a bicycle. You saw older kids doing it, but you had never done it yourself. No amount of explanation from your parents or your friends could help you understand what riding a bike feels like.

Fully understanding what SharePoint is can be an impossible task. With more than 15 years of experience working with SharePoint on a daily basis, I still don't know everything there is to know about the product – but neither does any one person at Microsoft. Despite this, there are many things that are easy to understand about SharePoint and how it can be a part of how you work. At the most basic level, SharePoint is a web-based system. That means all you need is a web browser to access SharePoint. The information you get from the web browser will vary somewhat, depending upon how SharePoint is being used. Let's first look at SharePoint as a collaboration tool, and from there, we can move on to how SharePoint can be a communication tool.

Collaboration Tool

One of my favorite things to ask is this: What does the word "collaboration" mean to you? The term is often used and rarely understood. Most people think it means "working together," which is somewhat odd because collaboration tools often allow you to work together – while being apart. The next time you hear the word collaboration, you might want to ask, "Do you mean to conspire with the enemy?" That is one of the dictionary definitions.

For the most part, there are two kinds of collaboration. The first kind is real-time: collaboration interactions that happen immediately or at the same time. This is the kind of collaboration that happens in a face-to-face meeting - that is, if any collaboration happens at all in the meeting. Real-time collaboration is all about the dialog, people interacting at the same time for a common goal.

The second kind of collaboration is – stunningly – non-real time. That is to say, the collaboration doesn't happen at the exact same moment for both parties but, rather, occurs after some elapsed time. The best example of this is email. You and a friend or colleague can be working together to plan a party or create a response to a request for proposal. Even though you are working together, it's unlikely that you're doing it at the exact same moment.

Microsoft (and others) offers solutions to the real-time communication problem, such as Microsoft Skype for Business (formerly Lync). While SharePoint integrates with whether someone is available or not (called "presence information") on a SharePoint page, SharePoint is not, itself, a real-time collaboration tool. SharePoint activates Skype for Business and displays an icon next to a person's name, indicating their status using the same iconography and coloring provided in the real-time communications tool.

In the non-real-time category of collaboration, SharePoint is like that Swiss Army knife – there are numerous tools that are available inside SharePoint to help you work with others, whether they're in the next office over or halfway around the world. There are really two key ways to think about the kinds of things on which users collaborate: documents and data.

Document Collaboration

The first key type of collaboration is with documents, such as working together to create a final output document. It could be a policy, a proposal, a PowerPoint presentation, or an Excel spreadsheet. Whatever the document is, you need to get the input from multiple people into the same single document. Historically, this has been handled through file shares, or more popularly through email. The problem with email is that it's difficult to find the right version and it consumes a lot of mailbox storage to keep pushing back and forth different versions of the same file.

SharePoint has a set of tools designed to manage the process of collaborating on documents. First, SharePoint offers version control. You can keep different versions of the same file on the system. This eliminates the problems associated with trying to manually track the file by incrementing a version number and prevents accidental overwriting of other users' work. The versioning feature, like most other features in SharePoint, is configurable, so that you can turn it off or on and even control how the versioning works. SharePoint allows you to limit the number of versions, as well as to control the type of versioning – either simple versioning or using major and minor versions.

Major and minor versions open up the concept of publishing – or approving – documents so that everyone can see the latest published version, but contributors – those with write access – can also see up-to-date working copies. This allows documents to be worked on in the same place that users consume them – if you want. Also, SharePoint allows you to require that documents be checked out before editing and can, by using out-of-the-box and custom workflows, even help to facilitate the approval process for a document.

You also have a set of records management functions that enable you to declare documents as official records for the organization, and therefore subject to a more restrictive set of policies for deleting or changing the record. SharePoint also has the ability to apply rights-management policies so that, even if a user downloads the document, it can still be protected from unauthorized access.

Another thing to know about how SharePoint manages documents is that SharePoint allows you to hold additional metadata for a document. Metadata literally means "data about data". In this case, it's the properties associated with the document. There are some automatic properties that all documents have, including those stored on your local computer. Files have names, sizes, creation dates, modification dates, etc. With the exception of the names, other automatic file properties are considered automatic metadata. It's information that the system added to the file for you.

SharePoint supports automatic metadata, but in contrast to a regular file system, you can add your own metadata to a file.

This custom metadata can be anything you want. Perhaps you want to store the customer's name, the lead referral source, the type of products being sold, or nearly anything else. Once the data is stored, you can then view the list of documents not just by name and folder, as you could on a hard drive, but also sorted, grouped, and filtered by any of the metadata that you've entered. This makes it easier to navigate large volumes of information easily. It also means that you can treat metadata about documents just like any other list of data.

Finally, SharePoint can work with the client application OneDrive for Business to synchronize files from SharePoint onto the file system of your local computer. This synchronization process allows you to work on files that are stored in SharePoint even when you're not online.

Data Collaboration

Document collaboration is what we do when we push documents back and forth via email, but there is other data that we collaborate on – or use to collaborate – that doesn't fit easily in documents. Consider for the moment a group that's working across the world. It might be useful to know what time zone each participant is in, what office they're located in, and perhaps their mobile telephone number. SharePoint allows you to create any kind of list data you want – very much like you would create columns in an Excel spreadsheet.

In the case of team members, it might be a matter of creating a new contacts list – one that has the kinds of fields that you would expect in an Outlook contact – and add fields for time zone, office, and mobile phone number. The list could then be accessible with these additional fields on the web to be sorted, grouped, and filtered.

Contacts may or may not seem like an obvious kind of data list with which you work. There are numerous others, though. Tasks lists are simply lists of tasks to be done. Calendars are simply a list of appointments. Announcements to communicate with the group are simply notes. However, there are two key differences between SharePoint and using a more traditional method, like storing the data in a spreadsheet.

The first is that SharePoint has a much richer set of options for the fields. Because a spreadsheet is designed to be rows and columns, it's sometimes hard to include pictures, or large blocks of formatted text. Since SharePoint treats each entry as a separate record and automatically generates a data entry form for you, it's easier to add fields that would be difficult to do in a spreadsheet.

Second, and perhaps more important, when you put a list of items in an Excel spreadsheet, only one person can work on that list at any given time. So Suzi and Fred can't both be completing their tasks at the same time. SharePoint, however, stores these as individual items in a collection and allows both Suzi and Fred to make updates to different items in the same collection at the same time.

Going further, SharePoint allows you to apply version control to an item. This allows you to keep older versions of the item for review. Consider the case where you have task items for a project. SharePoint can automatically track when updates were made and by whom, by keeping versions of the same record. This means that contributors don't have to be as focused on what each other is doing. They can simply do their work and allow SharePoint to do its job coordinating the activity.

Communications Tool

The ability to work on information together is just one piece of the puzzle. What about how to disseminate that information to the appropriate parties inside the organization? That's a fundamentally different problem than tracking revisions and enabling collaboration. As a communications tool, SharePoint has a set of key features that allow you as the user to control its appearance and how the data is displayed to the consumers.

Building Pages from Parts

Rarely does the user get to create his or her own web page. While some online portals allow users to select their components and the order that they appear, in most corporate environments, everything is pre-assigned and rigid. That isn't the case in SharePoint. One of SharePoint's key features is the ability for anyone to build a page from a set of components – called Web Parts. Even more impressive is that SharePoint allows you to configure these Web Parts to suit your needs.

Web Parts have what are called properties. These are settings that you – the user – can control; these properties make the Web Part behave the way you want it to. In some cases, the properties allow you to control which view is displayed in the Web Part. Other properties control the title and location of the Web Part on the page.

SharePoint ships with numerous Web Parts, including Web Parts for showing the members of a site, for allowing you to add static content, to insert other pages as a part of your page, etc. Developers in your organization and at third-party companies can write Web Parts, which are added to the gallery of available Web Parts that you can then add to a page.

More recently Microsoft has been migrating to a terminology of App Parts. Though App Parts are functionally equivalent to Web Parts, they're technologically different. For our purposes App Parts and Web Parts can be used interchangeably as they sometimes are in the SharePoint user experience.

Creating Your Own Pages and Sites

Your control of SharePoint isn't limited to adding parts to pages – you can add pages themselves. You can select from a template or create your own pages. These new pages can have Web Parts placed on them as well. The benefit of being able to create your own pages is that it allows you a way to show different contents to different people – or to contain different types of content that may not belong on the same page.

For truly separate topics, SharePoint allows you to create your own containers, called apps, which were formerly known as libraries or lists. Sites can have different security, navigation menus, and pages. Sites are like folders except more powerful. While SharePoint allows you to secure folders, sites allow you to change how users are grouped and assigned security. This allows you to tailor the experience of different groups of consumers based on varying sets of criteria.

Here too Microsoft is shifting terminology and you may sometimes hear List or Library used. Other times you'll hear Apps used. Further confusing things is that Microsoft used to call third party add-ins Apps – and they've not reverted to calling them add-ins. While the language may be confusing, the function is not. Apps, whether created internally or through a 3rd party add-in, add functionality to your site.

Quick Wiki

Wikis derive their name from the Hawaiian word for "quick." The wiki concept is designed to be quick and easy. There are several implementations of wiki – perhaps the most popular is Wikipedia, which rivals the information held by traditional encyclopedia companies. Wikis themselves are designed to allow untrained users to quickly create and connect information. Instead of the <A HREF="http://sharepointshepherd.com">SharePoint Shepherd</A> notation that a web page would require, a wiki allows you to build links by simply specifying the title that you want for the target. For instance, [[SharePoint Shepherd]] creates a link to a page titled SharePoint Shepherd.

What's better is that wikis included in a SharePoint implementation will automatically allow you to create the page after you've created (stubbed out) the link. By clicking on the link to SharePoint Shepherd, you'll be given the opportunity to create the page if it doesn't already exist. The net effect is that it takes very little effort to create knowledge repositories that are connected to one another.

SharePoint extends this model by allowing you to add Web Parts to a wiki page. This means that the content and links that you've created can sit side-by-side with a Web Part, showing the results of a query, the temperature in Alaska, or status from some third-party system.

The benefit of a wiki is plain in terms of speed to get content into the system. The negative to wikis is that pages tend not to have the same look and feel, nor does the navigation seem to have any structure to it.

Structuring Web Content

In communication environments, particularly where you're communicating with the public, the key concern isn't always how quick the content can be generated, but instead is how easy it is for the consumers to consume. This means that the pages should have a consistent page layout, and that the navigation should be created in a planned way – that is, architected. SharePoint allows you to publish structured content through a set of features called publishing features. These features allow for the creation of page layouts – page templates – into which content can be added. The page layouts are varied by content type so that some of the pages can have more fields than others. Users can create new pages by selecting a new page and the layout they want to use. The content is added into the entry boxes in the layout and, when completed, the output is merged into a single page that the user can see.

The beauty of this arrangement is that the page is stored relatively pre-built in the database so it can be returned to quickly, but it's also stored in its component parts so that it's easy to change the appearance of the page when the company changes its name or its branding. Power users can create the page layouts themselves so it's easy to create new types of content and layouts for it. It leaves the power of managing the appearance of the site to the user.

In addition to the ability to control – and change – the appearance of content, SharePoint includes several components designed to dynamically build the menus. By dynamically building menus to match the content that has been created, SharePoint minimizes the amount of effort that must be spent considering how to create the navigation and how to keep menus up-to-date. Further, SharePoint includes a page for Manage Content and Structure that allows you to move the content around, thereby changing the structure and menus which are dynamically generated. With all these tools, it's probable that your site will seem navigable. Of course, some users won't know how to navigate through your site's structure and will need another way to find the information they're looking for – that is where search comes in.

Leveraging the Power of Search

Unlike older systems that allowed you to only search for things within special fields, SharePoint includes a full-text search capability that can extract the text from documents and allow you to search that content for information. SharePoint ships with support for several of the most popular file formats, including text, xml, the Microsoft Office suite of applications, and Adobe's Acrobat PDF file format. There is also extensibility support to allow third-party vendors to plug their own search apps into SharePoint.

Beyond being able to search content stored in SharePoint, the search engine can be configured to index information in File Shares, Exchange, and nearly every kind of system that you can imagine if you're willing to build the XML file that specifies how to get to that content. The result is that SharePoint can be an enterprise-level tool for finding information.

SharePoint's full-text search capability can even reach out to other systems through federation. This allows you to run the same search on your intranet that you run on the Internet – at the same time. SharePoint also allows for the use of faceted search, using the metadata that SharePoint stores on a document or list or library item to further refine the result sets.

Consider that you're looking for a specific presentation on the topic of wind power that you know was given to the ABC Corporation in May. You can search for "wind power abc corporation" and receive a relatively large set of results and then click on a link on the set to limit your results to the PowerPoint presentation type. You can further refine the results to those where the client is identified as ABC Corporation by clicking on the dynamic list of customers that was generated from the results. Ultimately, you can even click into a date range to shrink the scope of the search results to a more manageable level. Often, one, two, or three facets will quickly reduce the number of results to a handful (less than a page). The impact of this is that it is easier to find the results that you're looking for – quickly.

Faceted search relies upon the correct metadata being filled out by users as they upload content to the system. That's something that is facilitated by the upload process – and by the Microsoft Office clients themselves.

Adding Office Client Applications

One of the key challenges in any content management system is getting users to apply metadata or storage location consistently. SharePoint is different than most other content management systems because SharePoint leverages the Office client applications to facilitate the addition of the metadata by the users when they're creating the document.

One Microsoft Word feature is QuickParts, which allows the user to enter data into the document directly and have that data promoted to metadata properties automatically. Another is the document information panel (DIP), with an InfoPath form that appears at the top of the document to specify properties. Both aid in the capture of metadata in the document. SharePoint promotes the properties in the documents to metadata in the SharePoint document library. This can dramatically simplify the process of capturing the metadata necessary to route documents (SharePoint's Content Organizer can move documents to new locations based on metadata).

Office client integration also includes the ability to take SharePoint data offline. and to synchronize calendars and contacts to Outlook. This means that SharePoint can be your storage repository for your data even if the primary way that you access that data is to leverage office tools like Microsoft Office and Outlook.

What is SharePoint Designer and Do I Need It?

For the most part, SharePoint is a web-based system. Most of the changes that you do for SharePoint are done from a web browser. There are some cases where you will use a free tool called SharePoint Designer. SharePoint Designer also allows you to create your own workflows so that you can create your own automatic responses to how data flows.

If you're allowed to install software and you're going to use SharePoint, then you should install SharePoint Designer and see if it can help you out.

Conclusion

There are dozens of features not mentioned in this brief introduction to SharePoint. The point here is to give you a flavor – not enumerate every feature. An enumerated feature list can be found at http://www.microsoft.com/sharepoint.

If you have a better way to explain what SharePoint is, please drop me a line at Shepherd@SharePointShepherd.com.

What is a Content Type?

Content types are mentioned more than occasionally in the SharePoint documentation that you see online and the guidance that you hear from experts speaking at conferences. It's one of those things that makes SharePoint very powerful – but in some ways equally confusing.

Let's start with the problem that content types are designed to solve. You have a set of different kinds of documents that you may want to work with that might really be best if stored in the same place. Consider the idea that you are in a sales role and that you work with customers on a variety of projects. Each time you need to do a proposal, there are several different kinds of documents that are needed. For instance, you might need to do a PowerPoint file as a face-to-face presentation for the customer. You might also need to develop a pro-forma profit and loss (P&L) analysis for approval by management. Further, you might also need to develop a formal offer letter.

The fact is, the files themselves are different and need different approval processes, and perhaps they differ in the amount and type of metadata that is required. For instance, doing a presentation to the customer may not require any approvals. The P&L might require approval by finance. The formal offer letter might require both financial and sales management approval.

On the metadata side, you might require that all the different documents require the customer ID number for the proposed project. You might require a projected one-year and three-year profit for the P&L. The formal offer letter might require an offer date and an offer expiration date.

SharePoint handles the need for different metadata and different approval processes with a content type. A content type collects a set of rules, including the fields and the processes around the content. The formal offer letter might include the fields as well as an approval workflow that includes both finance and sales management.

Content types form a hierarchy; that is, a content type can derive from another content type. So, in our example, we might create a content type called customer document, which includes the field for the customer ID. The formal offer letter could derive from the customer document type and pick up the customer ID field. In this way, you can make changes to a whole set of content types by modifying their shared parent content type.

The real magic of content types isn't in the ability to define fields and processes. The real magic is in the idea that you can put multiple content types in the same document library app. In the management of a list or library app, there's an option to enable content types. Once enabled, you can connect a library to an existing content type – in other words, to an existing definition. When you add the content type to the library, SharePoint automatically adds the fields of the content type to the library. Then, when a user saves a document as a specific content type, SharePoint displays the fields that apply to that content type on the edit form.

One benefit of the content type approach is that if you create lists in different subsites, you can ensure that all of the libraries have the same definition for the data – because they're using the same content type. Without content types, the creator would have to manually verify the creation of each field and ensure that the processes including workflows are assigned correctly.

With a basic understanding of what content types are, it would be natural to be curious when you might want to use them. Certainly one common scenario was laid out here – where there are several different kinds of documents in the same library with different data storage and processing needs; in other words, use them when you want to store dissimilar things in the same place. However, the opposite reason is also true.

Consider the idea of forms on your Intranet. Some forms come from IT. Some forms come from HR. Some forms come from Accounting. However, when someone wants a form, they don't want to have to know whether the form is a HR form or an IT form or an Accounting form. They want to be able to get the form they're looking for. By using the same content type in IT, HR, and Accounting, it's possible to leverage search to look only for items matching that content type. The net result is that you can get a searchable list of forms regardless of their source location. In this case, content types are good because they provide a way to bring together the same data located in different areas of the organization.

Content types aren't limited to just the columns, templates, and workflows we've discussed above. Content types are also a way to give developers a way to extend functionality in SharePoint. Some examples are customizing forms used for creating list or library items (New/Display/Edit forms), adding custom actions to a list or library app item (event receiver), or detailing specialized permissions (Information Rights Management).

How Do I Manage Versions?

Most people have struggled with version management at some point in their career. There's been some sort of a snafu where the wrong version of a letter, a presentation, or a spreadsheet was used. Many of us have gone back into email to try to find the "latest" version of some important document. Those of us with battle scars have taken to adding identification to the file itself in the form of a "V1" appendix to the regular file name. Others have settled on adding the date to the name of the file as a suffix. These strategies work when you have multiple versions to look at side-by-side, but fail miserably when you can't remember what the last version was and don't have time to hunt down all of the versions.

Luckily, SharePoint can save you from these challenges. SharePoint supports versioning for both list items and for files. You don't have to rename the file to know which version is which. Once enabled, SharePoint will automatically keep previous versions of the file – up to the limit you set – without any further action from you. This prevents the user errors that sometimes overwrite good versions of the file with bad changes, and makes it easier to be certain that you have the latest version.

Let me sidestep the conversation of document versioning for a moment, since that conversation is more detailed – and better understood. I have said that SharePoint supports versions of list items as well. This means that you can see who changed what in each item in a list. This can be very handy when you're trying to piece together what happened with a task, issue, or other item. Items support "simple" versioning, where each new version gets a new, incremental whole number. So the first version of an item is version 1, the second version is version 2, and so on.

The versioning settings are on the list or library settings page. They're important enough to get the second link from the top-left of the settings page. Enabling versioning for the list is as simple as turning on the *Version History* option. On libraries, the versioning information allows for enhanced features beyond the basic incremental versioning supported on lists.

In addition to basic versioning, files can have major/minor versioning enabled. This versioning takes each draft (non-approved) version and assigns it a new partial number. For instance, the first version of a draft document is 0.1 and the next non-published version is 0.2. Once published, the version number is converted to a whole number. So 0.2 could be come 1.0 if the version is approved.

The implication of major/minor versioning is that the public (those with Read permissions) can see the approved versions (whole numbers). Users with contribute access have access to see both the approved version as well as the current draft version.

Consider the scenario of an employee handbook. Most employees in the organization get to see the most recent approved version – and might be allowed to even see the previously approved versions. The HR department can work on the draft versions of the document in the same place that users are getting the previous approved version. When HR approves the latest draft, it immediately becomes available to all of the employees of the organization.

In some cases, simply managing versions isn't enough. There are times when it's possible to overwrite the changes of another user. If all the users are connected online to SharePoint when making changes, SharePoint will prevent a second user from opening a file up for edit if another user is editing it. This is very useful because it prevents most situations where there might be problems because of users overwriting each other's work. (If both users have Office 2010 or later, they may be given the option to co-edit the document.)

However, consider for a moment a user who is using Office to take files offline. They make changes while they are disconnected on an airplane. When they synchronize back, their changes may conflict with changes made on the server while they weren't connected. While Word has a very good set of conflict resolution tools, PowerPoint and Excel – as well as non-Office files – don't have the same benefit. In this case, SharePoint does allow a user to formally check out a file. Once a file is checked out, no other user can modify the file until the file is checked in or someone discards the check out.

It's possible to require checkout on an entire document library so all files must be checked out to be edited. In practice, this is rarely used because it's generally not worth the extra hassle to have to check out the document to edit it; again, SharePoint will handle letting folks know that a document is being edited if everyone is online.

SharePoint is good at notifying users that the file is checked out. It adds a small arrow marker over the bottom right of the document icon to indicate the file is checked out. Additionally, there's a "Checked Out To" field that will show the name of the user who has the file checked out. Finally, if you attempt to edit a document that is checked out, you'll receive a dialog prompt indicating that the file is checked out and isn't available for edit.

With all these features, it can be hard to decide how to best handle your situation. As a general rule, basic versioning is used in all collaborative cases where you just want to protect yourself from accidentally overwriting someone else's changes. Major/minor versioning is used when the documents are public documents that are revised by a small group of people. As already mentioned, the *Require Check Out* feature is used for special cases where there is zero tolerance for accidentally overwriting things. Finally, every user should check out a document they intend to edit before they go offline to indicate to other users that they intend to modify it.

The one thing that you won't have to do is append the version number to the file or a date to manually manage the versions yourself.

How Do I Get Notified of Changes?

Knowing when something changes is a trick in any organization. Of course, the person making the change can let you know that they've done it – if they know that you need to know about the change. SharePoint can help if you're interested, even if neither the data nor the person who updates the data knows that you want to know about the changes. There are three basic ways that you can be notified of changes.

Perhaps the most popular way to get notified of changes is to use the *Alert Me* feature that is found both on the Files and Library tabs. This allows you to receive an email alert for a particular file or for all of the files in a library. These alerts can be sent immediately, daily, or weekly. This allows you to be notified of changes automatically.

Another popular technology for monitoring changes is Really Simple Syndication, more frequently referred to by the acronym RSS.

SharePoint apps and searches are capable of providing an RSS feed via a specially formatted link. This becomes a summary of the latest data in the app. It's also possible for search to provide RSS. RSS feeds, as these links are called, can be displayed directly in Internet Explorer, in Microsoft Outlook, or in a dedicated news reader software. Additionally, these RSS feeds can be formatted and displayed on SharePoint pages.

The benefit of getting information as an RSS feed is that you can have the speed of an immediate alert with the efficiency of a daily or weekly alert. Immediate alerts are sent – surprisingly – immediately. That means that multiple changes will give you multiple emails. It also means that each individual change is found in a separate message. There is no summary view that can show you all of the recent changes together, as would happen with a daily or weekly alert message. An RSS feed allows you to see the summary of changes like those delayed emails with the ability to hit refresh and get immediately updated data.

Internet Explorer and Outlook allow you to track the same feeds in a shared space called the Windows Common Feed list. This means that Outlook can periodically check the RSS feeds and provide access to them offline like you would have with emails.

In addition to SharePoint Alerts and RSS feeds, there are other techniques you can use to get notified that something is changing. You can create workflows in SharePoint Designer that are designed to notify you only when certain criteria are met. For instance, let's say that you're a manager who has given your employees purchase order request signing authority for $1,000, but you want to know any time they submit a purchase order request for more than $250. You can create a workflow on the purchase order request document library. You can set a criterion of amounts more than $250 and have a special email sent to you. That email could contain additional information from the purchase request, including the requestor, the cost center, the vendor, etc. Anything that is promoted to the properties of the file/item can be used to form the message to you. The benefit of this is that you'll be able to better control the information you want to see without looking at the items themselves.

Whatever option you choose, SharePoint makes it easy to be notified of changes.

Content Containers: Site Collections, Sites, Libraries, Folders, and Pages

When gathering leftovers from a meal, sometimes one of the most challenging aspects is picking the size of the container to hold the food. On the one end of the spectrum, you have the option of one large container that you're sure will fit everything – but may have problems fitting into the refrigerator. On the other end, there's the smallest container but that runs the risk of not holding all the leftovers - and the need for another small container to hold what didn't fit. Then, when you're going to use the leftovers, you may be pulling from multiple containers.

The problem with deciding which SharePoint container is similar. There are benefits and drawbacks to both larger (site collection) and smaller (folder) containers inside of SharePoint. We'll walk through them so you can make the best educated guess on the right size container for your needs.

Scope

The place to start with what kind of container to create is much like where you would start with deciding how big a container to put in the refrigerator – that is, how much stuff are you trying to contain? If you're looking to create a space for a handful of documents, then the smallest container you can create – a folder – is likely (but not certainly) the right answer. Conversely, if you're looking to address the collaboration needs of an entire department, then you may be looking to create a large container (a separate site collection).

Site Collections

Site collections must be created by a SharePoint administrator; they can't be created by users. While they have a large number of specific benefits that the other container types don't have, they have a number of limitations as well.

The biggest benefit is that a site collection is a level of isolation for security. There isn't any way for someone who isn't in a site collection to be accidentally provided security. There's a hard security boundary for the site collection that is useful when security is the utmost concern.

Site collections are also the boundaries for managing storage and resource utilization quotas. If you're concerned about marketing overrunning your available storage by placing large pictures or videos online, then you may need a site collection to prevent them from consuming too much. Server resources for sandboxed user code host solutions is a lesser concern given the fact that Microsoft has deprecated that type of solution – but it's still a good boundary to have available to you.

The final benefit to site collections is the ability to scale. SharePoint's scalability and performance is really centered on the site collection level. Because of this, the more site collections you have, the greater ability you have to prevent one group from impacting another.

The deal breaker for most folks when it comes to using site collections is the requirement for an administrator to create them. If you're not an administrator and you can't request a site collection be created for you, then you're stuck without creating a site collection as an option.

Site collections also have separate navigation. If you're trying to keep navigation the same across your environment, then you'll have to use some special tricks to keep navigation the same between sites. It's easy enough to just copy navigation from one site collection to another when you get things started – however, if you end up with a dozen or more site collections and your navigation changes frequently, you'll soon wish you had the convenience of shared navigation.

Sites

Often you want to organize information into a hierarchy of containers. Site collections are always at the highest level, so you can't create hierarchy in them. However, sites allow you to create child sites of child sites and so on until you have created the kind of organizational structure that you want. While hierarchy is also available for the other smaller container types, the site has the unique benefit of being the only hierarchical container that can contain other sites, lists of items, pages and files.

While SharePoint is a powerful enterprise content management (ECM) system capable of managing large numbers of files with a high degree of control, it's also a great tool for managing lists of items, whether it's a list of contacts, a list of appointments, a list of tasks, or some custom list. A site can contain any kind of list as well as any kind of library. This means that sites are one of the most flexible containers available.

Also, since sites are designed to be viewed with multiple pages, they provide a place when you want to have the multiple views that different pages provide. Each page can display a different view of the data in the site.

Libraries

Libraries themselves are containers for files. However, libraries also allow you to do more than just hold files. You can define, by content types, the types of files you want to hold, with each having its own template, workflows, and fields. Libraries can also have specific retention schedules applied to them. That is to say, if your organization requires that some records be destroyed or reviewed at a certain time, you can set these settings at a library level.

Libraries are the container to use when you only need to store files but the files themselves have different requirements. From the way that versions are managed, to the fields that are collected for the document, libraries allow you to control how the files are handled.

The key limitation with libraries is that they're not hierarchical. They all exist at the root of the site. Thus they're not as flexible as folders. This is sometimes mitigated by placing libraries inside a hierarchy of sites, but with the disadvantage of needing an extra navigational click to get where you want to go.

Folders

Folders are a very common way of organizing files. They've been with us since nearly the beginning of computers. They're the lightest weight and smallest type of container that you can create in SharePoint, and what they lack in flexibility they make up for in sheer ease and simplicity.

If you know that you aren't going to need the additional capabilities that creating a library or a site will offer, why go to the trouble of creating them?

Page

A page is a different kind of container. Instead of containing documents (and other items or files), it contains text and web parts, which are often views into other areas of the site. The beauty of pages is that they allow you different views of the same information. They're at the heart of publishing sites and wiki libraries. Having multiple pages allows you to have filtered views of what's in a site, as well as view the same information from multiple perspectives.

Since pages aren't containers in their own right, they come up as a decision when you're wondering whether you should create a separate site for something. If you need to view the same information multiple different ways, it may not be that you need a separate site – you may just need a separate page.

	Advantages	Disadvantages
Site Collection	Storage and Resource Quotas Security Isolation Overall Scalability	Administrator Required Separate Navigation Separate Query
Site	Hierarchy Lists and Libraries	
Library	Content Types File Handling Settings	Files Only Non-Hierarchical
Folder	Hierarchical Simple	Limited
Page	Different Display	Not a container for files

Choosing the Right Site Template

SharePoint Server 2016 Enterprise Edition offers 18 site templates out of the box. Making a decision on which one to use for your site isn't exactly straightforward. However, by asking a set of yes or no questions, you can quickly walk through the key criteria for picking the right site template for you.

First, there are four templates that don't even make the decision tree. They're so specialized and designed for administrators that you'll probably never create them. They are:

- Developer – This template is used by developers who are creating solutions with Visual Studio for SharePoint.
- My Site Host – This is used by IT administrators who are setting up profiles on SharePoint.
- Community Portal – Used by IT administrators to create a place where users can find community sites on SharePoint.
- Product Catalog – A starting point for creating a product catalog on SharePoint for Internet publishing.

The decision tree has three basic sections. First, you get a set of screening questions to handle special-use cases; second there's a less-common section that handles less commonly-used cases; and finally, the last block of questions handles the most commonly-used cases. They're handled by first eliminating the odd and less-common templates, then making the decision among the core templates that you're likely to use most often.

In the screening group, there are three key questions and site templates:

- Journal or Blog – If the primary purpose of the site is a blog – or a running journal of information, then the Blog template may be the best choice. It's specifically designed for this purpose.
- Business Intelligence – If you're building a site for reporting on information and helping the business to make better decisions then the Business Intelligence Center is the way to go.
- Flowchart Library – If you are going to be creating a library for process flows in your organization using Visio, the Visio Process Repository may be the answer.

In the less common – but still important – category, there are two key questions: is the site for formal document management, and will its primary purpose be for search?

The first question in this group is whether the site will be for formal document management – that doesn't mean simple version control of documents, but rather a large-scale document management or knowledge management initiative with or without regulatory compliance needs.

If you're doing formal document management, the next question is whether the site will be an official repository for records. In this case, the right answer is the Record Center template, which is set up to handle records management. If not, you need to consider if you're creating the site to manage eDiscovery requests. eDiscovery are electronic discovery requests that are caused by legal cases or regulatory requests. You'll know if you need to create an eDiscovery center for compliance events. If not, you'll probably want to start with the standard Document Center template.

The second major decision in the less-common block is whether the site will be used primarily for search. If so, you'll have to decide whether you need multiple search interfaces in the same site – in other words, a tabbed interface. If yes, then you'll need to use the Enterprise Site template, which includes the built-in capability to include multiple search and result pages. If a simple site without tabs will do, then you can use the Basic Search Center.

The final block includes the most common templates. In this block, the major questions are whether the site will be used primarily for communication (vs. collaboration), whether the site will be project-specific, and finally whether you anticipate more than 100 users.

Communication sites are different than collaboration sites. If the site will be primarily intended for a small number of people to communicate with a large number of people, then it is a communication site. If it's a communication site, the next question is whether the information will be unstructured – in other words, a collection of random notes. If that's the case, an Enterprise Wiki with its less structured approach may be ideal.

If it's for structured communication, you simply need to decide whether you're going to have a formal approval workflow. Of the Publishing Site and Publishing Site with Workflow templates, the Publishing Site with Workflow template is used for more formal approval situations.

If the site won't be for communication, the next question is whether it is project-related. That is, will the site be associated with a single specific project; in that case, you'll probably want to use the Project Site template.

The last question is the basis of the site. Are you building a site to have conversations or manage documents? If you're doing a conversation-based site, you'll want to leverage the Community Site template. If instead you're focused around management of documents, you'll want to use the Team Site template.

With those questions answered, you should have determined which of the 18 site templates that may work best for your situation.

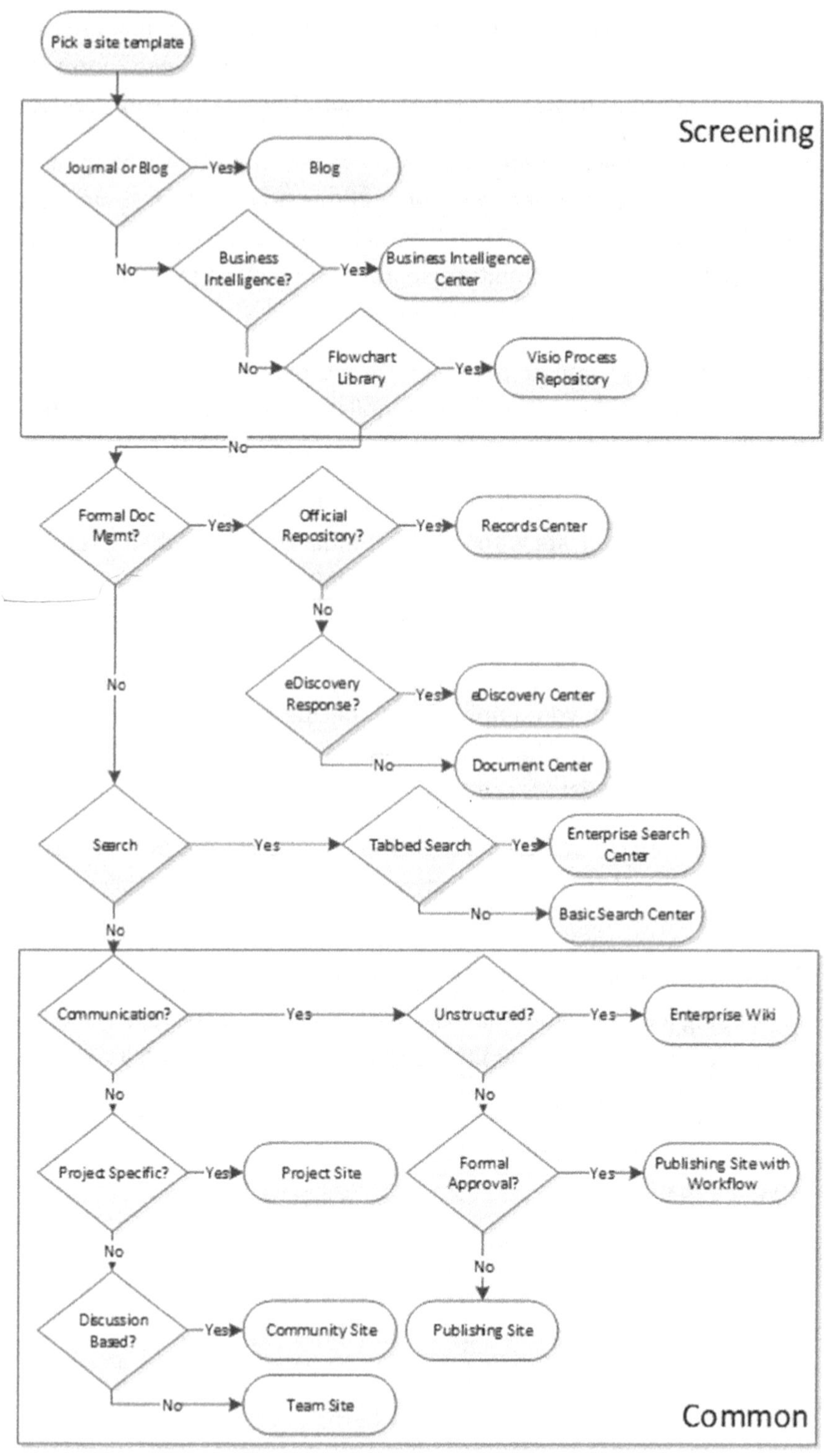
Pick a site template
Screening
Journal or Blog
Yes
Blog
No
Business Intelligence?
Yes
Business Intelligence Center
No
Flowchart Library
Yes
Visio Process Repository
No
Formal Doc Mgmt?
Yes
Official Repository?
Yes
Records Center
No
eDiscovery Response?
Yes
eDiscovery Center
No
Document Center
No
Search
Yes
Tabbed Search
Yes
Enterprise Search Center
No
Basic Search Center
No
Communication?
Yes
Unstructured?
Yes
Enterprise Wiki
No
Project Specific?
Yes
Project Site
No
Formal Approval?
Yes
Publishing Site with Workflow
No
Publishing Site
No
Discussion Based?
Yes
Community Site
No
Team Site
Common

Create a List or Library App

Starting in SharePoint 2013, the constructs of lists and document libraries have been merged into one unified name, known as "Apps". Despite their unified name, lists and libraries operate differently enough that it's important to know what kind of an app you're creating when you create a new list. SharePoint's document library apps have many features that are similar to list apps – particularly the capability to store additional metadata with the file. It can be confusing to decide whether you should be creating a list or a library app. There are certainly some limitations with creating a library app – but there are extra features as well.

As a starting point, it's useful to think of a library as a special case of a list. The key difference with a library is that a library has one and only one attachment per item. Document libraries still have all the same metadata that a list has but they also have a single attachment. There are additional features for document libraries, but the relationship between the metadata and the files is the most fundamental.

The first decision to make is whether you'll need to make the files (if there are files) available via File Explorer. This includes the ability to use OneDrive for Business to synchronize files from SharePoint to your local machine. These features are only supported via libraries, so you'll want to select a document library for your information.

The next consideration is whether you'll be using folders. Folders are technically possible in lists but are rarely done, and all of the user interface isn't optimized for the idea of having folders in a list. Thus, if you need to organize by folders, you'll want to use a library as well.

The next consideration is versioning. Major (sequential) versioning is available for both lists and libraries, but major-minor versioning with approvals and publishing is only available for libraries. So if you're going to want to have "published" versions of the content, you will likely need a library.

Similarly, the ability to promote properties in Microsoft Office documents to metadata and the ability to save to SharePoint directly from the Microsoft Office applications only works with files in libraries, not with attachments on lists. So if you need this functionality from Microsoft Office, you'll need a library.

The last decision is a bit trickier. On the surface, if you need data without a file or you need multiple files for a single item, you need a list. Lists allow for zero as well as multiple attachments.

However, since SharePoint 2010, we've had a workaround for wanting zero or more than one attachment by thinking of the problem in terms of a document set. Consider that you have some sort of an approval process which needs some information and perhaps some supporting documentation. In this case, even though there may be zero or more than one attachment, it may be possible to continue to use a library app – by leveraging the document set. A document set is really a folder that has properties – and the ability to have a customized start page to change the way the "folder" looks – different from the default metadata a list app has. Utilizing this approach, it's possible to work around the idea of having zero or more than one attachment. This workaround is something you would use only if you needed zero or multiple attachments and you needed some of the other functionality – if you don't need things like File Explorer access or direct access from Office applications, the effort of creating a document set isn't worth it.

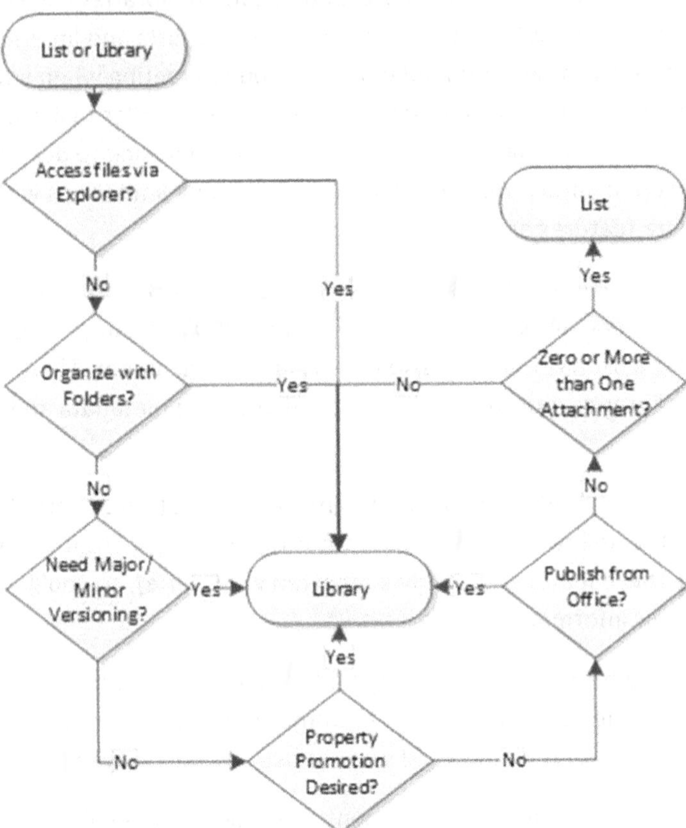

Organize with Folders or Metadata

The decision of whether to organize data with folders or with metadata is a classic problem that's been with SharePoint for years. The problem with this decision is that there are key limitations to both approaches, some of which require a difference in the way you think about the problem.

For instance, in the past, using metadata for storing information in SharePoint meant that you couldn't open the files in the Office client applications because they only understood the folder hierarchy. With Office 2010 (or greater) and SharePoint 2010 (or greater), it's possible to see a metadata view of the files – but only if metadata navigation is turned on in SharePoint.

On the other side, there are key limitations which cause issues with file names, including folders and host names that exceed 260 characters. In those cases, the Office client applications will refuse to open the files directly; they'll have to be saved locally, then opened in the Office client application – and then re-uploaded to SharePoint. Obviously, this isn't the most efficient way to operate.

The good news is that SharePoint's features – and the capability for Office to view metadata navigation when enabled – make it less difficult to find a balance between the two approaches.

The first deciding factor for whether you need to use folders for organization is whether you're using a method of access to the library app that doesn't support metadata navigation. The most common reasons for this are using the Explorer view of a folder, or synchronizing the folder via OneDrive for Business. These simply don't support viewing the files by metadata; they only support a folder concept. Similarly, if users are often opening files from Office client applications directly, folders may be necessary – unless all the locations they navigate to support metadata-based navigation and you can train users how to use that in the Office clients – some pretty big ifs.

The second key factor that might lead you to folders is the need to have individual security on files. Often documents in a library app have one set of security, but in some cases, it's necessary to have different permissions for different groups of documents. In this case, it's important to create folders. Performance with large numbers of access control lists (unique security) for each folder falls off quickly. By organizing contents with similar security into folders, the number of unique access control lists is minimized. This can be critical for larger libraries.

There are two factors that might lead to the decision that metadata is required. The first is that not all users navigate to the data in the same way. For instance, assume you're a clothing manufacturer that makes shirts in different colors and in different sizes and styles. If some of your users navigate first by size and others navigate first by style, you'll need something other than a folder structure to allow them to navigate in ways that they're comfortable with – and that's metadata-based navigation. Similarly, if you have a folder structure that would lead to more than 260 characters in the web address (URL) for the folder, you'll need to use metadata, since several problems happen once path lengths – including the host name – exceed 260 characters. Specifically, you won't be able to directly open the file in an Office client application.

If none of these criteria apply to you, then selecting either folders or metadata-based navigation should work fine. The bias is that metadata-based navigation is better from an information architecture perspective – but it's not enough to pull you away from a folder-based structure if that's what your users are able to work with.

However, SharePoint has two features that help mitigate the challenges of making a forced choice between folders or metadata. Default column values is a feature of document libraries that allows for default metadata to be set when the metadata is blank. This can be used to transform folder-based structures into the metadata that metadata navigation needs and that is useful for search.

Conversely, the *Content Organizer* feature allows for users to set metadata, and SharePoint then uses this metadata to migrate the content into the appropriate folder. This strategy allows you to start with metadata and end up with folders if you have a user (or a system) that is more comfortable with metadata than folders.

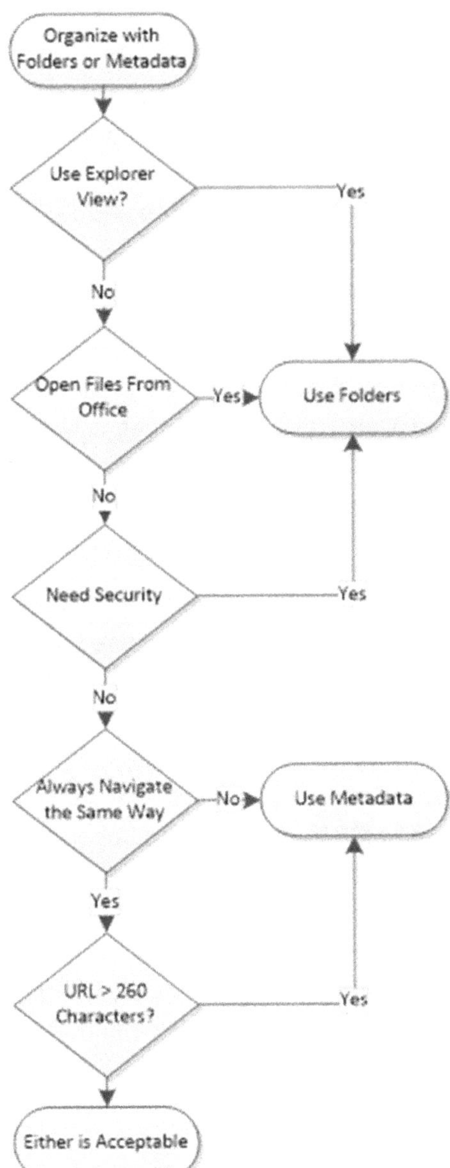
Organize with Folders or Metadata
Use Explorer View?
Yes
No
Open Files From Office
Yes
Use Folders
No
Need Security
Yes
No
Always Navigate the Same Way
No
Use Metadata
Yes
URL > 260 Characters?
Yes
Either is Acceptable

Managing Permissions with Active Directory Groups or SharePoint Groups

A common question about managing security in SharePoint is how to control the users who have – or do not have – access to the system. Obviously, individually managing permissions for individual users can be time-consuming and tedious – especially if the users all fall into one or two permission levels. It is much easier to add a user to a group that has the right permissions in the right places than to establish security individually for each user. While this is clear, the question about whether or not site administrators should use SharePoint groups or Active Directory groups isn't so clear.

It's first important to review the types of groups that SharePoint supports. The first type of group that SharePoint supports is a SharePoint group; that is to say, SharePoint knows the precise membership of the group, because every user has to be manually added in SharePoint. The obvious limitation to this approach is that the group is scoped to SharePoint – it can't be used for any other purpose except for security in SharePoint. Less obvious is the fact that a SharePoint group is scoped to the SharePoint site collection it was created in. That means the group cannot be used in another site collection on the same farm.

The second type of group that SharePoint supports is an Active Directory group, an identity management framework inherent in Windows servers. The Active Directory group looks to SharePoint to be just another user during the setup of security. The group is added to permissions – or to a SharePoint group – just like any other user. The benefit of an Active Directory group is that it can be used across site collections and can be used outside of SharePoint. The disadvantage of an Active Directory group is that it's not easy to display the membership of the group to a user who is curious about who is in the group. Similarly, in most organizations, not everyone can add or remove members of a group: generally, the IT administrators or the help desk must make changes to group membership. Because of this, managing Active Directory groups is generally harder for an end user than managing a SharePoint group. However, the consistency in being able to use the group in every site collection, and by non-SharePoint applications, may mean that the extra hassle is worth it.

Making the decision between an Active Directory group and a SharePoint group isn't always as simple as it could be. The following decision tree can help you decide between an Active Directory group or a SharePoint group.

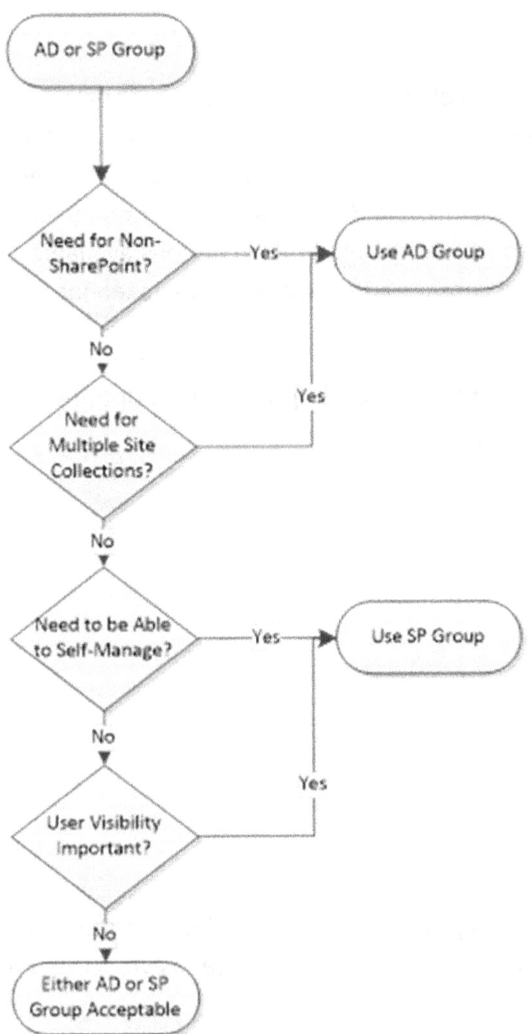
AD or SP Group
Need for Non-SharePoint?
Yes
Use AD Group
No
Yes
Need for Multiple Site Collections?
No
Need to be Able to Self-Manage?
Yes
Use SP Group
No
Yes
User Visibility Important?
No
Either AD or SP Group Acceptable

Creating Forms

The best way to create a form has plagued us since the dawn of personal computers. We've moved from an era when most forms were paper to one in which most forms are electronic. However, what technology should you use to create the forms that your organization needs? Part of the reason that this is even a question is that Microsoft and third parties offer many different ways to create forms for capturing data. Let's take a look at the major form options available for SharePoint installations, and then review the additional considerations that must be taken into account.

Form Types

Just out of the box, SharePoint and Office offer four different options for how to create forms. The expanded list of options includes:

- List Form
- Word Form
- InfoPath Form
- PowerApps
- Fillable PDF
- Third Party
- Excel

With any form, the objective is to pick the right answer for capturing the information you need. Each of these approaches has a set of benefits and weaknesses as we'll cover in the following sections.

List Forms

If you create a list in SharePoint, it will create for you a default form. The form will have the field names you've used, display the descriptions, and, more importantly, will implement any of the validation that you've defined for the fields and for the record itself. SharePoint creates this form automatically by default, so it's a good starting place for our discussion.

The challenge with the default list form is that it's fixed. Whatever SharePoint generates is what you get. You can't add an image or instructions to be displayed to help folks to fill out the form without going through some unnatural gyrations. Because the form is automatically generated, it does what it does and customization isn't really much of an option.

List forms directly publish the values to the list, and so the process of getting the data in SharePoint is straightforward.

Word Forms

Most of the forms in your organization currently are probably already Word forms. They may not officially be Word document templates, and they may not have fields for the users to fill in, but they've been saved and shared by administrative users throughout the organization for years.

Because users are familiar with Word forms, making more Word forms is easy. It's something that the administrative users, who have already been creating the forms, can be taught to do quickly and easily.

Built into SharePoint is a functionality called "property promotion". This allows properties in documents to be promoted into metadata for the list or library. Word has a feature called QuickParts, which allows document properties to be synchronized with the main text of the document. So, for instance, I can put a fill-in field for an invoice number on the form, and this will be converted to a property. Through property promotion, these values are further elevated to fields inside of SharePoint.

Thus, when users save their form, they're uploading the data values to the library. Because Word forms are actual documents, they're saved in a library rather than a list. The good news is that the metadata from that library can be exported and used in Excel or Access, just like any other list. The bad news is that you can't preconfigure the file name to save the document as. Your users will have to create their own file name for their document when they save it. This can be a real annoyance for some users.

Word forms also can't handle data that has a one-to-many relationship. One example of this is an expense report that has multiple lines on it. Capturing each line in an expense report would require multiple fields per line, and in practice this becomes very unwieldy quickly. Finally, the Word form will only do the validation that SharePoint can do for the fields. It can't do math or validate anything more than what SharePoint will do.

InfoPath Forms

SharePoint has had a long love affair with InfoPath. Despite InfoPath being a legacy technology, SharePoint list forms can still be designed with InfoPath Designer. InfoPath is a powerful forms tool built on XML technology. It's great at building forms with validation and supports a great set of tools for managing multiple views. However, its reliance on fixed schemas make the forms difficult to update.

InfoPath forms are substantially richer than either List Forms or Word forms. In addition to calculations and validations, InfoPath forms can directly read from other data sources to validate information. However, this richness comes with a learning curve that many people find hard to master, particularly for the everyday forms that administrative support team members create.

InfoPath forms tend to be the kind of forms which are complicated and for which IT helps build. Their basis on XML means that they're relatively easy to integrate into other systems when more complex data structures are needed.

In general, if you don't have InfoPath expertise today, you're unlikely to develop this skill just to create new forms for your organization. You'll want to look for another forms solution – unless the need for automation is so great that it justifies learning more about InfoPath.

PowerApps

If you have the option of using Office 365 and relying on a cloud-based service, you may be able to use PowerApps, which is Microsoft's cloud-based technology for forms creation. It's designed to be a native HTML forms generation tool that's easy to use and powerful. When coupled with Microsoft's Flow workflow technology, PowerApps forms have the potential to be a great way to capture information, and to handle the complex scenarios that InfoPath previously handled with less learning time and quicker returns.

Since this technology is evolving and not everyone has access to using it, it's unclear how effective the tool will be at being a form replacement.

Fillable PDF

It's relatively common for folks to ask about the ability to use fillable Adobe Acrobat PDF forms in their SharePoint sites. It is, after all, probably the most common electronic form technology on the planet. Unfortunately, SharePoint out of the box does not support fillable PDF forms.

There are third party options which enable fillable PDF forms to be used with SharePoint, but these are additional solutions that must be purchased. Additionally, to create a fillable PDF, you need the for-fee Adobe Acrobat Pro, which not everyone is licensed for.

As a result, fillable PDF forms aren't the best solution for SharePoint forms.

Third Party Forms Solutions

There are numerous third party forms solutions that plug into SharePoint. Some of them are integrated into the SharePoint environment, and others are hosted by other servers and the data is pushed to SharePoint. In either case, there's a cost associated with the third party forms solution in terms of installation effort, maintenance, and, of course, licensing fees.

Excel

Excel has a number of advantages as a form technology, including the ability to do calculations and validation. It's perhaps the second most popular form technology behind Word. Cell protection creates opportunities for the template to be protected while allowing users to enter data. These would seem to make it a great candidate for a form solution inside of SharePoint. Unfortunately, Excel doesn't promote any of the data it captures to SharePoint, and as a result it's difficult to capture and summarize data across individual files.

Form Considerations

Capturing the data is just one part of the problem. While it's the most visible, there are other considerations that need to factor into the overall decision.

Security

When a user submits a form, it sometimes contains sensitive data. That is, the data that the user provides might be personally identifiable information (PII) like a social security number. It might also be sensitive information that isn't necessarily PII, such as their annual salary. Because sensitive information may be provided, it's common to have users be able to see and edit only their own items. This can be accomplished through the use of workflows which restrict access to the form to just the user.

Workflows are included in SharePoint and can be used to secure the forms - as long as you realize that this needs to be done.

Workflow

The workflow capabilities inside of SharePoint allow you to take actions when an item is created, changed, or deleted. In addition, the document retention settings allow you to run a workflow after a specific date criterion is met for the content. This gives you the baseline support you need to deliver solutions, not just forms. In truth, we don't want forms or even electronic forms. We want to facilitate a business process with a form, but that's just the data component of the process. Workflows bring the data to life.

SharePoint offers two workflow engines. The first engine, introduced in 2007 and revised in 2010, is known as the SharePoint 2010 workflow engine. The second workflow engine was introduced in 2013, which is built on top of Azure Workflow Services. Both engines have their benefits and weaknesses, so it's not a forgone conclusion that you'll want to do workflows in the latest engine.

In addition to the two engines that are included in SharePoint, Microsoft has introduced a cloud-based service called Flow that is used in conjunction with PowerApps, which allows a different structure for workflows. Then there are third party offerings that have their own approaches, advantages and disadvantages.

When you're considering what forms technology to use, it's important to consider how the data will move once you have it, and that's either manually managing the data or using a workflow engine.

Why Not Both?

In most cases, there's no one answer for all of the forms in an organization. Most of the forms in the organization may be able to be accomplished as a Word form, but some may be more complicated and may need a different technology because of a different set of advantages and disadvantages. It's not abnormal to see more than one forms technology in use at an organization.

That's a good thing. It means that users are free to use the best solution to the problem rather than being locked into a rigid, one-size-fits-all approach to forms development. Obviously, it's possible to err on the side of allowing any kind of form, but the issues around training for both the development and filling out of these forms generally cause organizations to filter into a set of solutions that work.

When picking a forms solution, it's important to eliminate options that aren't good fits for your organization – but equally important to settle on one or two that are the recommended approaches for most of the forms.

	Advantages	Disadvantages
List Form	Quick / Easy	Difficult to customize
Word Form	Common / Well-Known	File Naming on Save
InfoPath Form	Flexible Calculations One-To-Many	Complicated Deprecated
PowerApps	HTML-Based	Unproven Technology
Fillable PDF	Easy to Create	Won't post data to SharePoint Need Acrobat to create
Third Party Forms	Flexible Feature-Rich	Additional Costs
Excel	Common / Well-Known	Doesn't promote data

Collaborate on Projects

In any business organization, public or private, the need to effectively communicate and collaborate in a timely manner is very important. Gone are the days of paper memos, and even group email has proved to be a cumbersome method of sharing information. Today, with mobile workers and shifting schedules, the tools of the Internet are the way to go. That's the overall function of SharePoint 2016: to allow users within organizations to collaborate and share work within a commonly accessed Web site framework. These Web sites are no different than any other Web site you might visit, except that with SharePoint, they can be custom-made to perform exactly the functions you and your team need to get the job done.

The sites that SharePoint creates are designed to be used by workgroups, committees, or a whole department of workers—the choices are entirely flexible to your own organization's needs, and you can organize SharePoint sites however you wish.

Sites can hold lists of things to do, libraries of documents that need work, and discussion boards to share ideas... among other tools.

In this section, you will learn how to handle the basics of collaboration:

- Create a Place for Teams to Work: Build a team site in which users can work.
- Share Your Site: Once a new site is created, you need to allow users access to that site.
- Accept an Invitation: When you are invited to a new site, you will need to accept the invitation to that site.
- Create a Microsoft Account: To accept an invitation to a SharePoint site, you must have either have an Office 365 account from your organization, or a Microsoft account.
- Create a New Group: While SharePoint provides some basic user groups to which you can assign your users, there may be instances where you will want to create new groups with very specific permissions.
- Assign Users to a Group: After groups have been created, users will need to be assigned to these groups.
- Remove Users from a Group: In the case of an in-company move or task reassignment, you will need to quickly remove the user from their old group.
- Edit Group Settings: Occasionally your group will need certain changes, such as who receives requests to join or leave.
- Remove a Group: To prevent site clutter from occurring, you can simply remove obsolete groups from SharePoint.

- Create a Project Site: Project sites include a Calendar, Task List, Document Library, and other basic apps to get things done. It can be best used as a temporary project site within a team or company site.
- Create an Alert: When you're multitasking, sometimes it can be difficult to keep track of the changes made to a document. SharePoint allows you to receive email alerts that tell you when something has been modified at the frequency you choose.
- Create an Alert for an App or Folder: Like alerts for individual documents or items, SharePoint also allows you to receive email alerts when someone adds, edits, or deletes any content in an app or folder.

Task: Create a Place for Teams to Work

Purpose: In any business organization, public or private, the need to effectively communicate and collaborate in a timely manner is very important. That's the overall function of SharePoint 2016: to allow users within organizations to collaborate and share work within a commonly-accessed website framework. These websites are no different than any other website you might visit, except that with SharePoint, they can be customized to perform exactly the functions you and your team need to get the job done.

Sites can hold lists of things to do, libraries of documents that require work or action, discussion boards to share ideas... or one of several other lists, as well.

Before any of these tools can be put to use, you will need to start with the basics: creating a team site where users can start working. If you have the appropriate permissions, you can create a new site very easily in SharePoint.

Steps:

1. Start Internet Explorer and type the URL for your organization's SharePoint server. The Start page will open. If you want your new team site located as a subsite of another site, navigate to that site.

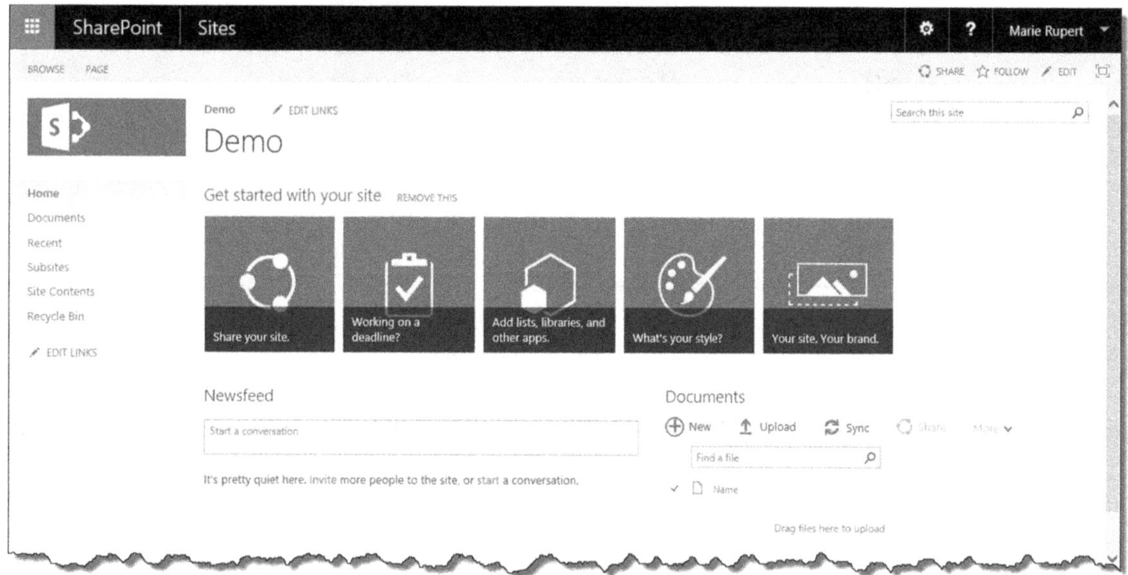

Figure 1: A Start Page for a SharePoint Site

2. Click the Settings menu drop-down control, which resembles a gear. The Settings menu will appear.

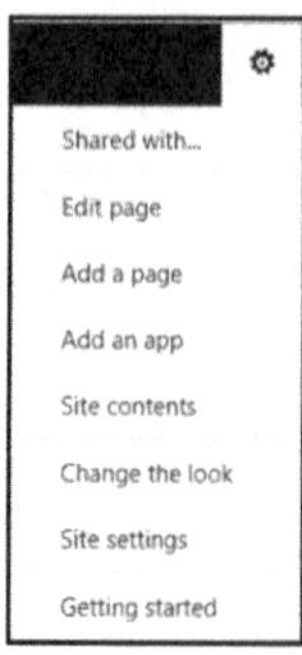

Figure 2: The Settings Menu

3. Click Site Contents. The Site Contents page will appear. If you do not see the new subsite option, you do not have the proper authorization. Please contact your administrator.

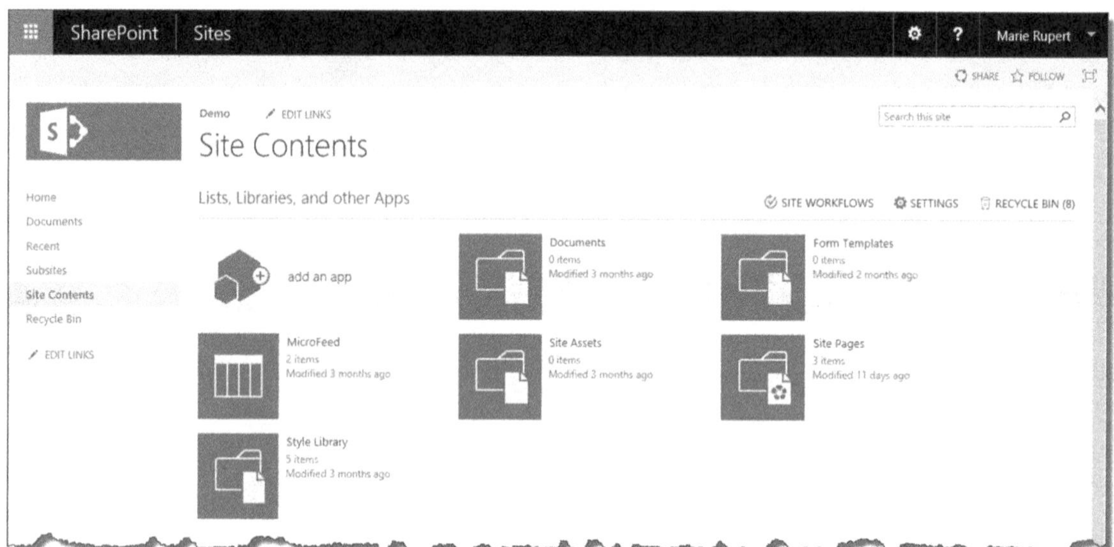

Figure 3: The Site Contents Page

4. At the bottom of the page, click the new subsite link. The New SharePoint Site page will open.

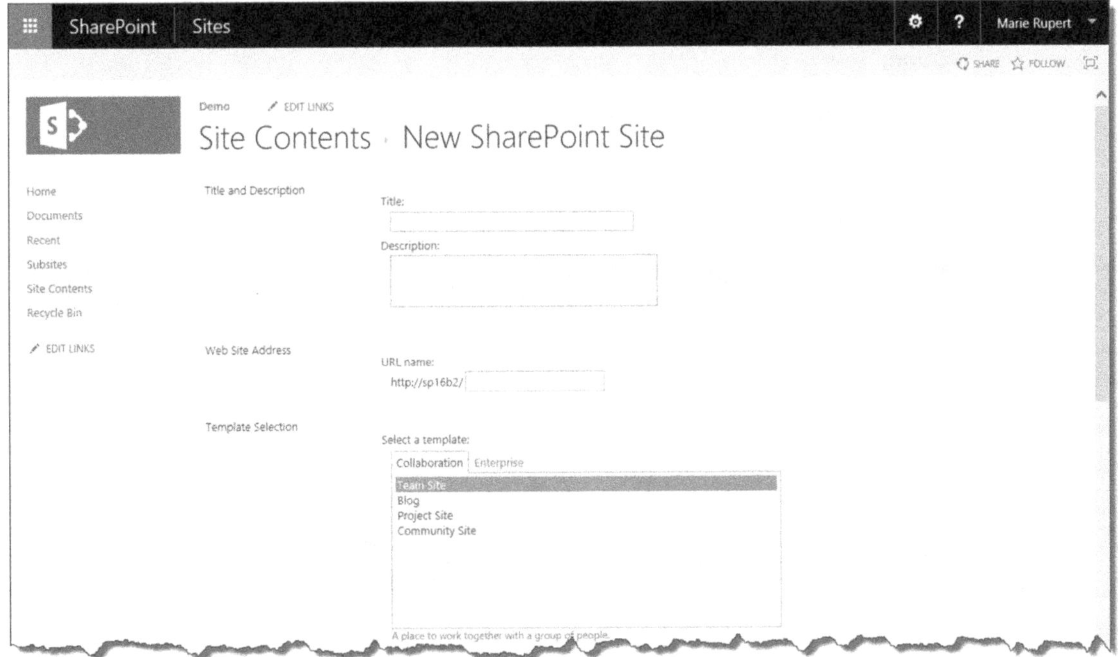

Figure 4: The New SharePoint Site Page

5. In the Title field, type a title for your site. The title of your site should be descriptive and can be up to about 50 letters before becoming intrusive. It will appear on the top of your new site.

6. In the Description field, type a description for your site. The description is like a sub-title that will be displayed on some of the pages. It should further clarify the title so that anyone can understand the site's purpose.

7. In the URL name field, type a short, descriptive name for your team. This will become part of the full website address for your new Team site. Some features don't work with long URLs, so keeping the name in the URL short but descriptive is recommended.

8. In the Template Selection section, click the **Team Site** option.

9. In the User Permissions field, select the **Use same permissions as parent site** option. You can change to unique permissions later as shown in "Assign Users to a Group."

Note: If the publishing feature is activated for your site, the **Display this site on Quick Launch** and **Display this site on the top link bar of the parent site** are not options on the New SharePoint Site page.

10. In the Display this site on the Quick Launch of the parent site field, select the **Yes** option.

11. In the Display this site on the top link bar of the parent site field, select the Yes option.
12. In the Use the top link bar from the parent site field, select the Yes option.
13. Click Create. The "Working on it ..." screen will briefly appear, followed by the new Team Site home page.

Figure 5: The New Team Site Home Page

Exception: If the Site Contents option or new subsite link don't appear, you do not have specific permissions to create subsites. Check the permissions settings to ensure you have the appropriate access rights.

Task: Share Your Site

Purpose: Once a new site is created, you need to allow users access to that site. You can do this by individually assigning permissions or by using groups. By default, SharePoint creates four groups:

Owner: Users who can control and administrate all aspects of a team site
Member: Users who can contribute to the site by viewing or editing its content
Visitor: Users who can only read a site's content
Viewers: Users who can only view a site

You can create other groups of users in SharePoint; however, these groups provide a good starting point. For the most part, you will want new users to have Member status: they can create new entries, or read and change existing entries, but they will not be able to change the layout of the pages, nor will they be able to create new lists.

Example: Once you have created the Action Group team site, the next order of business is to grant access to the site for team members.

Steps:

1. Start Internet Explorer and type the URL for your organization's SharePoint server. The Start page will open.
2. Navigate to the site where you want to add users to edit your site. The site's home page will open.

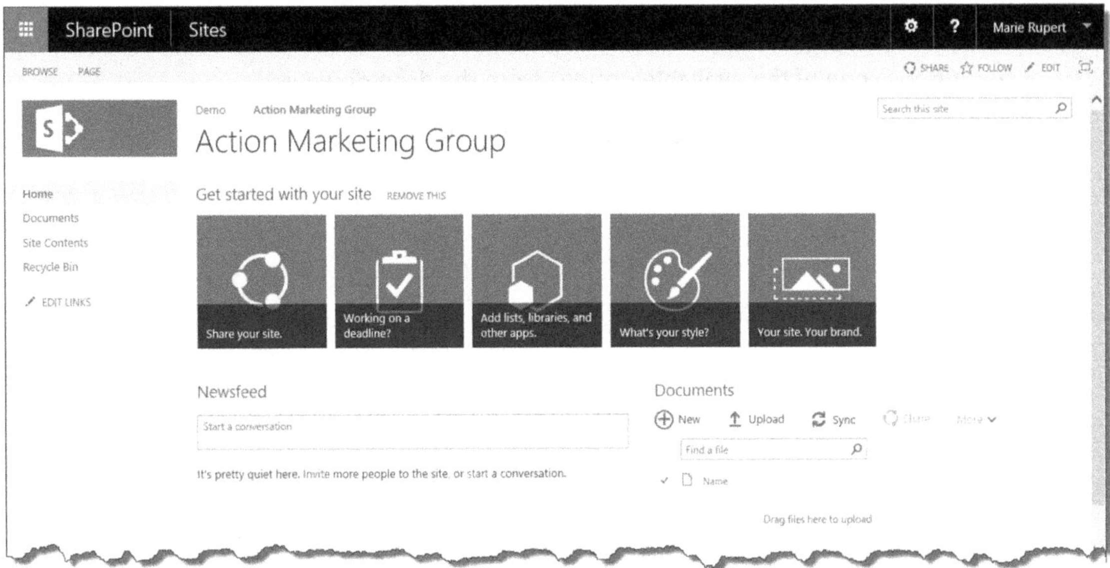

Figure 1: A Team Site Home Page

3. Click the **Share** link on the top right. The Share dialog box will open.

Figure 2: The Share Dialog Box

4. In the Invite people field, type the name or email address of the people you want to have on the site. As you type, list of matching personnel will appear. You can click on the name to complete the entry.

5. New shares are always added as Members. If you want to give the person more or less capabilities, click the Show Options link. The Select a Group or Permission Level section will appear.

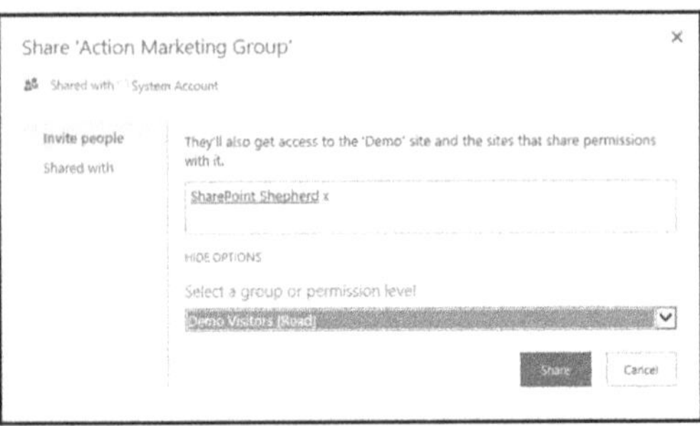

Figure 3: The Expanded Share Dialog Box

6. Choose one of the available options from the drop-down list.

7. Click Share. The person(s) will be added to the team site.

Task: Accept an Invitation

Purpose: From time to time, you may be invited to participate in a new SharePoint site collection within your organization, or an organization that you're working with. When someone shares their site with you, you'll receive an email notification with an invitation message. In this task, you'll accept an invitation message you've received.

Steps:

1. Open Outlook or the email host where you received the message. Locate the email sent by the SharePoint user and click on it to preview the invitation message. Then click on the SharePoint site's name to open a new browser window.

Figure 1: A Sample Invitation Message

2. If you have not logged into the site before, a Windows Security dialog box may appear. Enter your username and password, then click **OK** to log in. The SharePoint site will open.

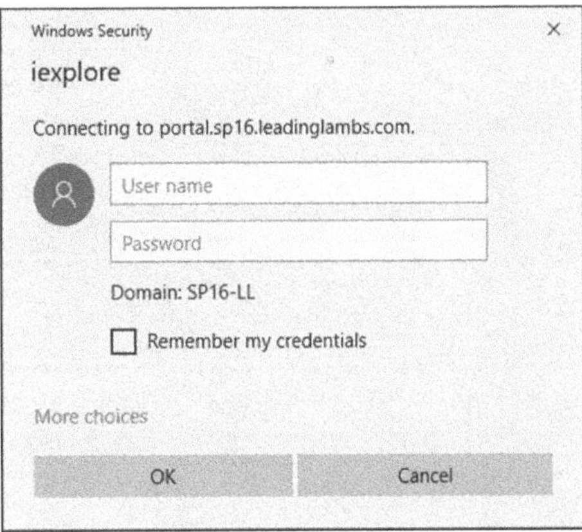

Figure 2: The Windows Security Dialog Box in Internet Explorer

3. If you have logged into the SharePoint site before, or if the site is a site collection within your organization, you will automatically be logged in and directed to the SharePoint site.

Task: Create a Microsoft Account

Purpose: In order to accept an invitation to a SharePoint site, you must have either an organizational account for logging into Office 365 or a Microsoft account. Microsoft accounts are free and can be created with your existing email account. In this task, we'll show you how to create a Microsoft account.

Steps:

1. Open Internet Explorer (or your favorite browser). In the address bar enter signup.live.com and press **Enter**.

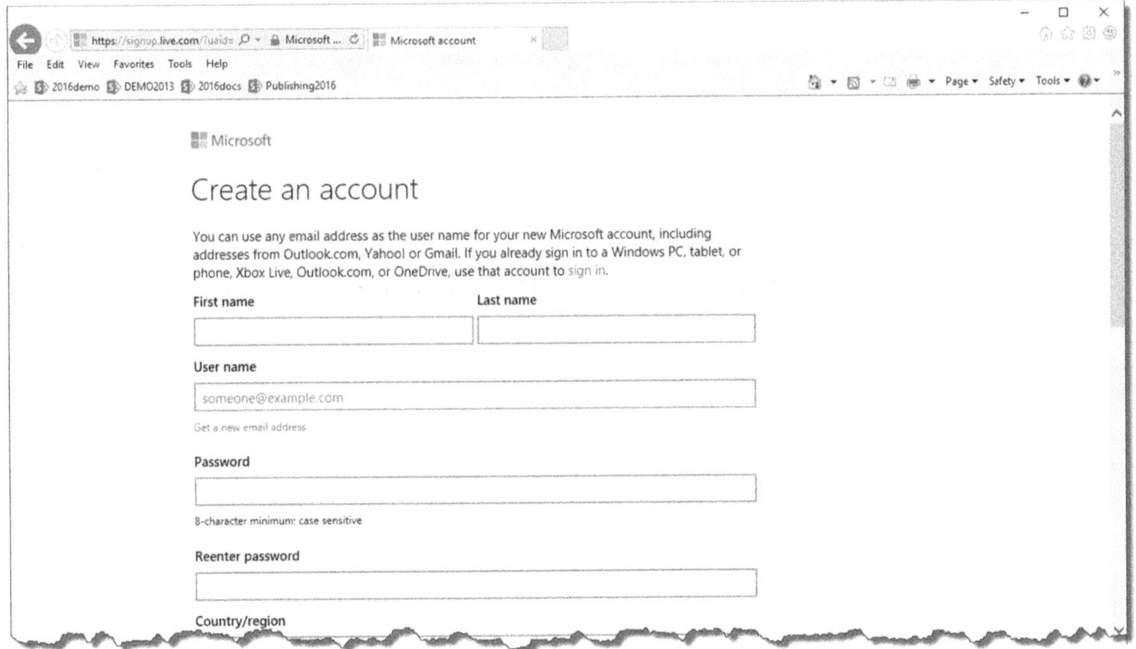

Figure 1: Create an account page

2. Enter the required information, including first and last name, the requested username (existing email address), password, country, zip code, birthday, gender, and phone number. The email address and phone number will be used to validate the account, so make sure that they're correct. Click the **Create account** button.

Note: The password you provide for your Microsoft account does not need to be the same password that you use to login to your email.

3. You will be automatically signed in, and the Verify email page will open. If you do not receive the email from the Microsoft account team, you can click the **Resend email** button to request another email be sent.

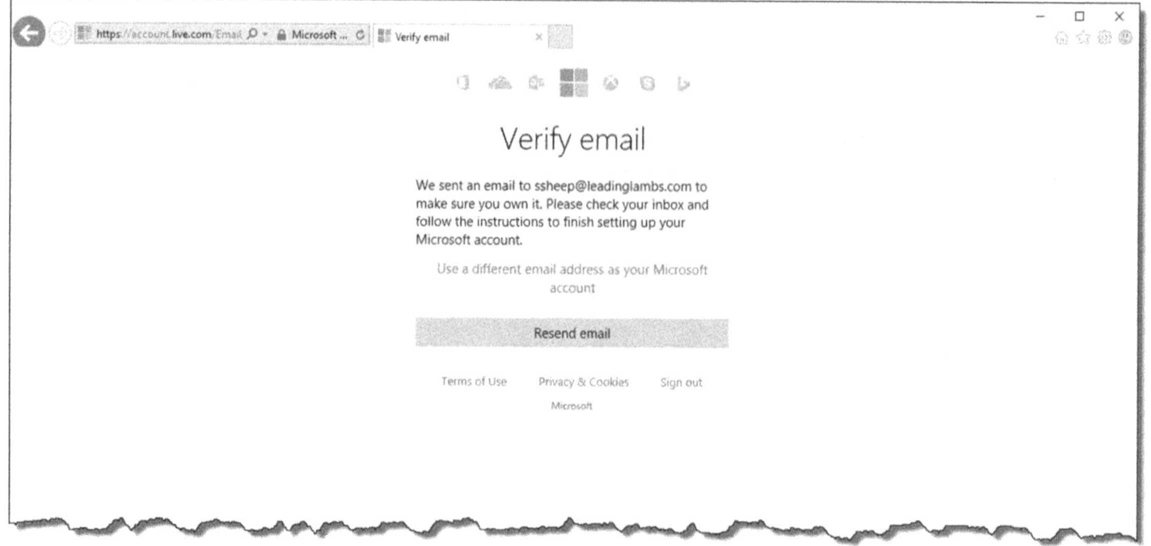

Figure 2: The Verify email page

4. Go to your email and open the "Verify your email address" email from the Microsoft account team. Within the email, click the button to verify your email address.

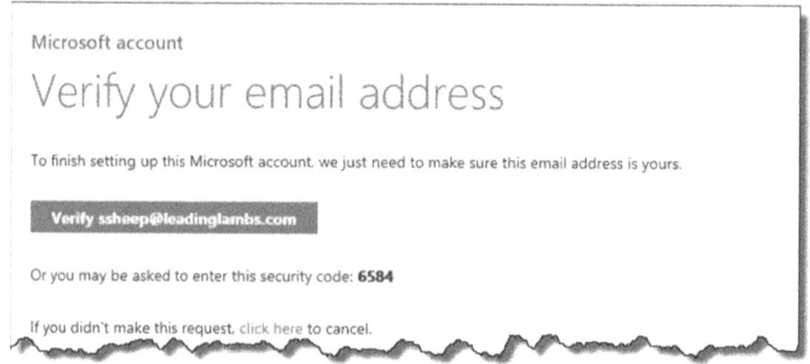

Figure 3: Verification Email

5. A new browser tab will open to show the Ready to go! page. Your Microsoft account is now successfully created and verified, and you can start using it for Microsoft services.

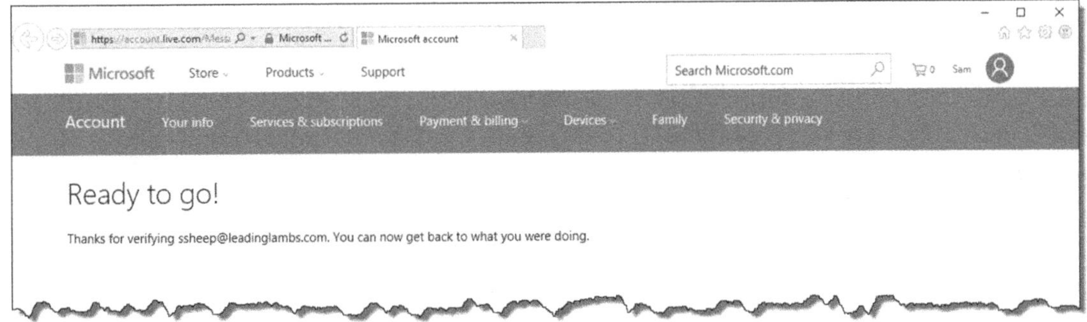

Figure 4: Ready to go! page

Task: Create a New Group

Purpose: While SharePoint provides some basic user groups to which you can assign your users, there may be instances where you will want to create new groups that will have different permissions.

An example of this type of group would be for team members who can only read and edit existing content. Because of your organization's culture, you might not want them to create documents.

When these kinds of access issues crop up, it is a big timesaver to create a unique group with specific capabilities and then assign users to that group as needed. You can even add your own permission levels, as demonstrated in "Create a Custom Permission Level."

Example: A few of your team members need to be assigned to a specific group for web development while working with the new team site. But before they can be assigned to this group, it needs to be created.

Steps:

1. Start Internet Explorer and type the URL for your organization's SharePoint server. The Start page will open.
2. Navigate to the site where you want to add a group. The site's home page will open.
3. On the **Settings** menu gear icon, click the **Site settings** option. The Site Settings page will open.

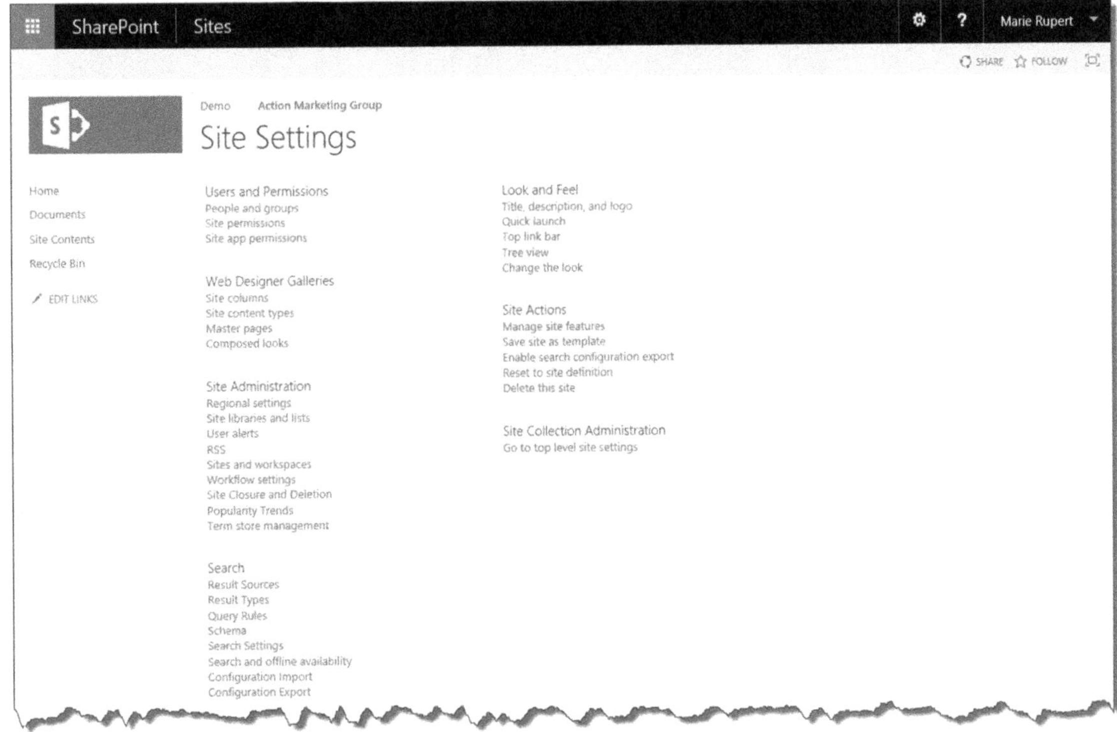

Figure 1: The Site Settings Page

4. In the Users and Permissions section, click the **Site permissions** link. The Permissions page will open.

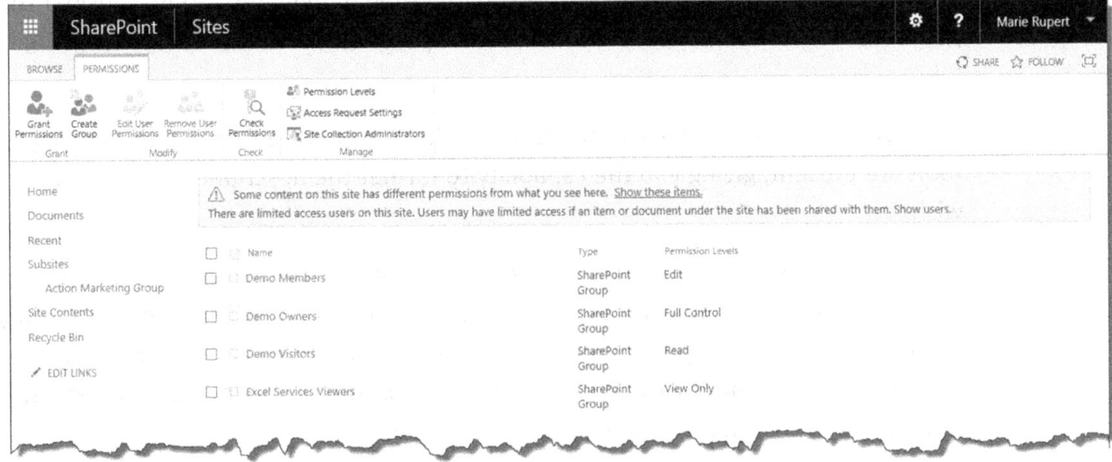

Figure 2: The Permissions Page

5. In the Permissions ribbon, click the **Create Group** button. The Create Group page will open.

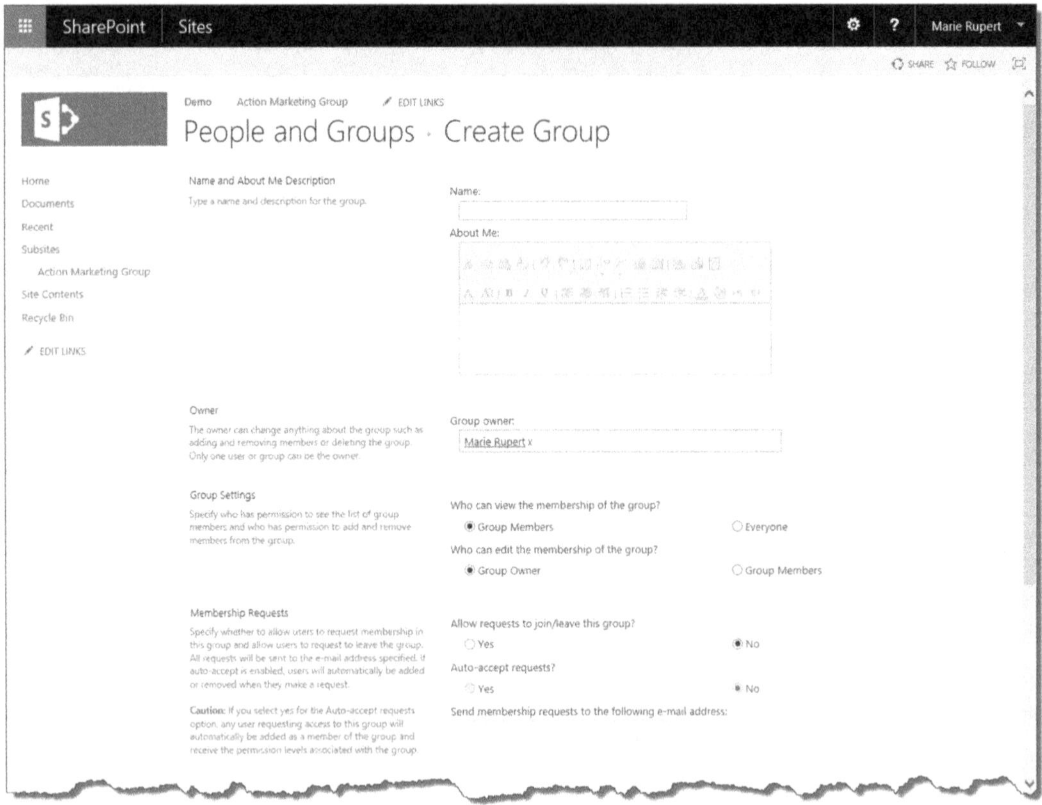

Figure 3: The Create Group Page

6. In the Name field, type a name for the group. When naming the group, consider the people that will be added, not necessarily the permissions that you'll be assigning to them.

7. In the About Me field, type a description for the group. Note that rich text editing tools are present, giving you the capability to format the description however you wish.

8. In the Group Owner field, if the owner of the group is not going to be you, delete your user name and enter the appropriate one in the text box. The owner will always be able to manage group membership. By changing the owner to someone else, you can allow them to modify the group. Users, such as Site Collection administrators, will also be able to modify the group membership.

9. In the Who can view the membership of the group field, click the **Everyone** radio button if you want all people with permissions to view your site to see who's in this group. Otherwise, leave **Group Members** selected. You might want to make the members private if the confidentiality of the members should be maintained.

10. In the Who can edit the membership of the group field, indicate who can edit members in the group by clicking the **Group Owner** or **Group Members** radio button. Typically, only the group owner can edit group membership. However, if all of the members are highly trusted, you have the opportunity to allow any of them to modify membership.
11. In the Membership requests field, click the appropriate option to allow requests to join or leave the group. You may want to allow requests to join or leave the group if you're setting up a volunteer team to support an initiative.
12. Select the appropriate option to auto-accept requests. It is recommended that you keep this option set at **No**. Auto-accepting could make it difficult to manage the comings and goings of your group. However, if you are working with a volunteer group, such as those helping with the company picnic, auto-accepting requests may be appropriate.
13. If you chose to allow requests, enter the appropriate email address to which users can send membership requests. Warning: not every server is properly configured to accept inbound email messages.
14. Click **Create**. The new group will appear in the People and Groups page. You can now add users, as explained in "Assign Users to a Group."

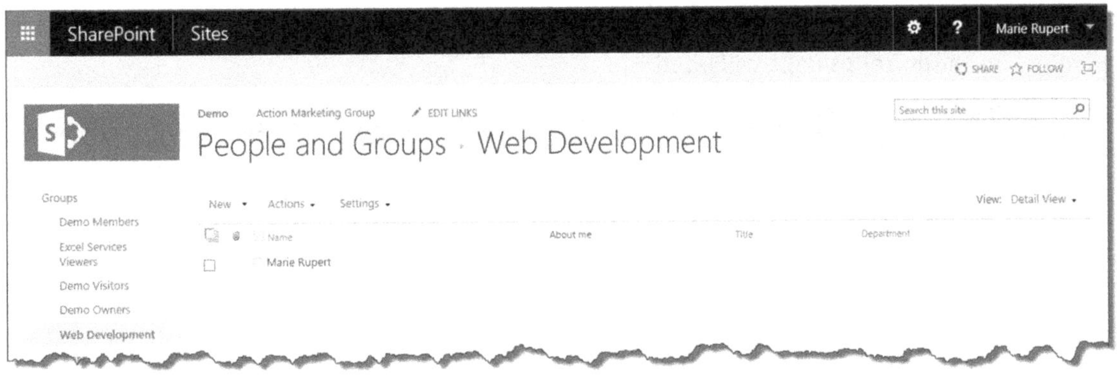

Figure 4: The New Web Development Group

Exception: If you can't add a group name, either the group name already exists or you do not have specific permissions to add groups. Check the permissions settings to ensure you have the appropriate access rights.

Task: Assign Users to a Group

Purpose: After groups have been created, users will need to be assigned to these groups. Unless you have chosen to allow your group to auto-accept requests to join or leave the group, someone will need to quickly add or remove users from the group as the need arises.

Even though this might seem a bit tedious, it's a good idea for someone to act as the "gatekeeper" for a group, if only to make sure the appropriate people are allowed in.

Example: The new Web Development group has been added to the Action Marketing Group's team site, and now you need to assign users to that group.

Steps:

1. Start Internet Explorer and type the URL for your organization's SharePoint server. The Start page will open.
2. Navigate to the site where you want to manage a group's users. The site's home page will open.
3. Click the **Settings** menu gear icon and then the **Site Settings** option. The Site Settings page will open.
4. In the Users and Permissions section, click the **People and groups** link. The People and Groups page will open.

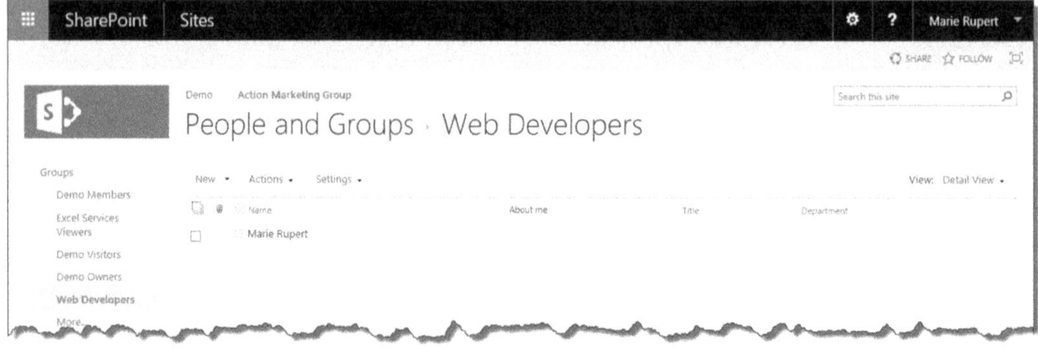

Figure 1: The People and Groups Page

5. In the Quick Launch under Groups, click the name of the group to which you want to add users. The Group's page will open.
6. Click the arrow beside **New** to open the drop-down menu, then click **Add Users**. The Share dialog box will open.

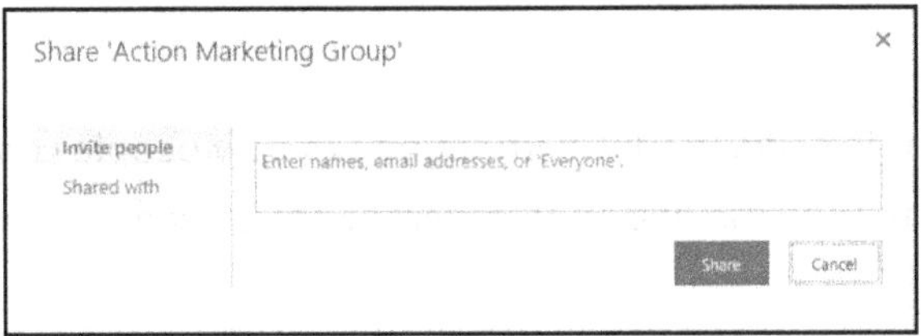

Figure 2: The Share Dialog Box

7. In the Add People field, type in the name of the user. As the name is typed, a list of matching results will appear. You can click on the name to add it to the list.
8. Add additional names as needed.
9. Click Share. The Share dialog box will close and the users will appear in the group list on the People and Groups page.

Figure 3: The New Group Members

Exception: If a red squiggly line appears under user names added in the Share dialog box, this indicates the user cannot be found.

Task: Remove Users from a Group

Purpose: Change is present in every work environment. As new people come in, veterans to an organization may find themselves moving on to different assignments, or even different jobs within the company.

When a user leaves a company altogether, their account will be removed from the various systems by the IT department. In that case, their removal from SharePoint's user roles will be automatic. But in the case of an in-company move or task reassignment, you will need to remove a user from their old group.

Example: One of the members of the Web Development group has transferred to a new team, and will need to be removed from the Action Marketing Group's team site.

Steps:

1. Start Internet Explorer and type the URL for your organization's SharePoint server. The Start page will open.
2. Navigate to the site where you want to manage a group's users. The site's home page will open.
3. Select the **Settings** menu gear icon, then the **Site Settings** menu option. The Site Settings page will open.
4. In the Users and permissions section, click the **People and groups** link. The People and Groups page will open.
5. In the Quick Launch under Groups, click the name of the group from which you want to remove a user. The Group's page will open.

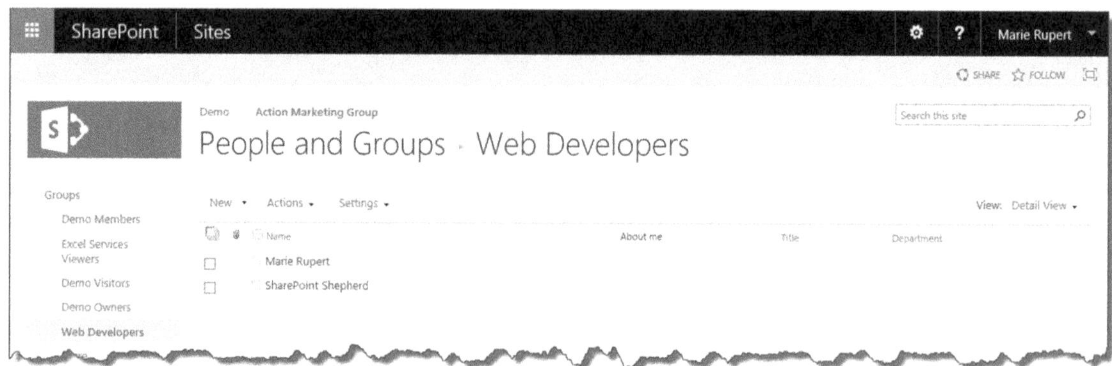

Figure 1: The Group Page

6. Click the **checkbox** of the user(s) you want to remove to select them.

7. Click the arrow beside **Actions** to open the drop-down menu, then select **Remove Users from Group**. A confirmation dialog box will open.

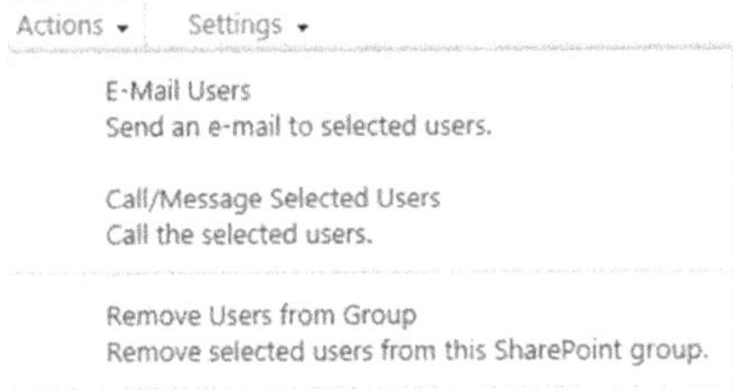

Figure 2: The Actions Menu

8. Click **OK**. The user(s) will be removed from the group.

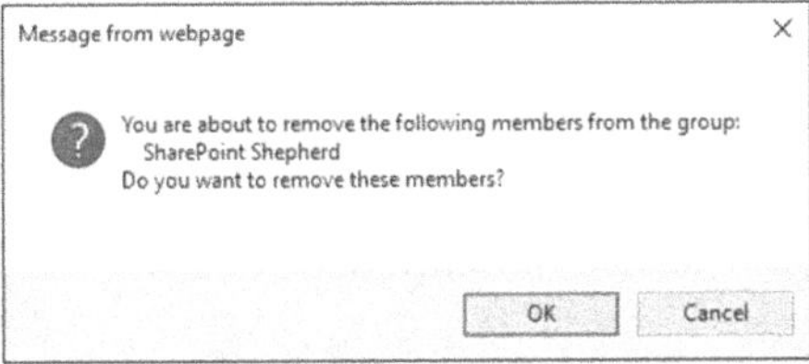

Figure 3: The Remove Users from Group Confirmation Dialog Box

Task: Edit Group Settings

Purpose: Occasionally your group will need to have changes made, such as changing the group owner who gets requests to join or leave the group. This doesn't happen very often, but SharePoint's flexibility allows you to make such changes easily.

Example: You have been asked to provide a description to the Web Development group in the team site to differentiate them from other web development groups within the company.

Steps:

1. Start Internet Explorer and type the URL for your organization's SharePoint server. The Start page will open.
2. Navigate to the site where you want to manage a group's settings. The site's home page will open.
3. Select the **Settings** menu gear icon, then the **Site Settings** option. The Site Settings page will open.
4. In the Users and Permissions section, click the **People and groups** link. The People and Groups page will open.
5. In the Quick Launch under Groups, click the name of the group you want to edit. The Group's page will open.
6. Click the arrow beside **Settings** to open the drop-down menu and select the **Group Settings** option. The Change Group Settings page will open.

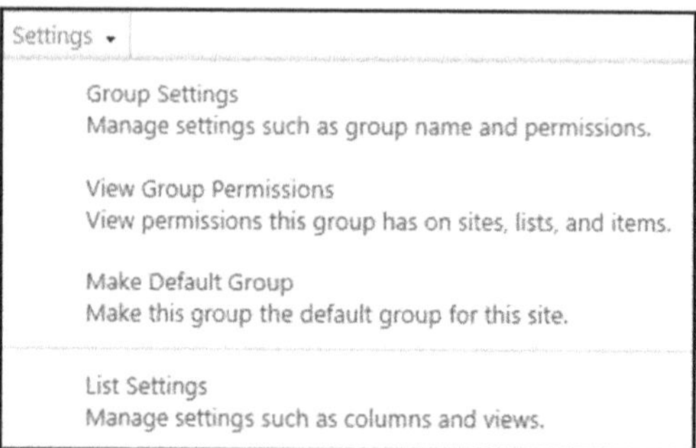

Figure 1: The Settings Menu

7. Make the changes you need, then click **OK**. The changes will be applied to the group. You'll find more information about the fields on this page and what they do in the task "Create a New Group."

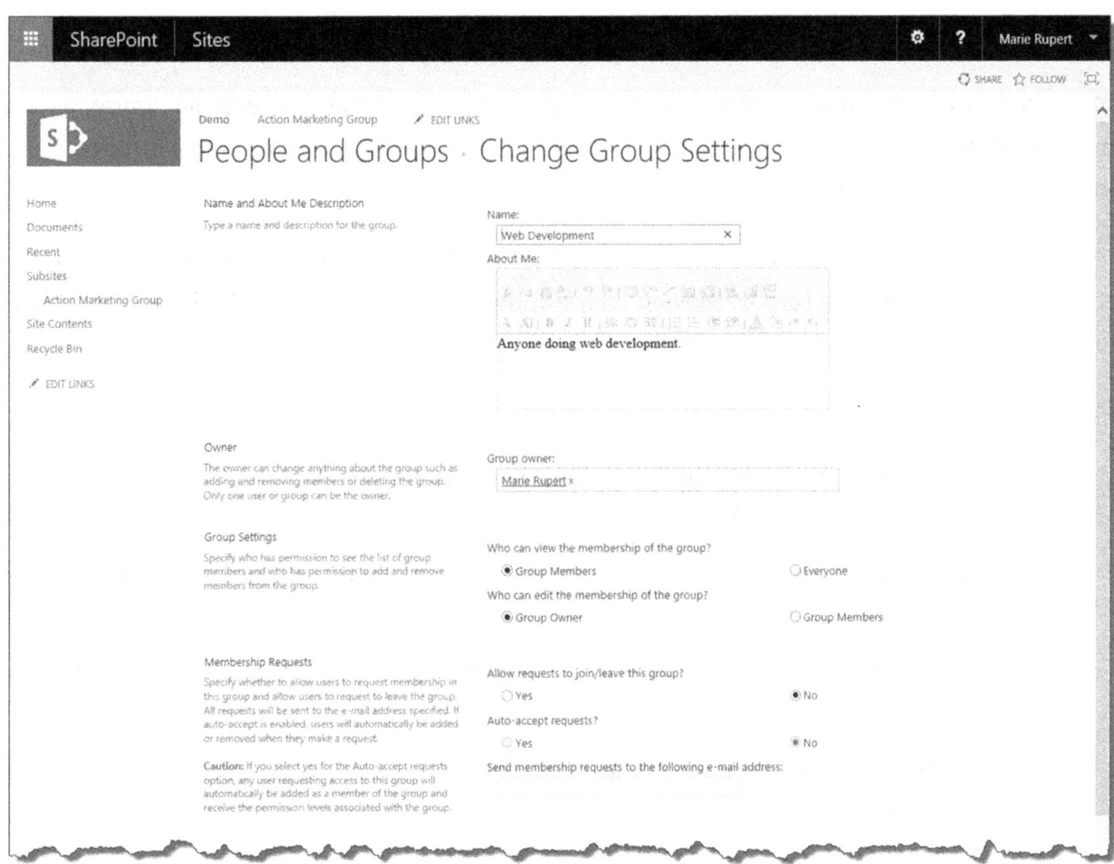

Figure 2: The Change Group Settings Page

Task: Remove a Group

Purpose: In SharePoint, adding groups is so simple that you might forget to keep old, unused groups from filling up your team site. To prevent such clutter from occurring, you can simply remove obsolete groups from SharePoint.

Example: The Web Development group within the Action Marketing Group has been folded into another team within Leading Lambs. Moving forward, there's no need to identify these employees as Web Developers in SharePoint, so the group will be removed.

Steps:

1. Start Internet Explorer and type the URL for your organization's SharePoint server. The Start page will open.
2. Navigate to the site from which you want to remove the group. The site's home page will open.
3. Select the **Settings** menu gear icon, then the **Site Settings** menu option. The Site Settings page will open.
4. In the Users and Permissions section, click the **People and groups** link. The People and Groups page will open.
5. In the Quick Launch under Groups, click the name of the group you want to remove. If your group does not appear in the list, click **More...** to see all groups, then click the group you want to remove. The Group's page will open.
6. Click the arrow next to **Settings** to open the drop-down menu, and select the **Group Settings** option. The Change Group Settings page will open.

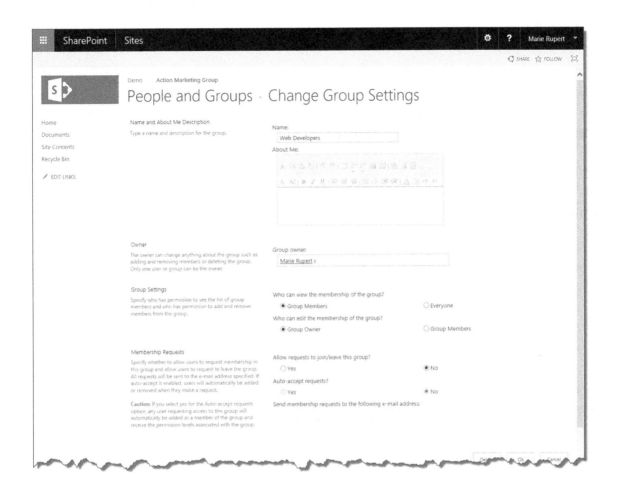

Figure 1: The Change Group Settings Page

7. On the bottom of the page, click **Delete**. A confirmation dialog box will open.

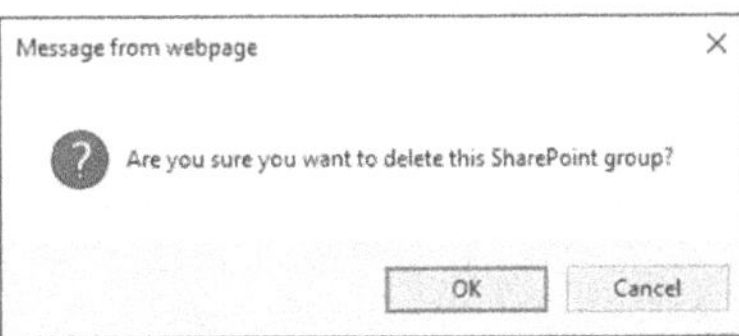

Figure 2: The Group Deletion Confirmation Dialog Box

8. Click **OK**. The Group page for the first group appearing on the Quick Launch menu will open, with the previous group no longer appearing in the groups list on the Quick Launch bar. Because only a few groups are listed on the Quick Launch menu, you may need to click the **More...** link in order to verify that the group has been removed.

Exception: If you can't delete the group, you do not have specific permissions to delete the group. Check the permissions settings to ensure you have the appropriate access rights.

Task: Create a Project Site

Purpose: One of the useful templates within SharePoint 2016 is the project site. At first glance, this may look and feel very much like a team site, and there are similarities. The project site includes a Calendar, Task List, Document Library, and other basic apps to get things done. It can be best used as a temporary project site within a team or company site.

Example: The Action Marketing Group has been tasked to put together a marketing campaign for Leading Lambs' newest product. A project site will allow team members as well as other Leading Lambs employees to collaborate on the project.

Steps:

1. Start Internet Explorer and type the URL for your organization's SharePoint server. The Start page will open. If you want your project site located as a subsite to another site, navigate to that site.
2. Click the **Settings** menu gear icon and click the **Site Contents** option. The Site Contents page will appear.
3. In the Subsites section, click the **new subsite** link. The New SharePoint Site page will open.
4. In the Title field, type a title for the project site. The title of your site should be descriptive and can be up to about 50 letters before becoming intrusive.
5. In the Description field, type a description for your site. The description is like a subtitle that will be displayed on some of the pages. It should further clarify the title so that anyone can understand the site's purpose.
6. In the URL Name field, type a short, descriptive name for your group. This will become part of the full website address for your new project site. Some features don't work with long URLs, so keeping the name in the URL short but descriptive is recommended.
7. In the Template Selection section, select **Project Site** as the template.
8. In the User Permissions field, select the **Use same permissions as parent site** option.

Note: If the publishing feature is activated for your site, the **Display this site on Quick Launch** and **Display this site on the top link bar of the parent site** are not options on the New SharePoint Site page.

9. In the Display this site on the Quick Launch of the parent site field, select the **Yes** option.
10. In the Use the top link bar from the parent site field, select the **Yes** option.

11. Click **Create**. The "Working on it…" screen will briefly appear, followed by the new Project Site page.

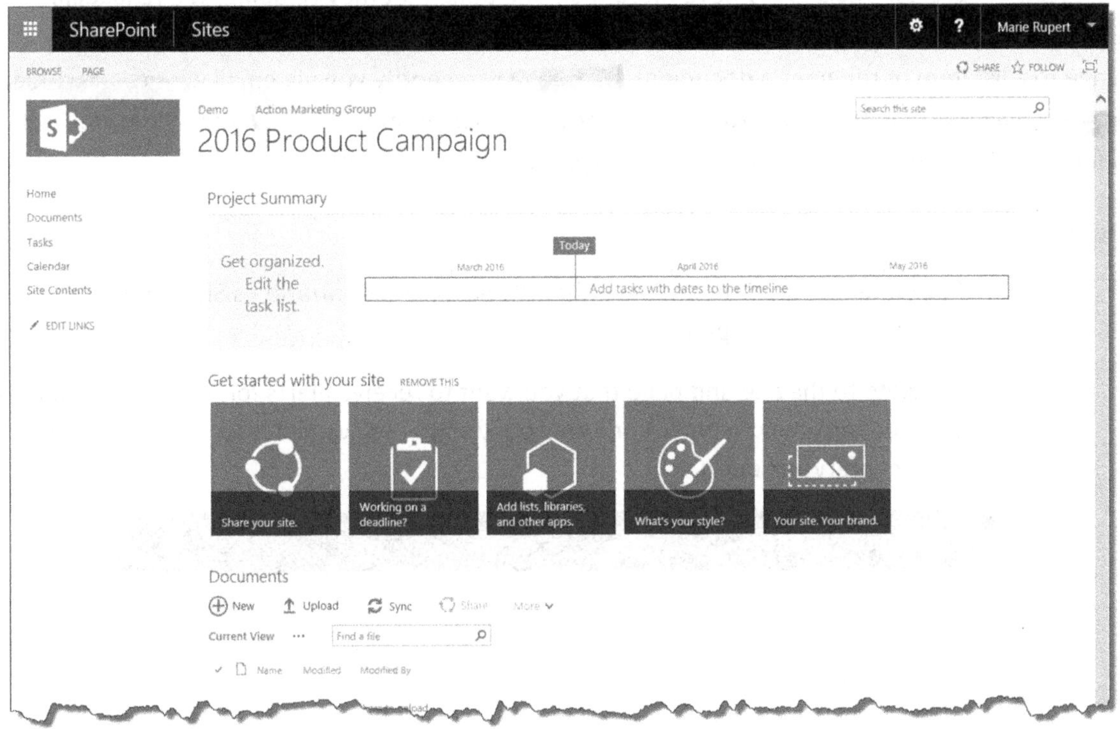

Figure 1: The New Project Site Home Page

Exception: If the desired site template is not listed, you do not have specific permissions to access the correct site templates. Check the permissions settings to ensure you have the appropriate access rights for creating project sites.

Task: Create an Alert

Purpose: Most professionals today have more than one thing that they're doing. We're juggling projects, clients, and responsibilities. There's rarely time to go check to see if someone makes a change to a list item or renames a document. SharePoint can notify you via email when a page, file, or item changes so you don't have to go check for changes in multiple places. In this task, we'll set ourselves up to receive alerts when our team page is modified by another user.

Steps:

1. Start Internet Explorer and type the URL for your organization's SharePoint server. The Start page will open.
2. Navigate to the site and page that you want to receive alerts for, or the list or library that contains the document or item you wish to receive alerts for. The site's page, list, or library will open.

Figure 1: A Team Page with the Ribbon on Browse

3. Click on the Page, Files, or Items tab to reveal the ribbon. To set an alert on a document or list item, click the check mark to the left of the document title or item to select it.

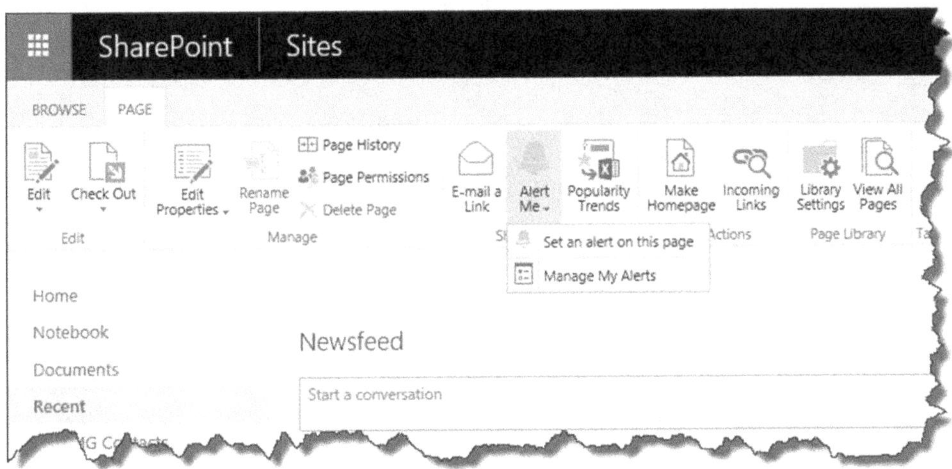

Figure 2: A Team Page with the Page-Ribbon Open

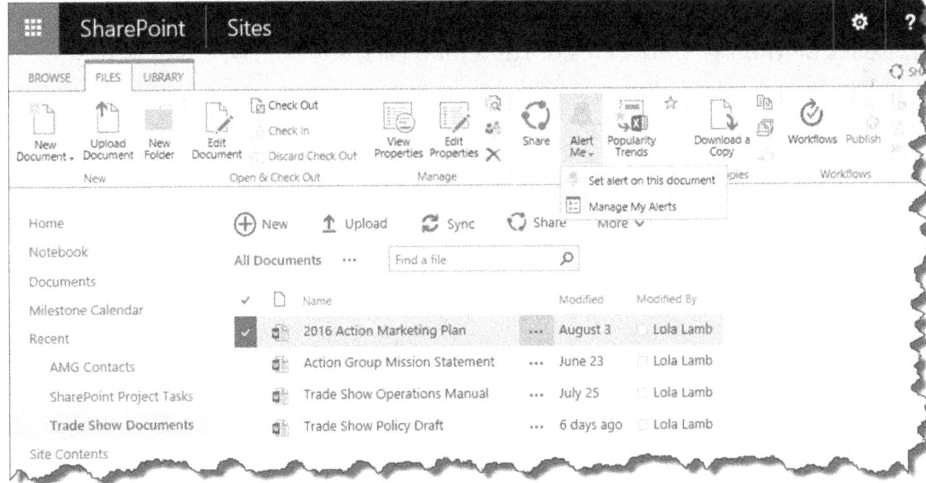

Figure 3: A Document Library with the Files Ribbon Open and Document Selected

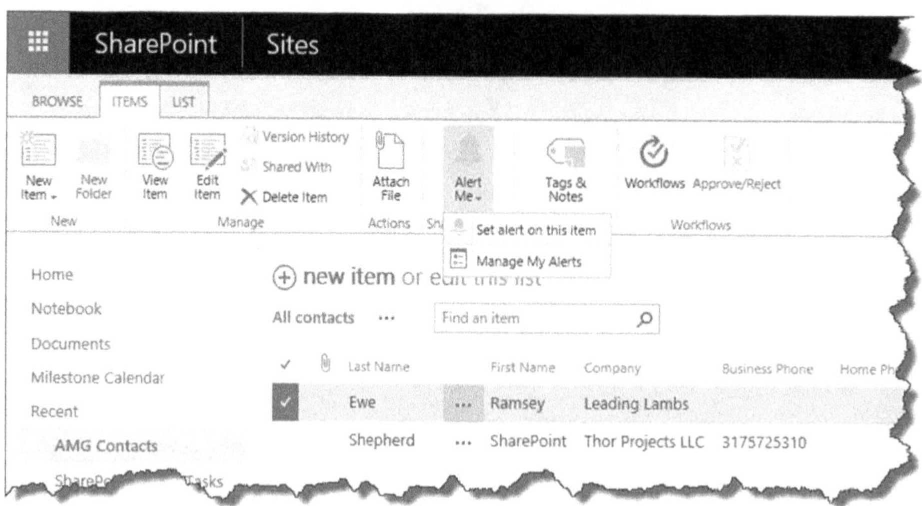

Figure 4: A List with the Items Ribbon Open and Item Selected

4. Click on the Alert Me bell icon, and then click Set alert on this page/document/item. The New Alert window will appear.

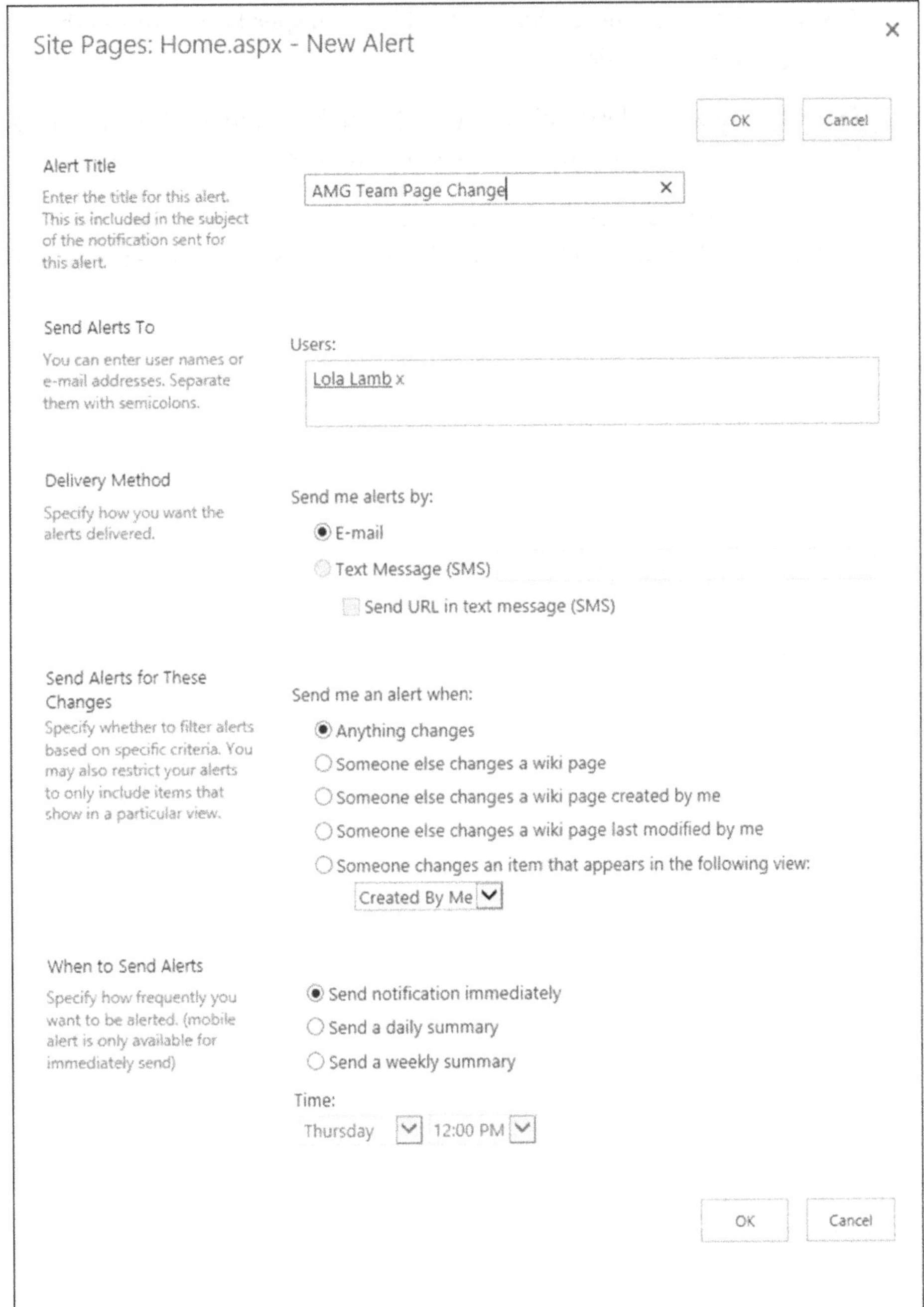

Figure 5: The New Alert Window for a Wiki Page Home Page

5. In the Alert Title field, enter a title for the alert. Especially if you have multiple alerts, it is good to keep your alert title short and specific.

6. In the Send Alerts To box, enter people to send alerts to. Your name will be in the list by default, but you can include others as well.

7. The Send Alerts for These Changes field lets you specify the criteria that must be met for you to receive an alert.
8. The When to Send Alerts field lets you choose how frequently you receive alerts, from immediately after changes are made, to weekly in summary form.
9. Click **OK** to save your new alert. The New Alert window will close. You will now start receiving notifications on the page, file, or item based on the settings you chose.

Task: Create a SharePoint Alert for an App or Folder

Purpose: Just like setting alerts for individual documents, SharePoint can notify you via email when changes are made to apps or folders. Occasionally you just need to know when someone else adds or removes an item from an app, and not receive an alert any time someone edits an individual item. In this task, we'll set ourselves up to receive alerts when someone else adds, modifies, or deletes items in a library app.

Steps:

1. Start Internet Explorer and type the URL for your organization's SharePoint server. The Start page will open.
2. Navigate to the site and library or list app that you want to receive alerts for. If you want to only receive an alert for items changing in a specific folder, navigate to the library app containing that folder.

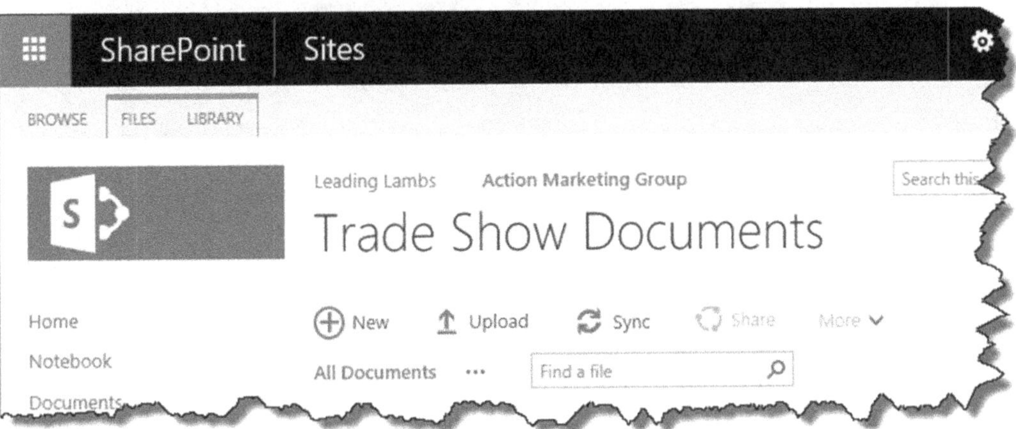

Figure 1: A Library App with the Ribbon on Browse

3. Click on the **Library** or **List** tab to reveal the ribbon. To set an alert on a specific folder, click the **check mark** to the left of the folder's name to select that folder, then click the **Files** tab to open the Files ribbon.

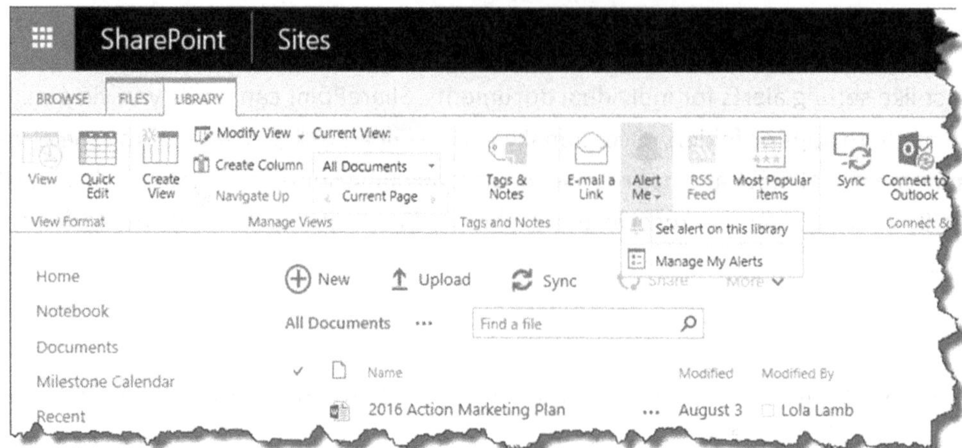

Figure 2: A Document Library with the Library Ribbon Open

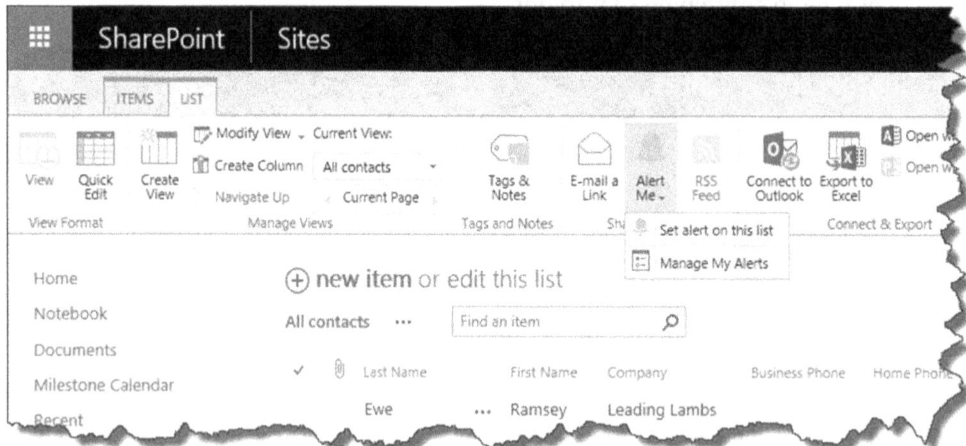

Figure 3: A List with the List Ribbon Open

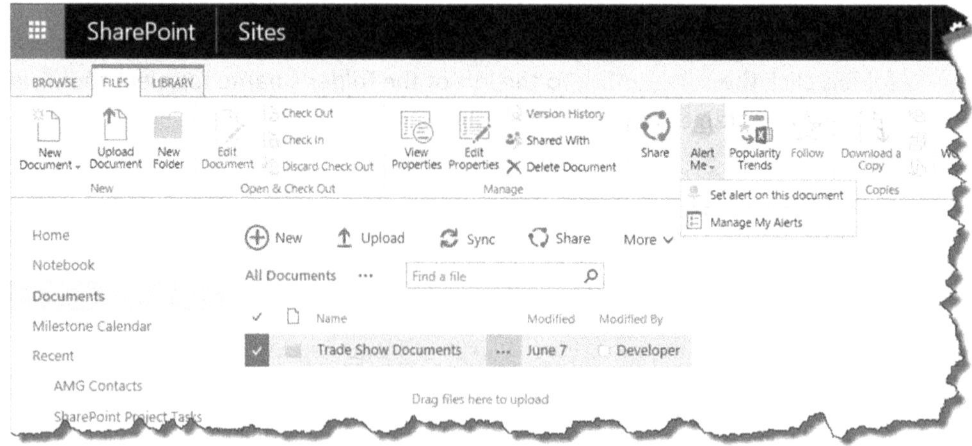

Figure 4: A Document Library with the Files Ribbon Open and Folder Selected

4. Click on the **Alert Me** bell icon and then select **Set alert on this library/list/document**. The New Alert window will appear.

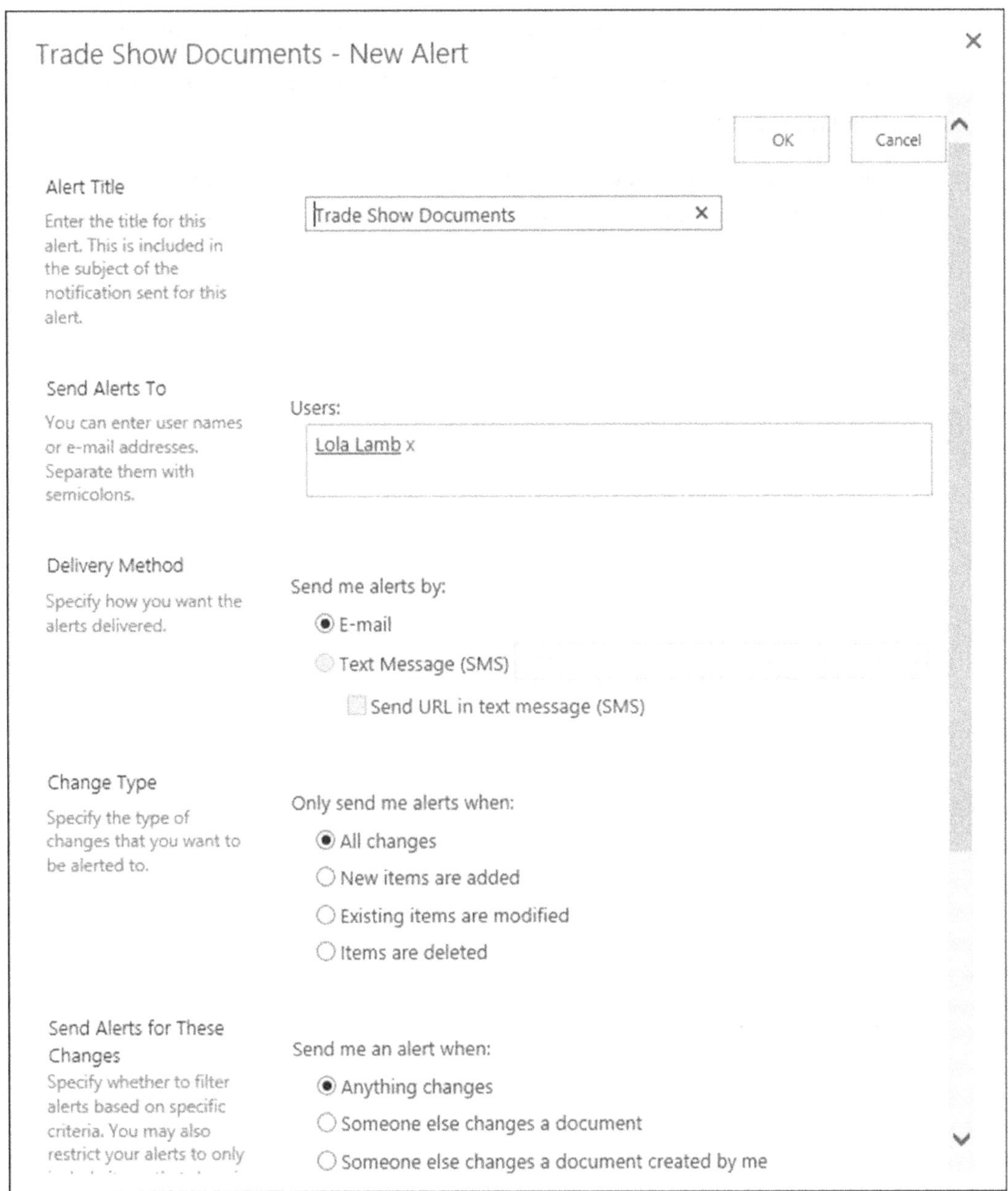

Figure 5: The New Alert Window for a Library App

5. In the Alert Title field, enter a title for the alert. Especially if you have multiple alerts, it is good to keep your alert title short and specific.

6. In the Send Alerts To box, enter the people to send the alerts to. Your name will in the list by default, but you can include others as well.

7. Set the Change Type to the type of changes that you want to see an alert for.
8. The Send Alerts for These Changes option allows you specify criteria for alerts, whether it's any change to any item, or only items that you created or last modified.
9. In the When to Send Alerts field, set the notifications to occur immediately, daily, or weekly, as desired.
10. Click **OK** to save your new alert. The New Alert window will close. You will now start receiving notifications on the app or folder based on the settings you chose.

Communicating Ideas

When group projects occur in the workplace, one of the old standbys for communication is the email discussion. Members of a team send emails back and forth, going over various approaches and ideas. But emails can be cumbersome. Which message had the file you needed for the annual statistics? Who was replying to whom about next week's meeting? Did you hit "reply" or "reply all"?

One good way to avoid these logistical problems is to use SharePoint's discussion board feature. In a discussion board, all the comments are in one place, for everyone to quickly see and read. Discussions are threaded, so their order and flow is easier to follow.

In this section, you will learn how to:

- Create a Discussion Board: By default, all new team sites created in SharePoint have a discussion board, but here's how to create one of your own.
- Start a New Discussion: Once a Discussion Board has been created, it is ready to be used by any member of the groups authorized to use the team site.
- Reply to a Discussion: After a discussion is started, you can add your own comments in much the same way you would create a regular email.
- Edit Discussions: From time to time, you may make a comment on a discussion board and then discover that you need to add something or change the original content of that comment.
- Delete Discussions: Once in a while, a comment might be completely in error, or applied to the wrong discussion.
- Remove a Discussion Board: Once the project is completed, you can remove the discussion board from the team site entirely.

Task: Create a Discussion Board

Purpose: When group projects occur in the workplace, one of the old standbys for communication is the email discussion. Members of a team send emails back and forth, going over various approaches and ideas. But emails can be cumbersome. Which message had the file you needed for the annual statistics? Who was replying to whom about next week's meeting? Did you hit "reply" or "reply all"?

One good way to avoid these logistical problems is to use SharePoint's discussion board feature. In a discussion board, all the comments are in one place, for everyone to quickly see and read. Discussions are threaded so their order and flow is easier to follow. By default, all new team sites created in SharePoint have a discussion board, but here's how to create one of your own.

> Caution: SharePoint's discussion board feature isn't a replacement for a full-fledged forum management or bulletin board system. It's effective for a relatively small number (less than 100) of original threads. Plan to create many individual discussion boards if you need a large number of topics. You may also want to consider other SharePoint/Office 365 features like Site Mailbox, Groups, and Yammer based on your needs.

Example: The Action Marketing Group would like to start a discussion board for issues concerning the team's goals. This discussion board should be viewable for all visitors to the Action Marketing Group site.

Steps:

1. Start Internet Explorer and type the URL for your organization's SharePoint server. The Start page will open.
2. Navigate to the site where you want to create a discussion board. The site's home page will open.
3. Click the **Settings** menu gear icon, then click the **Add an app** option. The Your Apps page will appear.

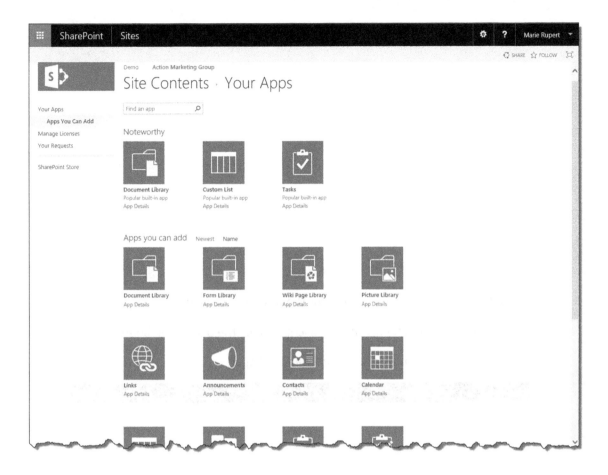

Figure 1: The Your Apps Page

4. Scroll down and click the **Discussion Board** icon. The Adding Discussion Board dialog box will appear.

Figure 2: Adding the Discussion Board Dialog Box

5. Click **Advanced Options**. The New Discussion Board page will appear.

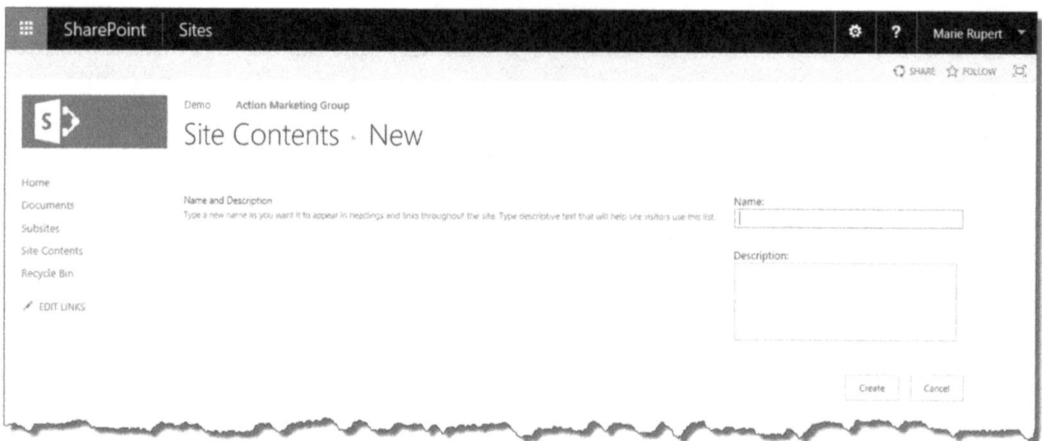

Figure 3: The New Discussion Board Page

6. In the Name field, type a name for the discussion board.
7. In the Description field, enter a description for the discussion board.
8. Click Create. The new discussion board will open.

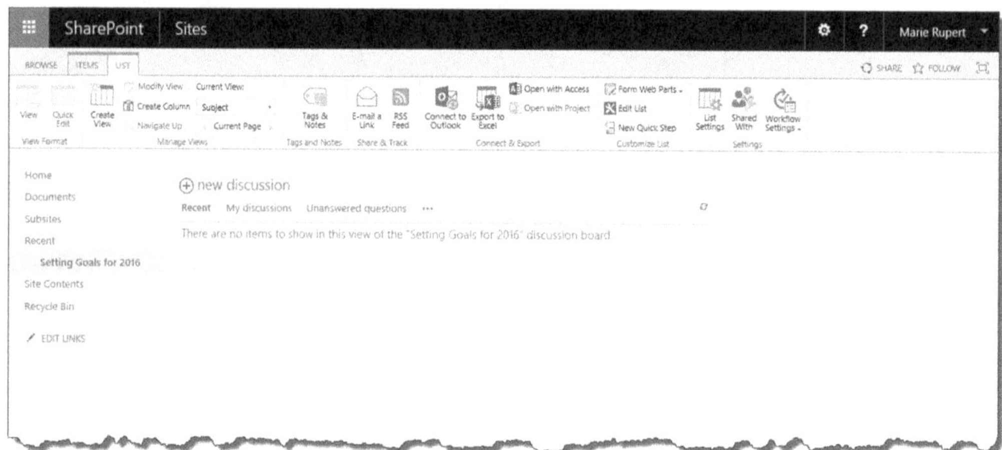

Figure 4: A New Discussion Board

Exception: If you cannot create a discussion board, there is an existing discussion board with the same name or URL or you do not have specific permissions to create a discussion board. Check the permissions settings to ensure you have the appropriate access rights.

Task: Start a New Discussion

Purpose: Once a Discussion Board has been created, it may be used by any user in the site. Discussions serve as topics for anyone to jump in and comment. All you need is for someone to get a conversation started.

Example: A new file relating to the yearly goals has been created, and the author wants to ask a question about the file via a post on the discussion board.

Steps:

1. Start Internet Explorer and type the URL for your organization's SharePoint server. The Start page will open.
2. Navigate to the site where you want to participate in a discussion. The site's home page will open.
3. Click the **Settings** menu gear icon, then the **Site Contents** option. The Site Contents page will open.
4. Find the discussion board you want to join and click on its name. The board's home page will open.
5. Click the **new discussion** link. The Discussion entry page will open.

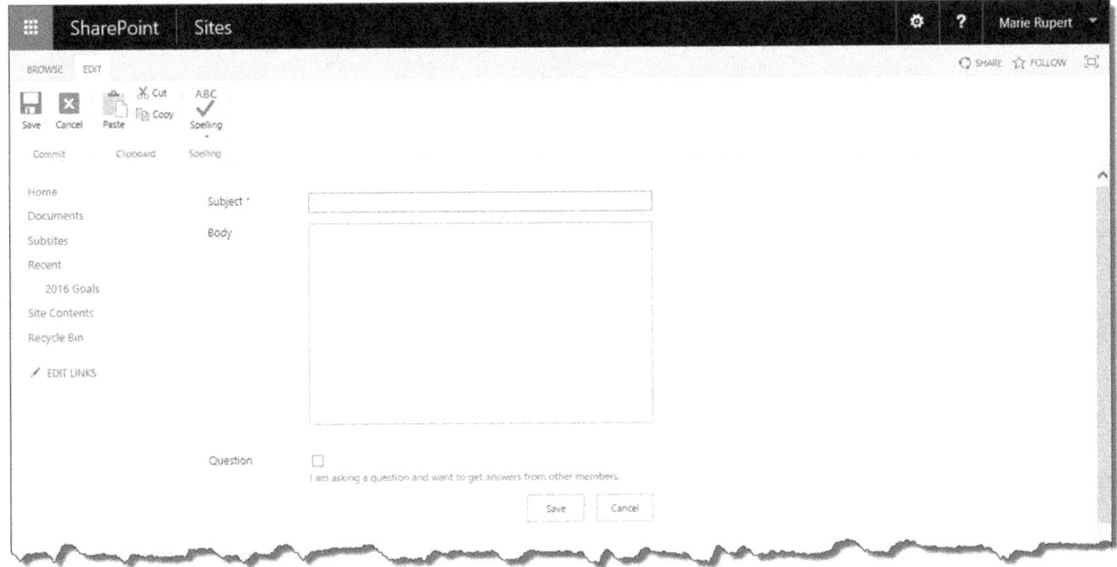

Figure 1: The Discussion Entry Page

6. In the Subject field, type a topic for the discussion. The subject field is the short description that will be displayed in the list.

7. In the Body field, add any message you want. The editing tools will appear. You can copy content in from a Word document, web page, or any other source of content.

8. Click Save. Your discussion topic will appear on the discussion board.

Exception: If you cannot create a discussion, you do not have specific permissions to create discussions on a discussion list. Check the permissions settings to ensure you have the appropriate access rights.

Task: Reply to a Discussion

Purpose: After a discussion is started, you can add your own comments in much the same way you would create an email. Replying to a discussion keeps the responses threaded together so they're easy to see and read.

Example: As discussions begin, members of the Action Marketing Group will want to join in and deliver their own responses.

Steps:

1. Start Internet Explorer and type the URL for your organization's SharePoint server. The Start page will open.
2. Navigate to the site where you want to participate in a discussion. The site's home page will open.
3. Click the **Settings** menu gear icon, then the **Site Contents** option. The Site Contents page will open.
4. Find the discussion board with the desired discussion and click on its name or icon. The board's home page will open.
5. Click the discussion topic to which you want to respond. The discussion page will open.

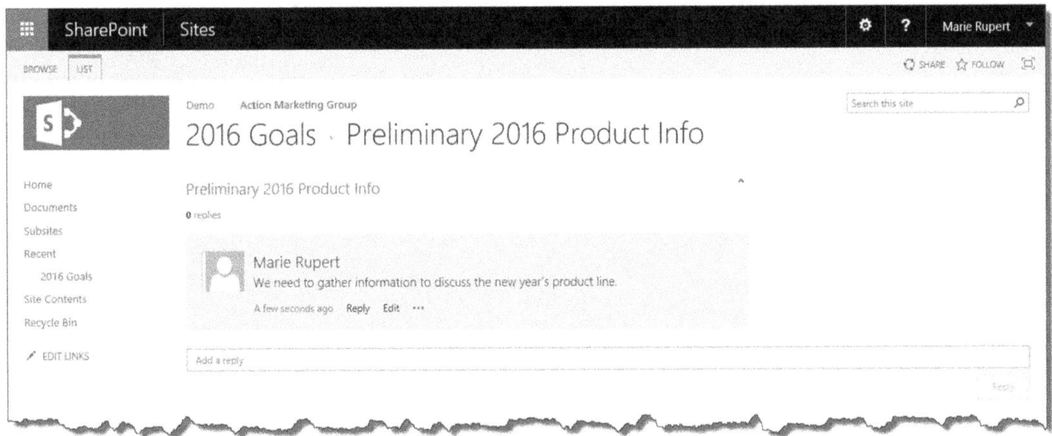

Figure 1: The Discussion Page

6. In the Add a Reply field, enter a reply.
7. Click **Reply**. The new comment will appear on the discussion page.

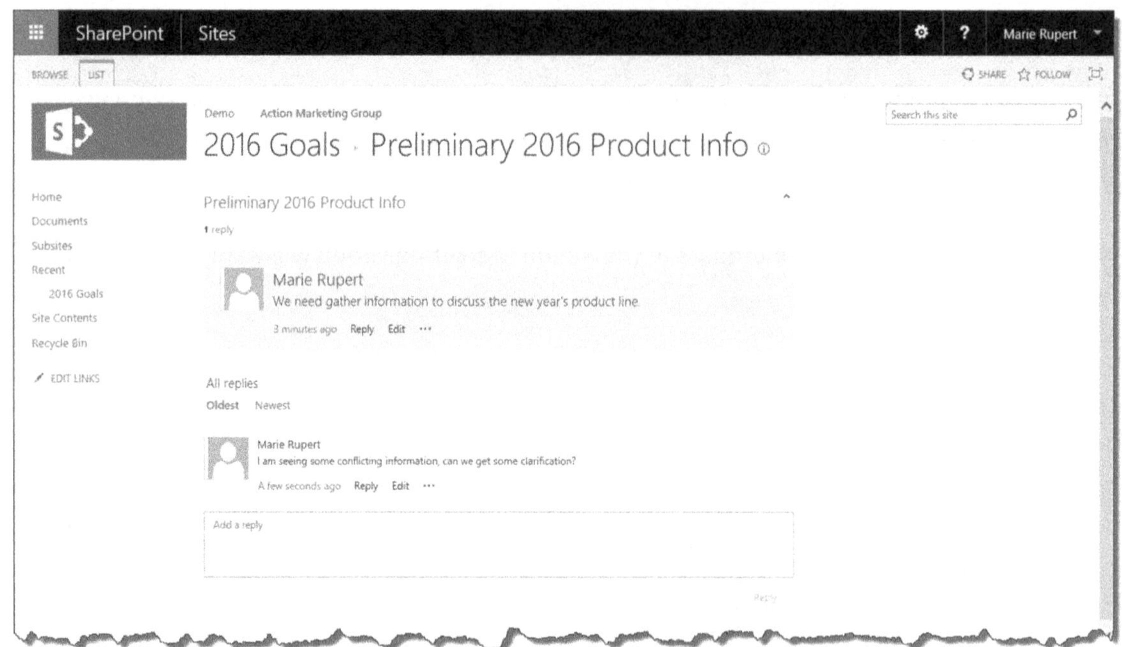

Figure 2: The Discussion Page with New Reply

Exception: If you can't reply to a discussion, you have read-only permissions and do not have specific permissions to create a reply. Check the permissions settings to ensure you have the appropriate access rights.

Task: Edit Discussions

Purpose: From time to time, you may make a comment on a discussion board and then discover that you need to add something or change the original content of that comment. SharePoint lets you, if need be, edit your own comments after they have been posted.

Example: The most recent comment in the discussion has an error, and the author would like to correct the mistake.

Steps:

1. Start Internet Explorer and type the URL for your organization's SharePoint server. The Start page will open.
2. Navigate to the site where you want to participate in a discussion board. The site's home page will open.
3. Click the **Settings** menu gear icon, then the **Site Contents** option. The Site Contents page will open.
4. Find the discussion board with the comment you wish to edit and click on its name or icon. The board's home page will open.
5. Click the discussion topic with your comment. The discussion page will open.
6. Find the comment you wish to edit and click **Edit**. The comment's text will be made available to edit.

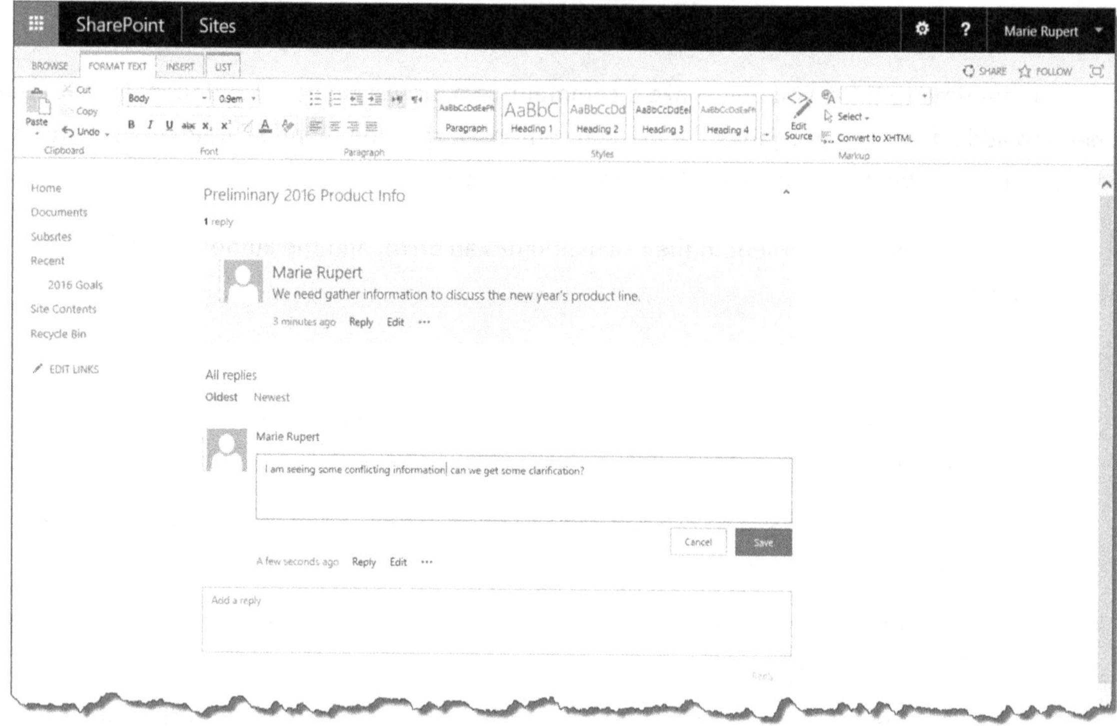

Figure 1: An Editable Comment

7. Edit the comment as needed and click Save. The edited comment will now appear in the discussion.

Note: If versioning is turned on for the list, prior versions of your comment will be available. Please see the task "Activate Version Control" for an example of how to access the version history of a SharePoint list item.

Exception: If you can't edit your response, you do not have specific permissions to edit discussions. Check the permissions settings to ensure you have the appropriate access rights.

Task: Delete Discussions

Purpose: Once in a while, a discussion board comment might be completely in error, or applied to the wrong conversation. In those cases, you may want to remove the comment altogether.

Example: After reviewing his comments, a user decides that he has replied to the wrong discussion topic, and just wants to remove his comment from the wrong thread altogether.

Steps:

1. Start Internet Explorer and type the URL for your organization's SharePoint server. The Start page will open.
2. Navigate to the site where you want to remove comments from a discussion board. The site's home page will open.
3. Click the **Settings** menu gear icon, then the **Site Contents** option. The Site Contents page will open.
4. Find the name of the discussion board you need to remove comments from and click on its name or icon. The board's home page will open.
5. Click the conversation topic with your comment. The discussion page will open.
6. Find the comment you wish to remove. Next to the Edit menu, click the **ellipsis** control found below the reply for that comment, and click **Delete**. A confirmation dialog box will open.

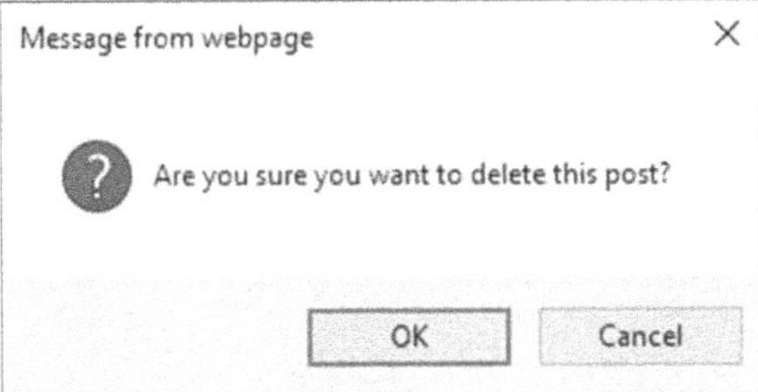

Figure 1: Delete Item Confirmation Dialog Box

7. Click **OK**. The comment will be removed from the discussion board.

Exception: If you cannot delete a conversation, you do not have specific permissions to delete conversations. Check the permissions settings to ensure you have the appropriate access rights.

Task: Remove a Discussion Board

Purpose: Depending on the activity of a team, you may find that you have to set up specific discussion boards for things like special projects. Once the project is completed, you can remove the discussion board from the team site entirely.

Example: After the feedback for the Action Marketing Group's goals has been gathered and analyzed, the site administrator decides to delete the board to prevent confusion.

Steps:

1. Start Internet Explorer and type the URL for your organization's SharePoint server. The Start page will open.
2. Navigate to the site with the discussion board you want to remove. The site's home page will open.
3. Click the Settings menu gear icon, then the Site Contents option. The Site Contents page will open.
4. Find the discussion board you wish to remove and click on its name or icon. The board's home page will open.
5. In the ribbon click the List tab. The List ribbon will open.

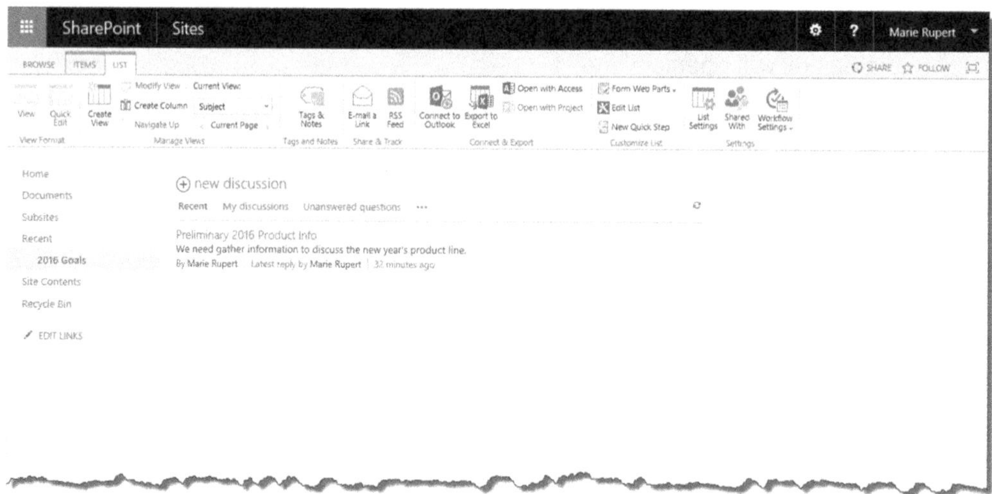

Figure 1: The List Ribbon

6. Click the List Settings button. The Discussion Board Settings page will open.

SharePoint Sites
Marie Rupert
SHARE FOLLOW

Demo Action Marketing Group

2016 Goals · Settings

Home
Documents
Subsites
Recent
2016 Goals
Site Contents
Recycle Bin
EDIT LINKS

List Information
Name: 2016 Goals
Web Address: http://sp16b2/AMG/Lists/2016 Goals/AllItems.aspx
Description: To discuss goals

General Settings
- List name, description and navigation
- Versioning settings
- Advanced settings
- Validation settings
- Audience targeting settings
- Rating settings
- Form settings

Permissions and Management
- Delete this discussion board
- Save discussion board as template
- Permissions for this discussion board
- Workflow Settings
- Generate file plan report
- Enterprise Metadata and Keywords Settings
- Information management policy settings

Communications
- RSS settings

Content Types
This list is configured to allow multiple content types. Use content types to specify the information you want to display about an item, in addition to its policies, workflows, or other behavior. The following content types are currently available in this list:

Content Type	Visible on New Button	Default Content Type
Discussion	✓	✓
Message	✓	

- Add from existing site content types
- Change new button order and default content type

Columns
A column stores information about each item in the list. Because this list allows multiple content types, some column settings, such as whether information is required or optional for a column, are now specified by the content type of the item. The following columns are currently available in this list:

Column (click to edit)	Type	Used in
Body	Multiple lines of text	Discussion, Message
Created	Date and Time	

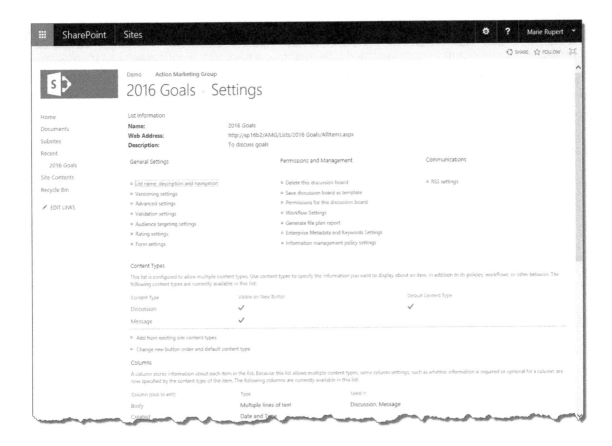

Figure 2: The Discussion Board Settings Page

7. In the Permissions and Management column, click Delete this discussion board. A confirmation dialog box will open.

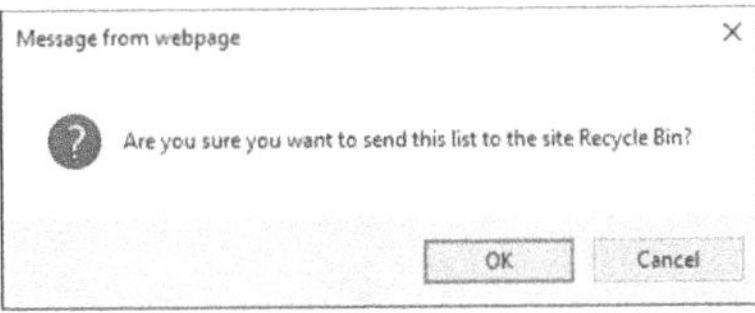

Figure 3: Delete Discussion Board Confirmation Dialog Box

8. Click OK. The discussion board will be removed from the site.

Exception: If you can't remove the discussion board, you do not have specific permissions to manage discussion boards. Check the permissions settings to ensure you have the appropriate access rights.

Conduct Effective Meetings

Collaboration comes in many forms. In the digital age, many people are encouraged to try online chats, shared document sessions, or email conversations to exchange ideas. Sometimes, though, a good old-fashioned face-to-face meeting is what's needed. SharePoint can create an online home for meetings, allowing attendees to be invited, agendas to be set, and tasks to be assigned.

Before all of this can happen, a new event must be created in the SharePoint calendar.

In this section, you will learn how to:

- Create an Event: The basics of creating an event are reviewed.
- Create a Recurring Event: Creating recurring events on your calendar is just a few steps more than creating a one-time event.

Task: Create an Event

Purpose: SharePoint can create an online home for meetings, allowing attendees to be invited, agendas to be set, and tasks to be assigned.

Before all of this can happen, a new event must be created in the SharePoint calendar.

This task will cover the creation of a one-time event; see the task "Create a Recurring Event" to make events that occur with regularity. Note: these events will be added to the SharePoint calendar, not the user's Outlook calendar.

Example: A client is planning to visit the Action Marketing Group offices, and the event needs to be posted on the team's calendar.

Steps:

1. Start Internet Explorer and type the URL for your organization's SharePoint server. The Start page will open.
2. Navigate to the site where you want to add the event. The site's home page will open.
3. In the Quick Launch for your site, click the name of your calendar. If the calendar you want to work with doesn't appear on the Quick Launch, you can click the **Settings** menu gear icon and the **Site Contents** link, and select the calendar from the list that appears. The Calendar page will open.

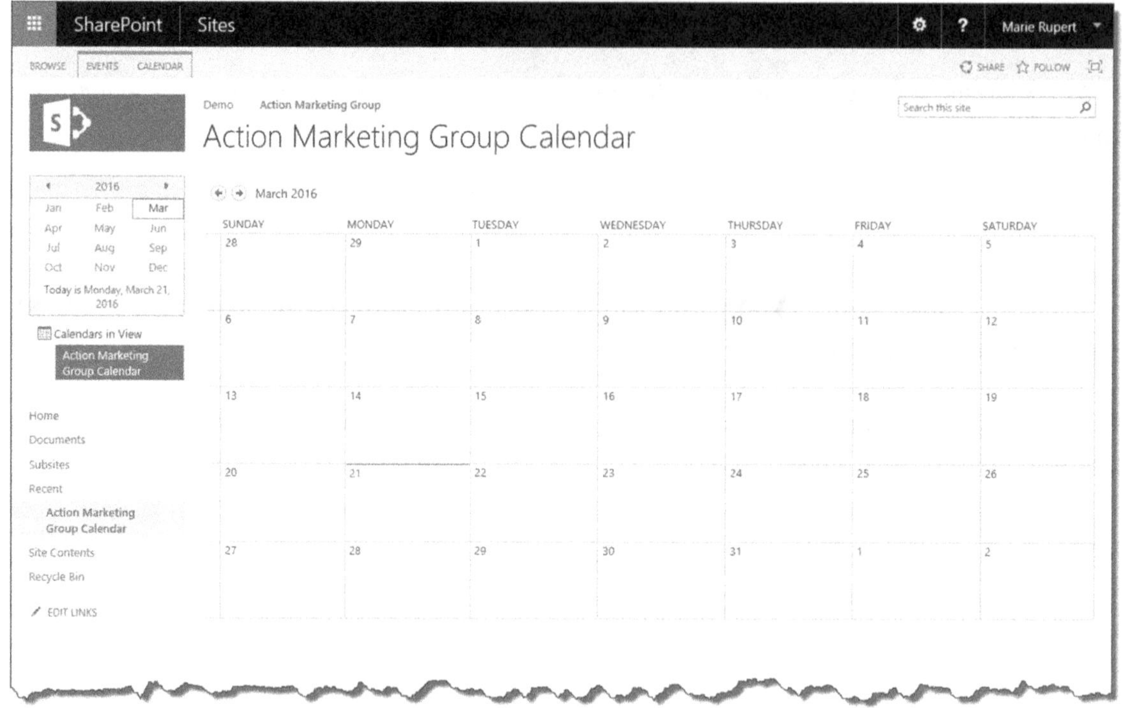

Figure 1: The Calendar Page

4. Hover over the date on which you want add the event and click the +Add link when it appears. The Calendar - New Item dialog box will open.

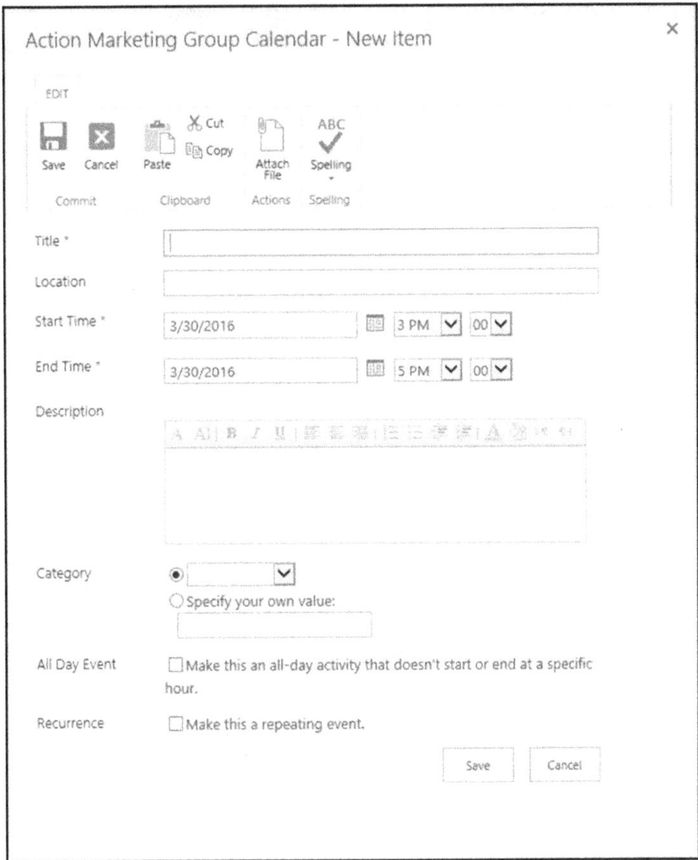

Figure 2: Calendar - New Item Dialog Box

5. In the Title field, enter the name of the event. This description is the one typically used when looking at a summary of events, or at the events in the calendar view.

6. In the Location field, enter a place for the event. This could be the room number for a meeting, or the city, state, and country for larger events.

7. Specify the Start and End Times. It is possible to customize the list such that events don't have times associated with them. If you want to create events without times, click the **All Day Event** checkbox.

8. In the Description field, enter a description of the event.

9. Select a classification for the event in the **Category** drop-down list, or select the **Specify Your Own Value** option and enter your own.

10. Click **Save**. The Calendar - New Item dialog box will close and the event will appear in the Calendar on the Calendar page.

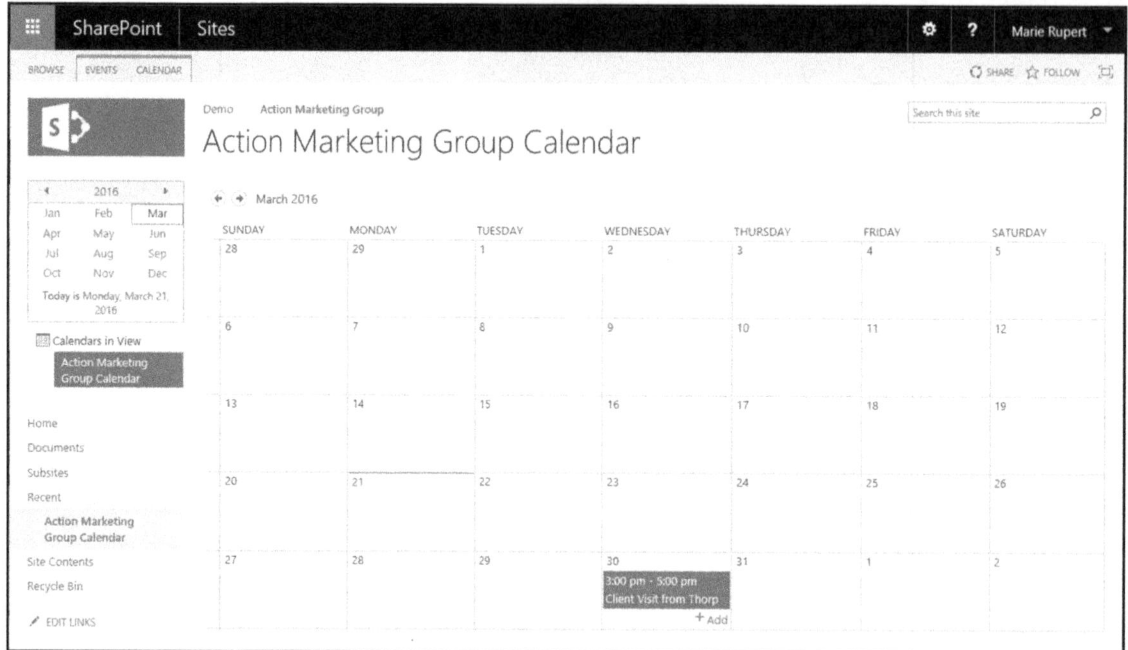

Figure 3: The New Event on the Calendar Page

Exception: If you can't add an event to a calendar, you do not have specific permissions to change content within this calendar. Check the permissions settings to ensure you have the appropriate access rights.

Task: Create a Recurring Event

Purpose: Some events take place on a regular basis, such as the weekly staff meeting or the quarterly analysts briefing. Creating recurring events on your calendar requires just a few steps more than creating a one-time event.

Example: The Action Marketing Group works with several interns during the year, and as part of the program, a bi-weekly status meeting is needed to keep up-to-date on all interns' progress.

Steps:

1. Start Internet Explorer and type the URL for your organization's SharePoint server. The Start page will open.
2. Navigate to the site where you want to add the event. The site's home page will open.
3. In the Quick Launch for your site, click the name of your calendar. If the calendar you want to work with doesn't appear on the Quick Launch, you can click the **Settings** menu gear icon and the **Site Contents** link, and select the calendar from the list that appears. The Calendar page will open.
4. Hover over the date on which you want to add the event and click the **+Add** link when it appears. The Calendar - New Item dialog box will open.
5. In the Title field, enter the name of the event. This description is the one typically used when looking at a summary of events, or at the events in the calendar view.
6. In the Location field, enter a place for the event. This could be the room number for a meeting, or the city, state, and country for larger events.
7. Specify the Start and End Times. It is possible to customize the list such that events don't have times associated with them. If you want to create events without times, click the **All Day Event** checkbox.
8. In the Description field, enter a description of the event.
9. Select a classification for the event in the **Category** drop-down list, or select the **Specify Your Own Value** option and enter your own.
10. Click the **Recurrence** checkbox. The recurrence controls will appear.

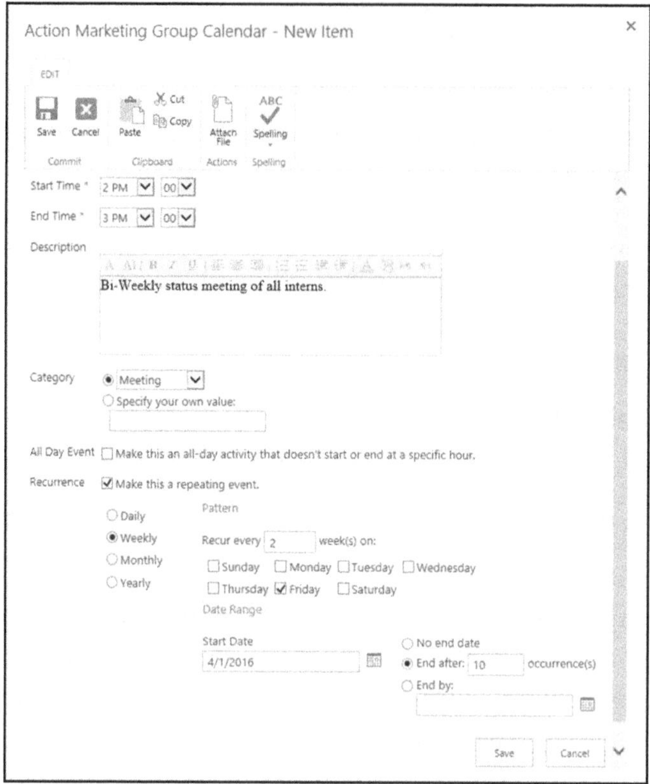

Figure 1: The Recurrence Controls for an Event

11. For a bi-weekly event, click the **Weekly** option. The Pattern section will change to accommodate a weekly recurrence. Each type of recurrence has its own pattern.
12. In the Pattern section, enter 2 in the Recur every __ week(s) field.
13. Select the **Start Date** for the recurring event. This is the first date when the event should appear.
14. Select an **End Date** option. In this case, enter a date near the end of summer.
15. Click **Save**. The new recurring events will appear on the calendar.

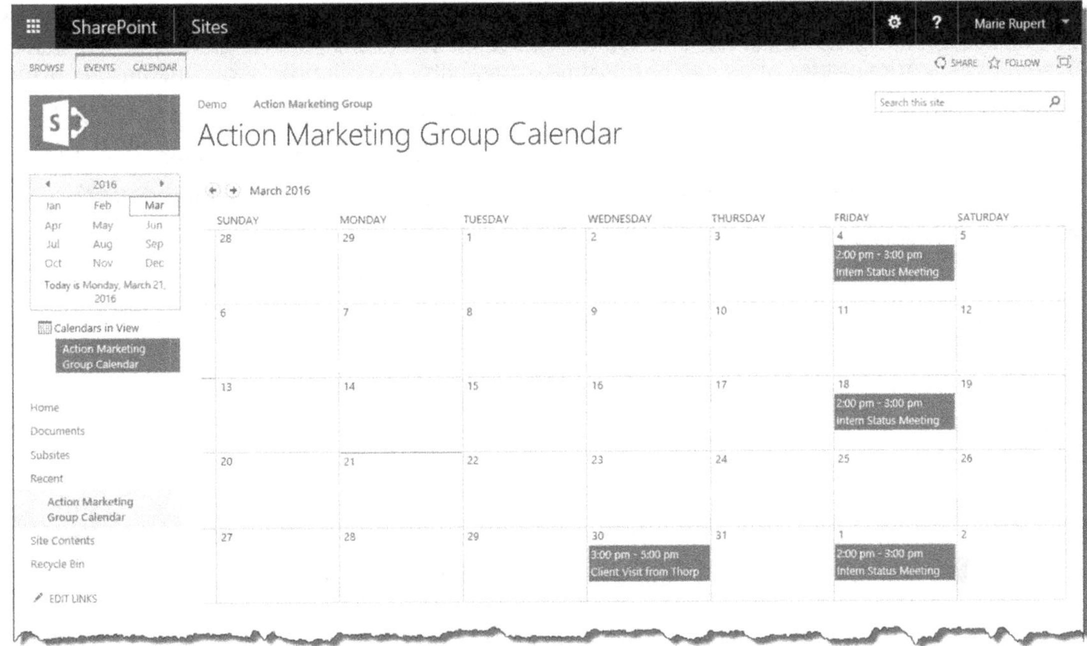

Figure 2: The New Recurring Events on the Calendar Page

Exception: If you can't add a recurring event to a calendar, you do not have specific permissions to change content within this calendar. Check the permissions settings to ensure you have the appropriate access rights.

Work Together on Content

One of the biggest advantages of using SharePoint is the ability to collaborate on documents using the Office Web Apps, or Office Online tools, which enables users to discuss, contribute to, and edit documents together, with changes updating in real time. While OneDrive for Business has replaced SkyDrive Pro, SharePoint still allows users to save a local copy of files and documents to their devices, and will notify users when a file has been updated on the server. SharePoint is also tightly integrated with Microsoft Office – so much so, you can use any Office application to work with SharePoint. These tools, when used together, establish a powerful collaboration infrastructure for any team.

In this section, you'll learn how to:

- Open and Save Documents using Office Web Apps: Because Office Web Apps automatically saves changes to your documents, you can open documents from SharePoint and others can view your changes to the file almost instantly.
- Sync Documents with OneDrive for Business: You can synchronize the contents of a document library into a folder on your local machine using OneDrive for Business.
- Changing Document Permissions in SharePoint: You can also grant more users access to a document in SharePoint itself.
- Check Out a Document in Office 2013: If many users are working on the same document, it is better to formally check the document out while making edits, to prevent other users from overwriting your changes.
- Check Out a Document in Office 2016: If many users are working on the same document, it is better to formally check the document out while making edits, to prevent other users from overwriting your changes.
- Check Out Documents in SharePoint: You can also check out a document directly from within SharePoint.
- Check In a Document in Office 2013: After you have completed your edits on a checked out document, you will need to check it back in to the document workspace so other users can see your changes.
- Check In a Document in Office 2016: After you have completed your edits on a checked out document, you will need to check it back in to the document workspace so other users can see your changes.
- Check In Documents in SharePoint: You can directly check in a document from within SharePoint.
- Connect an Approval Workflow: How a site administrator can tag a library, list, or workspace for improvement using the workflow process.

- **Follow a Document**: Use SharePoint's social tools to automatically track the status of a document.
- **Save a Site as a Template**: Learn how to create a template from any site, which can be reused to create other sites.
- **Activate Version Control**: SharePoint supports versioning for both list items and for files, so you can see what changes were made and by whom.

Task: Open and Save Documents Using Office Web Apps

Purpose: If you are already working within a SharePoint site, you can open documents directly from SharePoint and view them right inside your browser. Because Office Web Apps will automatically save your changes to SharePoint, this is a great method to ensure your edits are quickly saved into the document for others to view.

Example: Open a spreadsheet from within SharePoint to view and edit it.

Steps:

1. Start Internet Explorer and type the URL for your organization's SharePoint server. The Start page will open.
2. Navigate to the library app where you want to edit a document. The library app's page will open.

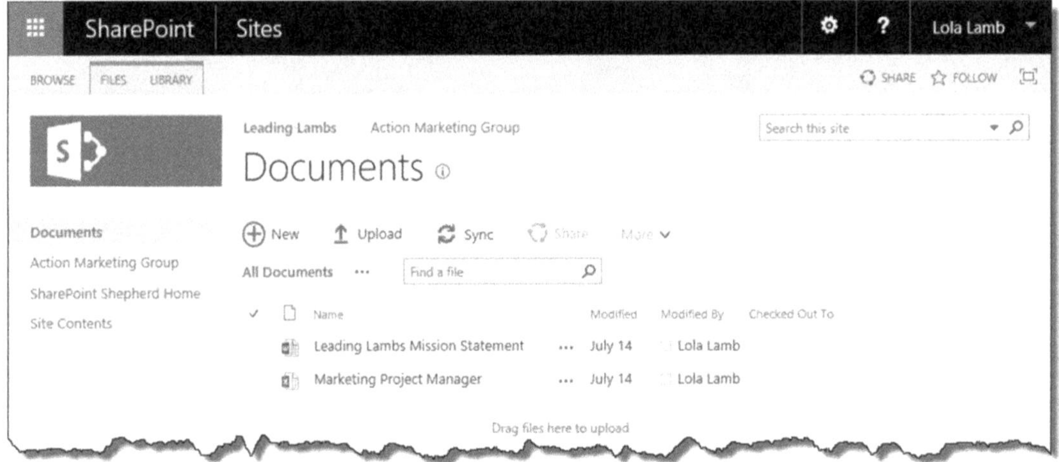

Figure 1: A Document Library

3. Find the document you wish to open and click the **ellipsis** control next to the document title to open the document's menu.

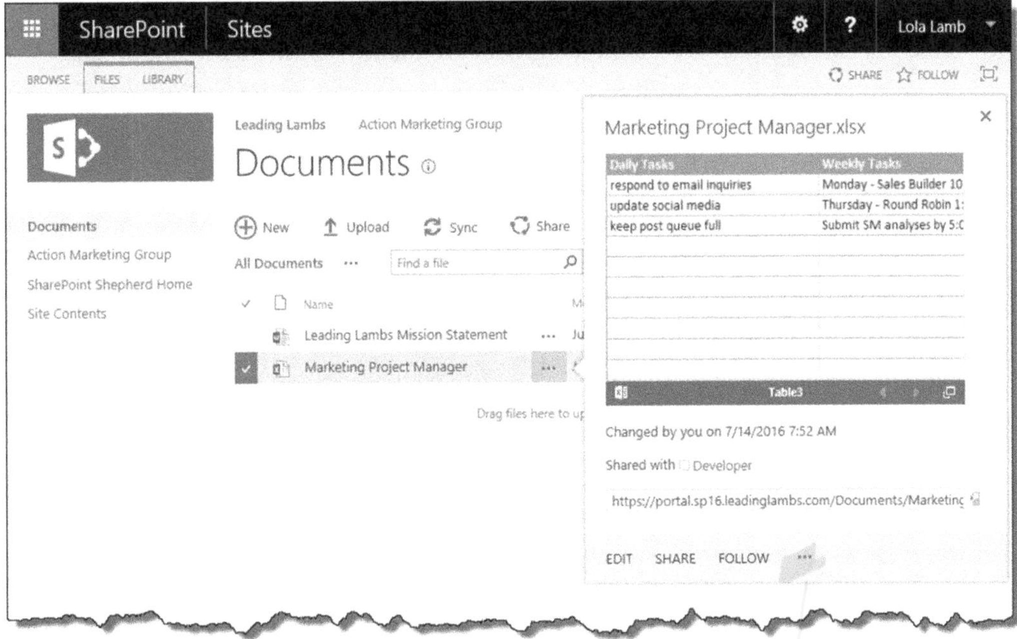

Figure 2: The Document Menu

4. At the bottom of the document's menu, click the ellipsis control to open the Options menu.

Figure 3: The Document Options Menu

5. Click the Open in Excel Online option. The Excel Web App will open in Edit mode.

Note: Depending on your library settings, clicking the document title may automatically open the document in the Office Web App in read-only mode. To edit the document in Office Web Apps, click the **Edit Workbook** menu and then click the **Edit in Excel Online** option.

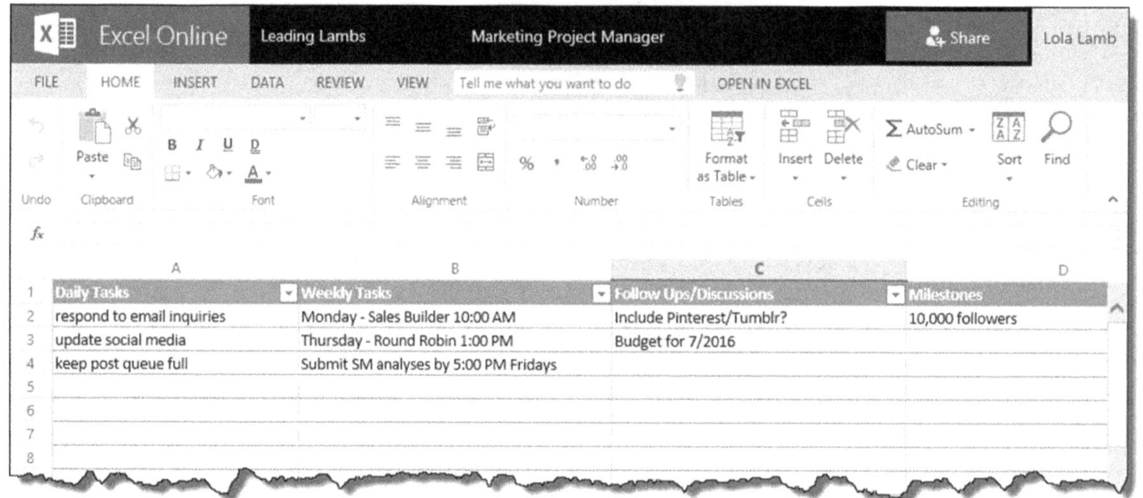

Figure 4: The Document Ready to Edit in the Browser

6. Once editing is enabled, changes are automatically saved to the file. At the top of the screen next to the title of your document, "Saving..." will be displayed while the changes are being saved. When the document is finished saving, "Saved" will be displayed instead, and you are safe to close the document or navigate to a different page.

7. To save a copy of the file online, or to rename the file, click the File tab and select Save As from the menu. The Save As screen will appear.

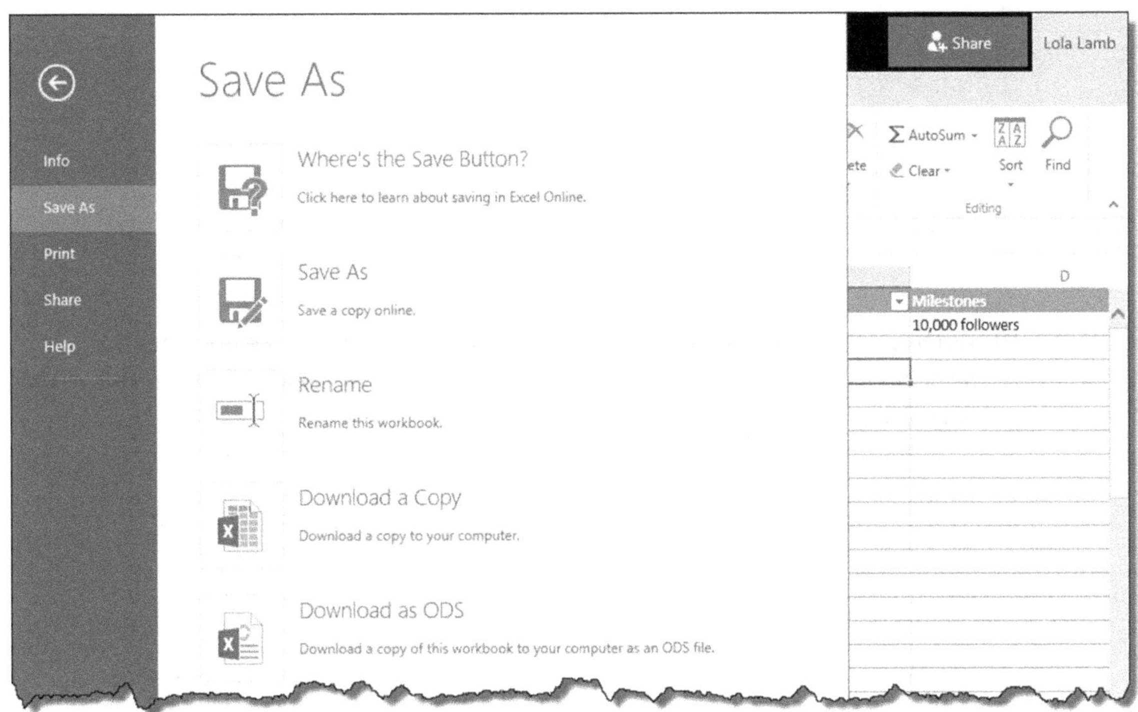

Figure 5: The Save As Screen

8. To save a copy of the document online, click **Save As**. The Save As dialog box will appear. You will be prompted to rename the copy of the document, or select **Replace existing file** if you would like to replace the existing document with the new copy. Click **Save** to save your changes.

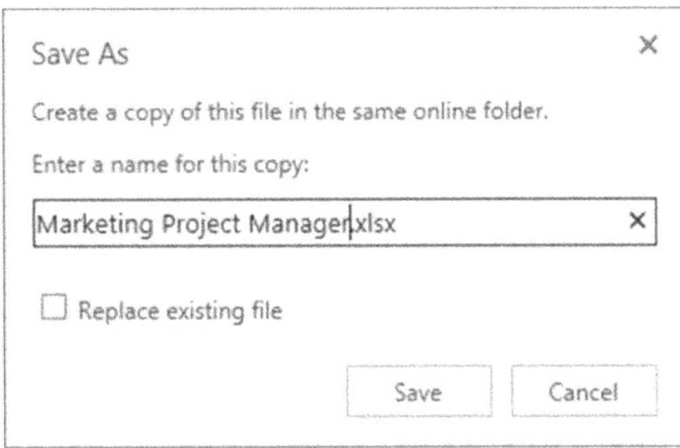

Figure 6: The Save As Dialog Box

9. To rename the document you're currently working on, click **Rename**. The Rename dialog box will appear. Type a new name for the document, then click **OK** to save your changes.

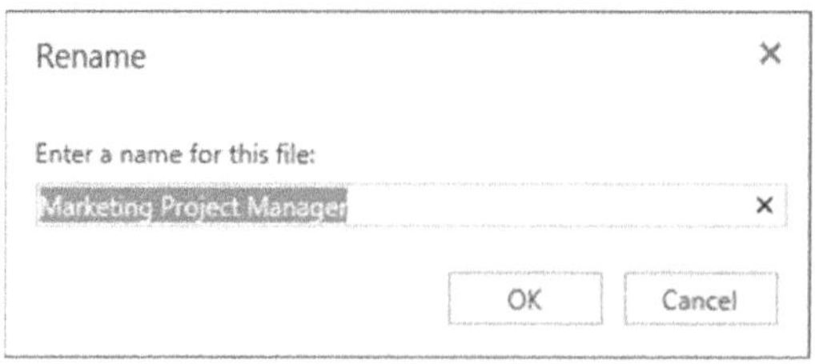

Figure 7: The Rename Dialog Box

10. When you are finished editing the document, you can close the document or navigate to a different page. Your changes are automatically saved to the file in the library app.

Task: Sync Documents in OneDrive for Business

Purpose: OneDrive for Business lets you synchronize the contents of a document library into a folder on your local machine. This is great for any user who needs to access documents while offline.

Example: One of the Action Marketing Group team members wants to synchronize shared documents in the Action Marketing Group library on their computer.

Steps:

1. Start Internet Explorer and type the URL for your organization's SharePoint server. The Start page will open.
2. Navigate to the document library that you want to synchronize to your device. The document library page will open.
3. Click the Library tab. The Library ribbon will open.

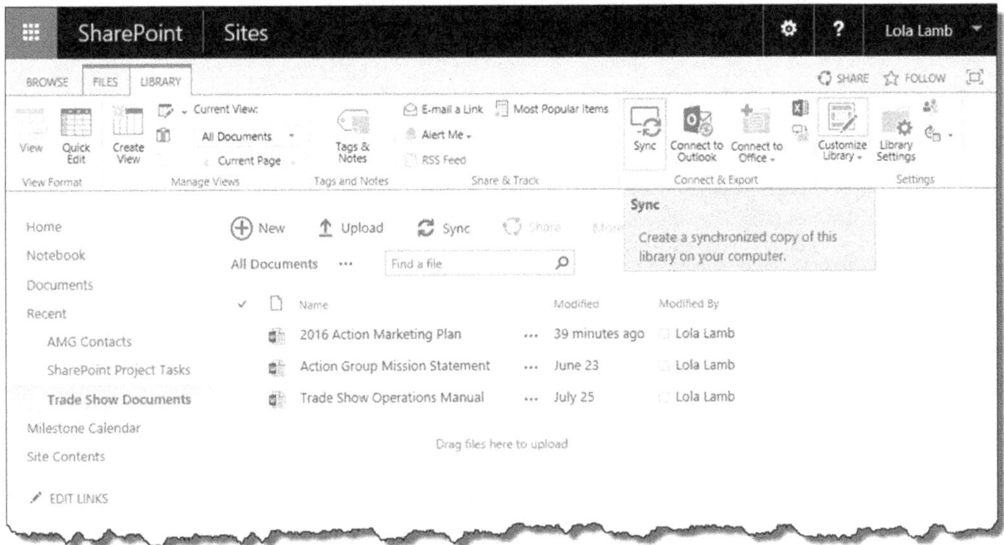

Figure 1: Library Ribbon with Sync Button

4. Click the Sync button. The Sync Now dialog box will open.
5. Click the Sync Now button to sync your documents. The Microsoft OneDrive for Business dialog box will appear.

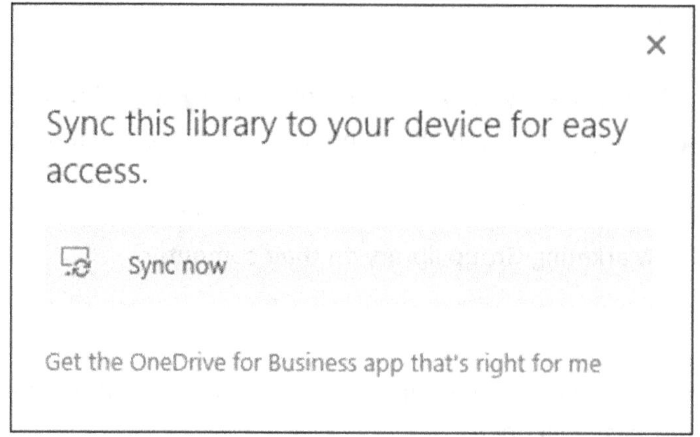

Figure 2: The Sync this library dialog box

6. If this is the first time you are using OneDrive for Business, it will give you a default location to save your documents. If you want to choose a different folder, click the Change link and browse for the location to synchronize files to, then press OK. Click the Sync Now button to sync your documents.

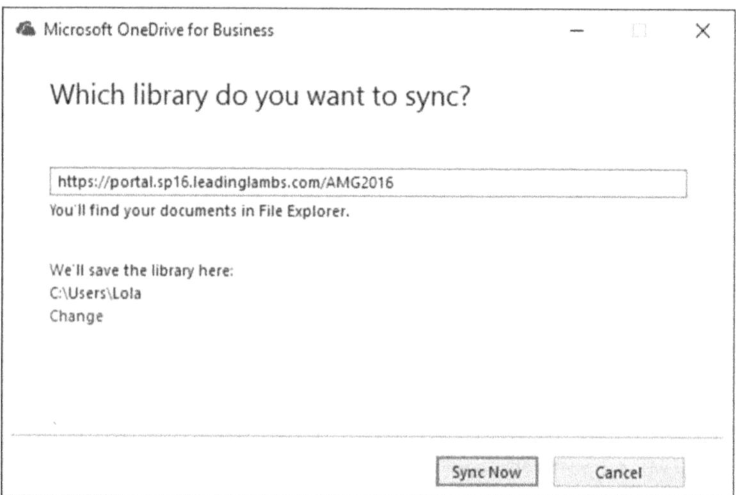

Figure 3: First Time Syncing a Library

7. If you have already used OneDrive for Business, your library will be saved in the same location as any other library you have previously synced. Click the Sync Now button to sync your documents.

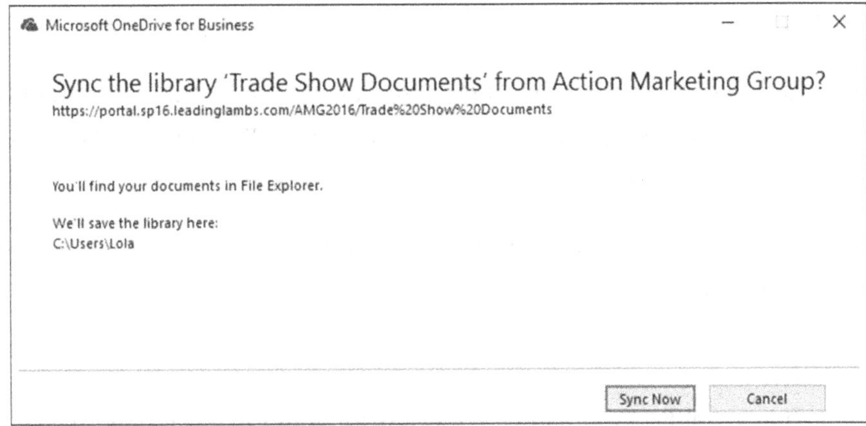

Figure 4: Syncing a New Library

8. After clicking Sync Now, or if you have already synced this library before, the Microsoft OneDrive for Business Dialog Box will appear. Click the Show my files button in order to access your synced document files.

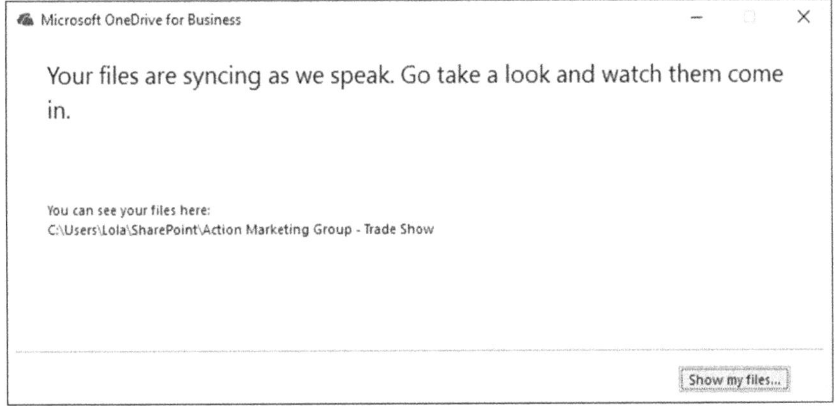

Figure 5: Files are Syncing

Task: Changing Document Permissions in SharePoint

Purpose: When a document is assigned to a library, the collaborators of the document are typically the same users who were originally granted access to that library. You can, however, grant more users access to a document library within SharePoint itself.

Example: The marketing plan document is starting to be created, and at this time you only want to restrict access to a few people.

Steps:

1. Start Internet Explorer and type the URL for your organization's SharePoint server. The Start page will open.
2. Navigate to the document library where the document you wish to modify is located. The document library page will open.

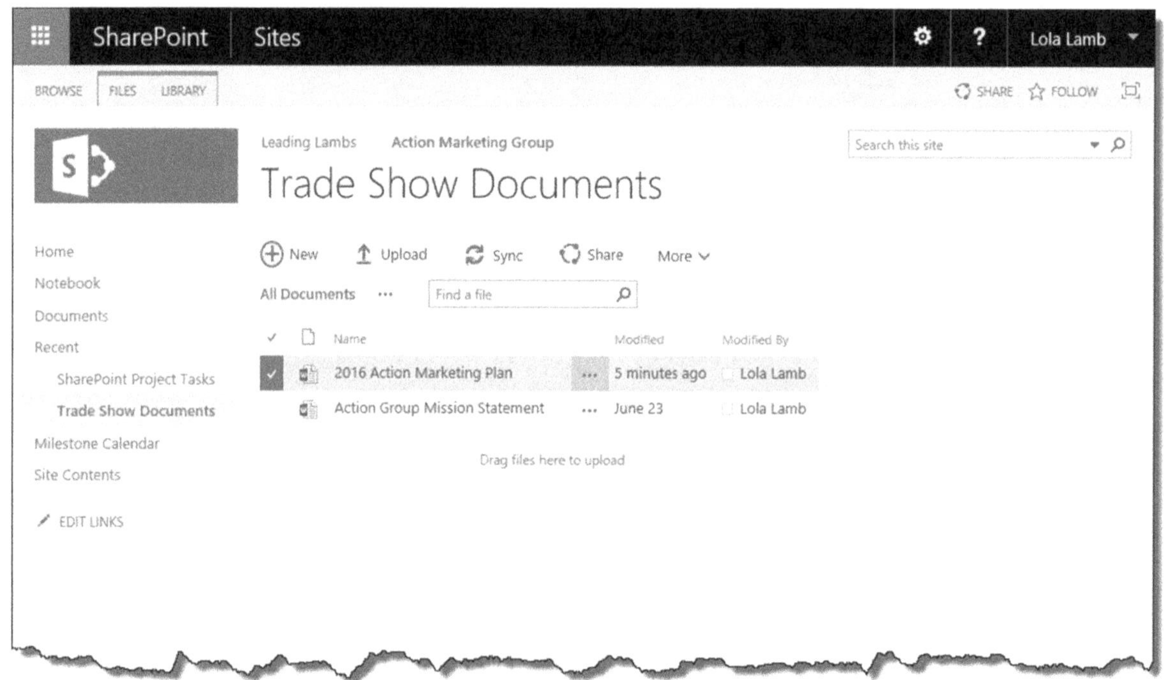

Figure 1: A Document Library

3. Find the document you wish to edit, then click on the ellipsis control next its name. The document's menu will appear.

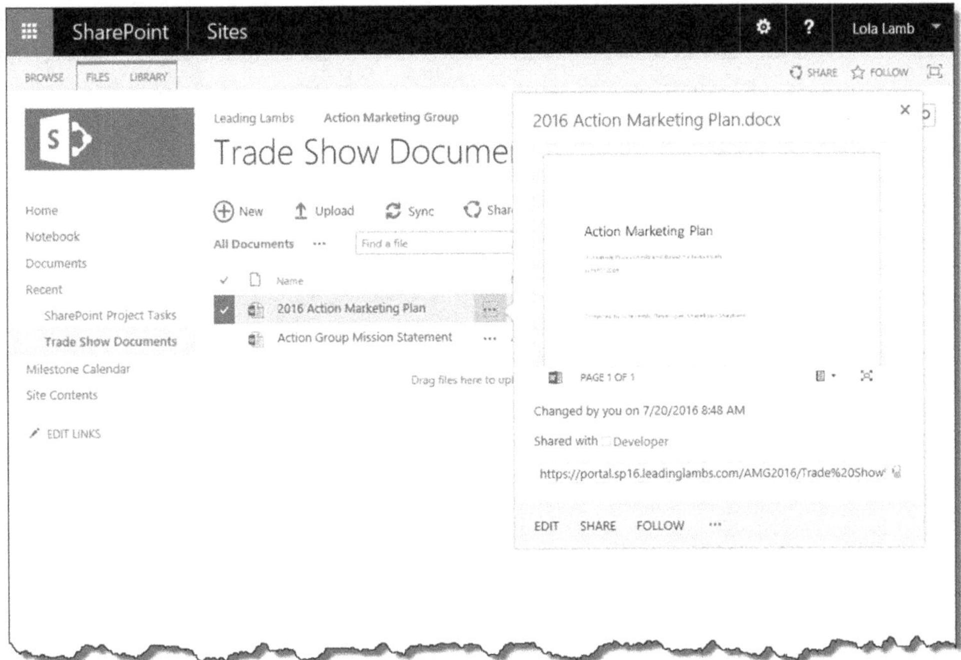

Figure 2: The Document Menu

4. At the bottom of the document menu, click **Share**. The Share dialog box will open.

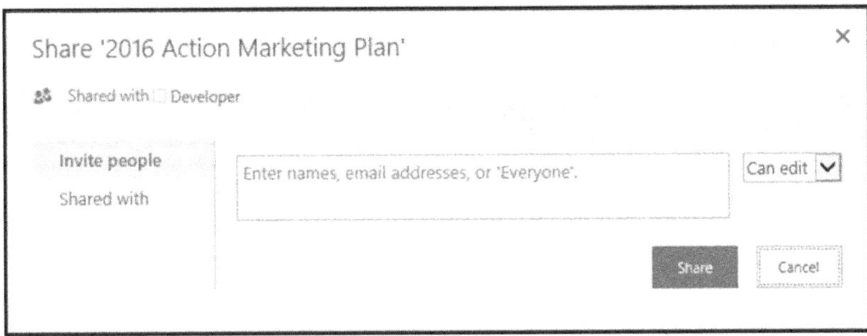

Figure 3: The Share Dialog Box

5. Click the **Shared with** tab. The Shared with screen will open.

6. Click the **Advanced** link and the Permissions page will open.

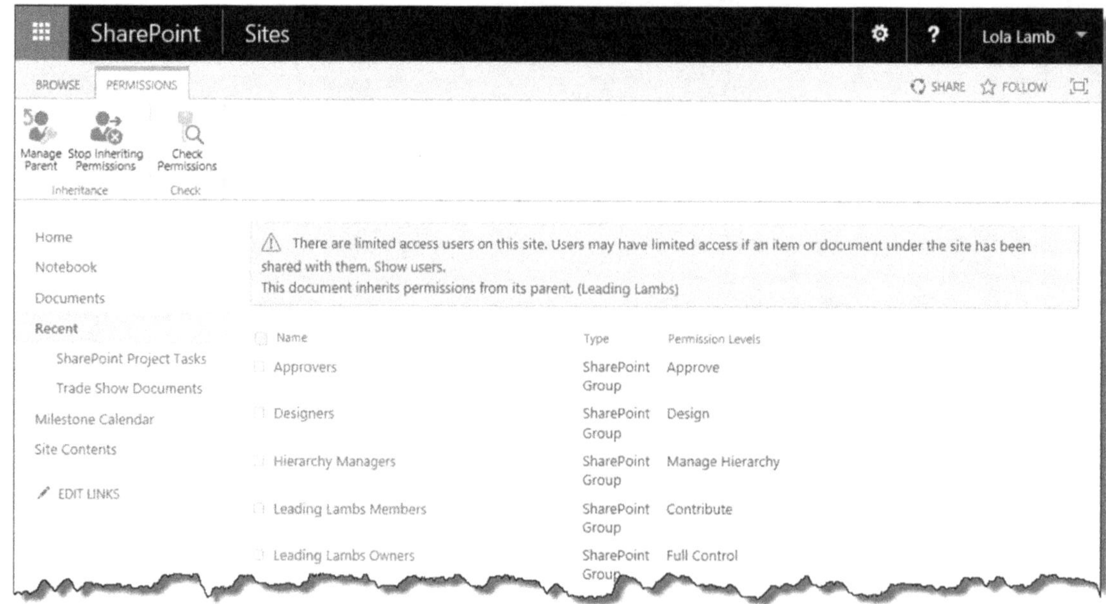

Figure 4: The Permissions Tools Page

7. In the Permissions ribbon, click the Stop Inheriting Permissions button. A confirmation dialog box will appear.

8. Click OK. The confirmation dialog box will close, the document will no longer have the same permissions set, and a new set of tools will appear on the page.

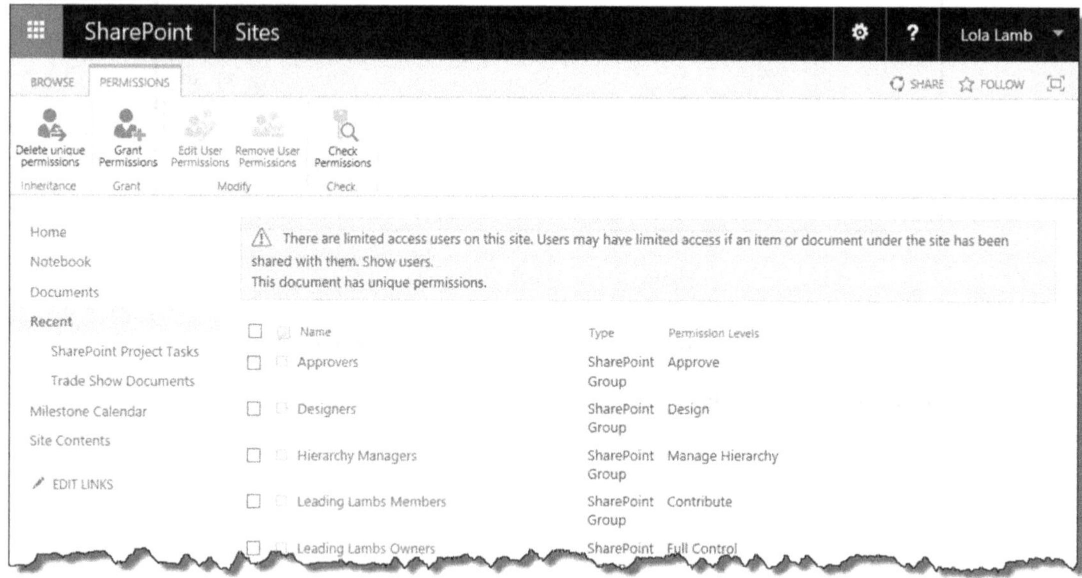

Figure 5: The Permissions Tools Page, Without Permission Inheritance

9. In the Permissions ribbon, click the **Grant Permissions** button. The Share dialog box will open.

10. In the Add People field, type in the name of the user. As the name is typed, a list of matching results will appear. You can click on the name to add it to the list.

11. Add additional names as needed.

12. Click **Share**. The Share dialog box will close and the users will now appear on the Permission page. Repeat Steps 9-12 to grant other users different permission levels.

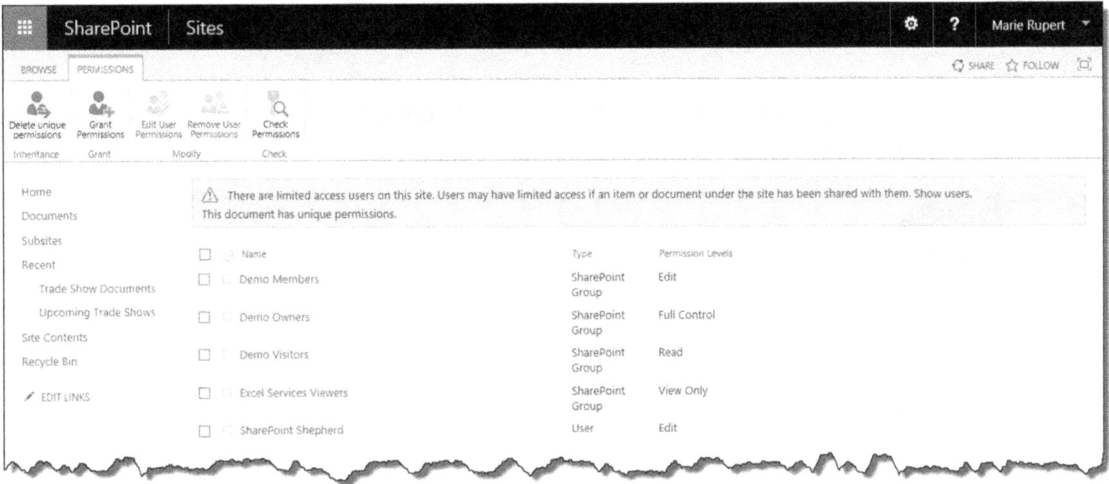

Figure 6: New Users Listed in the Permissions Tools Window

13. Click the **checkboxes** next to the names of the users and groups you do not want to have access. The users and groups will be selected.

14. Click the **Remove User Permissions** icon. A confirmation dialog box will appear.

15. Click **OK**. The confirmation dialog box will close and the user(s) will be removed from the user list.

Task: Check Out a Document in Office 2013

Purpose: When a document is being edited from a document library, a user can quickly open the document, make changes, and then save the document back into the workspace. If there are many users who may be working on the same document at the same time and you intend to work on the document offline, it may be better to formally check the document out.

Example: When you have a document opened from a SharePoint document library, you can check it out from the Office application.

Steps:

1. With the document open in the Office 2013 application, click the **File** tab and select **Info** from the menu. The Info screen will appear.

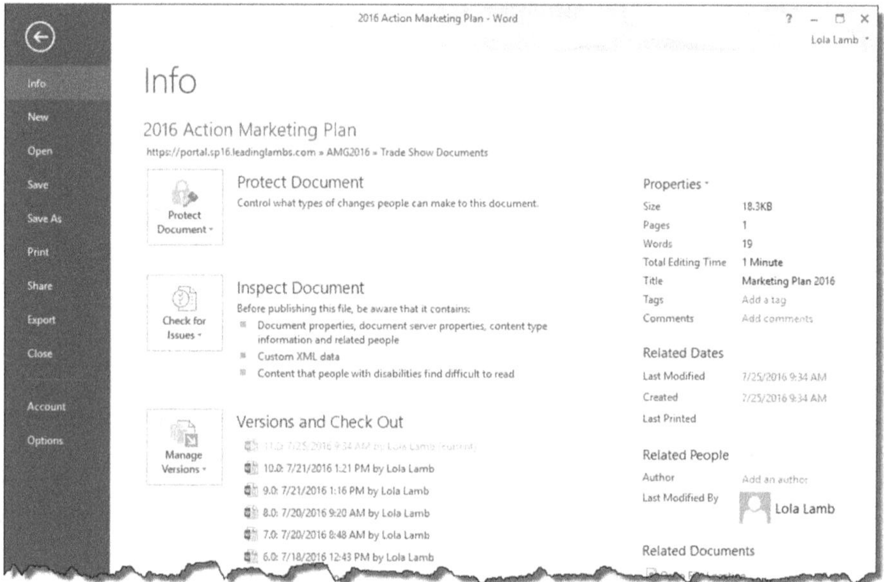

Figure 1: The Document Info Screen

2. Click the **Manage Versions** button, then click the **Check Out** option. The document will be checked out to you, but will remain stored on the SharePoint system.

Task: Check Out a Document in Office 2016

Purpose: When a document is being edited from a document library, a user can quickly open the document, make changes, and then save the document back into the library. If many users are working on the same document, however, it is better to formally check the document out while making edits to prevent other users from overwriting your changes. Depending on the library's properties, you may be required to check out a document before making any changes. Here's how to check out a document in Office 2016.

Example: When you have a document opened from a SharePoint document library, you can check it out from the Office application.

Steps:

1. With the document open in the Office 2016 application, click the **File** tab and select **Info** from the menu. The Info screen will appear.

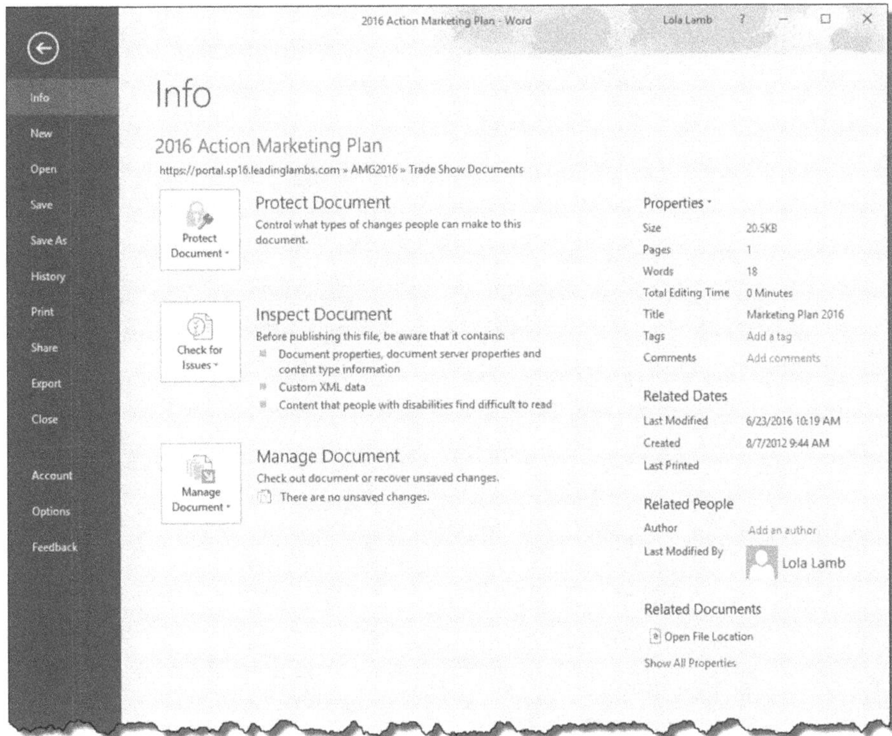

Figure 1: The Document Info Window

2. Click the **Manage Document** button, then click the **Check Out** option. The document will be checked out to you, but will remain stored on the SharePoint system.

Note: To view the version history of your document, click on **History** from the menu. Previous versions will appear in a sidebar on the right side of the document.

Task: Check Out Documents in SharePoint

Purpose: When a document is being edited from a document workspace, a user can quickly open the document, make changes, and then save the document back into the workspace. If many users are working on the same document, however, it is better to formally check the document out while making edits, to prevent other users from overwriting your changes.

Example: You need to check out a marketing plan document that you've already synchronized to your machine via OneDrive for Business so that you can work on it during your commute home.

Steps:

1. Start Internet Explorer and type the URL for your organization's SharePoint server. The Start page will open.
2. Navigate to the document library where the document you wish to check out is located. The document library page will open.
3. Find the document you wish to edit and next to the document title, click the ellipsis control to open the document's menu.

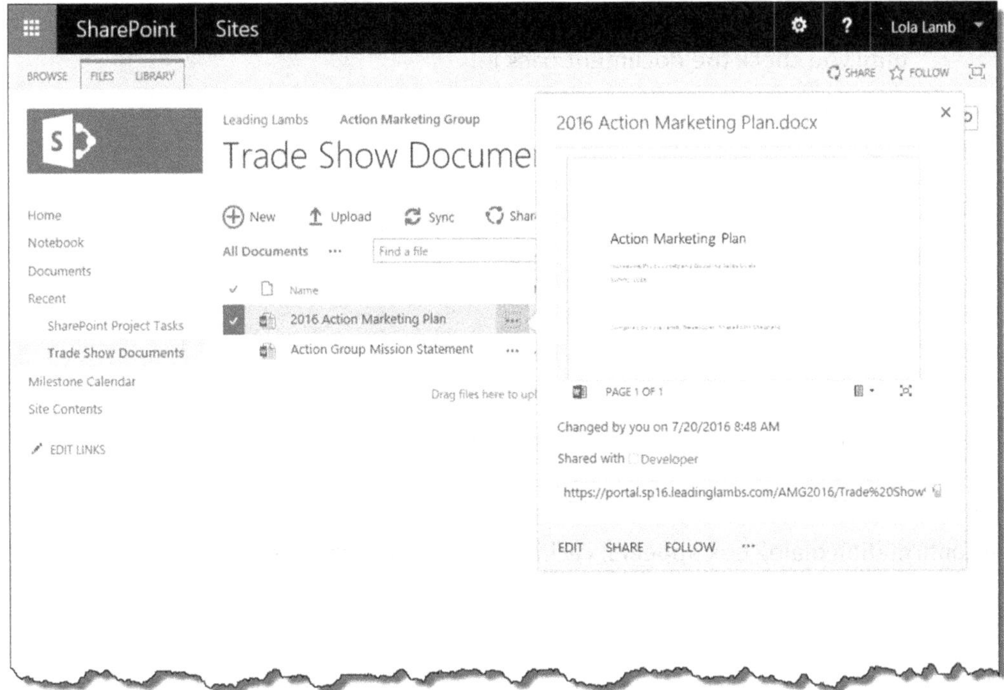

Figure 1: The Document Menu

4. At the bottom of the document's menu, click the ellipsis control to open the Options menu.

Figure 2: The Document Options Menu

5. Hover over **Advanced** to show the Advanced Options menu, then click the **Check Out** option. The document will be checked out to you and can be edited by you alone until you check the document back in.

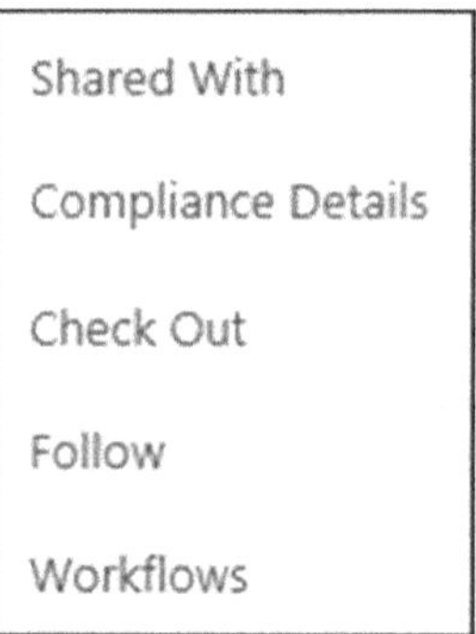

Figure 3: The Advanced Options Menu

Note: If a confirmation dialog box appears, click **OK** to complete the process.

Task: Check In a Document in Office 2013

Purpose: After you have completed your edits on a checked out document, you will need to check it back in to the document workspace so others can edit the document.

Example: After making changes to the marketing plan in Word 2013, you check the document back in so others can add their portions to the document.

Steps:

1. When your edits are complete in the checked out document, click the **File** tab and select **Info** from the menu. The Info screen will appear.

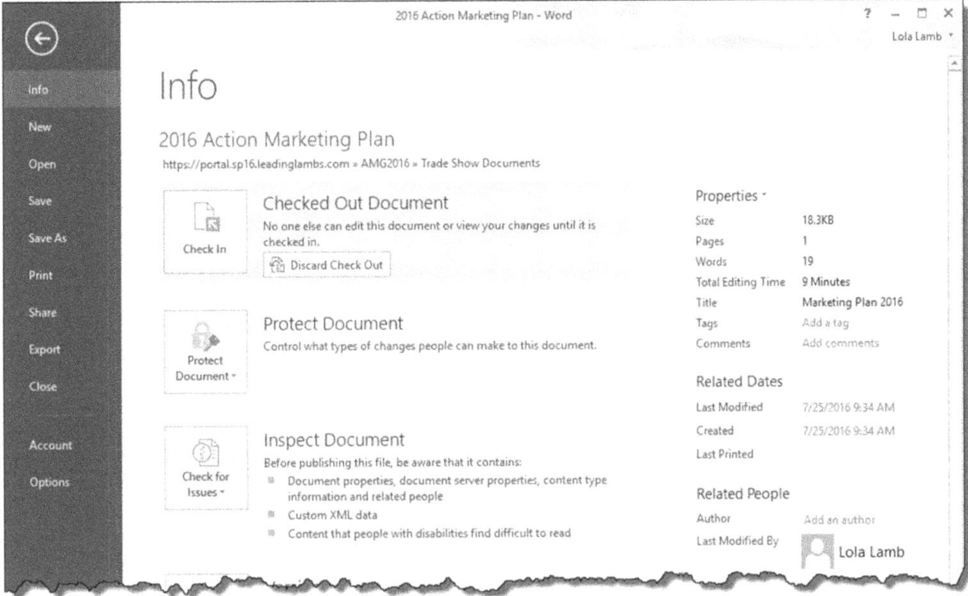

Figure 1: The Document Info Screen

2. Click the **Check In** button. The Check In dialog box will appear.

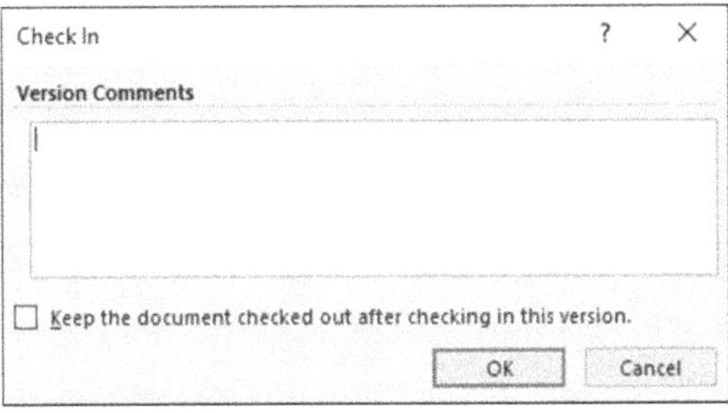

Figure 2: The Check In Dialog Box

3. In the Version Comments field, enter any notes.

4. Click **OK**. The document will be checked back in to the document workspace. Although the document has been checked in, the document will remain open, but read-only.

Task: Check In a Document in Office 2016

Purpose: After you have completed your edits on a checked out document, you will need to check it back in to the document workspace so others can edit the document

Example: After making changes to the marketing plan in Word 2016, you check the document back in so others can add their portions to the document.

Steps:

1. When your edits are complete in the checked out document, click the **File** tab and select **Info** from the menu. The Info screen will appear.

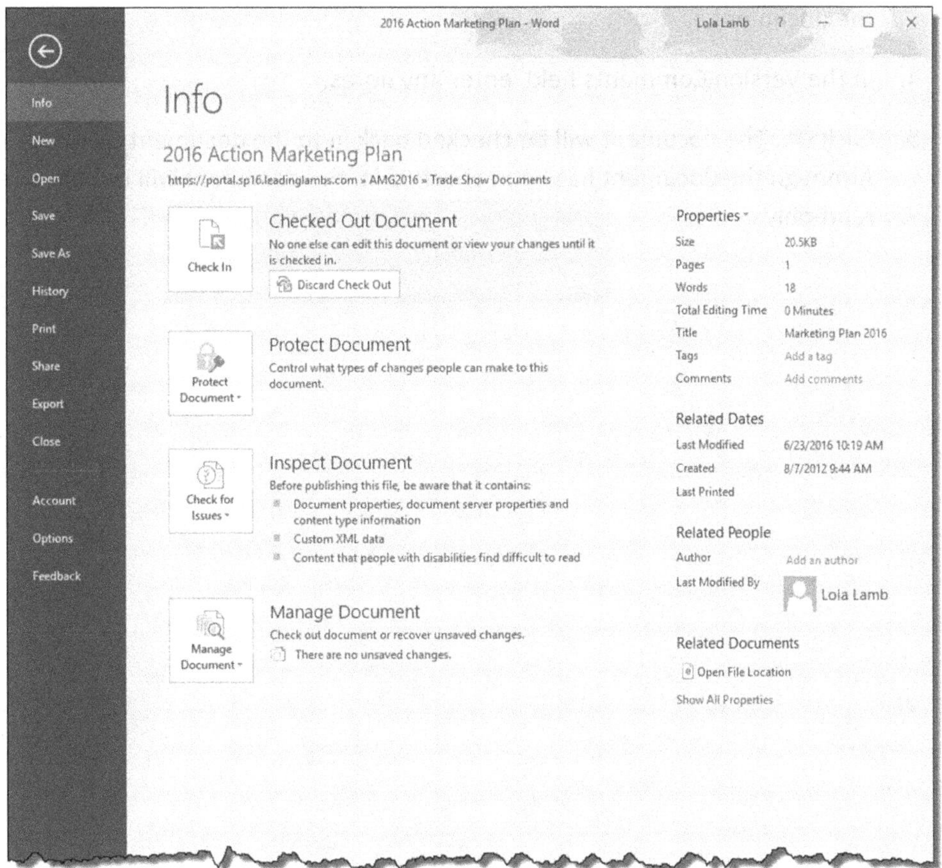

Figure 1: The Document Info Screen

2. Click the **Check In** button. The Check In dialog box will appear.

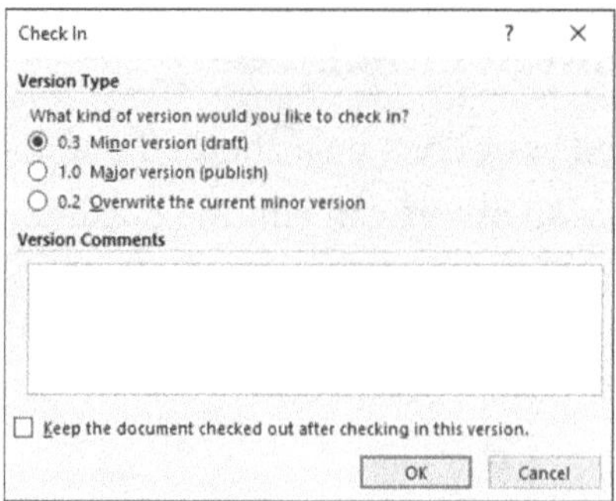

Figure 2: The Check In Dialog Box

3. If versioning is enabled in your document library, select which type of version to save the document as.
4. In the Version Comments field, enter any notes.
5. Click OK. The document will be checked back in to the document workspace. Although the document has been checked in, the document will remain open, but read-only.

Task: Check In Documents in SharePoint

Purpose: After you have completed your edits on a checked out document, you will need to check it back in to the library app so others can see your changes and/or edit the document themselves.

Example: After making changes to the marketing plan, you check the document back in so others can add their portions to the document.

Steps:

1. Start Internet Explorer and type the URL for your organization's SharePoint server. The Start page will open.
2. Navigate to the document library where the document you wish to check in is located. The document library page will open.
3. Next to the title of the document you need to check in, click the ellipsis control to open the document's menu.

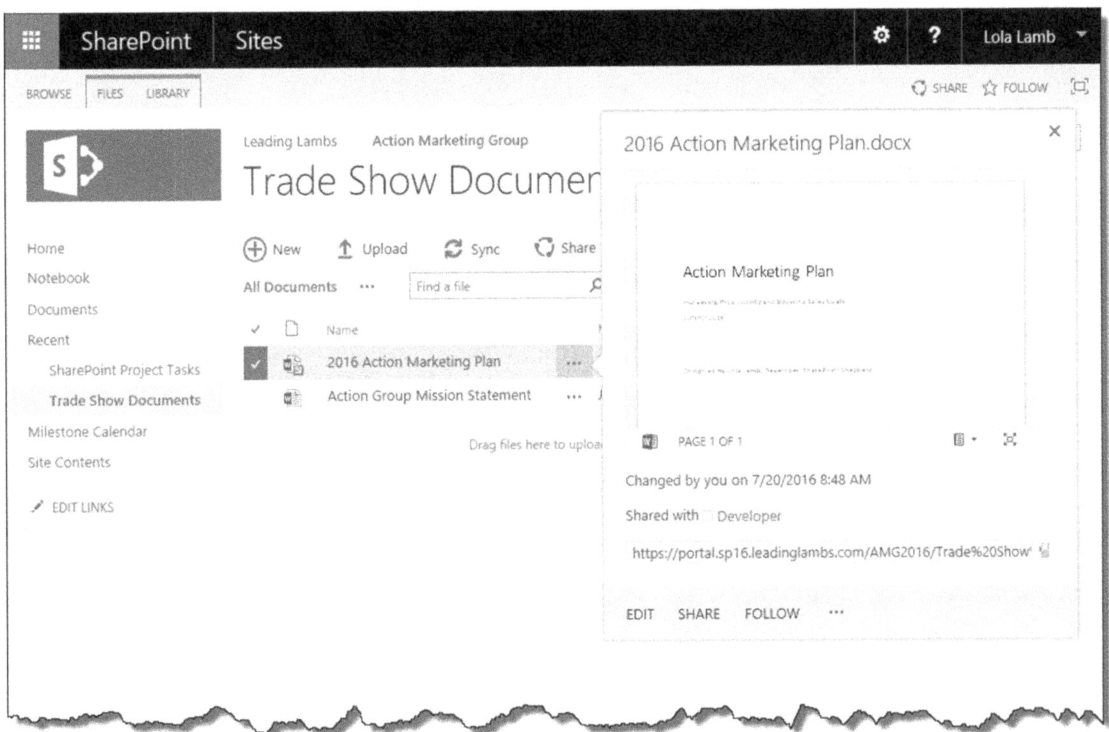

Figure 1: The Document Menu

4. At the bottom of the document's menu, click the ellipsis control to open the Options menu.

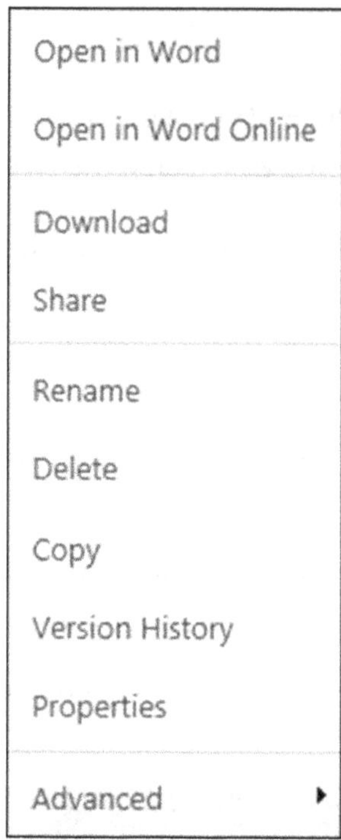

Figure 2: The Document Options Menu

5. Hover over **Advanced** to show the Advanced Options menu, then click **Check In**. The Check In dialog box will appear.

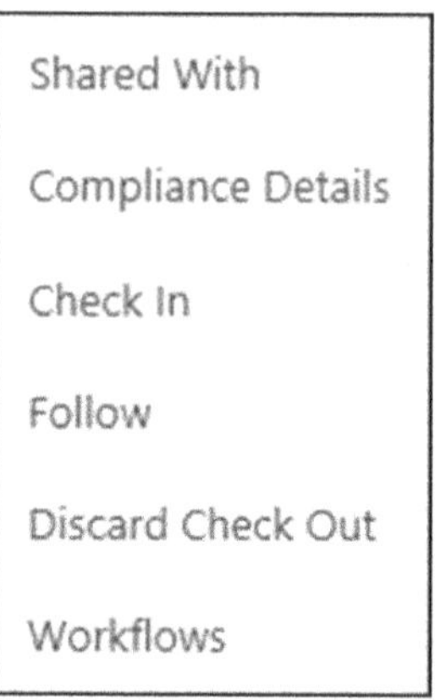

Figure 3: The Advanced Options Menu

6. In the Retain Check Out section, choose if you want to keep the document checked out after checking in this version.
7. In the Comments field, type any notes about this version of the document.

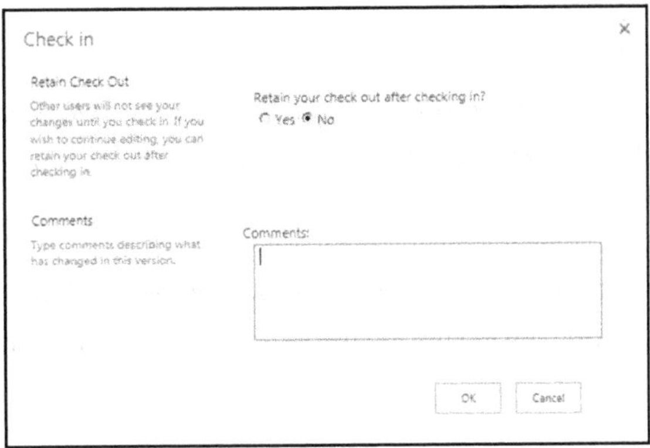

Figure 4: The Check In Dialog Box

8. Click OK. The document will be checked in.

Task: Connect an Approval Workflow

Purpose: Maintaining control of content is a problem for all websites. By connecting an approval workflow, you can ensure that all of the content added to the library goes through an approval process.

Example: Action Marketing Group policies must be approved before being published to the employees. Associating an approval workflow ensures that every new piece of content is reviewed before being published.

Steps:

1. Start Internet Explorer and type the URL for your organization's SharePoint server. The Start page will open.
2. Navigate to the document library that needs a workflow started.
3. In the ribbon click the **Library** tab. The Library ribbon will open.
4. Click the **Library Settings** button. The Document Library Settings page will open.

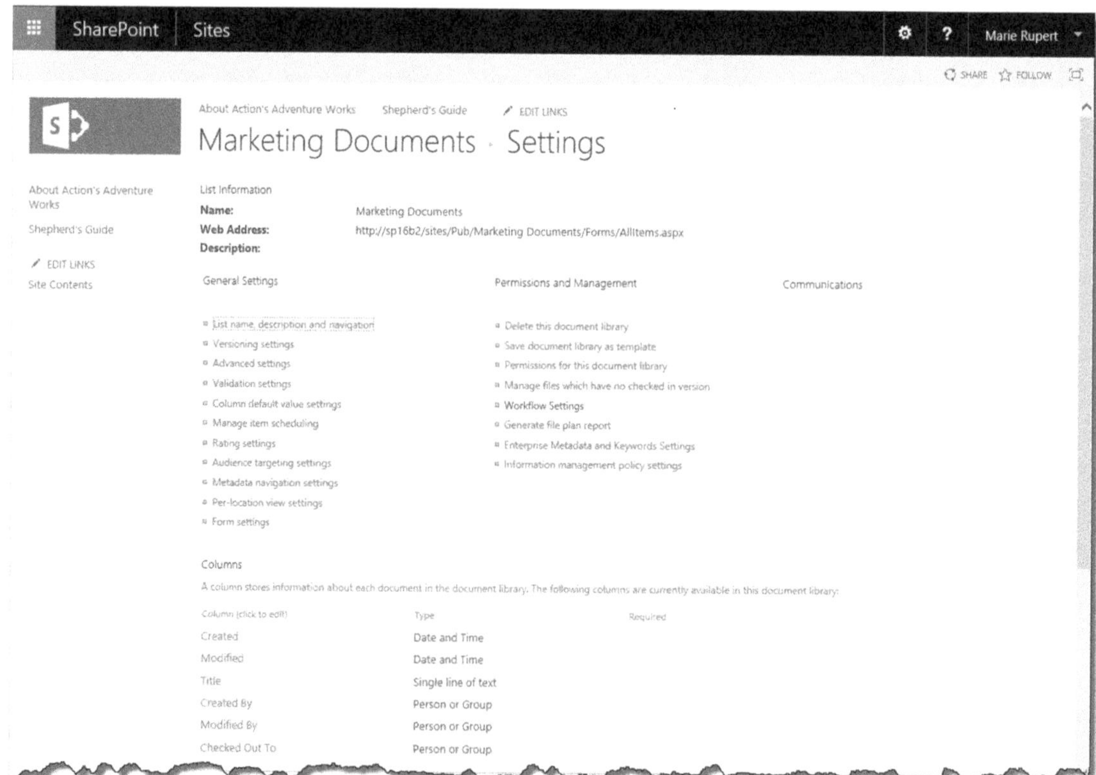

Figure 1: The Document Library Settings Page

5. In the Permissions and Management section, click the **Workflow Settings** link. The Workflow Settings page will open.

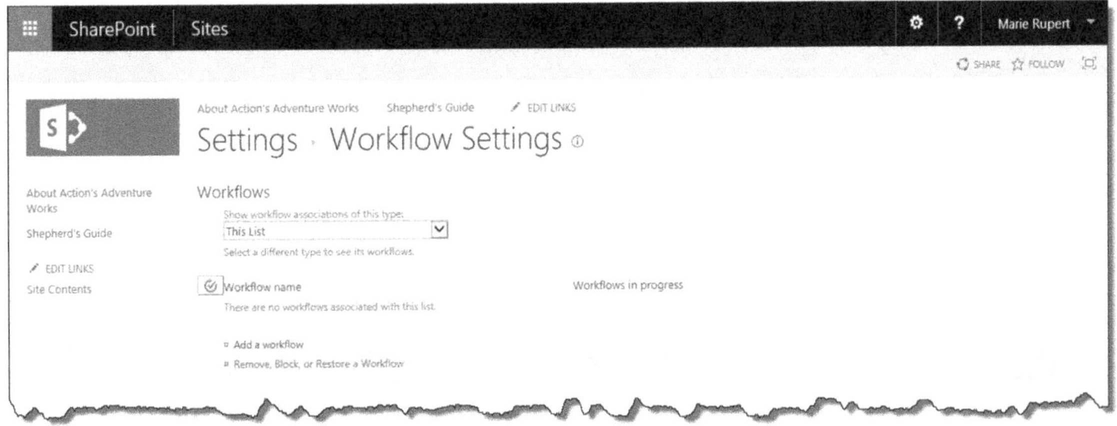

Figure 2: The Workflow Settings Page

6. At the bottom of the page, click the **Add a workflow** link. The Add a Workflow page will open.

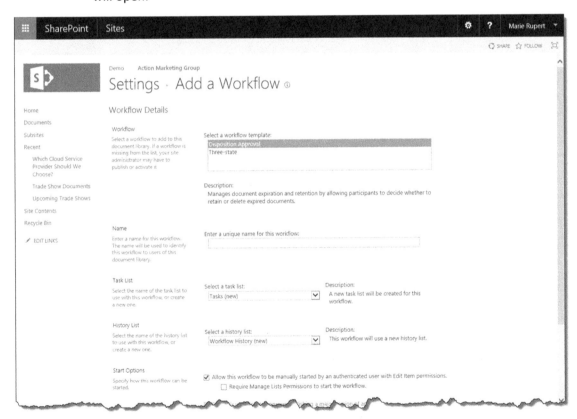

Figure 3: The Add a Workflow Page

7. In the Workflow section, click the **Publishing Approval** option.

Note: Workflow templates for sites must be set up by the site administrator or created in SharePoint designer. If you do not have any workflows available, contact the site administrator.

8. In the Name section, enter a title for the workflow.

9. In the Task List section, select **Tasks (new)**.

10. In the Start Options section, click the **Creating a new item will start this workflow** checkbox.

11. Click **Next**. The Publishing Approval settings page will appear.

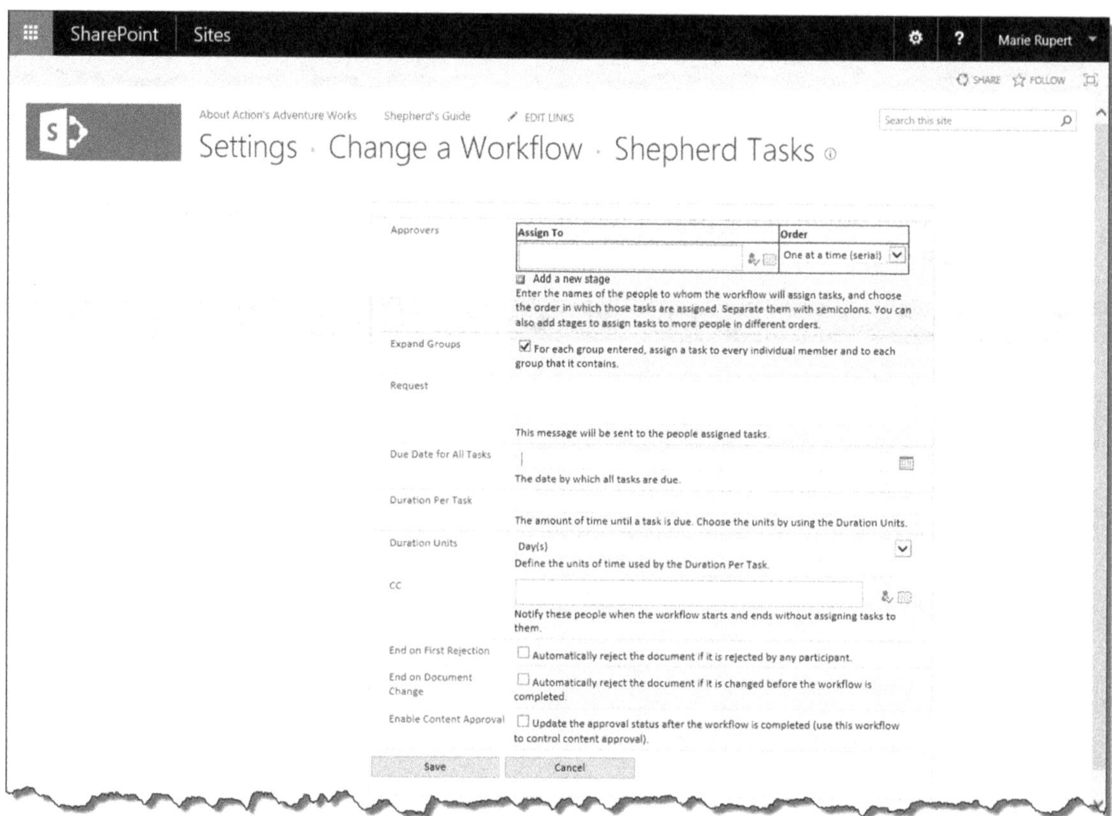

Figure 4: The Publishing Approval Settings Page

12. In the Approvers Section's Assign To field, enter the user name of the people you want to approve documents, separating multiple names with semicolons.

13. Click the **People Picker** icon to validate the user name(s).

14. In the Order field, select the approval type: **Serial** or **Parallel**.

15. In the Request section, type in the message you want each approval recipient to receive.

16. Enter either a single due date or a length of time you want the approval to be completed.

17. Select the **End on First Rejection** checkbox to stop the workflow if a rejection is made.

18. Select the **End on Document Change** checkbox to stop the workflow if any changes to the document are made.

19. Select the **Enable Content Approval** checkbox to ensure this workflow controls content approval.

20. Click **Save**. The Workflow Settings page will appear with the new workflow added.

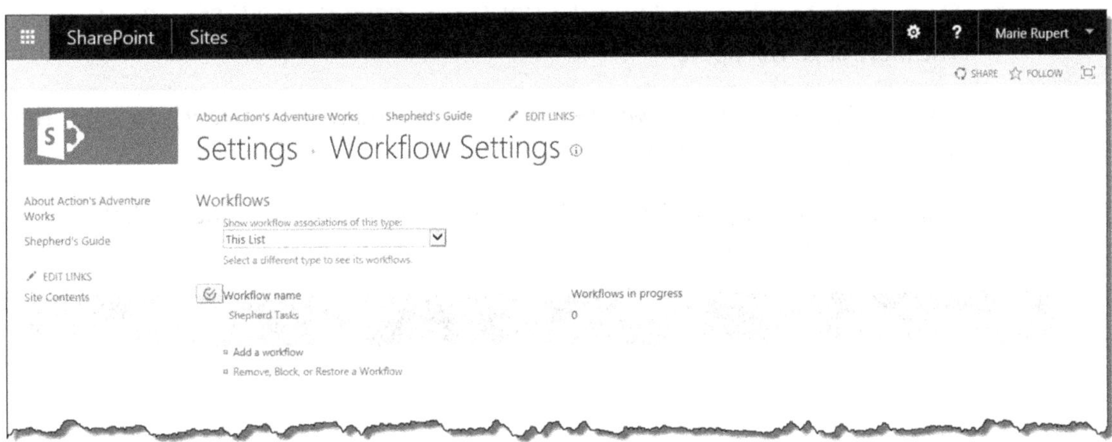

Figure 5: The Workflow Settings Page

Task: Follow a Document

Purpose: Keeping tabs on all of the documents in the organization that you're interested in isn't practical. SharePoint allows you to "follow" documents that are interesting to you so that you can be notified when they change. The changes appear in your newsfeed so you don't have to go looking for the documents that have changed.

Example: Action Marketing Group has a policy regarding vendor samples. As a purchasing manager you want to know when it changes so you can make sure you're following the right procedures.

Steps:

1. Start Internet Explorer and type the URL for your organization's SharePoint server. The Start page will open.
2. Navigate to the library app where the document you wish to follow is located. The library app's page will open.
3. Find the document you wish to edit and next to the document title, click the **ellipsis** control to open the document's menu.

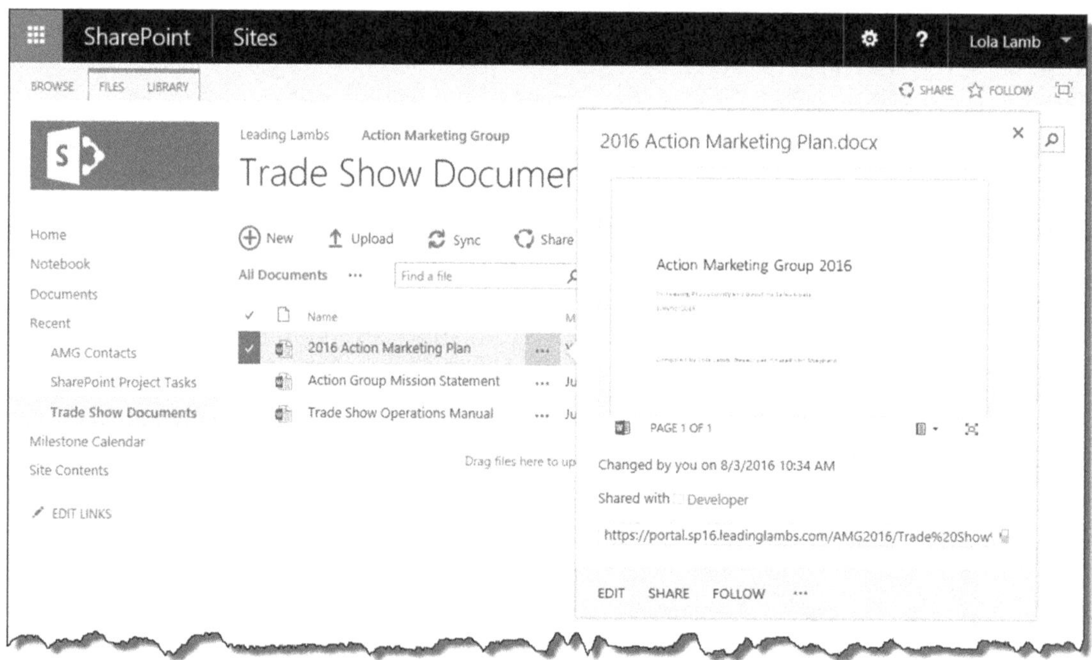

Figure 1: The Document Menu

4. At the bottom of the document's menu, click **Follow**. The document will be followed.

5. To see documents that are followed or the changes to the documents, people, and sites you follow, in the Suite bar at the top of the page, click the **Application Launcher** (waffle icon), and then the **Newsfeed** icon. The Newsfeed page will open.

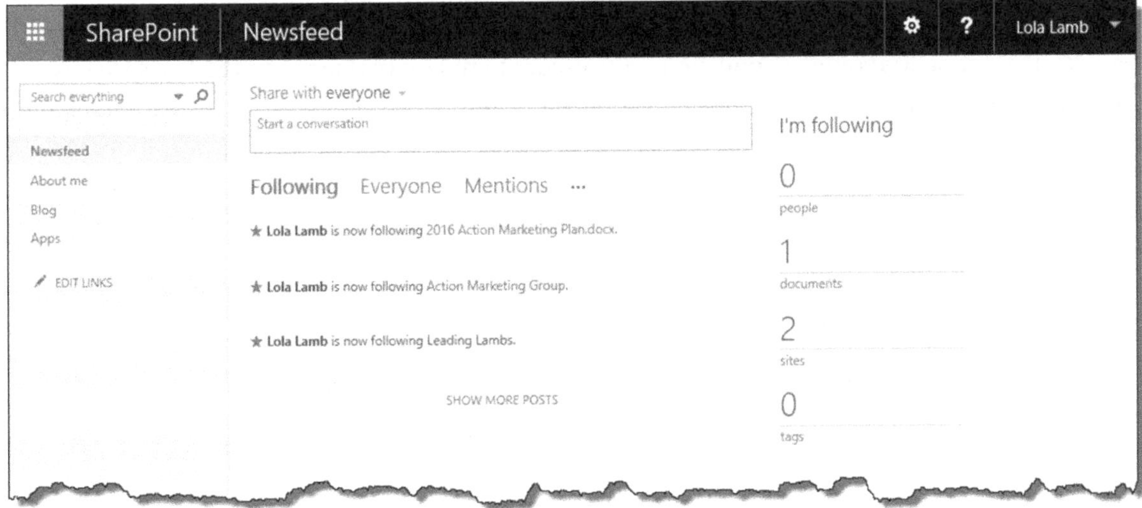

Figure 2: The Newsfeed Page

Task: Save a Site as a Template

Purpose: Once you have a site the way you want it; you can turn it into a template to create other sites by saving it as a template.

Example: The Action Marketing Group created a project template that includes the tasks that every project must do and the documents which must be filled out. They will save the template to be used for future projects.

Steps:

1. Start Internet Explorer and type the URL for your organization's SharePoint server. The Start page will open.
2. Navigate to the site to be templated. The site's home page will open.
3. Click the **Settings** menu gear icon and select **Site Settings**. The Site Settings page will open.
4. In the **Site Actions** section, click the **Save site as template** link. The Save as Template page will open.

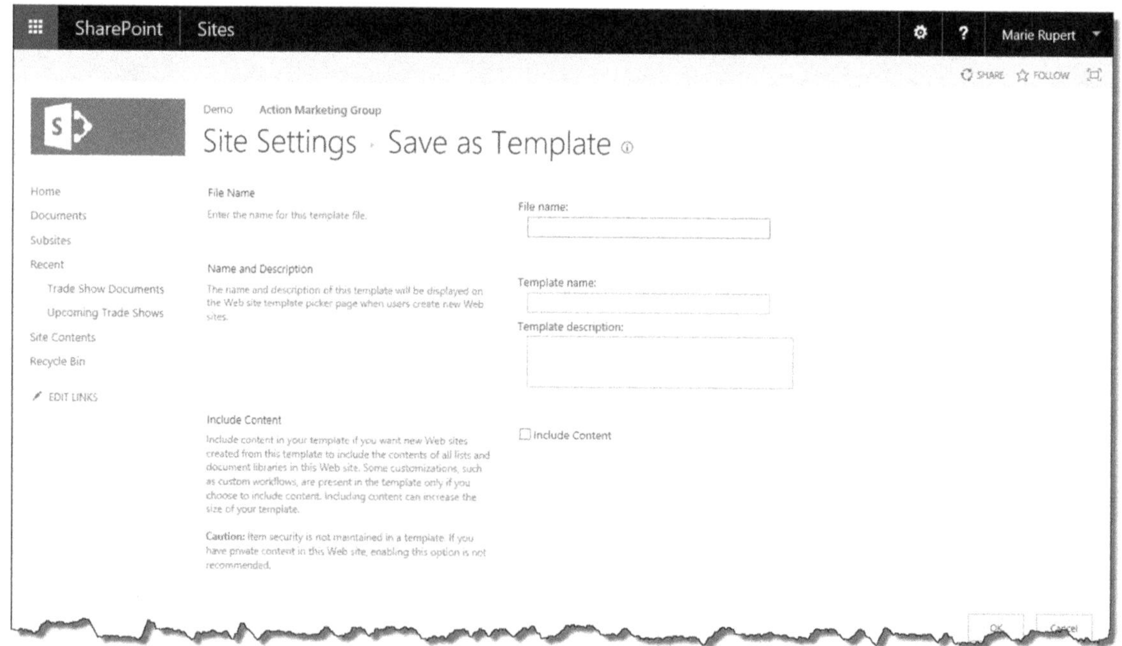

Figure 1: The Save as Template Page

5. In the File Name, Template Name, and Template Description fields, enter the pertinent information.

6. To capture any items and files that have been added to the site, click the Include Content checkbox.
7. Click OK. The site will be saved as a template in the Solutions Gallery for later use in SharePoint.

Task: Activate Version Control

Purpose: From time to time, you may need to find an earlier version of letter, a presentation, or a spreadsheet and then discover there are multiple prior versions or no prior versions. SharePoint supports versioning for both list items and for files.

Example: The most recent document has an error, and the author would like to find out what changes were made and by whom.

Steps:

1. Start Internet Explorer and type the URL for your organization's SharePoint server. The Start page will open.
2. Navigate to the list or library where you would like to turn on version control. The list or library's page will open.
3. Click the **List/Library** tab, and then the **List/Library Settings** option. The app's Settings page will open.
4. In the General Settings section, click the **Versioning settings** option. The Versioning Settings page will open.

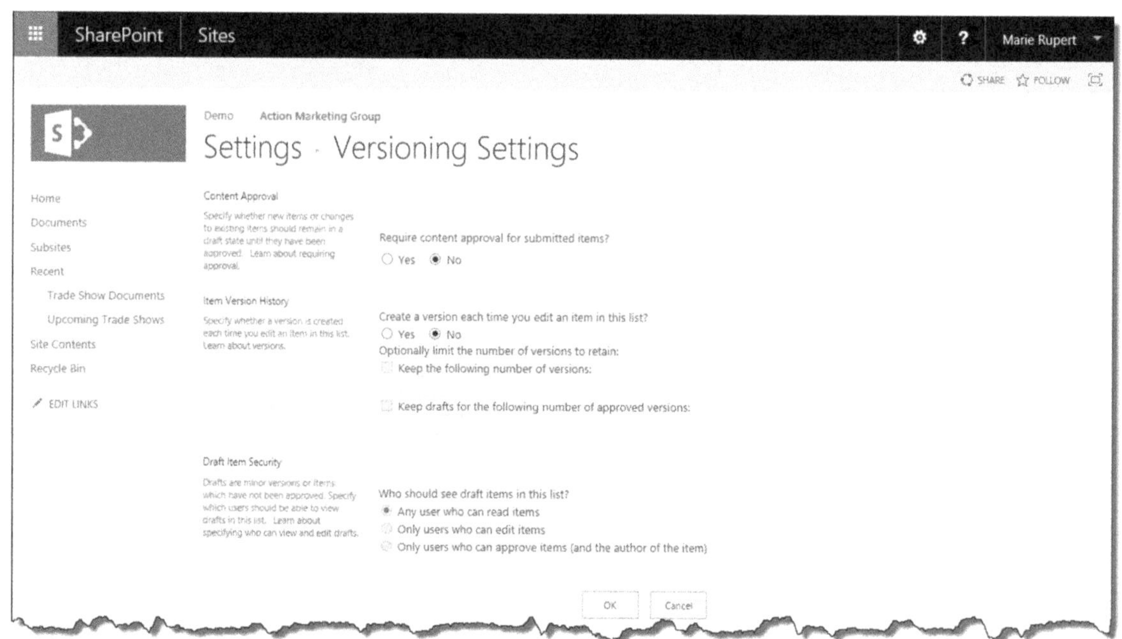

Figure 1: Versioning Settings

5. Under Content Approval, select **Yes** if you want items submitted for approval.

6. In the Version History section, select Yes for create a version each time you edit an item in this list. For the option to limit the number of versions to retain, consider what the purpose of the list and how many users will have access to make changes and select your number.

7. For the Draft Item Security section, make a selection based on the users that will have access and determine who will have read only, edit or approval permissions.

Exception: If you can't edit Versioning Settings, you do not have specific permissions to change Versioning Settings. Check the permissions settings to ensure you have the appropriate access rights.

8. Click OK. Versioning will be enabled for the app.

Manage Apps

In SharePoint 2016, information and files can be stored within apps. These collections combine the functionality and features of what were formerly known as libraries and lists.

A library app is simply a specialized app that contains, instead of just items of data, items with separate documents and files. These files can be photos, audio clips, Office documents... anything you can use on a PC, only better. That's because with a SharePoint server hosting your files, you get the added benefits of version control, having multiple views of your data, and the capability to add metadata to your content that will enable you and other users to quickly find the file you are seeking.

A list app in SharePoint is a valuable tool for organizing data. Many of the tools built into SharePoint are specialized lists: Contacts, Calendar, Tasks, and Surveys are just a few. But if none of the existing tools work for you, you can quickly build a new, custom list that collects exactly the kind of data you need.

In this section, you'll learn how to:

- Create a Custom List App: The basics of creating a custom list.
- Create a Library App: The basics of creating a library.
- Create a File in a Library App: Once you have a library app created, you can add items to that library fairly quickly.
- Upload a Single File to a Library App: Not only can you create a document and save it directly to a document library, you can also upload existing documents from your local PC to the SharePoint library.
- Upload Multiple Files to a Library App: If you have a lot of documents to upload, you don't have to upload them one at a time. You can simply upload them all at once.
- Create a New Folder in a Library App: Instead of just listing library items in a flat list, you can organize the library's contents by creating folders for the items.
- Import a Spreadsheet to Create a List App: Rather than retyping all of the data into SharePoint, you can quickly import an Excel spreadsheet and create a list or library.
- Create a New Item for a List App: Once you have an app created, you can add items to that app fairly quickly.
- Add New List or Library App Columns: When you add columns to the app, you are also providing additional fields to enter information.
- Edit Existing List or Library App Columns: Besides adding new columns to an app, you can also edit existing columns in case you need to make a correction or change.

- Delete List or Library App Columns: If a column in your app proves to be unnecessary, you can remove it from the app altogether.
- Edit a List or Library App in Quick Edit View: You can shift to Quick Edit view, which looks and functions very similarly to a spreadsheet, allowing you to edit a lot of app data at once.
- Subscribe to a List or Library App RSS Feed: SharePoint allows you to subscribe to an RSS feed that will notify you when an app's content has changed.
- View Library Item Properties: You can easily see a library app item's information on the item's properties page.
- View List Item Properties: List apps make it fast and easy to view all of a list item's properties in one place.
- Edit List or Library Item Properties: When you need to edit one item in an app, you can access all of their properties, not just those in the datasheet view.
- Manage List Item Permissions: Occasionally, you may need to adjust an item's permissions to make sure only the right people are allowed to edit it.
- Edit a Library App Item in a Preferred Application: Learn how to edit compatible documents directly from SharePoint, just like opening a file from your local hard drive.
- Download a Library App File: Occasionally, you will have files in your library app that are important to the context of the library, but they may not be in a SharePoint-compatible format.
- Move a File to Another Library App: You can move files to another library app anywhere on your SharePoint site.
- Email a Link to a Library App: If you want to get many users involved in the editing/creation process for a document, an efficient way is to send a link to the document in an email.
- Edit a List or Library App View: By default, apps are displayed in a certain way within SharePoint. You can change these aspects of an app's view very easily.
- Add a List or Library App View: It is possible to create whole new app views, just the way you want them, rather than heavily modifying the All Items view.
- Export a List or Library App to a Spreadsheet: Rather than retyping all of the data from SharePoint into Excel, you can quickly export an app to an Excel spreadsheet.
- Delete a Library App File: If you need to remove an item from an app, it's a quick operation.

- **Recover a List or Library Item from the Recycle Bin**: How to retrieve deleted items from the app Recycle Bin.
- **Edit List or Library App Content Types**: You can customize the types of content to be stored in your app.

Task: Create a Custom List App

Purpose: A list in SharePoint is a valuable tool for organizing data. Many of the tools built into SharePoint are specialized lists; Announcements, Contacts, Calendar, Tasks, and Surveys are just a few examples of specially-formatted SharePoint lists. But if none of the existing tools work for you, you can quickly build a new, custom list that collects exactly the kind of data you need.

Example: The Action Marketing Group wants to create a collaborative list of trade shows that team members will be attending or participating in during the coming year.

Steps:

1. Start Internet Explorer and type the URL for your organization's SharePoint server. The Start page will open. If you want this custom list to appear in one of your subsites, navigate to that site.
2. Click the **Settings** menu gear icon, then click **Add an App**. The Your Apps page will appear.

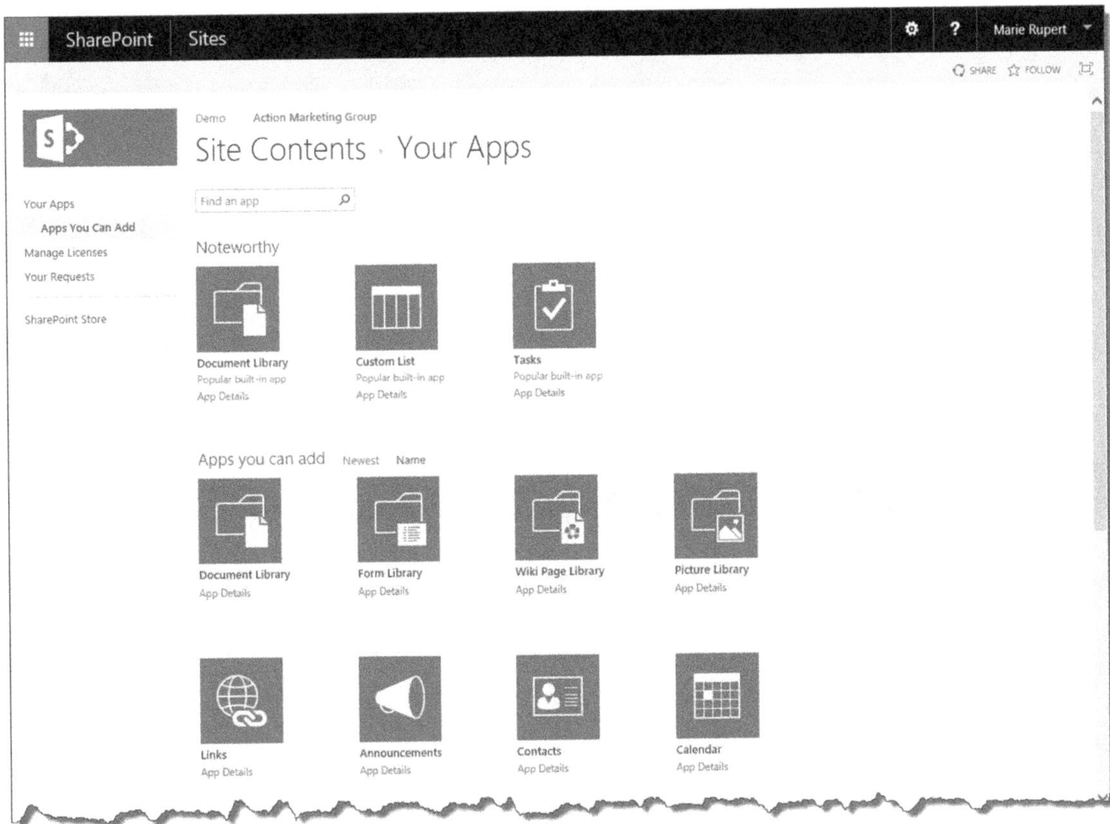

Figure 1: The Your Apps Page

3. Click the **Custom List** icon. The Adding Custom List dialog box will open.

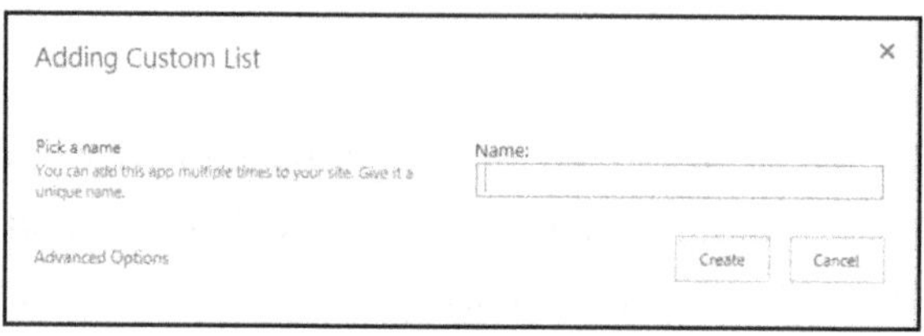

Figure 2: The Adding Custom List Dialog Box

4. Click Advanced Options. The Site Contents – New page will open.
5. In the Name field, enter a title for the new list. This is used to identify the list throughout SharePoint.

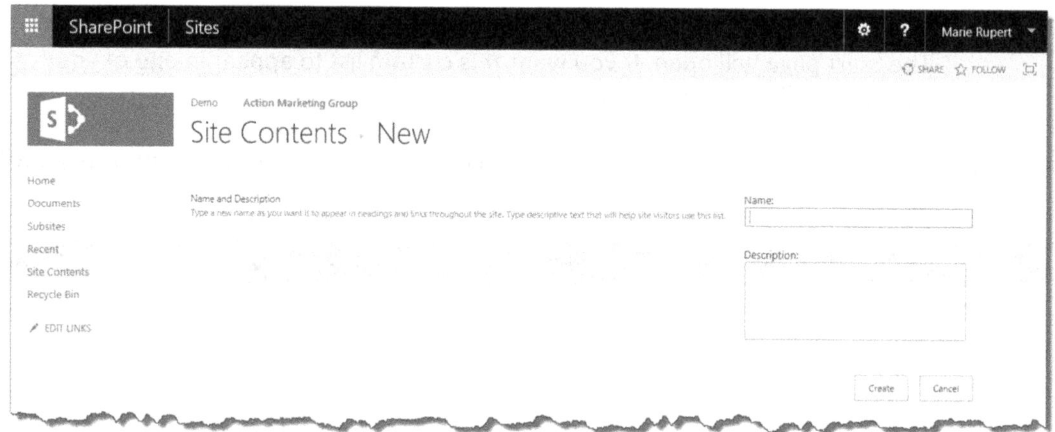

Figure 3: The Site Contents – New Page

6. In the Description field enter any notes about the new list. This appears as an information icon next to the list name when your list is open in SharePoint.
7. Click Create. The new list will be created.

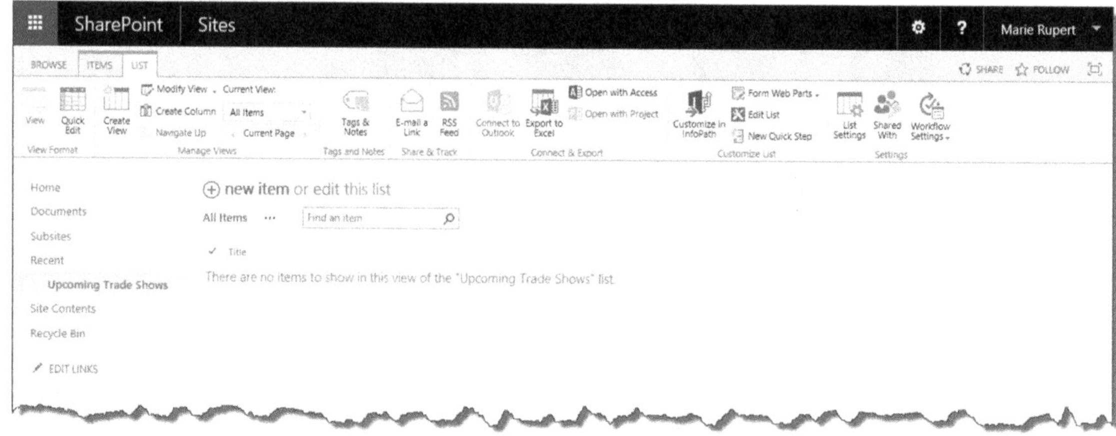

Figure 4: The New List

Note: When a custom list or library is created, it initially has just a few columns. For more information on adding columns to your list, see the task "Add New List or Library App Columns."

Exception: If you don't see the entry to create a custom list, you do not have specific permissions to view that app. Check the permissions settings to ensure you have the appropriate access rights.

Task: Create a Library App

Purpose: A library in SharePoint is very much like all the other list apps, though it has the specialized purpose of managing files. Creating a library allows you to have a place to store files.

Example: The Action Marketing Group wants set up a new document library for storing trade show documentation and marketing materials.

Steps:

1. Start Internet Explorer and type the URL for your organization's SharePoint server. The Start page will open. Navigate to the site or subsite that you wish to create the new app in.
2. Click the **Settings** menu gear icon, then click **Add an App**. The Your Apps page will appear.
3. Click the **Document Library** icon. The Adding Document Library dialog box will open.

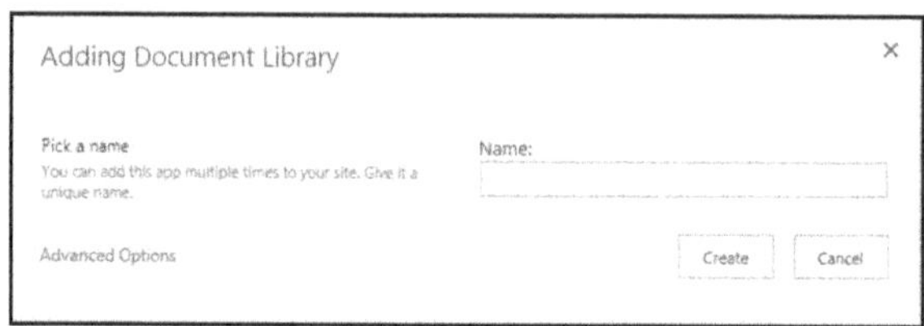

Figure 1: The Adding Document Library Dialog Box

4. Click **Advanced Options**. The Site Contents – New page will open.

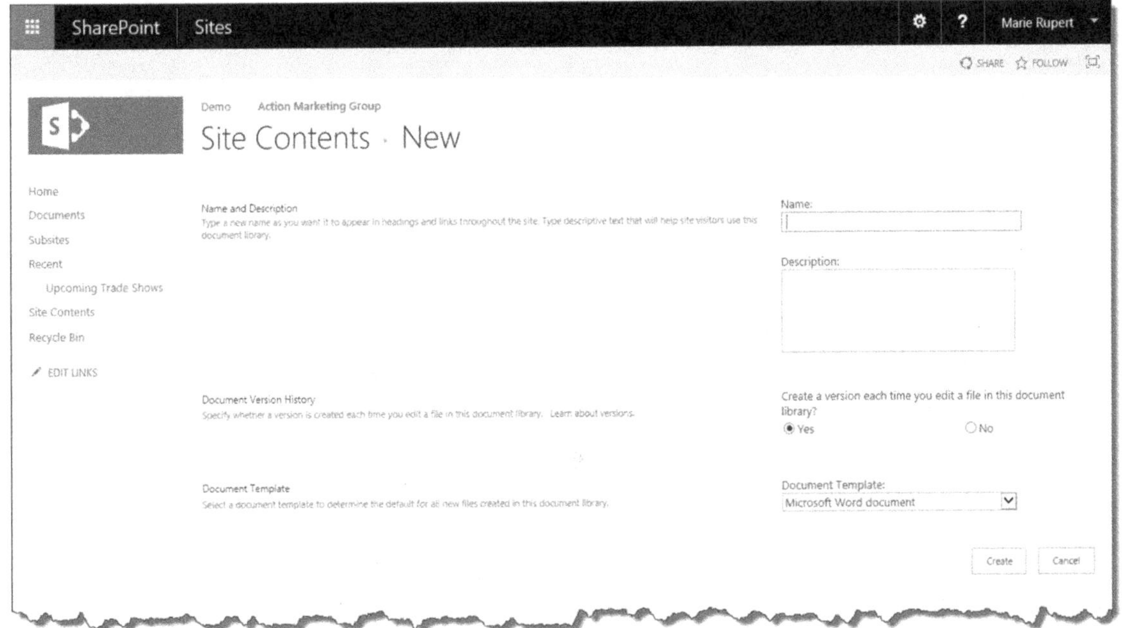

Figure 2: The Site Contents – New Page

5. In the Name field, enter a title for the new library. This is used to identify the library throughout SharePoint.
6. In the Description field enter any notes about the new library. This appears as a sub-heading when your library is open in SharePoint.
7. In the Document Version History section, click **Yes**.
8. Select the Document Template option you would like to use as the default file type for the library.
9. Click **Create**. The new library will be created.

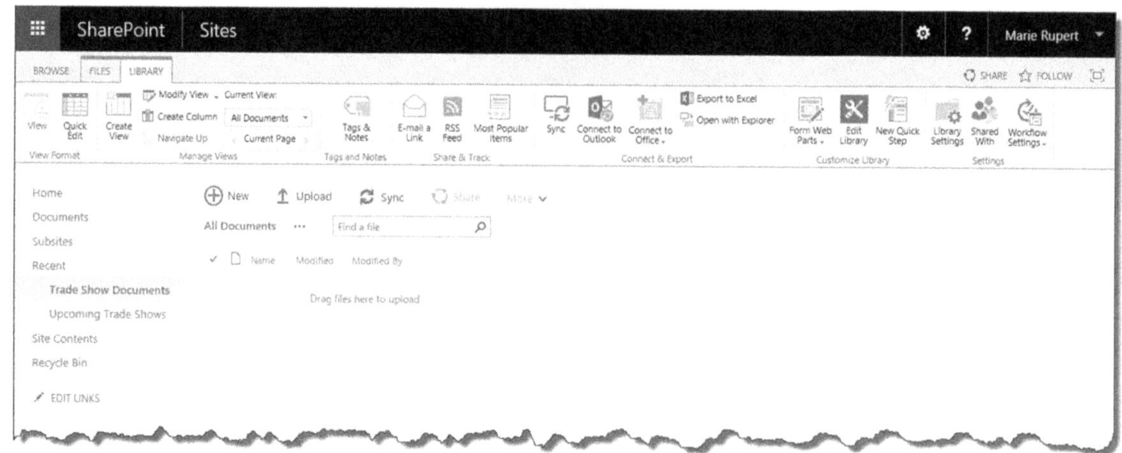

Figure 3: The New Library

Note: When a library is created, it initially has just a few columns. For more information on adding columns to your library, see the task "Create New List or Library App Columns."

Exception: If you don't see the app to create a library, you do not have specific permissions to view the app. Check the permissions settings to ensure you have the appropriate access rights.

Task: Create a File in a Library App

Purpose: Once you have a library app created, you can add items to that library fairly quickly. In this example, we will create a new document for a document library using the default document type defined for a library. You can directly upload documents to a library, which is covered in the task "Upload a Single File to a Library App".

Example: A new trade show document needs to be created in the new library.

Steps:

1. Start Internet Explorer and type the URL for your organization's SharePoint server. The Start page will open.
2. Navigate to the library where you want to add an item. The library page will open.
3. In the ribbon click the **Files** tab. The Files ribbon will appear.

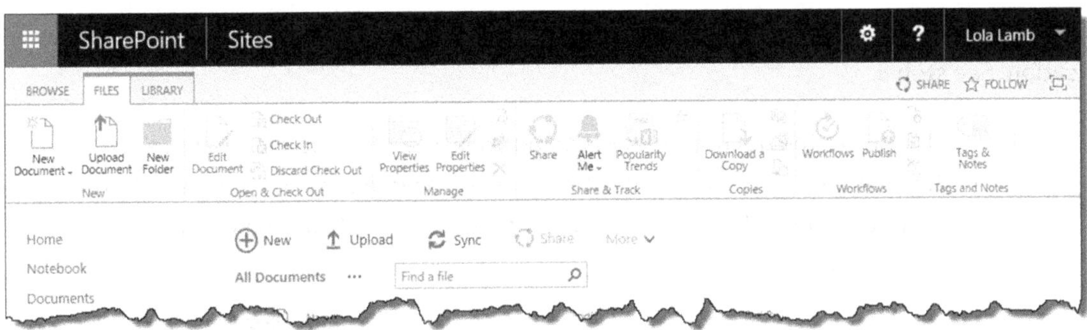

Figure 1: The Files Ribbon

4. Click the **New Document** button. You can also click the **New** icon (plus sign) to open the Create a new file menu, and select which file type to create – in this case, a Word document. A new document will open in the Office Web App.

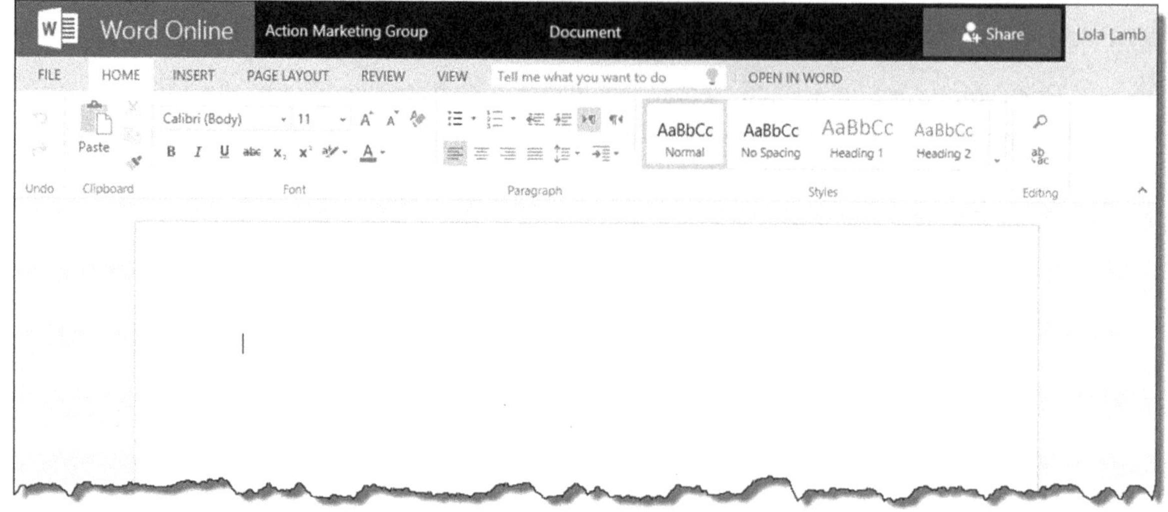

Figure 2: The New Document Open in Word Online

Note: Depending on your library app settings, the new document may be created in the Office client application. See step 8.

5. Changes to the document are automatically saved to the file. However, your document will have a default title, such as Document or Document 1. To rename your document, click the File tab and select Save As from the menu. The Save As screen will appear.

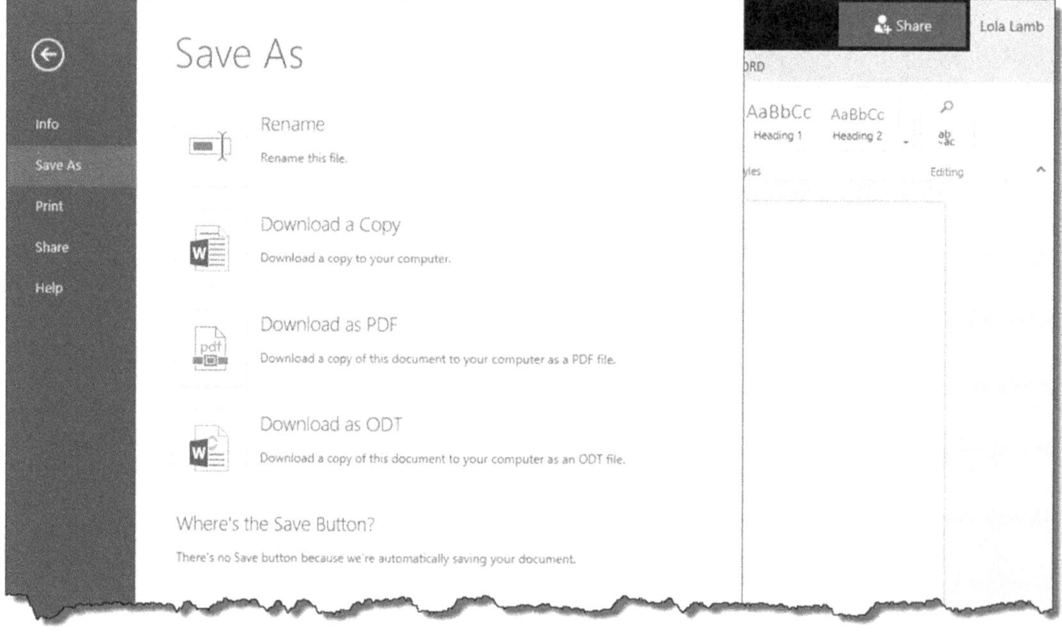

Figure 3: The Save As Screen

6. Click Rename, and the Rename dialog box will appear. Enter a name for your file, then click OK to save your changes.

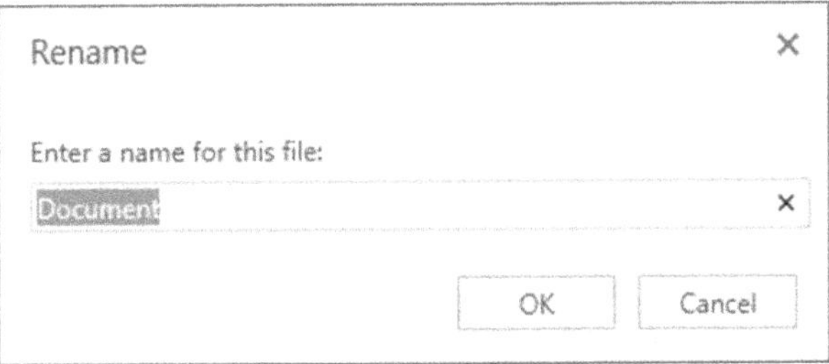

Figure 4:The Rename Dialog Box

7. When you are finished editing the new document, you can close the document or navigate to a different page. Your changes are automatically saved, and the library app page will now contain your new document.
8. Depending on your library app settings, your new document may open in the Office application. A Microsoft Office confirmation dialog box may appear to confirm that you would like to open the Microsoft Office application.

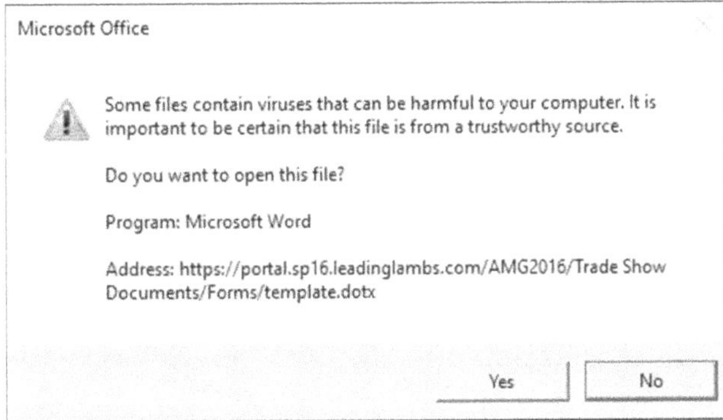

Figure 5: The Microsoft Office Confirmation Box

9. Click Yes. The Office application will open and a new document will appear.

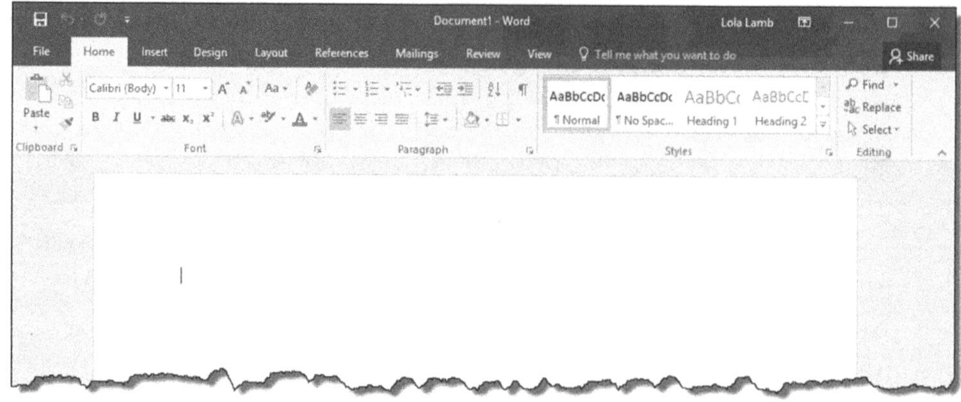

Figure 6: The New Document Opened using the Basic Document Template

10. Click the Enable Editing button if it appears to make changes in the Office application.

11. When you are finished editing the document, click the File tab and select Save As from the menu. The Save As screen will appear.

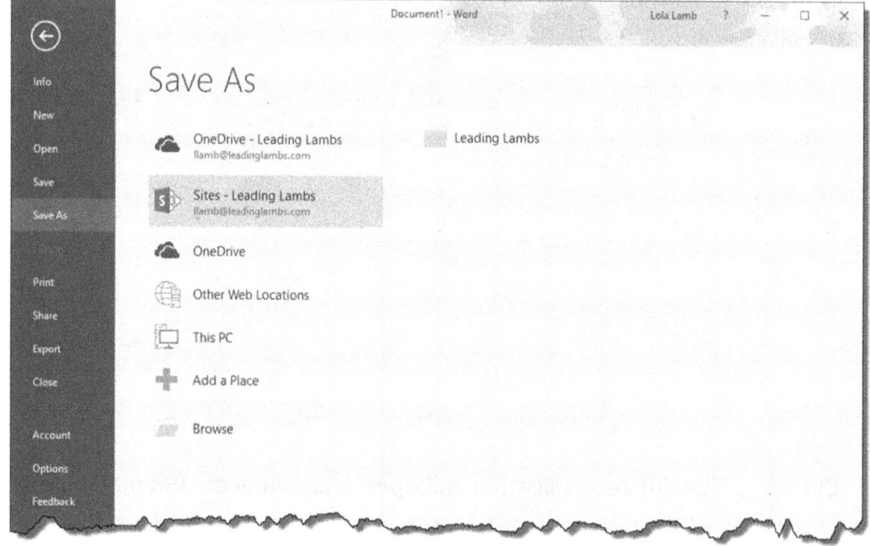

Figure 7: The Save As Screen

12. Click the folder icon representing the SharePoint library where the document was created, or click Browse. The Save As dialog box will open.

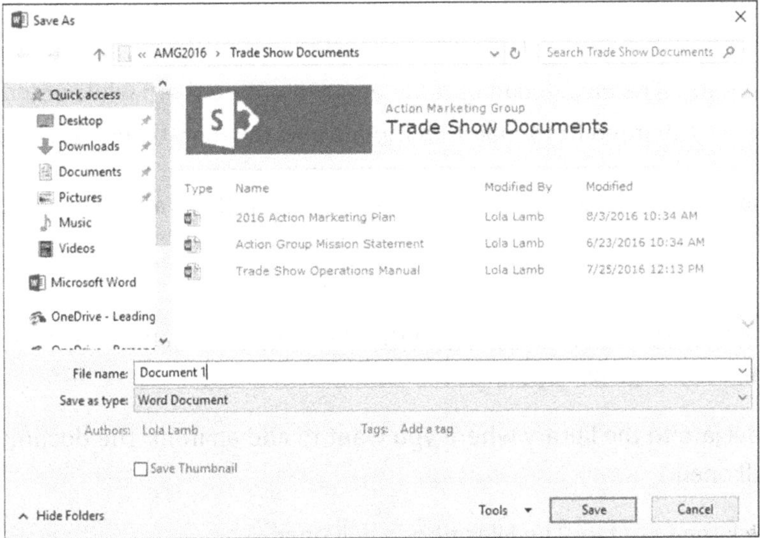

Figure 8: The Save As Dialog Box

13. In the File Name field, enter a name for your document.
14. Click Save. The document will be saved directly to the SharePoint library instead of your local hard drive.
15. Exit the Office application. The library app page will refresh and the library will now contain the new document.

Task: Upload a Single File to a Library App

Purpose: Commonly you'll receive documents via email or create them while you're not online and need to upload them to SharePoint to maintain the file and collaborate with others.

Example: The Action Marketing Group needs to upload files to the Trade Show Materials library.

Steps:

1. Start Internet Explorer and type the URL for your organization's SharePoint server. The Start page will open.
2. Navigate to the library where you want to add an item. The document library page will open.
3. Click the **Files** tab. The Files ribbon will open.
4. Click **Upload Document**. The Add a document dialog box will open.

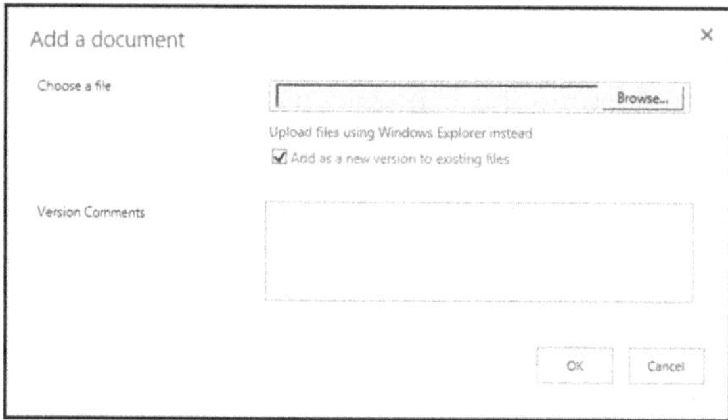

Figure 1: The Add a Document Dialog Box

5. Click the **Browse** button. The Choose File to Upload dialog box will appear.

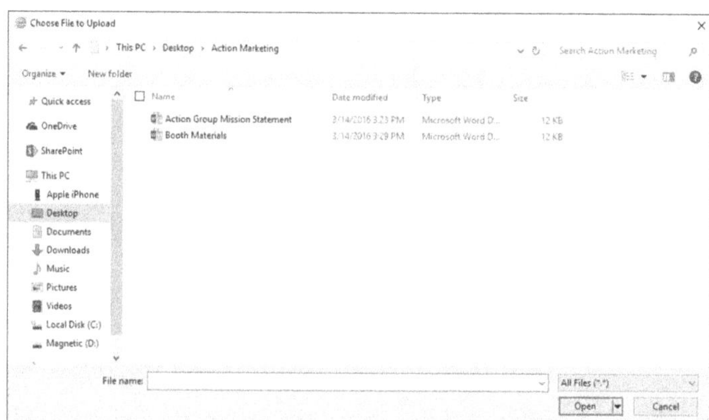

Figure 2: The Choose File to Upload Dialog Box

6. Select a file and click **Open**. The file and its file path will appear in the Name field of the Upload Document dialog box.

7. In the Version Comments field, add any notes about the document if you have Versioning enabled on the library.

8. Click **OK**. The file will be uploaded and will appear on the document library page.

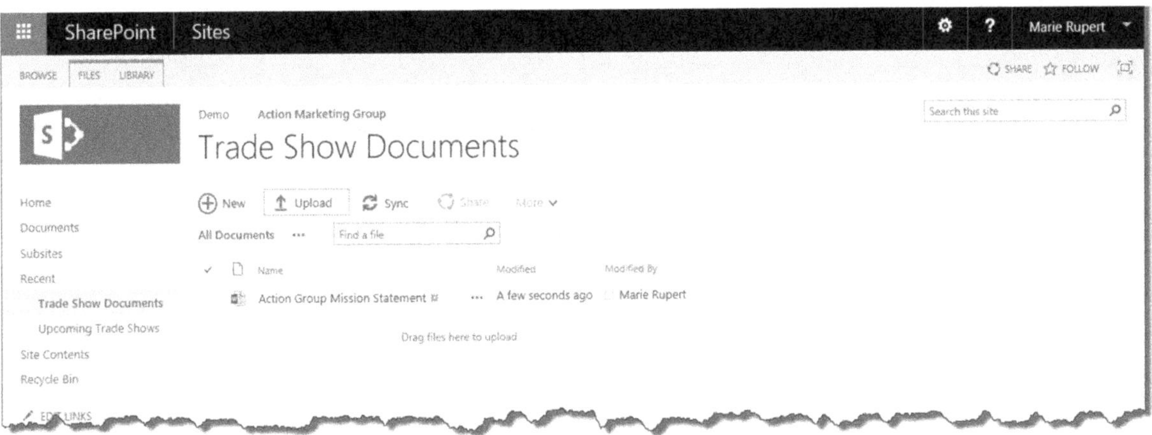

Figure 3: The New Uploaded Document on the Document Library Page

Task: Upload Multiple Files to a Library App

Purpose: While you can individually upload multiple files one at a time, it's more convenient to select a set of files and upload them all at once.

Example: The Action Marketing Group has multiple files from the recent tradeshow that they want to upload to SharePoint quickly.

Steps:

1. Start Internet Explorer and type the URL for your organization's SharePoint server. The Start page will open.
2. Navigate to the library where you want to upload documents. The library app's page will open.
3. Open Windows Explorer and navigate to the files you want to upload.
4. Drag and drop the documents into the Drag Files Here section. The files will be uploaded and will appear on the library app's page.

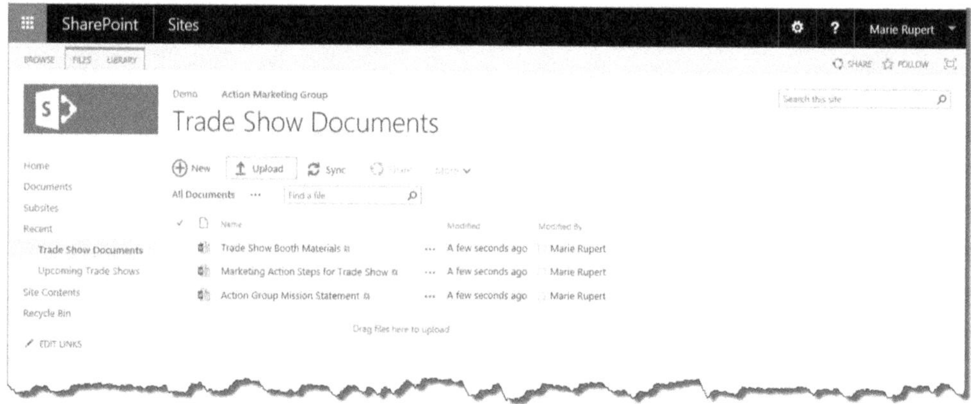

Figure 1: The New Uploaded Documents on the Document Library Page

Task: Create a New Folder in a Library App

Purpose: Nearly everyone is used to using folders on their computer to organize files. SharePoint document libraries allow you to use nested folders to organize files.

Example: The marketing team would like to have its documents organized separately from the general trade show documents. Creating a folder is the most familiar solution. For the best solution, see the Decision Tree "Organize with Folders or Metadata".

Steps:

1. Start Internet Explorer and type the URL for your organization's SharePoint server. The Start page will open.
2. Navigate to the library where you want to add a folder. The document library page will open.
3. On the ribbon click the **Files** tab. The Files ribbon will appear.
4. Click the **New Folder** button. The Create a folder dialog box will open.

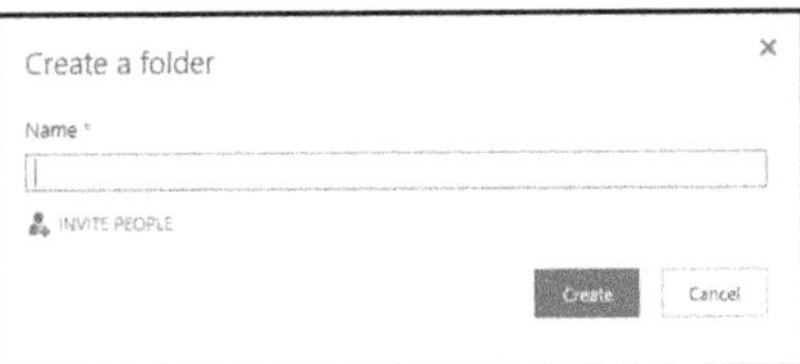

Figure 1: The Create a Folder Dialog Box

5. In the Name field, type a label for the folder.

6. Click Create. The folder will appear in the document library.

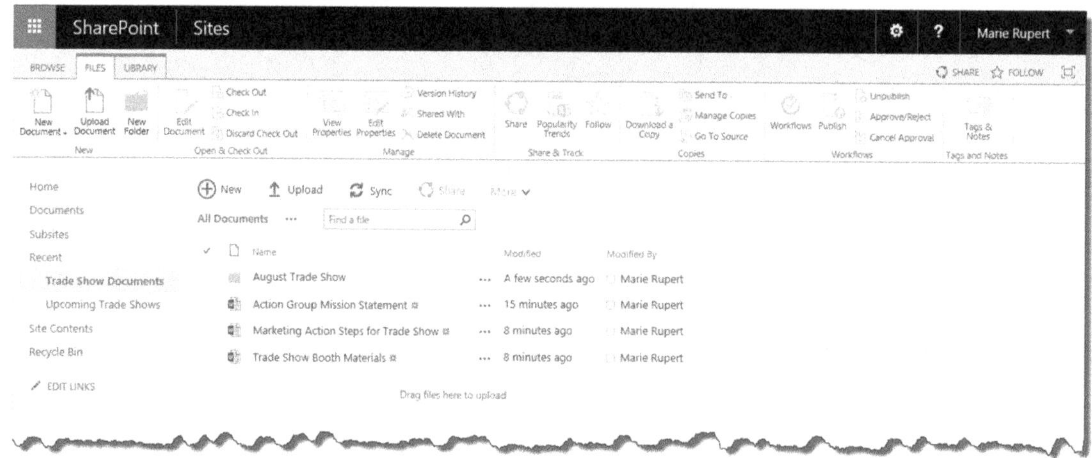

Figure 2: The New Folder on the Document Library Page

Task: Import a Spreadsheet to Create a List App

Purpose: List apps are essentially collections of data that SharePoint lets you publish for other users to see and change. In many organizations, such collections of data already exist in the form of Excel spreadsheets. Rather than retyping all of the data into SharePoint, you can quickly import an Excel spreadsheet and create a list from it.

Example: The Action Marketing Group has a list of VIP customers that they want to import into SharePoint.

Steps:

1. Start Internet Explorer and type the URL for your organization's SharePoint server. The Start page will open. If you want your new site located as a subsite of another site, navigate to that site.
2. Click the **Settings** menu gear icon, then click **Add an App**. The Your Apps page will appear.
3. Scroll down and click the **Import Spreadsheet** icon (you may have to click on the next app page to view this app). The Site Contents – New page will open.

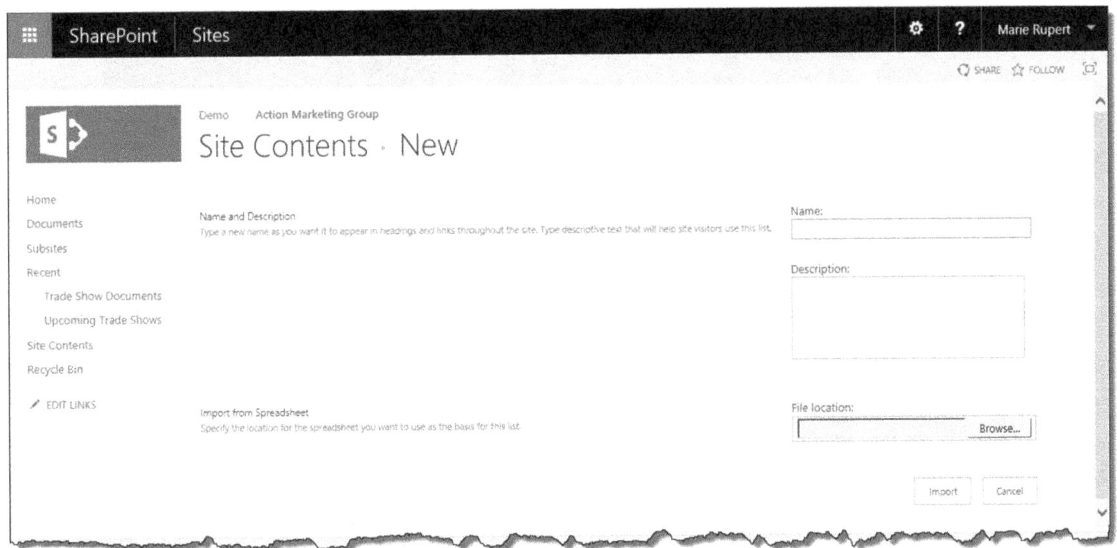

Figure 1: Site Contents - New Page for Importing Spreadsheets

4. In the Name field, enter a title for the new list. This will be the title of the list shown in any of the Site Content pages.
5. In the Description field, enter any notes about the new list. This should be a good description of what the list contains.

6. In the Import from Spreadsheet section, click **Browse**. The Choose File to Upload dialog box will appear.

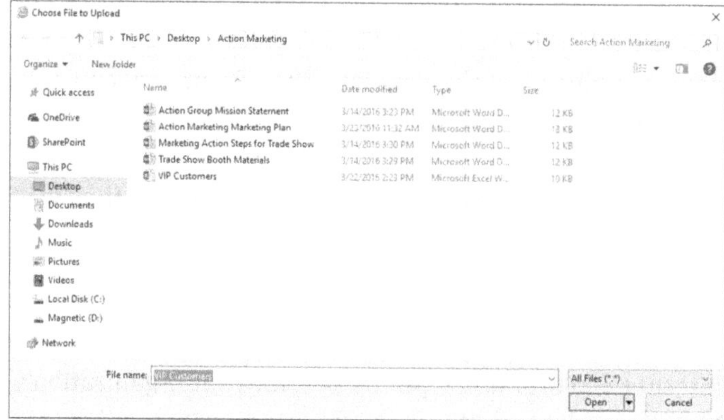

Figure 2: The Choose File to Upload Dialog Box

7. Click the spreadsheet to import, then click **Open**. The Choose File to Upload dialog box will close and the file name and path for the spreadsheet will appear in the File Location field on the New list page.

8. Click **Import**. The spreadsheet will open in Excel and the Import to Windows SharePoint Services list dialog box will appear.

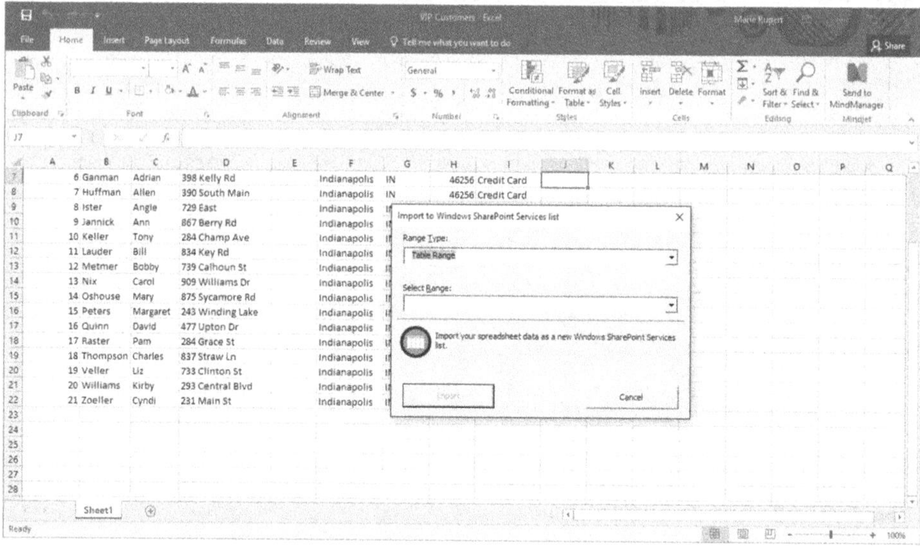

Figure 3: The Import to Windows SharePoint Services List Dialog Box

9. Excel spreadsheets can often contain specific table ranges or named ranges. If you have a table range or named range within Excel that you want to import, choose the appropriate option in the Range Type field and the desired range in the Select Range field.

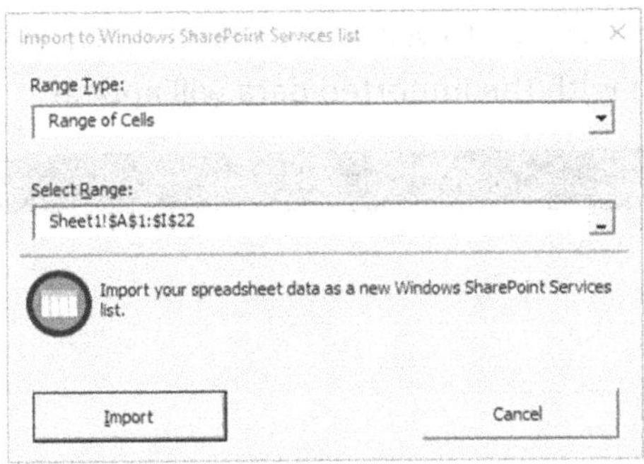

Figure 4: The Configured Range of Cells Range Type in the Import Dialog Box

10. If there is no range of cells within Excel that have been set as a named range or table that you want to import, select Range of Cells in the Range Type field and click the control in the Select Range field. Use the mouse cursor to highlight the appropriate range on the spreadsheet and press Enter. Alternatively, enter the cell range in the Select Range field.

11. Click **Import**. The Import to Windows SharePoint Services list dialog box will close and the new list with the imported data will appear.

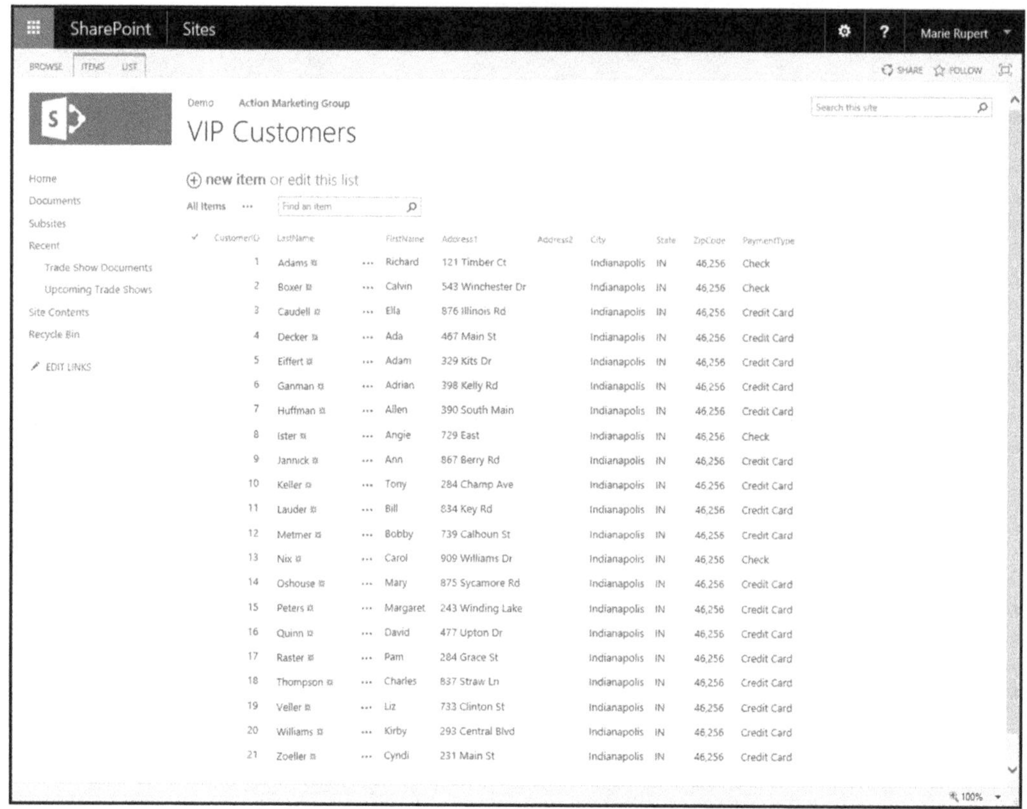

CustomerID	LastName	FirstName	Address1	Address2	City	State	ZipCode	PaymentType
1	Adams	Richard	121 Timber Ct		Indianapolis	IN	46,256	Check
2	Boxer	Calvin	543 Winchester Dr		Indianapolis	IN	46,256	Check
3	Caudell	Ella	876 Illinois Rd		Indianapolis	IN	46,256	Credit Card
4	Decker	Ada	467 Main St		Indianapolis	IN	46,256	Credit Card
5	Eiffert	Adam	329 Kits Dr		Indianapolis	IN	46,256	Credit Card
6	Ganman	Adrian	398 Kelly Rd		Indianapolis	IN	46,256	Credit Card
7	Huffman	Allen	390 South Main		Indianapolis	IN	46,256	Credit Card
8	Ister	Angie	729 East		Indianapolis	IN	46,256	Check
9	Jannick	Ann	867 Berry Rd		Indianapolis	IN	46,256	Credit Card
10	Keller	Tony	284 Champ Ave		Indianapolis	IN	46,256	Credit Card
11	Lauder	Bill	834 Key Rd		Indianapolis	IN	46,256	Credit Card
12	Metmer	Bobby	739 Calhoun St		Indianapolis	IN	46,256	Credit Card
13	Nix	Carol	909 Williams Dr		Indianapolis	IN	46,256	Check
14	Oshouse	Mary	875 Sycamore Rd		Indianapolis	IN	46,256	Credit Card
15	Peters	Margaret	243 Winding Lake		Indianapolis	IN	46,256	Credit Card
16	Quinn	David	477 Upton Dr		Indianapolis	IN	46,256	Credit Card
17	Raster	Pam	284 Grace St		Indianapolis	IN	46,256	Credit Card
18	Thompson	Charles	837 Straw Ln		Indianapolis	IN	46,256	Credit Card
19	Veller	Liz	733 Clinton St		Indianapolis	IN	46,256	Credit Card
20	Williams	Kirby	293 Central Blvd		Indianapolis	IN	46,256	Credit Card
21	Zoeller	Cyndi	231 Main St		Indianapolis	IN	46,256	Credit Card

Figure 5: The New Imported List

Task: Create a New Item for a List App

Purpose: Data entry into SharePoint is quick and easy. SharePoint creates a dialog that matches the fields in your list. Entering data one item at a time can be a good way to process individual transactions.

Example: A few of the Action Marketing Group VIP customers were missed when the list was created, they need to add them to the VIP Customers List.

Steps:

1. Start Internet Explorer and type the URL for your organization's SharePoint server. The Start page will open.
2. Navigate to the list to which you want to add an item. The list page will open.
3. Click the new item link. The New Item page will open.

Note: The New Item page is tailored automatically by SharePoint to match the list. Your view may be slightly different.

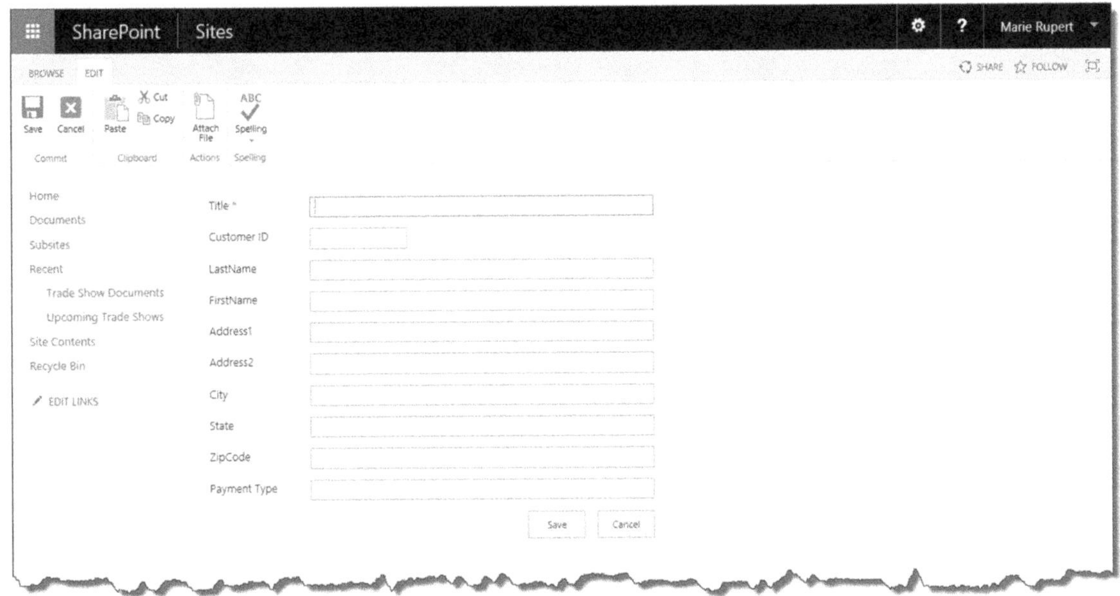

Figure 1: The New Item Page

4. Enter the information for the new item in the required fields (and enter information for any additional fields that may be listed).
5. Click Save. The item will be added to the list.

Task: Add New List or Library App Columns

Purpose: In any list or library app that you create, you can customize the columns that you want to use. This provides additional places to enter data about each item or file.

Example: The Action Marketing Group wants to capture the last contact date for their VIP customers in a new column.

Steps:

1. Start Internet Explorer and type the URL for your organization's SharePoint server. The Start page will open.

2. Navigate to the list you want to modify. The list page will open.

3. Click the **List** tab. The List ribbon will open.

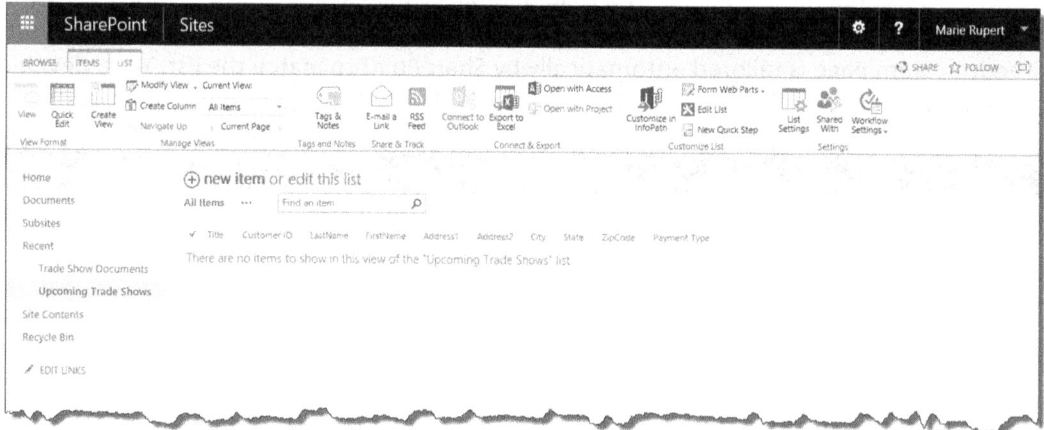

Figure 1: The List Tools Ribbon

4. Click **Create Column**. The Create Column dialog box will open.

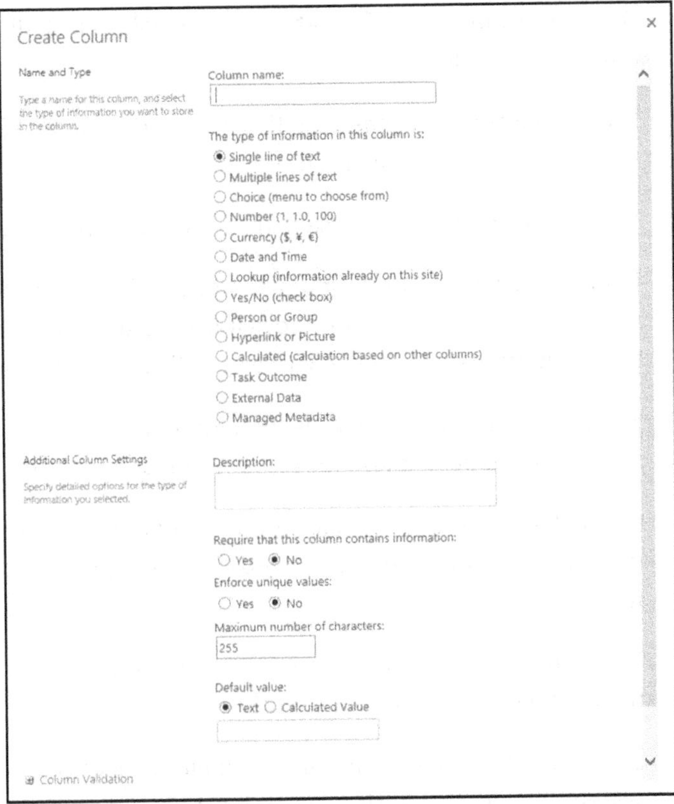

Figure 2: The Create Column Dialog Box

5. In the Column name field, enter a name for the new column.
6. Specify the type of information that will be contained in the list column. The options are:
    - Single Line of text – Good for short descriptions, titles, and information of less than 255 characters.
    - Multiple lines of text – Good for notes, comments, and other places where there may be a great deal of text to be entered.
    - Choice – Good for single-level predefined values including statuses, states, and conditions. Great for grouping.
    - Number – Good for numeric data including counts and values. Great when you'll need to sort the data numerically. Supports minimum and maximum values as well as integers and floating point numbers.
    - Currency – Good for currency values. Defaults the formatting to look good for your country's currency.

- Date and Time – Good for date and time values including values that are date or time only.
- Lookup – Good for connecting this list to other data in SharePoint. This references the values in another list.
- Yes/No – Good for checkboxes, true/false, and yes/no type data.
- Person or Group – Good for assignment of the item to a person or group for management, or to indicate the last user to use the system. Will be validated to your network or optionally to a specific group of people.
- Hyperlink or Picture – A special field that includes both the hyperlink (location) and description for either a link or a picture.
- Calculated – The value is calculated from other columns and static information in the item. Calculated fields are great for transforming different fields.
- Task Outcome – A special choice field variant that allows the results of the field to be used as a part of a workflow.
- External Data – SharePoint has the ability to access data stored in other systems in your enterprise. If this has been set up, you can connect your list data to your master customer list.
- Managed Metadata – A hierarchical collection

7. In the Description field, add notes for the column. This will appear in the New and Edit Item pages to tell users what information is needed, but will not appear on the View Item page.
8. Specify if the column is required to contain information. If it is required, the field will be denoted as such in the New and Edit Item pages.
9. Depending on the type of information selected in Step 6 above, additional settings may be needed. Set them as desired.
10. Click OK. The column will be added to the list.

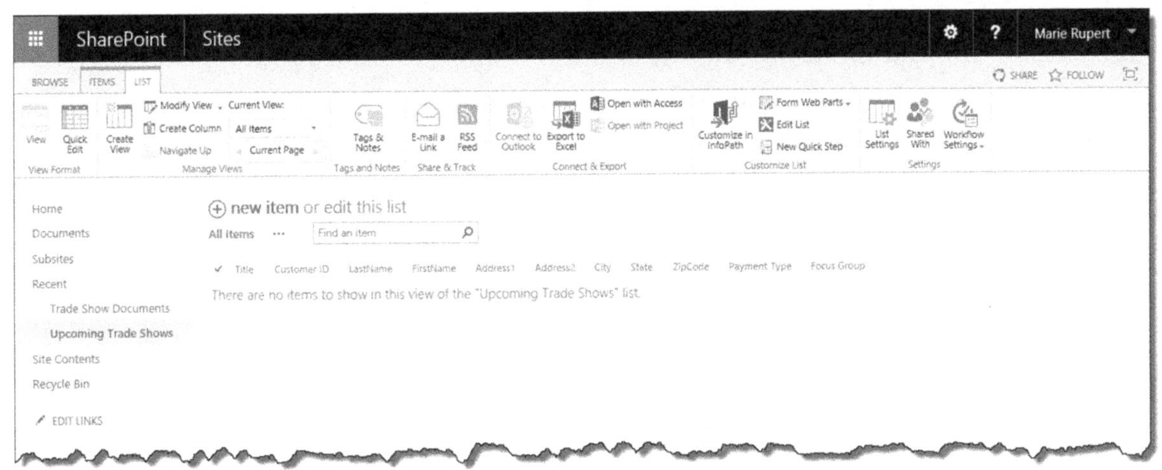

Figure 3: The New Column Added to the List Page

Task: Edit Existing List or Library App Columns

Purpose: Sometimes when you set up a column in a list, you don't get all the settings right. Perhaps you need to add an additional option to a choice field or edit the limits for a number. SharePoint allows you to adjust field settings after they have been created.

Example: When the Action Marketing Group imported the VIP Customer List, some of the column names in the spreadsheet were cryptic. They need adjusted to be friendlier.

Steps:

1. Start Internet Explorer and type the URL for your organization's SharePoint server. The Start page will open.
2. Navigate to the list you want to edit. The list page will open.
3. In the ribbon, click the **List** tab. The List ribbon will open.
4. Click the **List Settings** button. The list's Settings page will open.

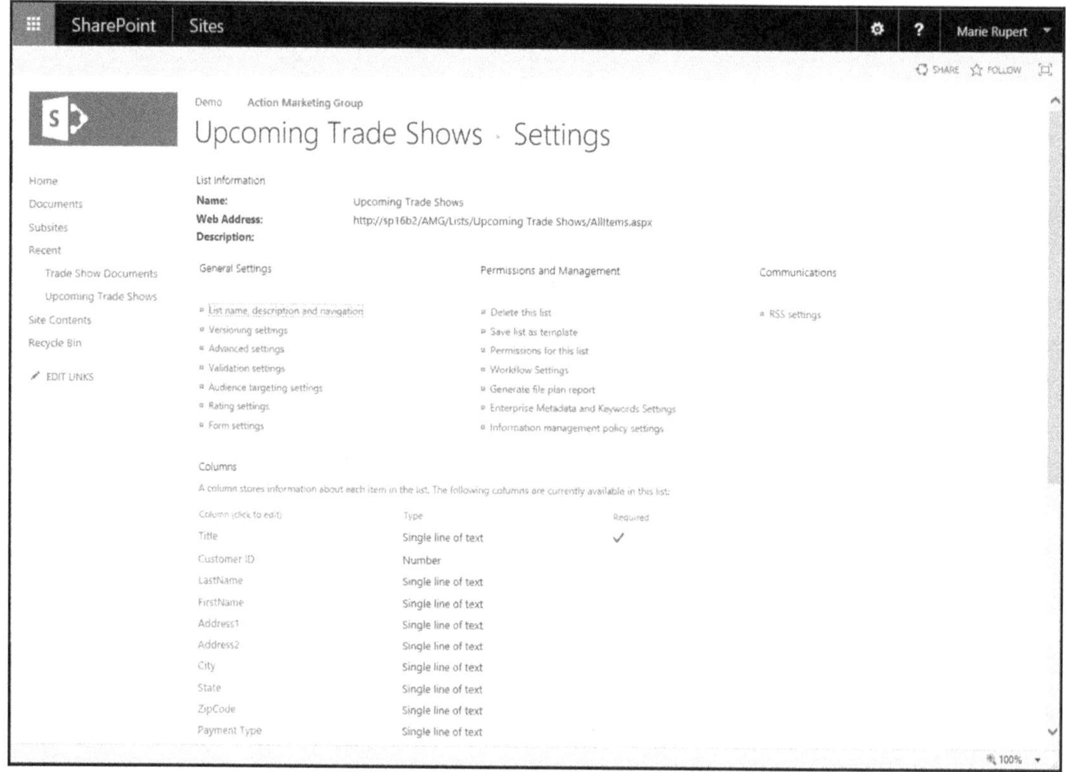

Figure 1: The List's Settings Page

5. In the Columns section, click on the name of the column you want to edit. The Edit Column page will open.

Note: The Edit Column page will vary, depending on what column/field you are trying to edit. You may also note that, depending on the column selected, your editing choices might be rather limited. Some columns cannot even be renamed.

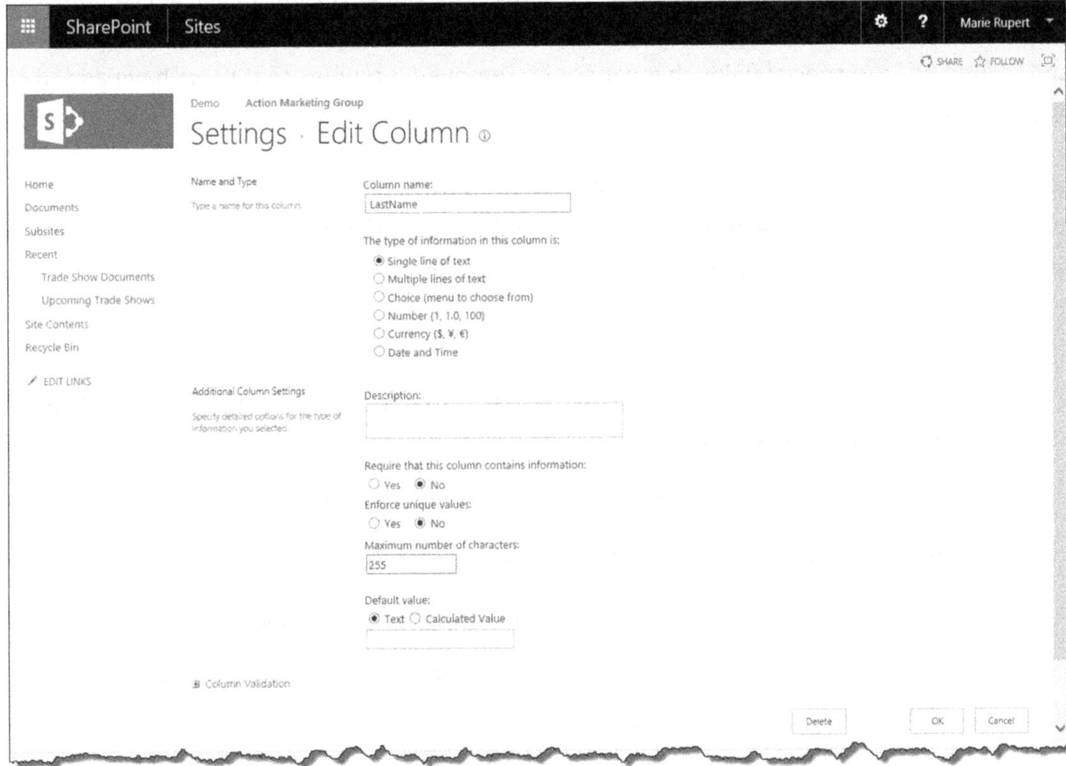

Figure 2: The Edit Column Page

6. Enter or add the information you want to change about the column in the appropriate field.
7. Click **OK**. The List Settings page will open again, with the changes indicated in the **Columns** section.

Task: Delete List or Library App Columns

Purpose: If a column in your list proves to be unnecessary, you can remove it from the list altogether. An important thing to note, however, is that you can only remove certain columns. Some columns, including the default columns used by SharePoint, such as "Title," "Created By," "Modified By," and "Modified" are special fields that cannot be removed. Columns that users have added can always be removed.

Example: Initially, the Action Marketing Group wanted to track product payment information for its VIP Customers, but after being warned of the potential for this information being misused, they have decided to remove the information from the VIP Customer list.

Steps:

1. Start Internet Explorer and type the URL for your organization's SharePoint server. The Start page will open.
2. Navigate to the list you want to edit. The List page will open.
3. In the ribbon click the **List** tab. The List ribbon will open.
4. Click the **List Settings** button. The List Settings page will open.
5. In the Columns section, click on the name of the column you want to remove. The Edit Column page will open.

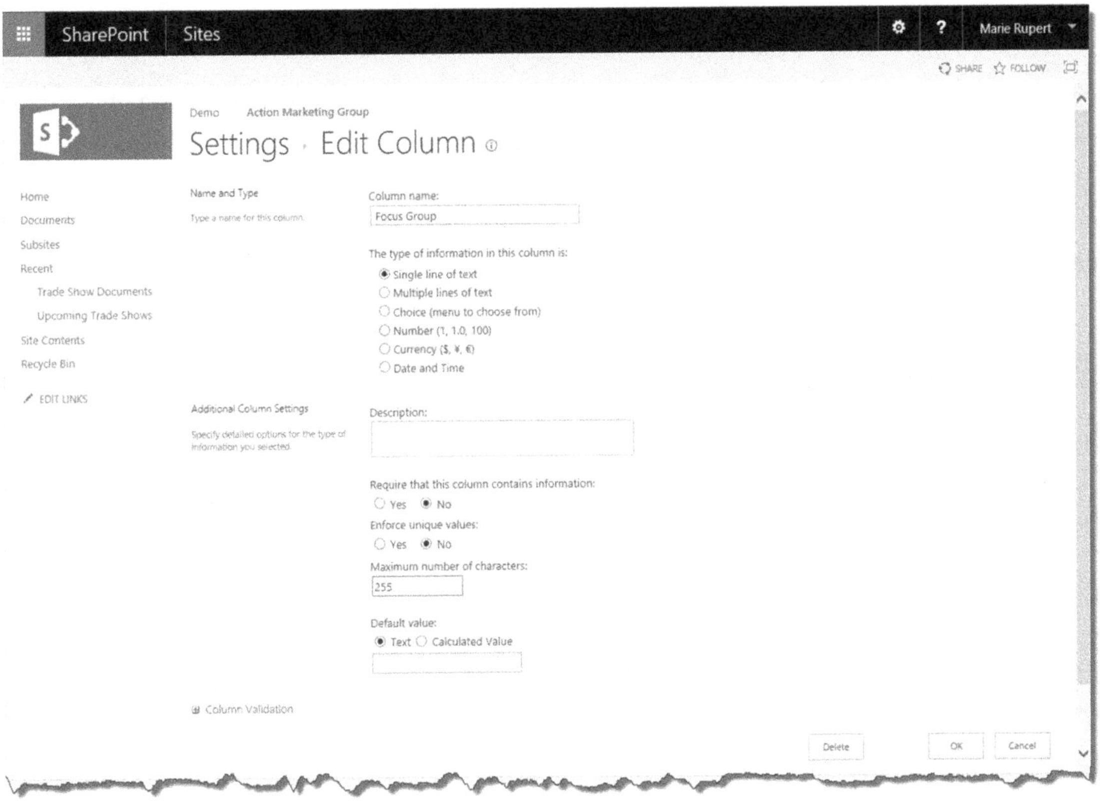

Figure 1: The Edit Column Page with Delete Button

6. Near the bottom of the page, click **Delete**. A confirmation dialog box will open.

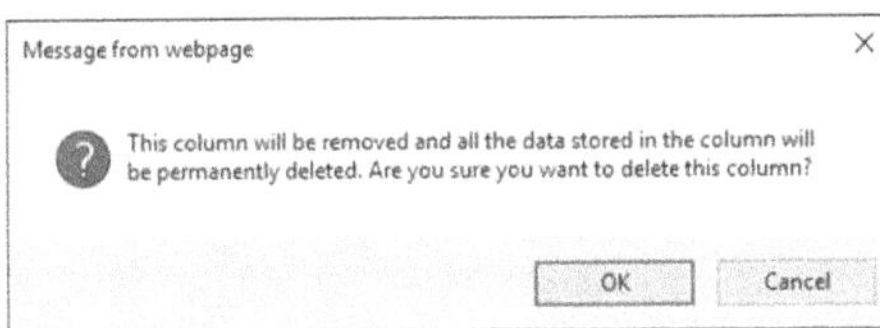

Figure 2: The Delete Column Confirmation Dialog Box

7. Click **OK**. The List Settings page will open again, with the column removed from the Columns section.

Task: Edit a List or Library App in Quick Edit View

Purpose: As you work with lists, you will note a distinct similarity to another collection of data: the spreadsheet. This is made even clearer if you have imported a spreadsheet from Excel to SharePoint. But editing information in a SharePoint list can be time consuming if you have to open up one item at a time. Fortunately, you can shift to Quick Edit view, which looks and functions very similarly to a spreadsheet, allowing you to edit a lot of list data at once.

Example: When Action Marketing Group imported the VIP Customer List, some of the data was not accurate. This data needs to be quickly updated.

Steps:

1. Start Internet Explorer and type the URL for your organization's SharePoint server. The Start page will open.
2. Navigate to the list you want to edit. The list page will open.

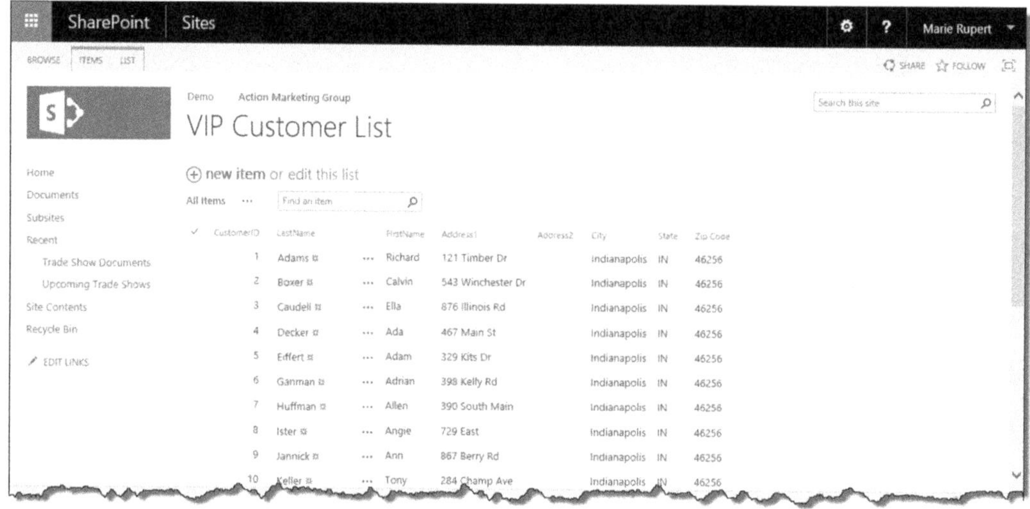

Figure 1: A List in Standard View

3. In the ribbon click the List tab. The List ribbon will open.
4. Click the Quick Edit button. The list will now appear in the Quick Edit view. You can also click the edit this list link to open Quick Edit view.

Note: Quick Edit View will work in any web browser that fully supports HTML5 including Internet Explorer 11 and current versions of Chrome and Firefox. Quick Edit will work in Internet Explorer 9 if Microsoft Office is installed.

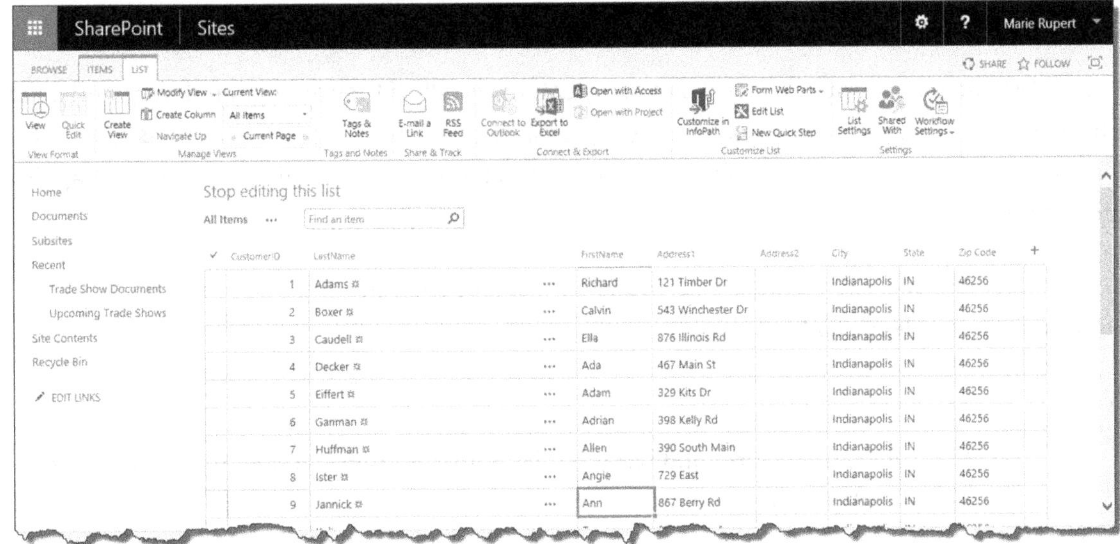

Figure 2: A List in Quick Edit View

5. Click a cell you want to edit to select that cell, and make any changes that are needed.

6. Repeat step 5 to edit other cells as needed.

7. Click the **Stop** editing this list link or click the **View** button to save your changes. Quick Edit View will close and the list will return to the Standard view.

Task: Subscribe to a List or Library App RSS Feed

Purpose: List and library apps in SharePoint are great, especially if they are updated frequently. But the best list in the world isn't going to do much good if no one actually comes back to look at it. If you are interested in an app, you can subscribe to an RSS feed that will notify you when that app's content has changed.

Example: Now that the VIP Customers list has been created, you can subscribe to the list's RSS feed using your preferred feed reader.

Steps:

1. Start Internet Explorer and type the URL for your organization's SharePoint server. The Start page will open.
2. Navigate to the list whose RSS feed you wish to subscribe to. The list page will open.
3. In the ribbon click the **List** tab. The List ribbon will open.
4. Click the **RSS Feed** button. The RSS feed page will open.

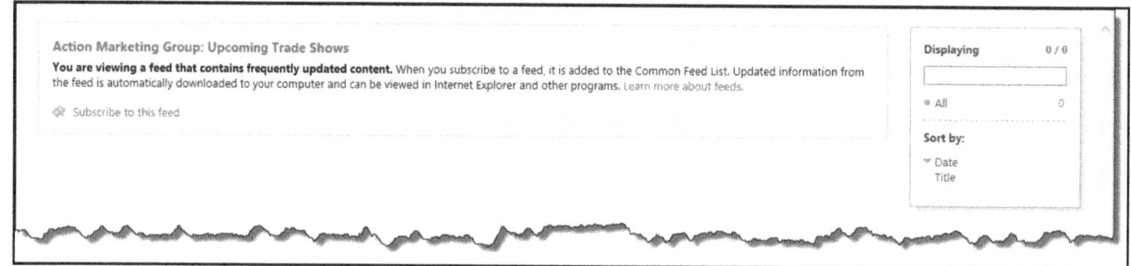

Figure 1: A List RSS Feed

5. Click the **Subscribe to this feed** link. The Subscribe to this Feed dialogue box will open.
6. The name of your list will appear in the Name field.
7. In the Create in section, decide if you want to create a new folder to hold your RSS feed.
8. Click the **checkbox** next to Add to Favorites Bar if you want to add the RSS feed to the Favorites Bar.
9. Click **Subscribe** button and you will be subscribed to the feed.

Task: View Library Item Properties

Purpose: Views in a library app are sometimes necessary to be able to look at all of the information for documents in detail. SharePoint allows you to quickly view all of the properties of a document.

Example: One of the Action Marketing Group's sales representatives is going to make a call to a VIP customer and needs to review the marketing plan prior to speaking with them.

Steps:

1. Start Internet Explorer and type the URL for your organization's SharePoint server. The Start page will open.
2. Navigate to the library where you want to view library item properties. The library page will open.

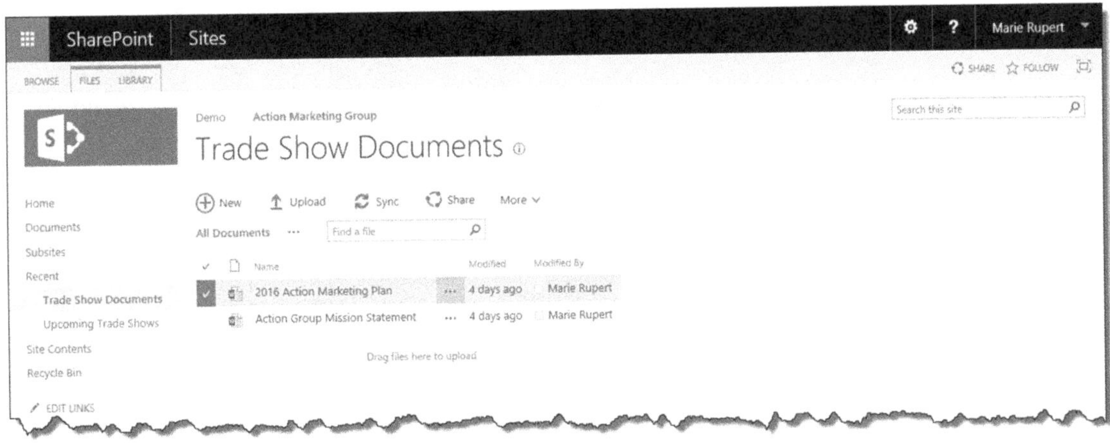

Figure 1: The Document Library

3. Click the Files tab. The Files ribbon will open.

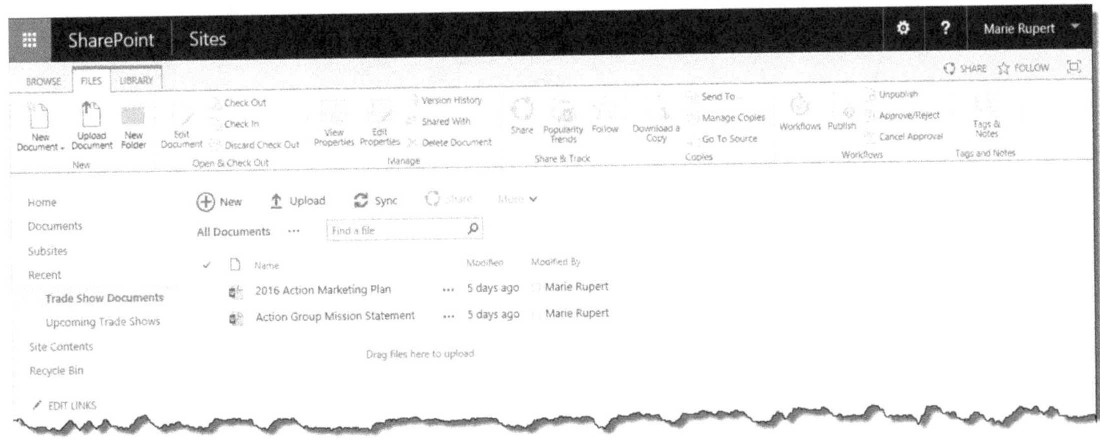

Figure 2: The Files Ribbon

4. Select a file by clicking the **checkmark** icon to the left of the document's title, then click the **View Properties** button. The View Document Properties page will open.

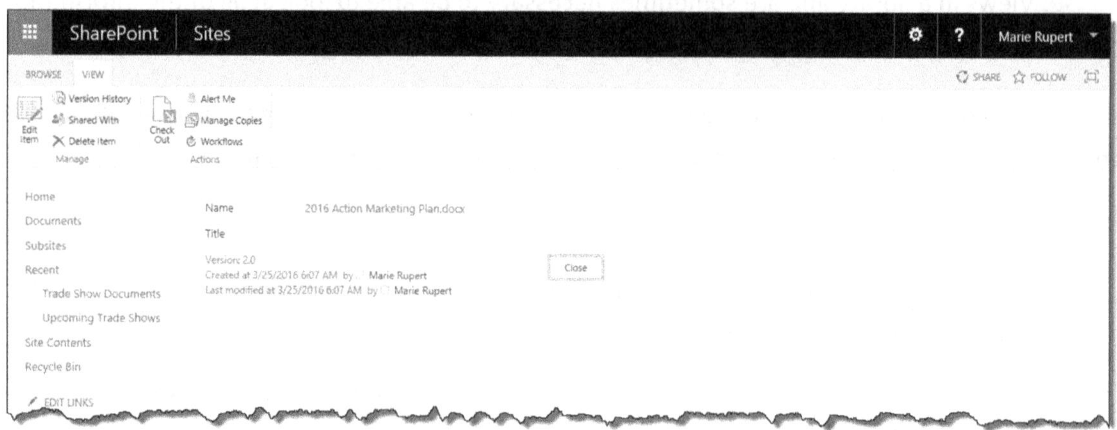

Figure 3: The View Document Properties Page

5. Click **Close** when finished. The View Document Properties page will close and the library page will appear.

Task: View List Item Properties

Purpose: Views of a list are necessary to make list apps manageable, but removing columns necessarily means removing list item properties from that view. SharePoint allows you to quickly view all of the properties of a list item. There are multiple ways to do this, and each will be shown here.

Example: One of the Action Marketing Group's sales representatives is going to make a call to a VIP customer and needs to view the list properties prior to speaking with them.

Steps:

1. Start Internet Explorer and type the URL for your organization's SharePoint server. The Start page will open.

2. Navigate to the list with the items you wish to view. The list's page will open.

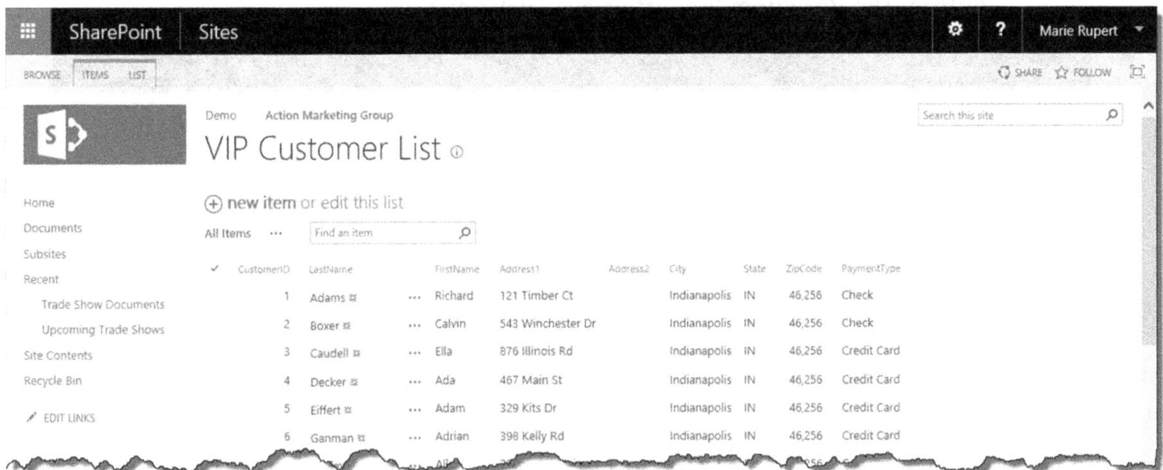

Figure 1: The List Page

3. The first way to view an item's properties is to click the title of the item. More specifically, click the column entry that is linked to the edit menu. The View Item Properties page will appear.

4. The second way to view an item's properties is to find the item you would like to view, and click the ellipsis control. The item's menu will appear.

5. Click View Item. The View Item Properties page will appear.

6. The last way to view an item's properties is to click the Items tab. The Items ribbon will open.

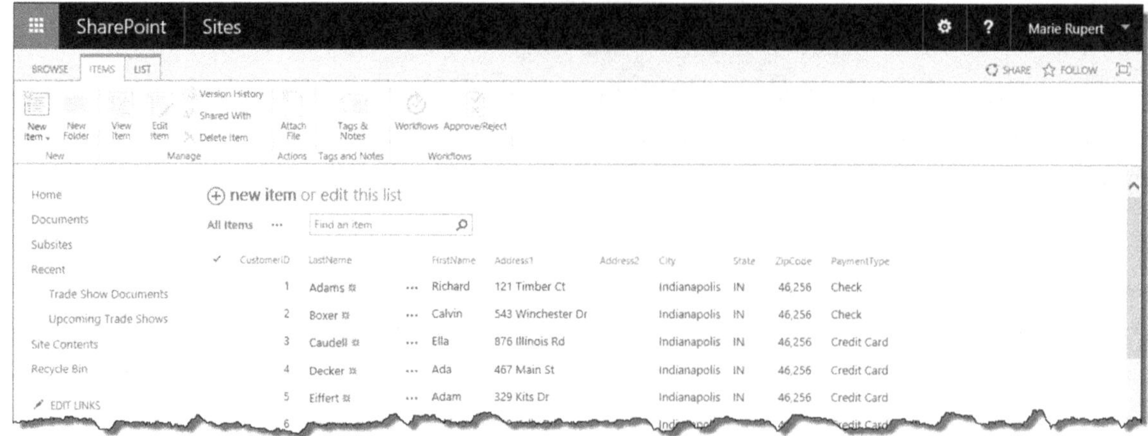

Figure 2: The Items Ribbon

7. Click the **checkmark** to the left of the list item to select it, then click the **View Item** button. The View Item Properties page will open.

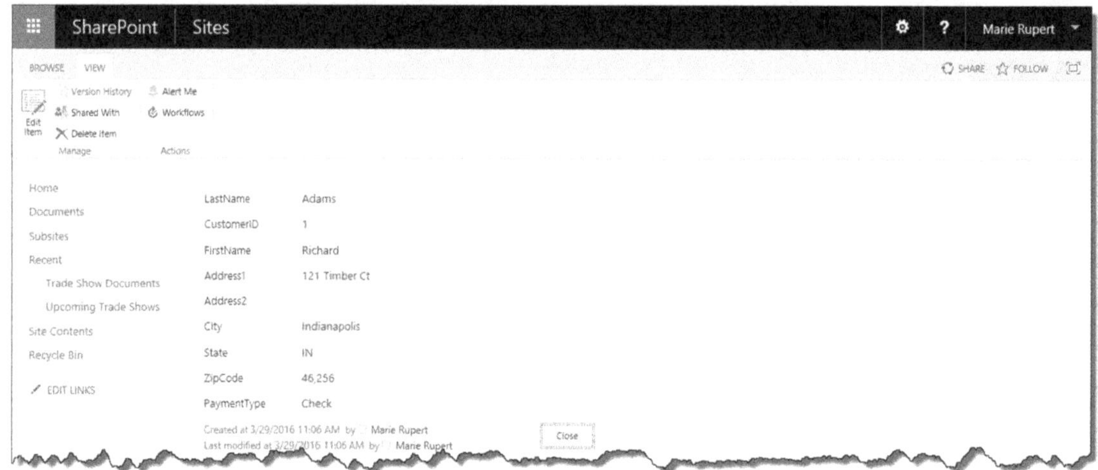

Figure 3: The View Item Properties Page

8. Click **Close** when finished. The View Item Properties page will close and the list page will appear.

Task: Edit List or Library Item Properties

Purpose: Sometimes it's more efficient to edit items in a view which provides better editing controls, descriptive text, and warnings while editing. SharePoint's edit form allows you to edit properties more richly than the Quick Edit view. There are two ways to do this – both will be shown here.

Example: The Action Marketing Group's VIP customer list has a customer with a bad address which needs corrected.

Steps:

1. Start Internet Explorer and type the URL for your organization's SharePoint server. The Start page will open.
2. Navigate to the list in which you are interested. The list page will open.
3. The first way to edit an item's properties is to find the item you wish to edit, then click the **ellipsis** control. The item's menu will appear.
4. Click **Edit Item**. The Edit Item Properties page will appear.
5. The second way to edit the list item's properties is to click the **Items** tab. The Items ribbon will open.
6. Click the **checkmark** to the left of the item's title to select the item, then click the **Edit Item** button. The Edit Item Properties page will open.

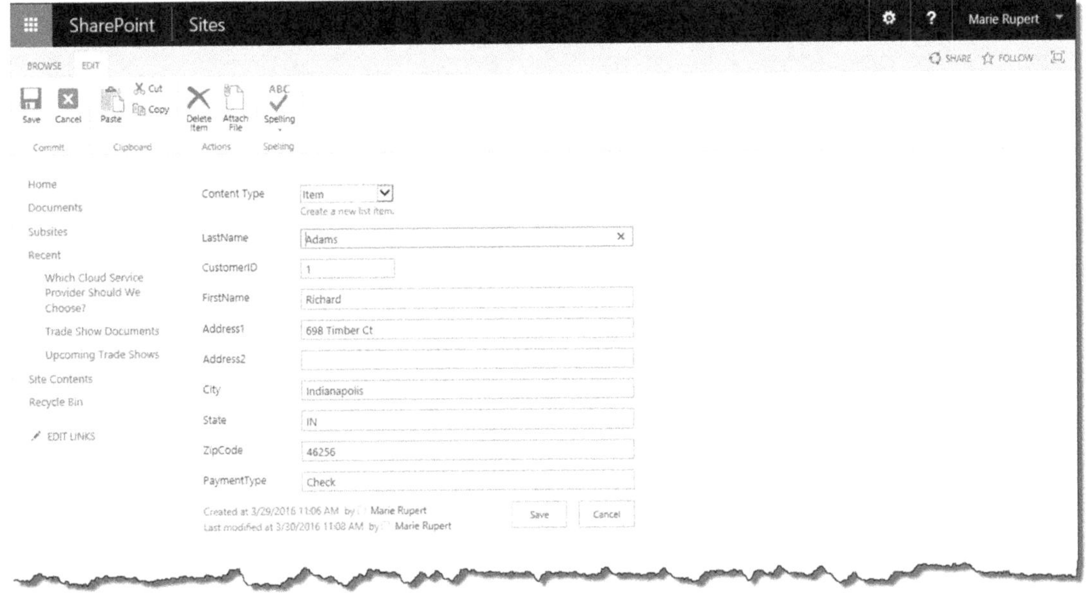

Figure 1: The Edit Item Properties Page

Note: The Edit Item page may look different depending on the columns your list contains and the list settings.

7. When you are finished editing the item's properties, click **Save**. The list page will appear with the updated item information.

Task: Manage List Item Permissions

Purpose: For the most part, permissions are set at a site, library or folder level. However, some list items may need different permissions. SharePoint allows you to set the permissions of a list item individually when necessary.

Example: The Action Marketing Group needs to limit the people who can modify the strategic plan.

Steps:

1. Start Internet Explorer and type the URL for your organization's SharePoint server. The Start page will open.
2. Navigate to the list app in which you are interested. The list page will open.
3. Click the ellipsis control for the item you want to change permissions for. The item's menu will open.

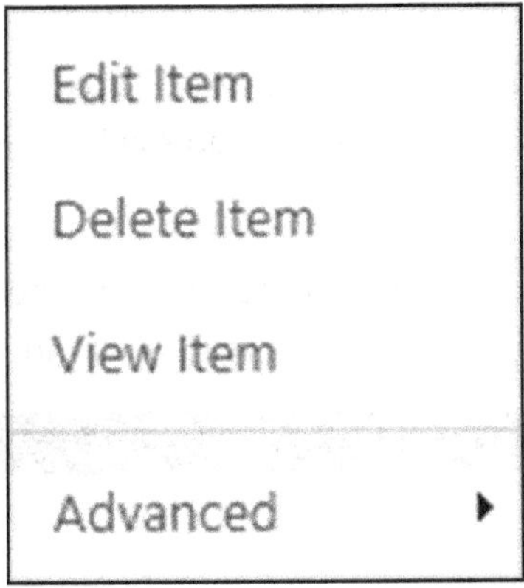

Figure 1: The Item Menu

4. Hover over Advanced to show the Advanced Options menu, then click Manage Permissions. The Permissions page will open.

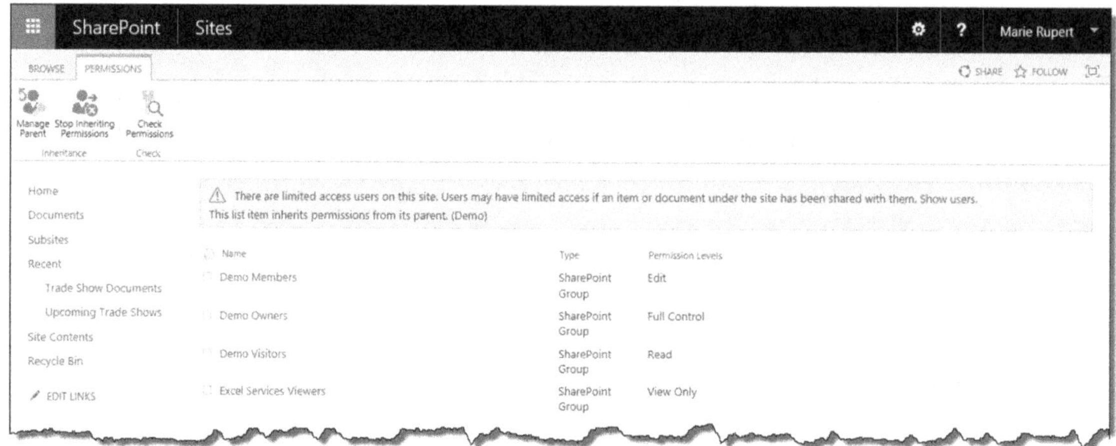

Figure 2: The Permissions Page

5. In the Permissions ribbon, click the **Stop Inheriting Permissions** button. A confirmation dialog box will appear.

6. Click **OK**. The confirmation dialog box will close, the list item will no longer have the same permissions set. A new set of tools will appear in the Permissions ribbon on the Permission page.

Note: Steps 5 and 6 will break the inherited permissions from the parent list. Any permissions changes made to the parent list may need to be repeated for individual items.

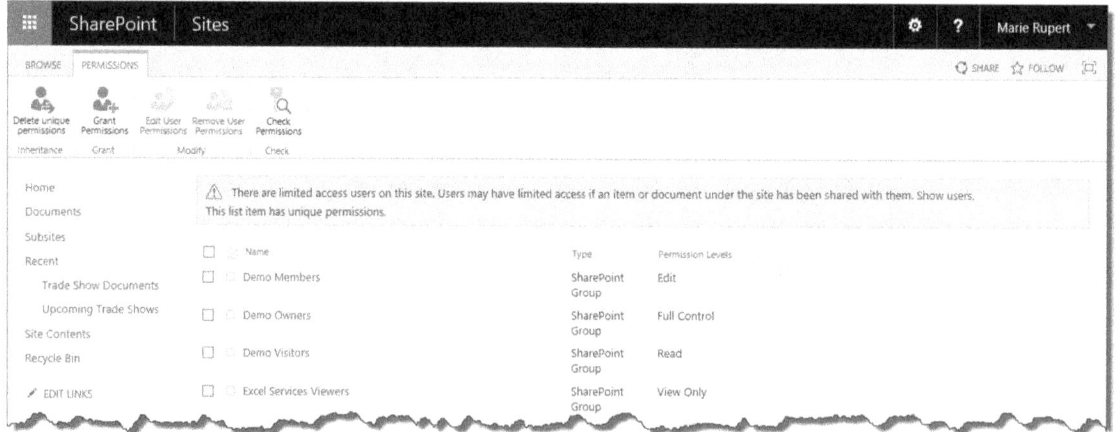

Figure 3: The Permissions Tools Page Without Permission Inheritance

7. In the Permissions ribbon, click the **Grant Permissions** button. The Share dialog box will open.

8. In the Invite people field, enter user names.

9. Click the **Show Options** link. The Select a permission level field will appear.

10. Select the permission level you wish to grant this set of users for this list item.
11. Click Share. The Share dialog box will close and the users will now appear on the Permissions page. Repeat Steps 7-11 to grant different permission levels to additional users.
12. You can also choose to undo custom permissions for the list item and resume inheriting the parent list's permissions. To do this, in the Permissions ribbon, click the Delete unique permissions button. A confirmation dialog box will appear.
13. Click OK. The confirmation dialog box will close, and the list item will resume inheriting parent permissions.

Note: Steps 12 and 13 will cause all custom permissions for a list item to be lost. Any permission changes to the parent list will be reflected in the list item.

Task: Edit a Library App Item in a Preferred Application

Purpose: Most Microsoft applications, and applications from many other vendors, can edit files directly from SharePoint. SharePoint launches the client application and the application saves the revised file back to SharePoint.

Example: The marketing manager needs update the Action Marketing Group plan in Word and save it back to the library.

Steps:

1. Start Internet Explorer and type the URL for your organization's SharePoint server. The Start page will open.
2. Navigate to the library app in which you are interested. The library page will open.
3. Find the document you wish to open and click the ellipsis control next to the document title. The document's menu will appear.

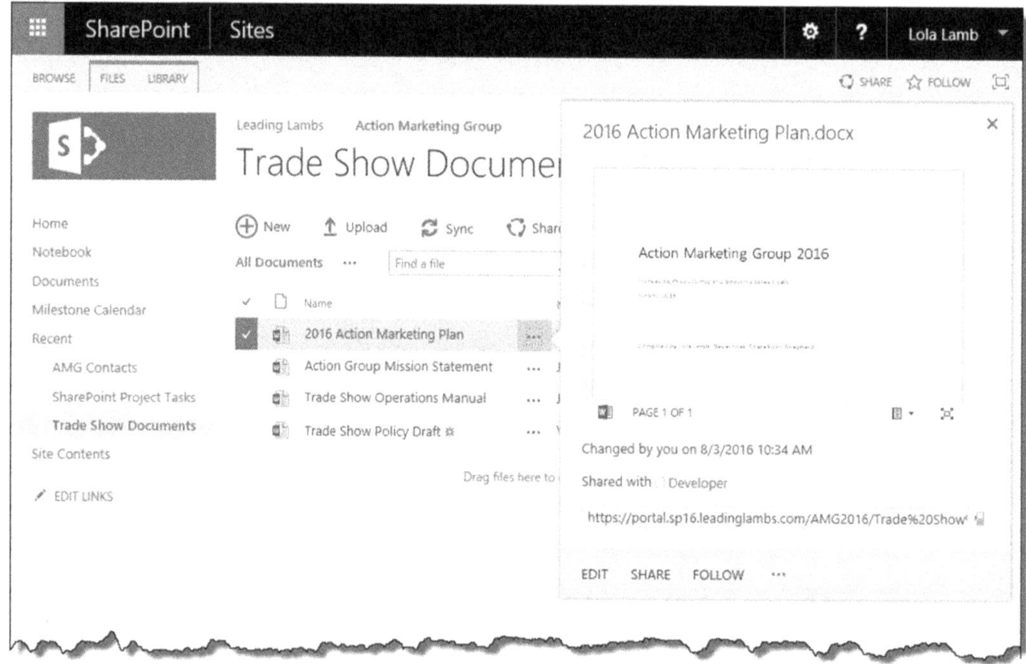

Figure 1: The Document Menu

4. At the bottom of the document menu, click Edit.

Note: If your library settings are configured correctly, clicking the document title may also open the document in the client application.

5. Depending on your security settings, a Microsoft Office confirmation box may appear. Click **Yes**.

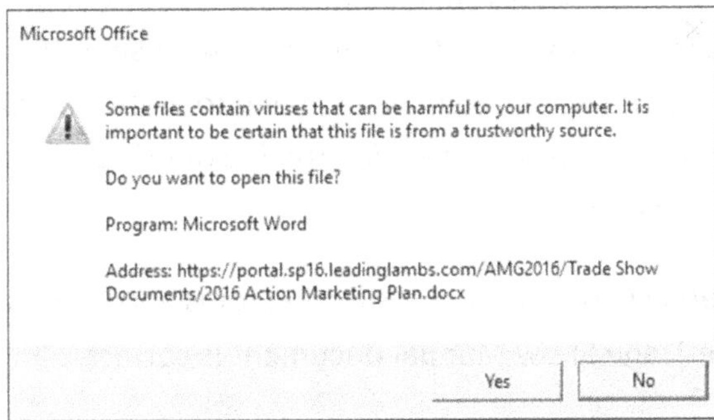

Figure 2: The Microsoft Office Confirmation Dialog Box

6. If prompted, login to the library item with the appropriate credentials. The document will be opened in the appropriate client application.

Note: Some applications, particularly Office applications, open documents from untrusted sources in a protected view. You may need to click the **Enable Editing** button to edit the document.

7. When you are finished editing the document, click **Save** in the application and close it. All changes will be saved to the file in the SharePoint document library.

Task: Download a Library App File

Purpose: Sometimes you will want to download a file rather than editing it directly from SharePoint. You might have an application that isn't directly compatible with SharePoint, you may want to bring a single file with you while you travel, or you may just need to grab a file to work on during the commute home. You may want to consider checking the file out if you suspect you and others may be modifying the file at the same time.

Example: The Action Marketing Group's trade show director is getting ready to get on a plane and needs to make sure that the Trade Show Manual document is correct.

Steps:

1. Start Internet Explorer and type the URL for your organization's SharePoint server. The Start page will open.
2. Navigate to the library app in which you are interested. The library page will open.
3. Next to the title of the document you wish to download, click the **ellipsis** control. The document's menu will appear.

Figure 1: The Document Menu

4. At the bottom of the document menu, click the **ellipsis** control to open the Options menu. Select the **Download** option. Your browser's download notification will appear.
5. Click the drop-down arrow next to the **Save** button and click **Save As**. The Save As dialog box will appear.

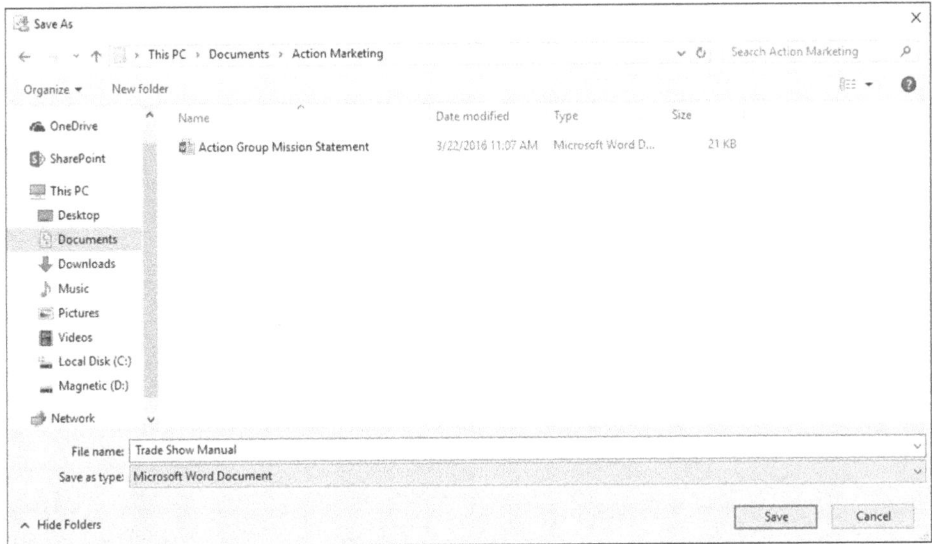

Figure 2: The Save As Dialog Box

6. Navigate to the location where you want to save the document and click **Save**. The file will be saved to the specified location. You've successfully downloaded the file.

7. After you complete editing, you may wish to save you changes to the file on SharePoint. When you have edited and saved the changes to your copy of the file, return to the document library in SharePoint.

8. In the ribbon click the **Files** tab. The Files ribbon will open.

9. Click the **Upload Document** button. You can also click the **Upload** up arrow icon from your Library view. The Add a Document dialog box will open.

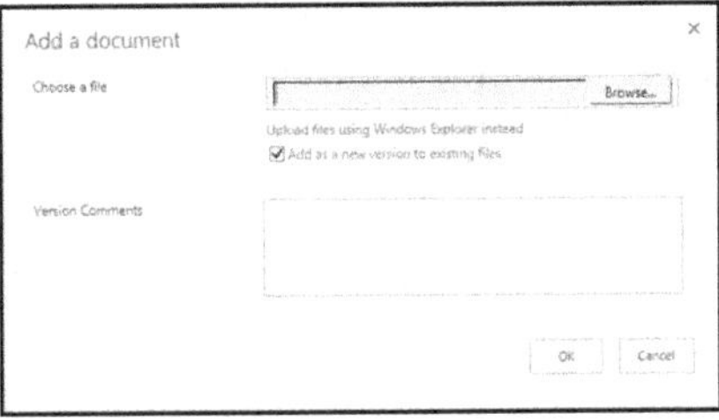

Figure 3: The Add a Document Dialog Box

10. Click the **Browse** button. The Choose File to Upload dialog box will appear.

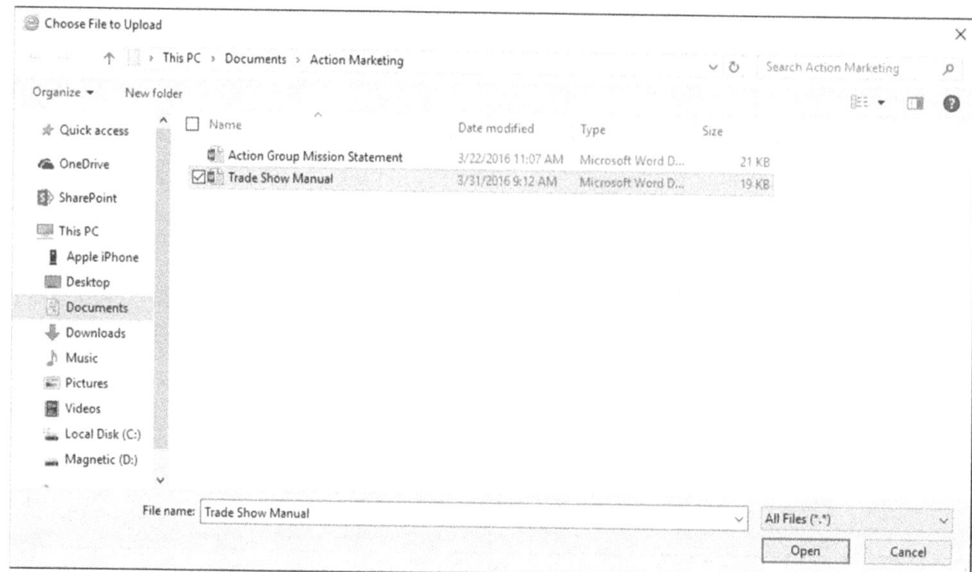

Figure 4: The Choose File to Upload Dialog Box

11. Select the local copy of the file and click Open. The file and its file path will appear in the Name field.
12. Verify that the Add as a new version to exiting files checkbox is checked.
13. Add any comments in the Version Comments field and click the OK button. The Add a document dialog box will close.

Note: If the Add as a new version to existing files checkbox is not checked, a dialog box will appear, stating that a file by that name already exists in the library. Click Replace It to save the document as a new version of the file.

14. The file will be uploaded and will appear in the library.

Task: Move a File to Another Library App

Purpose: Many times you will have a document that needs to be moved between library apps. You can use SharePoint 2016's drag-and-drop functionality to move a file to another library anywhere on your SharePoint site.

Example: The Action Marketing Group's trade show manager needs to move one of the trade show documents to the upcoming trade show documents because it was misfiled.

Steps:

1. Start Internet Explorer and type the URL for your organization's SharePoint server. The Start page will open.
2. Navigate to the target library where you want to move the document. The library page will open and the library will appear in the Quick Launch under the Recent section.
3. Click the **Settings** menu gear icon and click the **Site Contents** option. The Site Contents page will open.
4. Click the icon next to the library where the document you wish to move is located. The library page will open.
5. Click the **checkmark** icon next to the item or document title to select it.

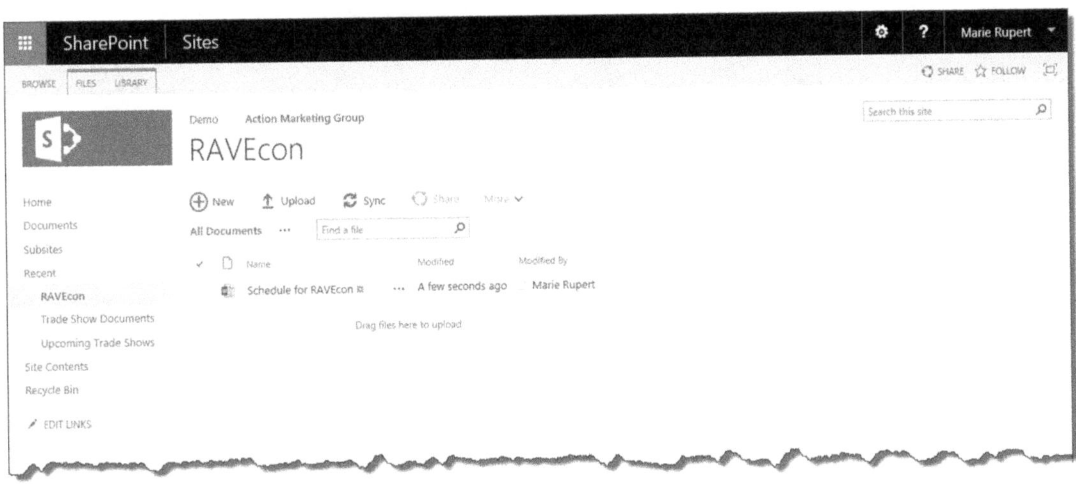

Figure 1: The Origin Library's Selected Item

6. Click and drag the item's link to the target library in the Quick Launch and release the mouse button. The file will appear in the destination library.

Note: If a circle with a slash appears, you will not be able to drag the file to the new library app. One of the most likely causes of this is that the site collection administrator has enabled the site collection feature Publishing Infrastructure, which disables this functionality.

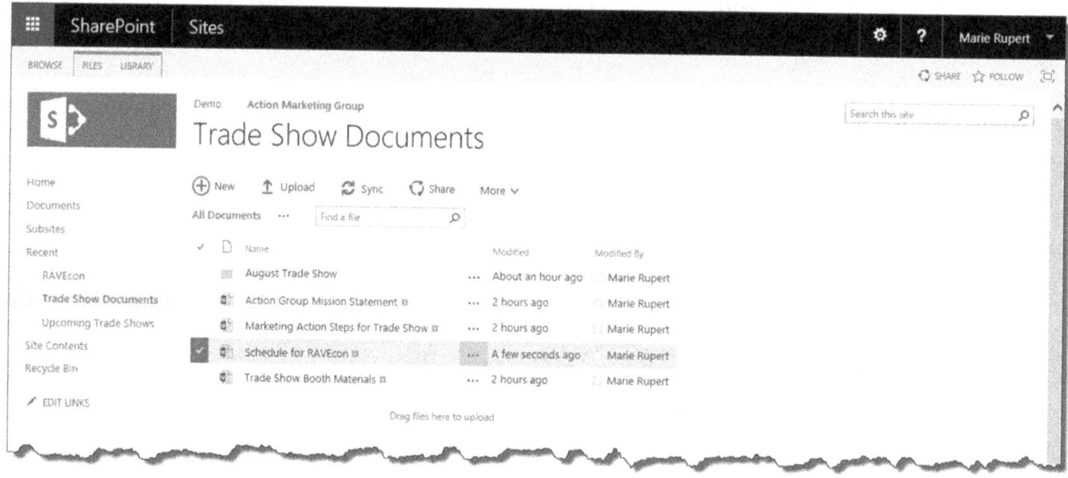

Figure 2: The Item in the Destination Library

Task: E-Mail a Link to a Library App

Purpose: If you want to get many users involved in the editing/creation process, an efficient way is to send a link to the library app in an email. Then they can click on the link and get right to work.

Example: One of your coworkers would like quick access to a document in the Trade Show Materials library. You want to send the link as quick as possible so you can get back to your work.

Steps:

1. Start Internet Explorer and type the URL for your organization's SharePoint server. The Start page will open.
2. Navigate to the library in which you are interested. The library page will open.
3. In the ribbon click the **Library** tab. The Library ribbon will open.

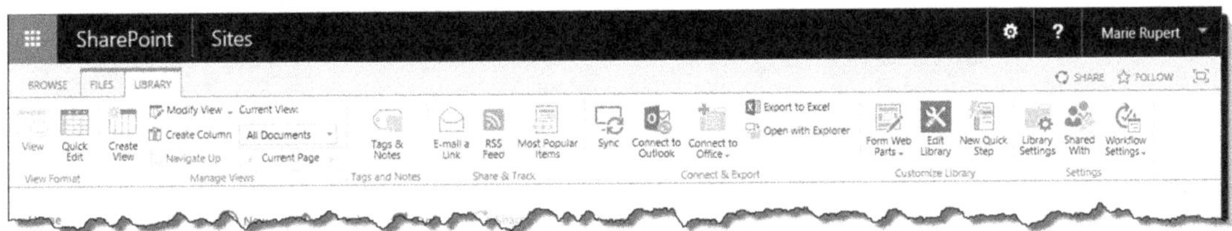

Figure 1: The Library Ribbon

4. Click the **Email a Link** button. An Outlook message window will appear.

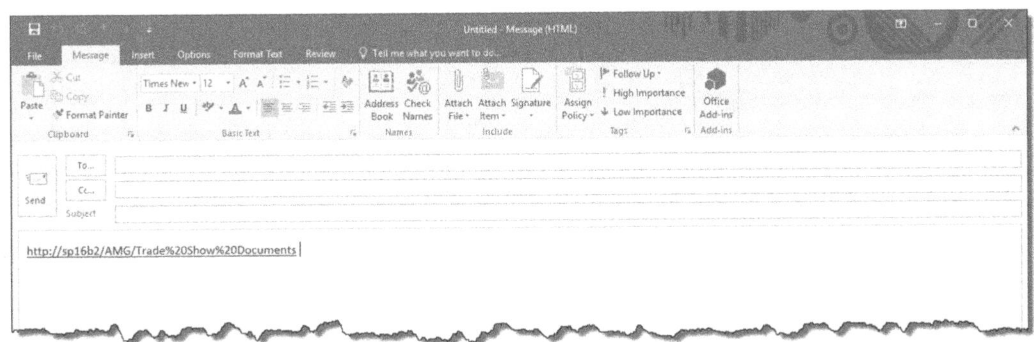

Figure 2: The Outlook Message Window with the Library Link

Note: If Microsoft Outlook is not your default email program, you will see a Compose Email window that contains a link to the document in the body of the email.

5. In the To field, type email address(es).
6. In the Subject field, enter a subject.
7. In the body of the email message, you can add a message along with the link.

8. Click **Send**. The message will be sent.

Task: Edit a List or Library App View

Purpose: Views are powerful in SharePoint. They allow you to have different ways to see the same information in a list or library differently. Editing views allows you to create views that match what you need to see and enables you to quickly find the right information.

Example: The Action Marketing Group's office manager does an occasional spot-check for the number of files that have changed recently. The manager's existing view doesn't filter items that are more than a week old. She wants to modify the view to minimize the work she does checking files.

Steps:

1. Start Internet Explorer and type the URL for your organization's SharePoint server. The Start page will open.
2. Navigate to the library app in which you are interested. The library app's page will open.
3. In the ribbon click the **Library** tab. The Library ribbon will open.
4. Click the **Modify View** button. The Edit View page will open.

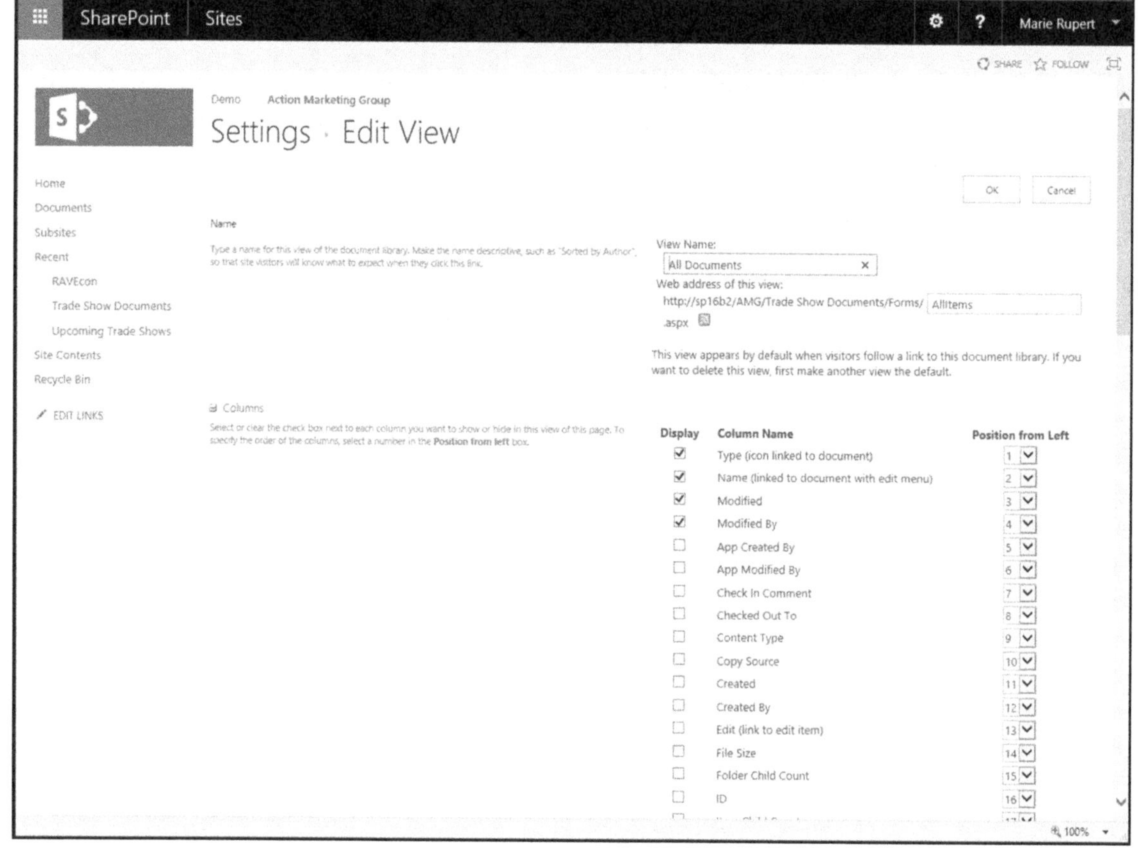

Figure 1: The Edit View Page

5. In the Columns section, click the **checkbox** under Display for any fields you wish to be visible in the view.
6. To move a column's position, select a new **Position from Left** value for that column. The other values will adjust automatically.
7. In the Sort section, select the column by which you want to sort the items.

Note: Some column names aren't really columns but are instead columns with additional formatting. This is important because you may not wish to have Name of Event and Name of Event (Linked to Item) both appear.

8. Click **OK**. The Edit View page will close, and the library app will open with the new view configuration.

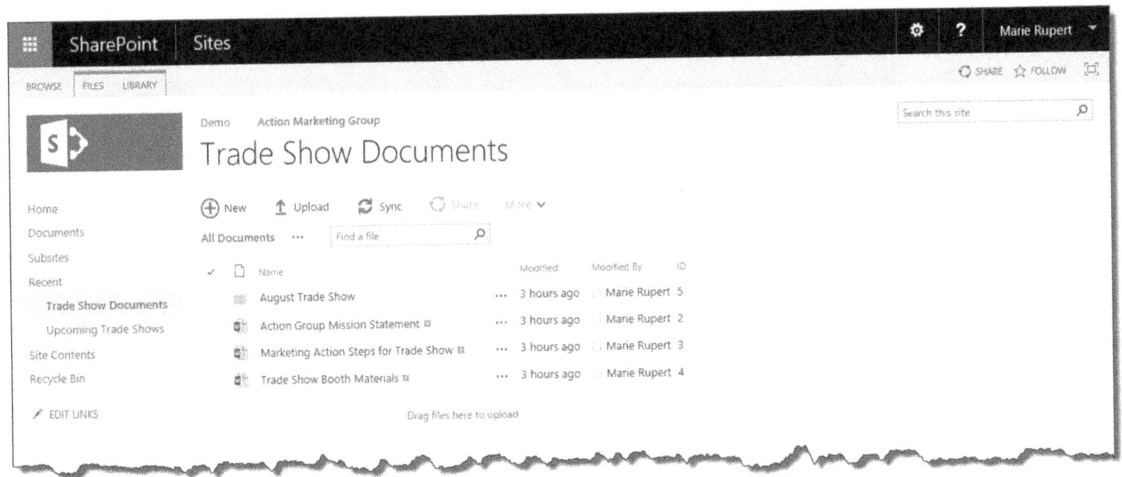

Figure 2: The New View of the Library App

Task: Add a List or Library App View

Purpose: New SharePoint list and library apps start with an All Documents or All Items view. However, you can create many views allowing you to have different looks for the list or library based on the information that you need. This task allows you to create your own custom views for the list or library.

Example: It is possible to create new list or library views, just the way you want them, rather than always modifying the default views.

Steps:

1. Start Internet Explorer and type the URL for your organization's SharePoint server. The Start page will open.
2. Navigate to the library app that you wish to add new view to. The library's page will open.
3. Click the **Library** tab. The Library ribbon will open.
4. Click the **Create View** button. The View Type page will open.

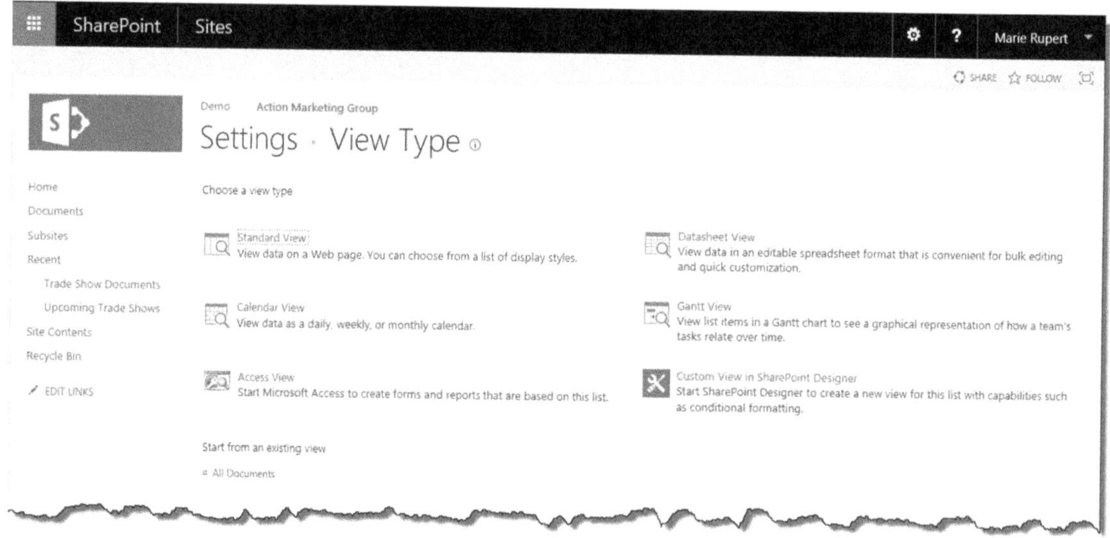

Figure 1: The View Type Page

Note: There are five view formats provided with SharePoint: Standard, Calendar, Datasheet, Access database, and Gantt views. A sixth option allows you to create a custom view in SharePoint Designer. For more information about views in SharePoint, see Appendix D, "Views."

5. Click a view format or select from the list of existing views. The Create View page for that format will open.

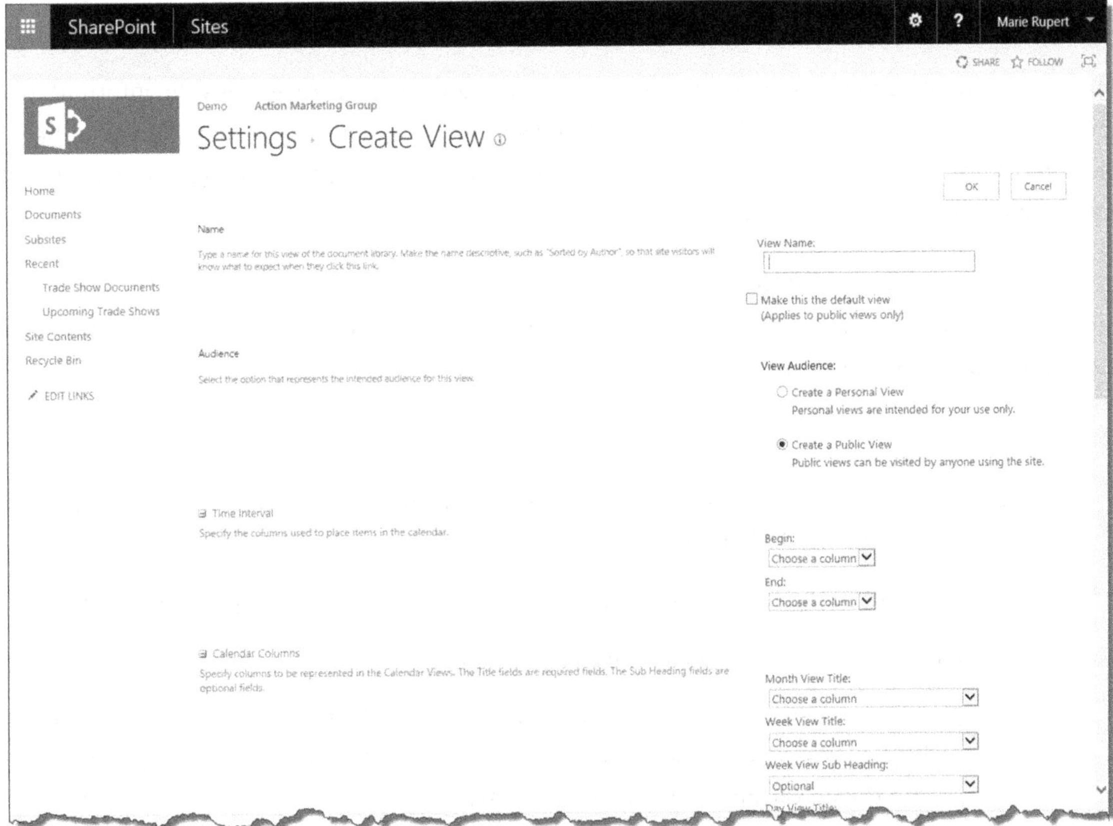

Figure 2: The Create View Page

6. In the View Name field enter a title for the view. This name will appear at the top of your library view.
7. You can select the **Make this the default view** option. This will make this view appear by default every time you open the library.
8. You can also select the intended audience for this view. By default, the **Create a Public View** option is selected, which means the new view can be visited by anyone using the site. Select **Create a Personal View** if you intend for this view to be for your use only.
9. Depending on the type of view you are creating, select the appropriate values to configure the view.
10. Click **OK**. The library or list will be displayed in the new view.

Task: Export a List or Library App to a Spreadsheet

Purpose: The columns that you enter data in for both lists and libraries resembles the information you would keep in a spreadsheet. While SharePoint views are powerful, they don't allow you the same level of flexibility that having an Excel Spreadsheet does. SharePoint allows you to export both List and Library App views to an Excel Spreadsheet.

Example: The Action Marketing group wants to review the documents in the library to evaluate when they were last updated for employee productivity. To do that, they choose to export the library to Excel and work with the information in Excel.

Steps:

1. Start Internet Explorer and type the URL for your organization's SharePoint server. The Start page will open.

2. Navigate to the library you want to edit. The document library page will open.

3. Click the **Library** tab. The Library ribbon will open.

4. Click the **Export to Excel** button. One or more security warnings as well as a login dialog box may appear, depending on your personal computer's settings. If you accept these warnings, the file will be downloaded to your local machine and opened in an Excel workbook as a worksheet.

Note: Changes made in the exported spreadsheet file will not be reflected in the library.

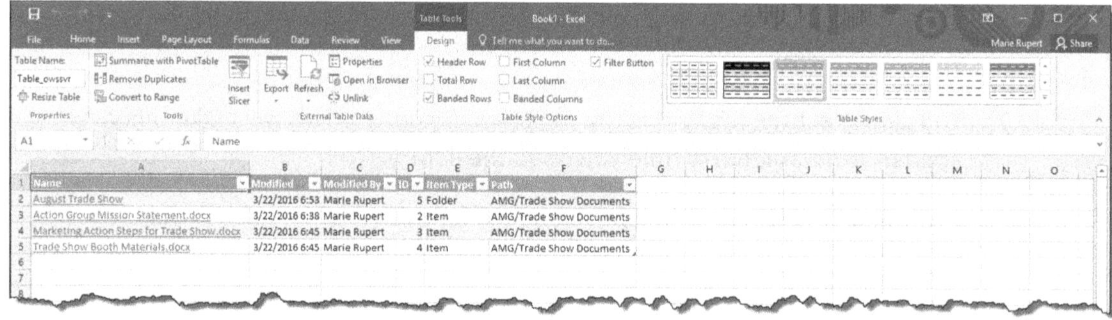

Figure 1: The Exported Spreadsheet

Task: Delete a Library App File

Purpose: If you need to remove an item from a library, it's a quick operation. And if you mistakenly delete a library item, it will be placed in the site's Recycle Bin, ready to be recovered. For more information, see the task "Recover Items from the Recycle Bin."

Example: The administrator for the Action Marketing Group accidentally uploaded a document which contained salary information to a publicly-accessible library, and it needs to be deleted.

Steps:

1. Start Internet Explorer and type the URL for your organization's SharePoint server. The Start page will open.
2. Navigate to the library in which you are interested. The library app will open.
3. In the ribbon click the **Files** tab. The Files ribbon will open.
4. Next to the title of the item you wish to delete, click the **checkbox** to select that item, then click the **Delete Document** button. A confirmation dialog box will open.

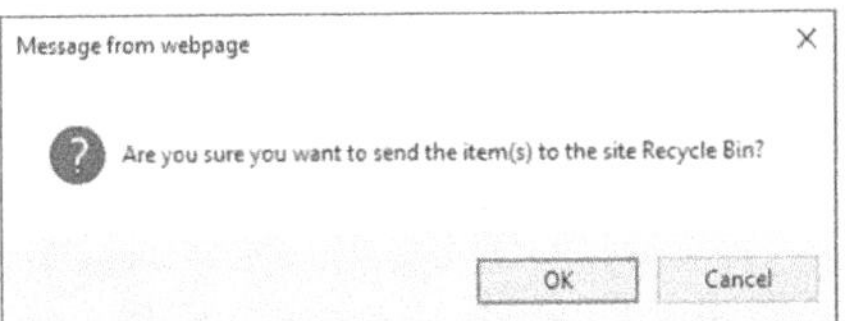

Figure 1: The Delete Document Confirmation Dialog Box

5. Click **OK**. The item will be removed from the library.

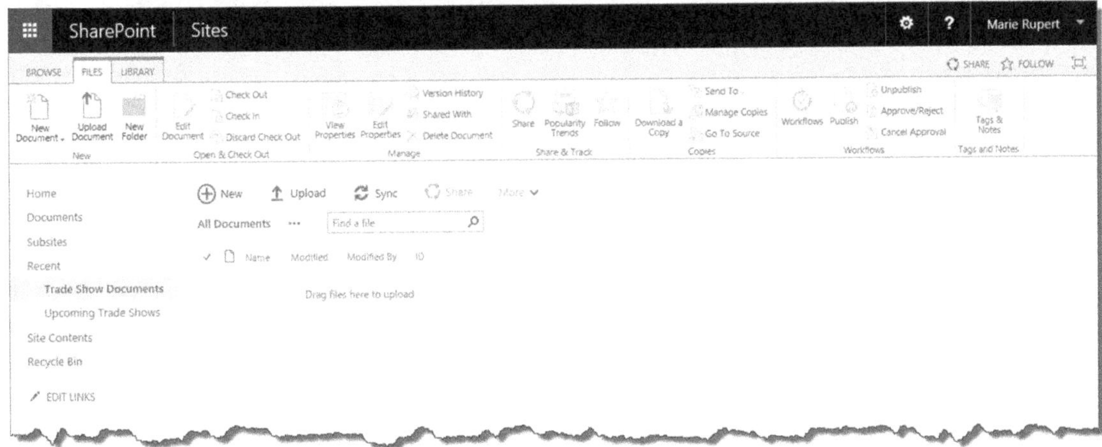

Figure 2: The Item is removed from the Library App

Task: Recover a List or Library Item from the Recycle Bin

Purpose: Sometimes files are accidentally deleted. On your computer you have a recycle bin so that you can recover an accidentally deleted file. SharePoint has a recycle bin as well to allow you to recover accidentally deleted files. Unlike your computer's recycle bin, the SharePoint recycle bin is automatically emptied of files and items. Typically, this is every 30 days but the specific time can be changed by the administrator.

Example: The only copy of the trade show manual was mistakenly deleted from the library app, and must be recovered.

Steps:

1. Start Internet Explorer and type the URL for your organization's SharePoint server. The Start page will open.
2. Navigate to the site from which you want to recover an item from the Recycle Bin. The site's home page will open.
3. Click the **Settings** menu gear icon. The Settings menu will appear.
4. Click the **Site Contents** option. The Site Contents page will open.
5. Click the **Recycle Bin** link near the top right of the page. The Recycle Bin page will open.

Note: The Recycle Bin only displays the removed content for the site where it's located. You need to navigate to that site first to see the correct set of removed files.

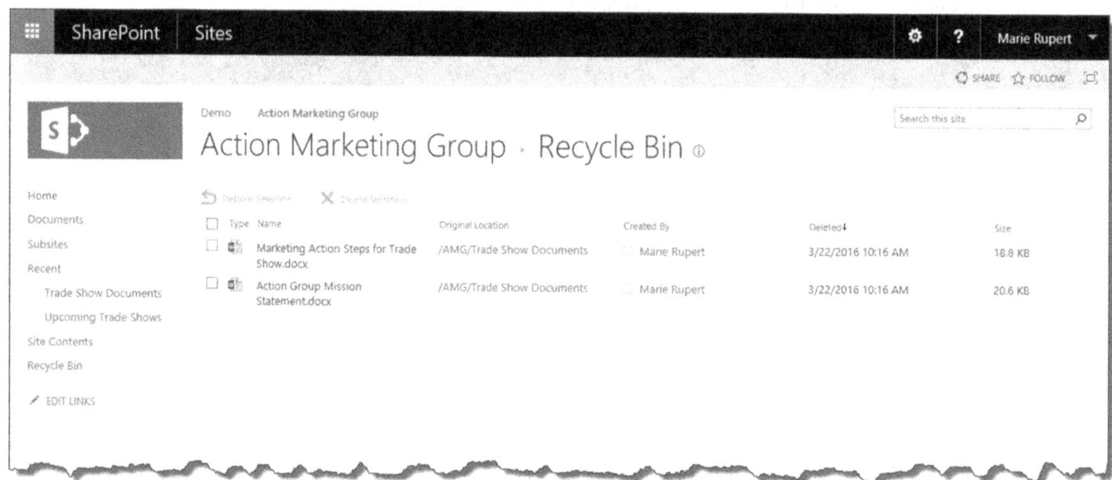

Figure 1 The Recycle Bin Page

6. Click the **checkbox** icons next to the items you want to restore to select these items.

7. Click Restore Selection. A confirmation dialog box will open.

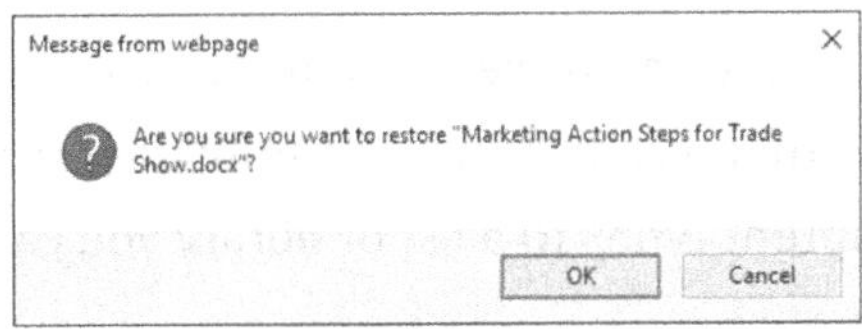

Figure 2: The Restore Selection Confirmation Dialog Box

8. Click OK. The selected items will be removed from the Recycle Bin and put back in their original location on the site.

Note: If you want to clean out the Recycle Bin, click the checkbox icons next to the items you want to permanently delete to select those items. Then click Delete Selection and another confirmation dialog box will open. Click OK and the selected items will be permanently deleted from the site. Permanently deleted items and documents cannot be restored or recovered after this action is taken.

Task: Edit List or Library App Content Types

Purpose: SharePoint allows you to have multiple content types in a single list or library app. A content type defines the columns that will be entered, templates, and rules for how the item will be processed. By adding multiple content types to a list or library you can encourage users to enter the right data for the right needs.

Example: The Action Marketing Group team wants to track contracts and proposals in the same library and will use content types to do this so that the right templates are used for each type of document.

Steps:

1. Start Internet Explorer and type the URL for your organization's SharePoint server. The Start page will open.
2. Navigate to the library in which you are interested. The library app will open.
3. In the ribbon click the **Library** tab. The Library ribbon will open.
4. In the ribbon click the **Library Settings** button. The Settings page will open.

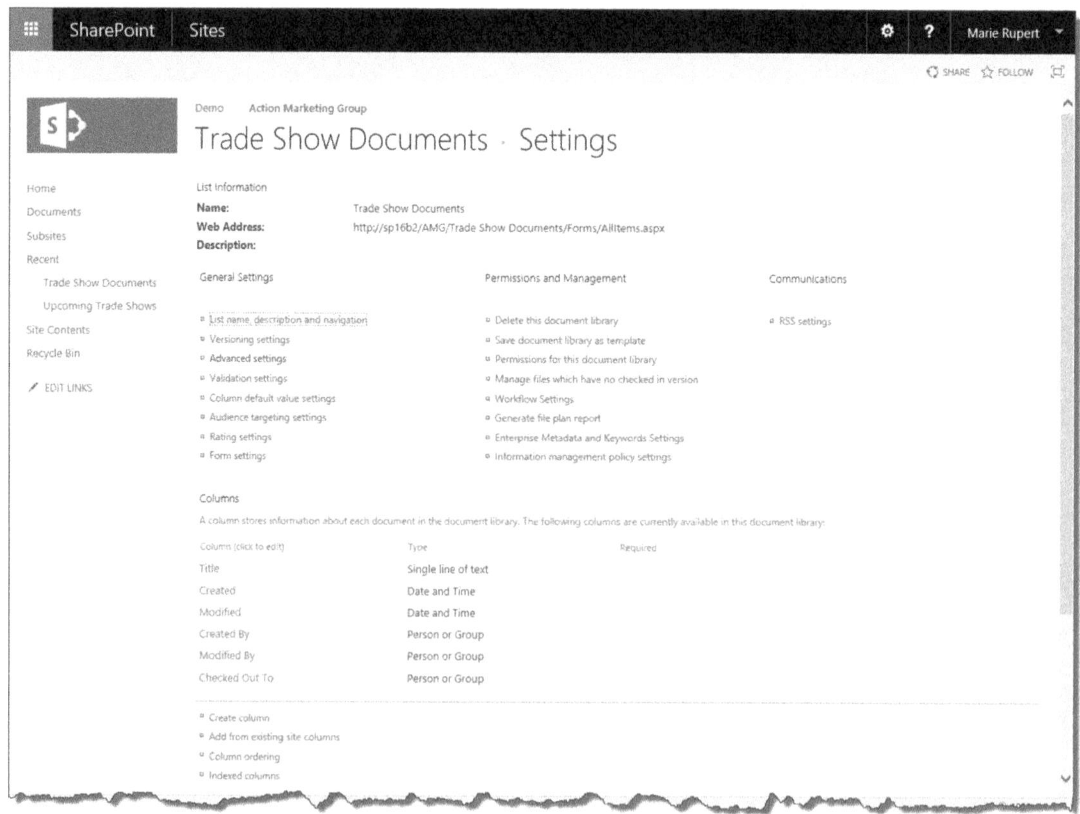

Figure 1: The Library Settings Page

5. In the General Settings section, click **Advanced Settings**. The Advanced Settings page will open.
6. In the Content Types section, click **Yes** to allow multiple content types.
7. Click **OK**. The Settings page will reopen.
8. In the Content Types section, click the **Add from Existing Site Content Types** link. The Add Content Types page will open.

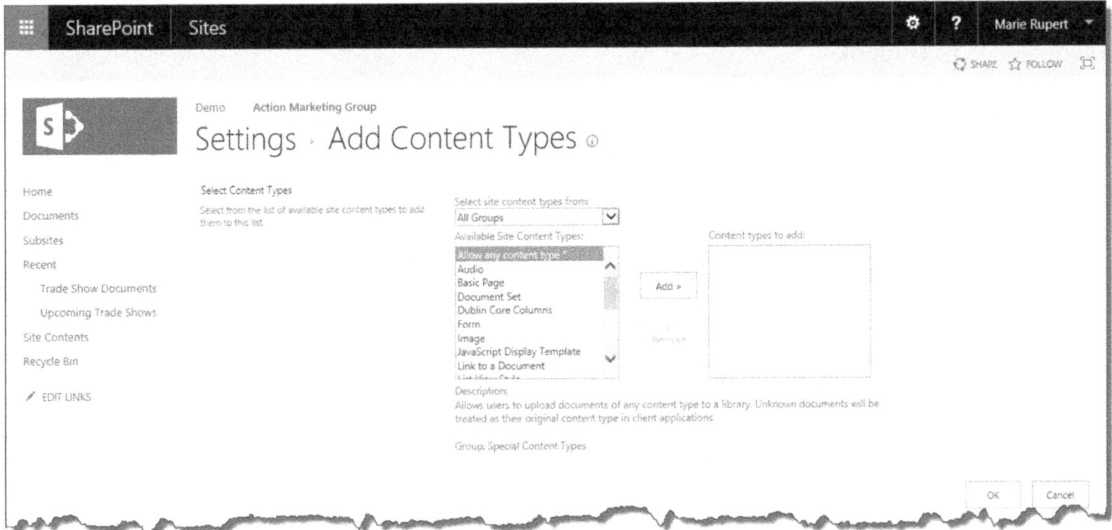

Figure 2: The Add Content Types Page

9. Select the content types you want to use, then click **Add**.
10. When complete, click **OK**. You will be returned to the Settings page and the content types will be added to the **New** button for the list or library.

Use Outlook for Sharing

SharePoint is very tightly integrated to the Microsoft Office applications, including Microsoft Outlook, which allows for much more efficient communication of SharePoint-hosted information. SharePoint will allow you to connect its document libraries, task lists, and calendars directly to Outlook 2016 or 2013.

In this section, you'll learn how to:

- Connect a SharePoint Library to Outlook: The basics of connecting from SharePoint to Outlook.
- Connect a SharePoint Calendar to Outlook: Shared calendars in SharePoint allow you to post dates, connect users to key information on a timeline, and allow them to work better together.
- Connect SharePoint Contacts to Outlook: SharePoint allows you to connect Contacts apps to Outlook so you can view and modify SharePoint contacts via Outlook.
- Connect SharePoint Tasks to Outlook: SharePoint supports connecting Tasks apps to Outlook to make them easier to edit.
- Share Connected SharePoint Content with Outlook: After an app is connected to Outlook, you can use Outlook to quickly share the contents of that resource with other users.
- Edit Library App Files in Outlook: After you have connected a library app to Outlook, you can access and edit the files in the library directly from Outlook without connecting to the SharePoint server.
- Edit a SharePoint Calendar in Outlook: Editing SharePoint calendar entries in Outlook makes it easier to edit and consider team member schedules.
- Remove a Connected Document from Outlook: There may be instances where you won't need a copy of every document or file in the app. Here's how to remove offline copies of documents from Outlook.
- Remove a Library App from Outlook: Once you no longer need a connection to a SharePoint resource, you can remove it from Outlook with ease.
- Share SharePoint Content with a Sharing Message: SharePoint allows you to invite others to view or edit a resource by sending a Sharing Message, which will appear in their Outlook inbox.

Task: Connect a SharePoint Library to Outlook

Purpose: Sometimes you travel and need to synchronize files that don't change very often or aren't a part of your core job. Other times you want to be able to see SharePoint files from inside Outlook. SharePoint allows you to connect libraries to Outlook and take files offline for editing.

Example: The Action Marketing Group's trade show team is going out to an offsite meeting in the woods where there will not be any Internet connectivity. They decide to bring a copy of the latest trade show manual with them via Outlook.

Steps:

1. Start Internet Explorer and type the URL for your organization's SharePoint server. The Start page will open.
2. Navigate to the library you want to connect to Outlook. The library's page will open.
3. Click the Library tab. The Library ribbon will appear.
4. Click the Connect to Outlook button. A confirmation dialog box will open.

Note: In order to connect to Outlook, you may need to set up the web site in the Intranet zone within Internet Explorer's security options.

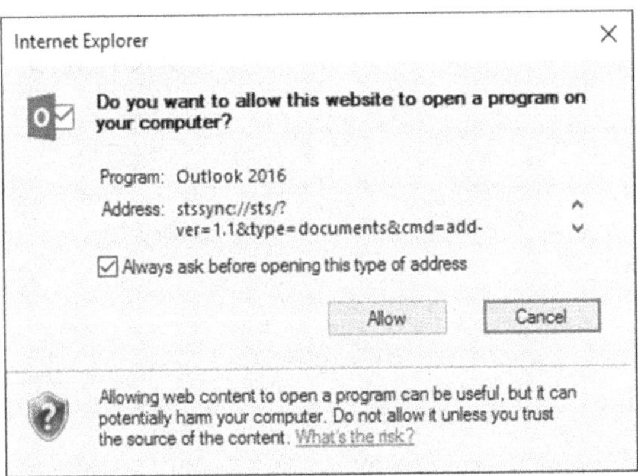

Figure 1: The Allow SharePoint to Open Outlook Confirmation Dialog Box

5. Click Allow. Outlook will open and a Connect to Outlook dialog box will appear.

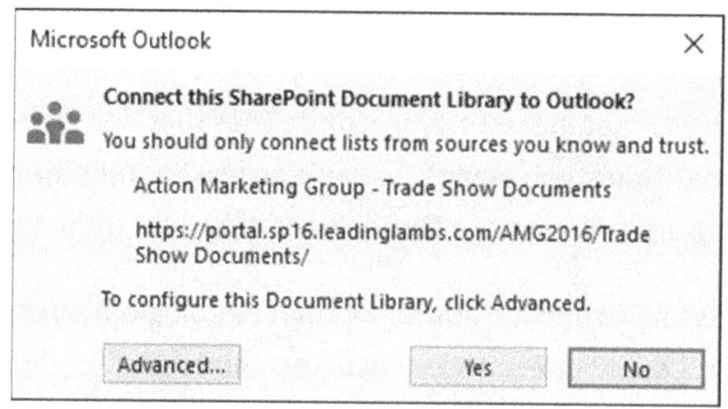

Figure 2: The Connect this Document Library to Outlook Dialog Box

6. Click Yes. The library will appear in the Mail view of Outlook under SharePoint Lists.

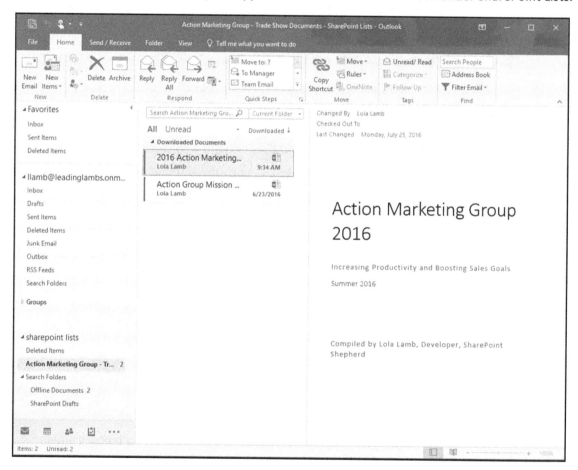

Figure 3: The Connected Document Library in Outlook

Task: Connect a SharePoint Calendar to Outlook

Purpose: Shared calendars in SharePoint allow you to post dates, connect users to key information on a timeline, and allow them to work better together. However, working with a calendar in SharePoint isn't as easy or as flexible as working on the calendar in Outlook. SharePoint allows you to connect a Calendar App so that you can view and edit it in Outlook.

Example: The Action Marketing Group manager wants to see the milestone calendar in Outlook so she can review it while approving vacation requests.

Steps:

1. Start Internet Explorer and type the URL for your organization's SharePoint server. The Start Page will open.
2. Navigate to the calendar you want to connect to Outlook. The calendar's page will open.
3. In the ribbon click the Calendar tab. The Calendar ribbon will appear.
4. Click the Connect to Outlook button. A confirmation dialog box will open.

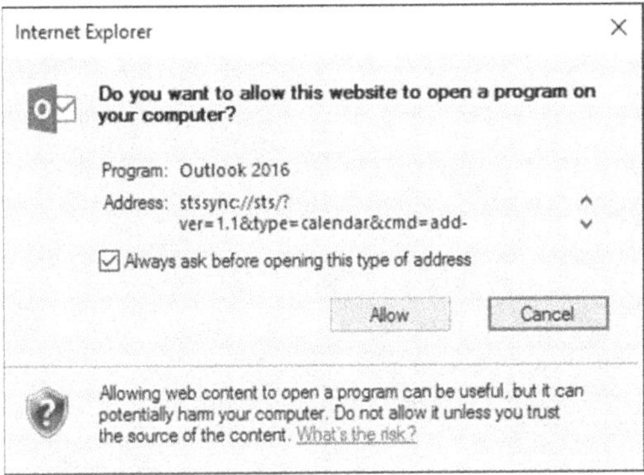

Figure 1: The Allow SharePoint to Open Outlook Confirmation Dialog Box

5. Click Allow. Outlook will open and a Connect to Outlook dialog box will appear.

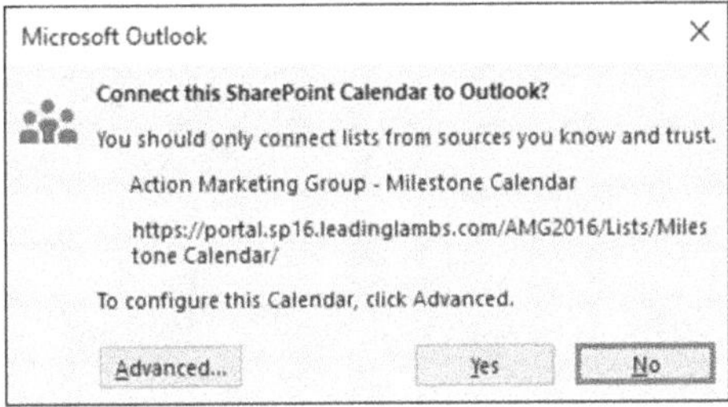

Figure 2: The Connect this SharePoint Calendar to Outlook Confirmation Dialog Box

Note: Clicking the **Advanced** button will display the SharePoint List Options dialog box, which will allow you to add more descriptive information, if needed.

6. Click **Yes**. The calendar will appear in the Calendar view of Outlook under Other Calendars.

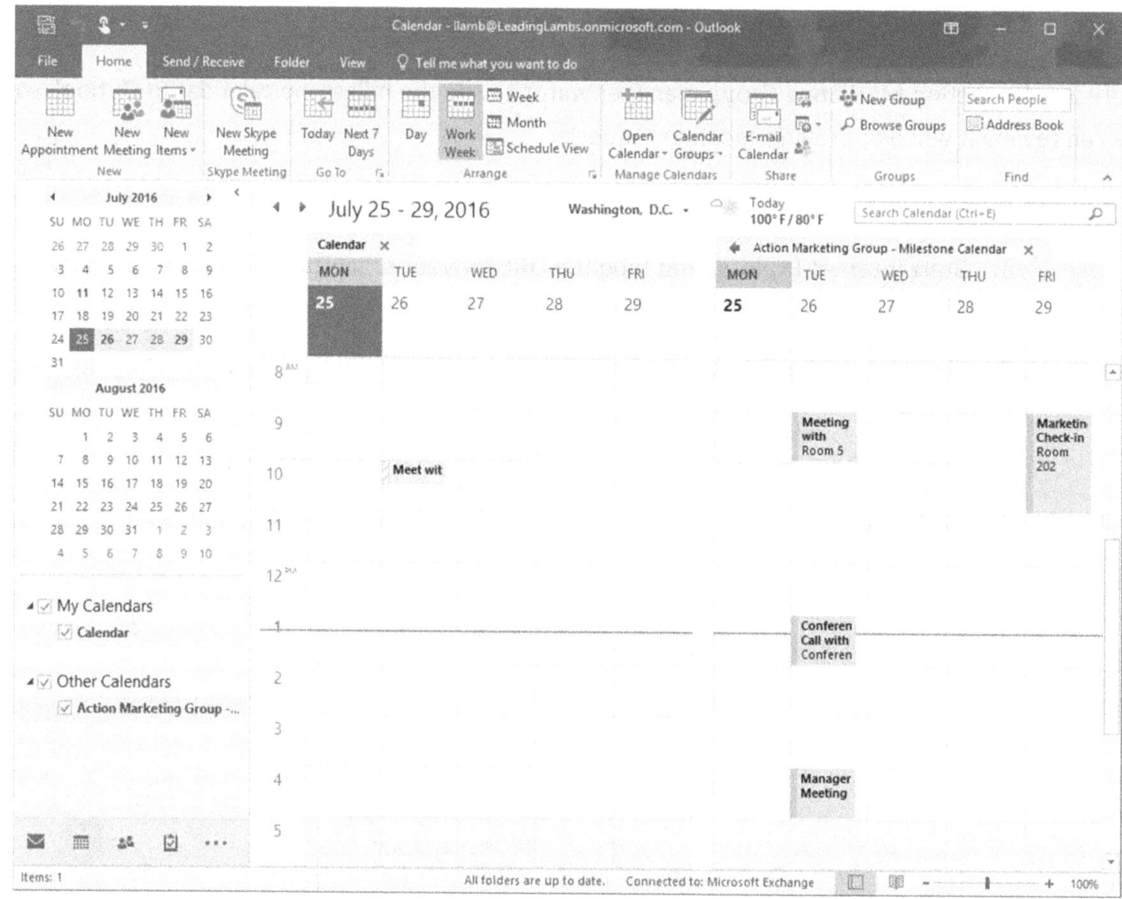

Figure 3: The Connected Calendar in Outlook

7. If you want to see both calendars at once to check for conflicts, right-click the SharePoint calendar's tab and select the **Overlay** option. The calendars will be merged.

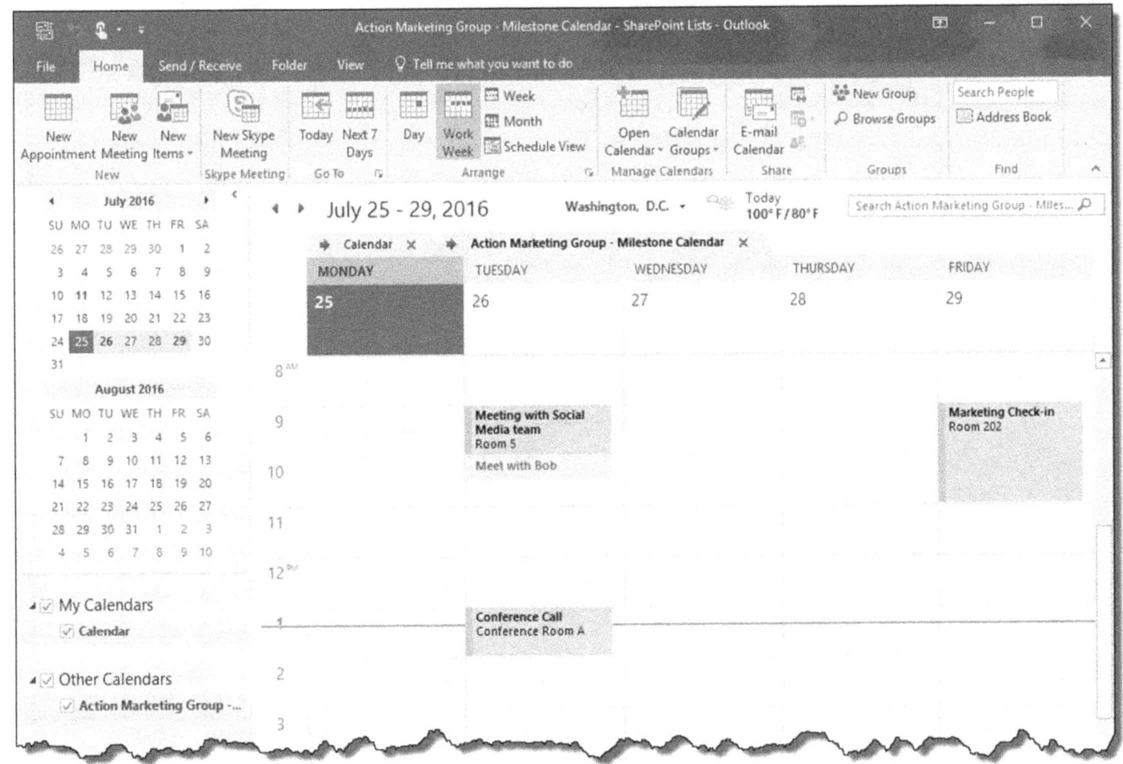

Figure 4: The View in Overlay Mode

8. To return to the default view, right-click either of calendar tabs and de-select the Overlay option. The calendars will be separated.

9. To view just the SharePoint calendar, under the My Calendars heading, click the calendar's checkbox to de-select it. The local calendar will close, and only the SharePoint calendar will be visible.

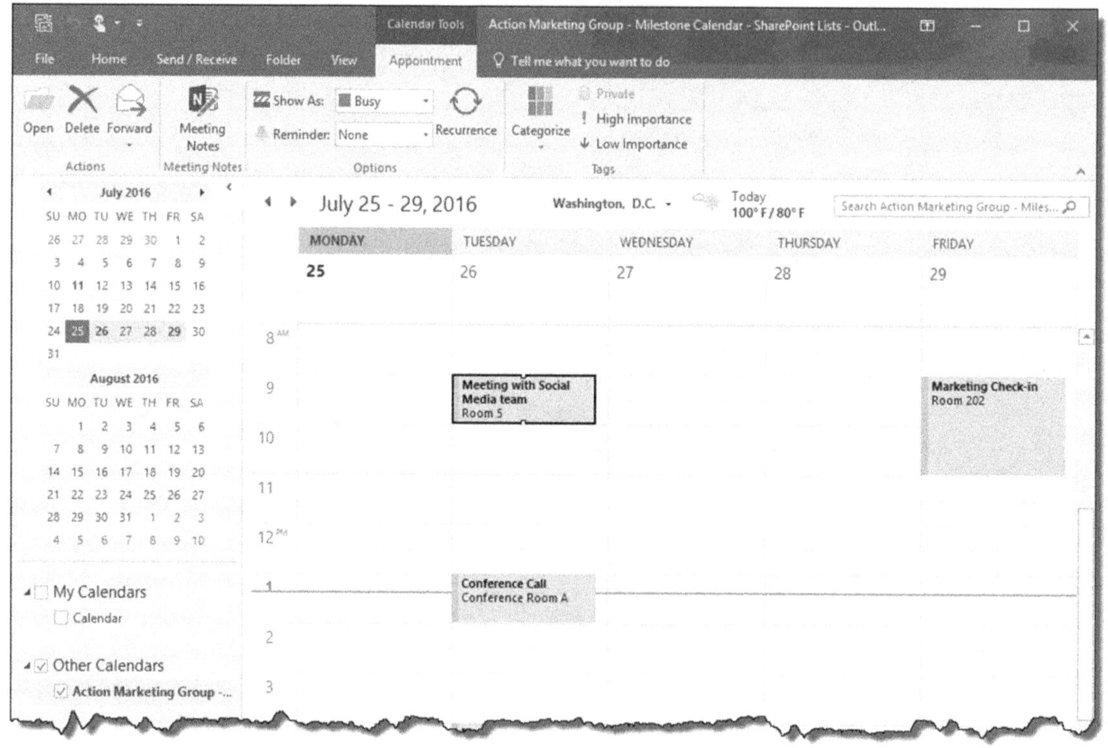

Figure 5: The Remote Calendar

Task: Connect SharePoint Contacts to Outlook

Purpose: Keeping libraries of contacts makes them available for multiple users, where having each user maintaining their own contacts would be inefficient. However, sometimes users are more comfortable using Outlook to manage contacts. SharePoint allows you to connect Contacts List Apps to Outlook so you can view and modify SharePoint contacts via Outlook.

Example: You want to share vendor contact information among the members of the purchasing team. The purchasing team spends most of their time in Outlook and wants to access those vendor contact records in SharePoint.

Steps:

1. Start Internet Explorer and type the URL for your organization's SharePoint server. The Start page will open.
2. Navigate to the contacts list you want to connect to Outlook. The contacts list's page will open.
3. In the ribbon click the **List** tab. The List ribbon will appear.
4. Click the **Connect to Outlook** button. A confirmation dialog box will open.

Note: In order to connect to Outlook, you may need to set up the web site in the Intranet zone within Internet Explorer's security options.

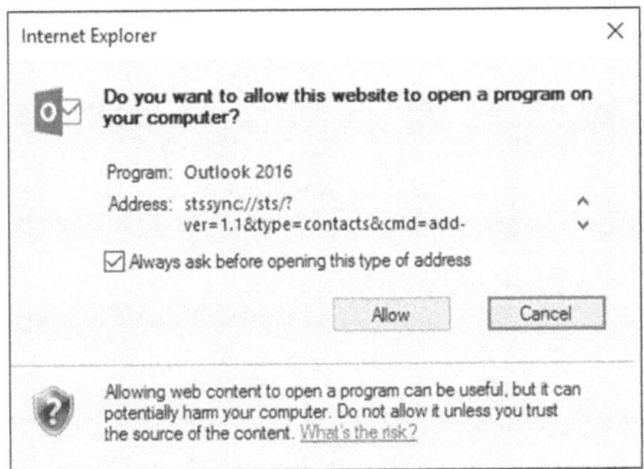

Figure 1: The Allow SharePoint to Open Outlook Confirmation Dialog Box

5. Click **Allow**. Outlook will open and a Connect to Outlook dialog box will appear.

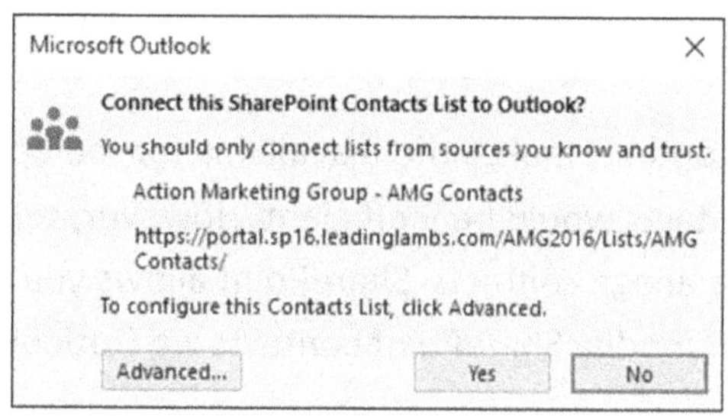

Figure 2: The Connect this SharePoint Contacts List to Outlook Dialog Box

6. Click Yes. The list will appear in the People view of Outlook under Other Contacts.

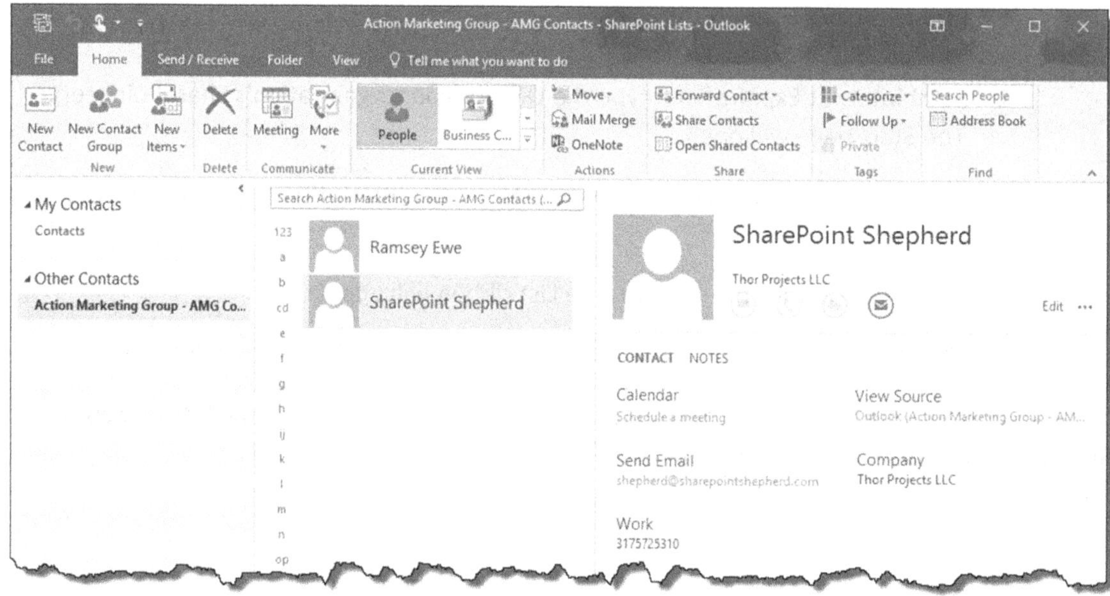

Figure 3: The Connected Contact List in Outlook

Task: Connect SharePoint Tasks to Outlook

Purpose: Managing shared tasks in SharePoint helps to coordinate what members of the team are doing. However, using the web interface to update the status of tasks isn't always easiest. SharePoint supports connecting Tasks List Apps to Outlook to make them easier to edit.

Example: The project team created a Tasks list on the SharePoint site and now needs to make the tasks available in Outlook.

Steps:

1. Start Internet Explorer and type the URL for your organization's SharePoint server. The Start page will open.
2. Navigate to the tasks list you want to connect to Outlook. The tasks list's page will open.
3. In the ribbon click the List tab. The List ribbon will appear.
4. Click the Connect to Outlook button. A confirmation dialog box will open.

Note: In order to connect to Outlook, you may need to set up the web site in the Intranet zone within Internet Explorer's security options.

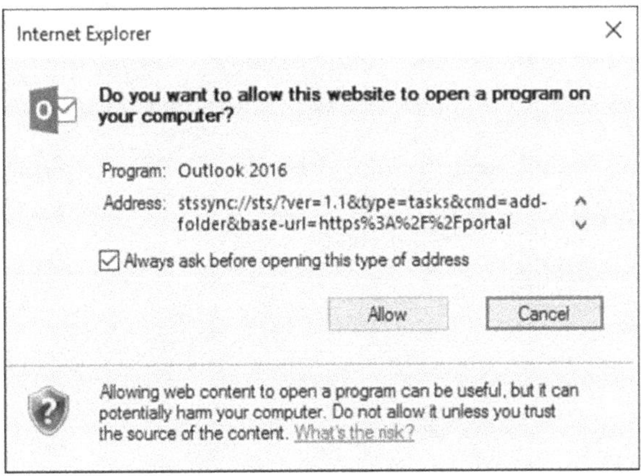

Figure 1: The Allow SharePoint to Open Outlook Confirmation Dialog Box

5. Click Allow. Outlook will open and a Connect to Outlook Dialog Box will appear.

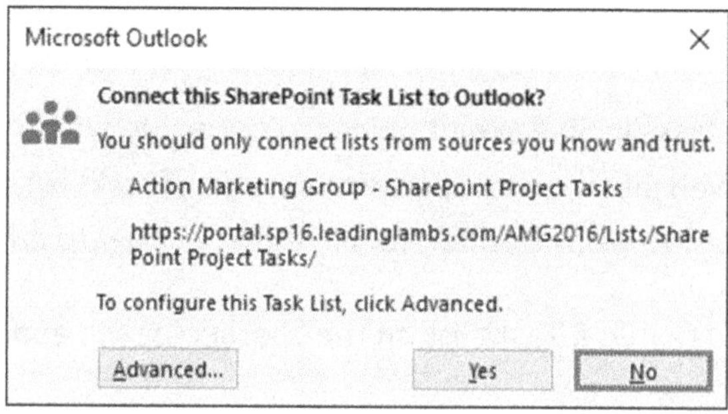

Figure 2: The Connect this SharePoint Task List to Outlook Confirmation Dialog Box

6. Click Yes. The tasks will appear in the Task view of Outlook under Other Tasks.

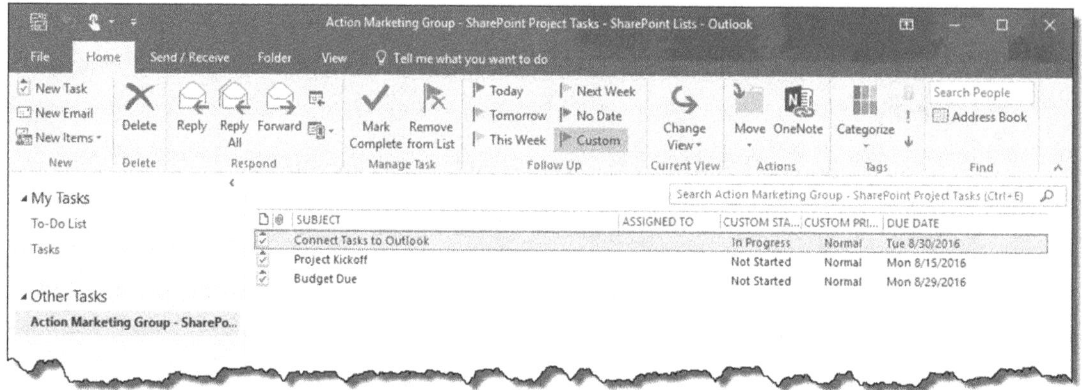

Figure 3: The Connected Task List in Outlook Task View

Task: Share Connected SharePoint Content with Outlook

Purpose: After a library or other SharePoint resource is connected to Outlook, you can use Outlook to quickly share the contents of that resource with other users. This is done by sending a message containing a special link that will automatically connect other users' Outlook installations to the SharePoint server.

Example: The Action Marketing Group wants to get the word out to employees about their Marketing library, and using Outlook to email a link to the folder is the fastest way.

Steps:

1. In Outlook, navigate to the Mail view.

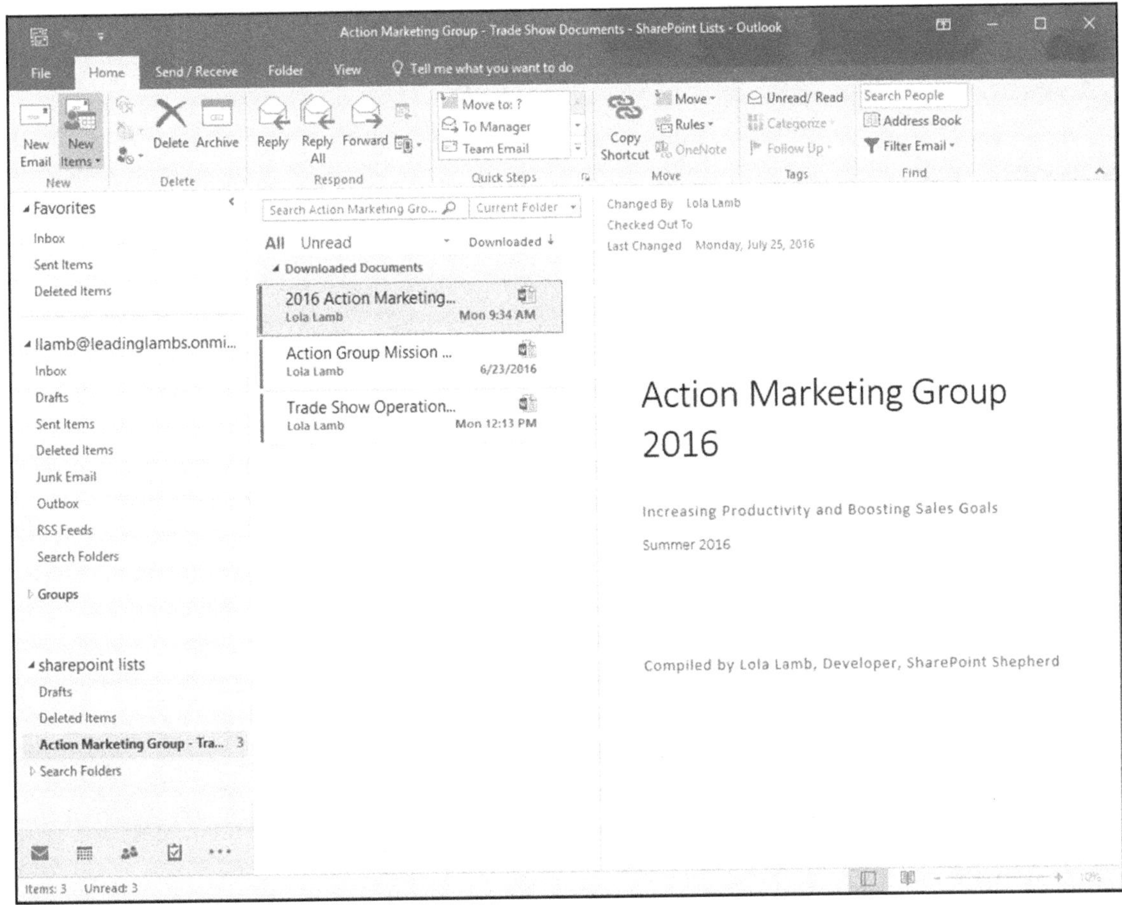

Figure 1: SharePoint Content in Outlook

2. Right-click the folder for the SharePoint resource you want to share. The context menu will appear.

3. Hover over the Share option, then click Share this Folder. A message window will open with a predetermined subject detailing the contents of the library.

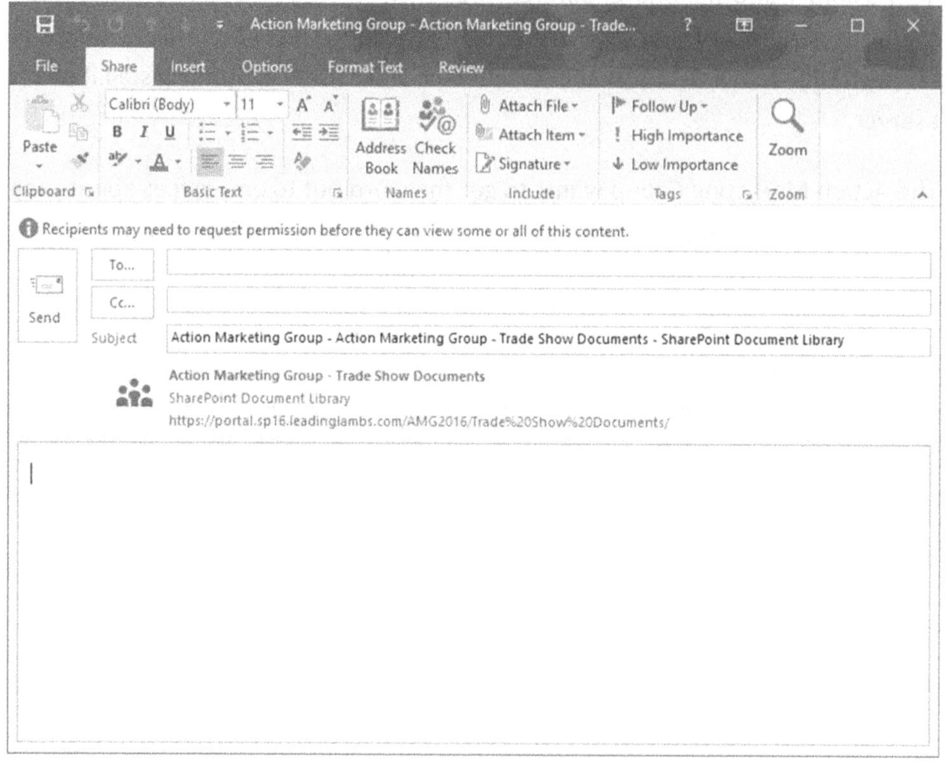

Figure 2: New Email Window with Folder to Share

4. In the To field, enter the email address(es) of the person(s) you want to share the content with.

5. Click Send. The message will be sent.

Task: Edit Library App Files in Outlook

Purpose: After you have connected to a library in Outlook, you can access and edit the files in the library directly from Outlook, without connecting to the SharePoint server.

Example: The Action Marketing Groups' trade show manager is on the plane to the show and needs to add a few new procedures to the manual which she has synchronized to Outlook.

Steps:

1. In Outlook, navigate to the Mail view.
2. Under the SharePoint Lists heading, click the folder with the name of the library. The contents of the library app will appear in the document listing pane.
3. In the document listing pane, double-click a document. The document will open in the appropriate application in read-only form.

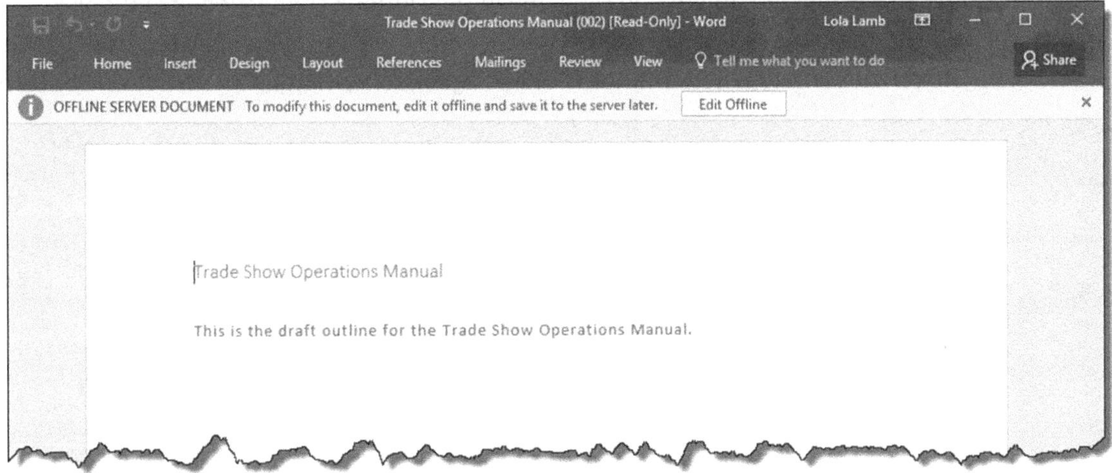

Figure 1: The Document in Read-Only Form

4. Just above the document, click the **Edit Offline** button. The Edit Offline dialog box will open.

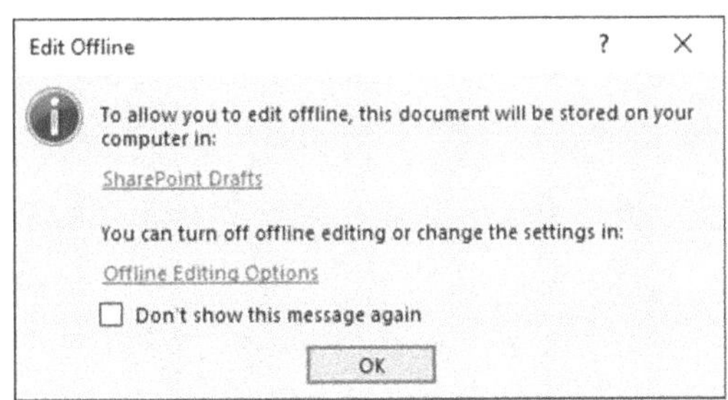

Figure 2: The Edit Offline Dialog Box

5. Click OK. The Edit Offline dialog box will close and the document will be stored in the SharePoint Drafts folder and can now be edited.

6. When you are finished editing the document, click Save within the client application.

7. Close the document. The Edit Offline dialog box will appear again. If you are online, you may be required to log into the SharePoint library app.

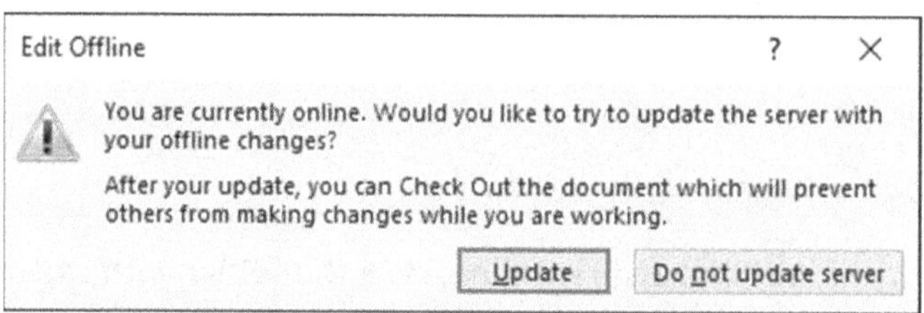

Figure 3: The Edit Offline Dialog Box

8. Click Update. The Edit Offline dialog box will close and the changes will be saved to the SharePoint document and reflected in the Outlook connection. If Outlook is offline, then any changes made to the document will be communicated back to the SharePoint library when Outlook is online again, or by clicking Send/Receive button.

Task: Edit a SharePoint Calendar in Outlook

Purpose: SharePoint calendars are a great way to centralize events, but often scheduling group events needs to take into account users' personal schedules. Editing SharePoint calendar entries in Outlook makes it easier to edit and consider team member schedules.

Example: Action Marketing Group wants to schedule a team recognition lunch and will review personal calendars before deciding on a time.

Steps:

1. In Outlook, navigate to the Calendar view.
2. Under the Other Calendars heading, click the desired SharePoint calendar's **checkbox** to select that calendar. The calendar will open. If it is already checked, the calendar is already open.

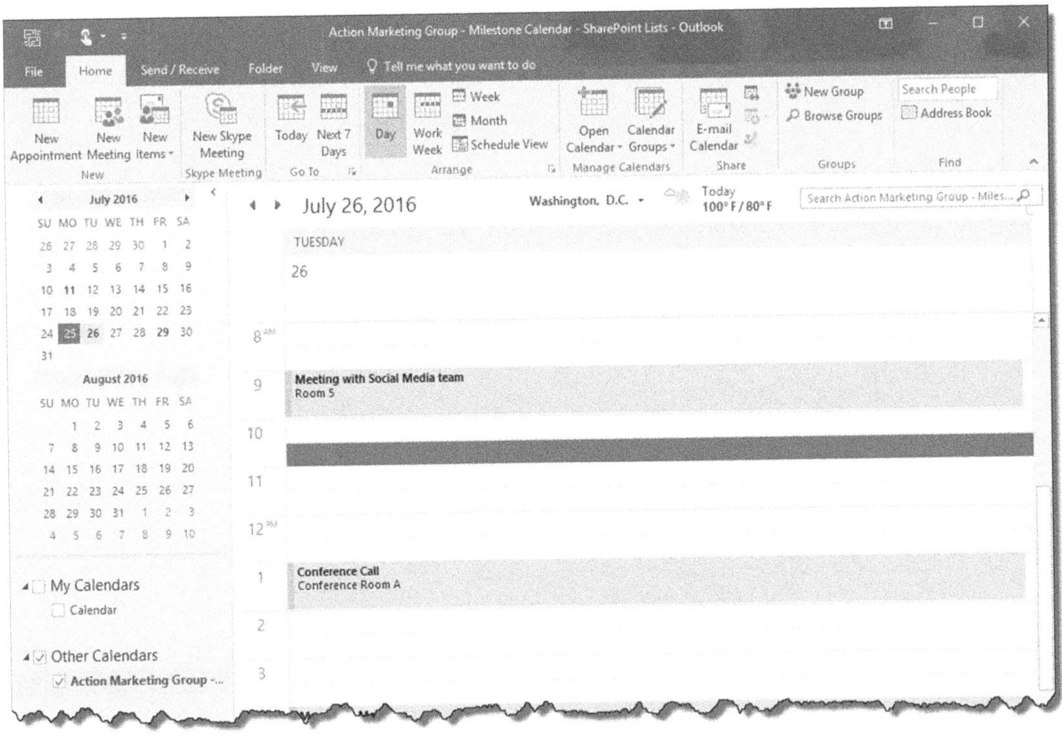

Figure 1: The Remote Calendar in Outlook

3. Click the **New Appointment** button. The Untitled Appointment dialog box will open.

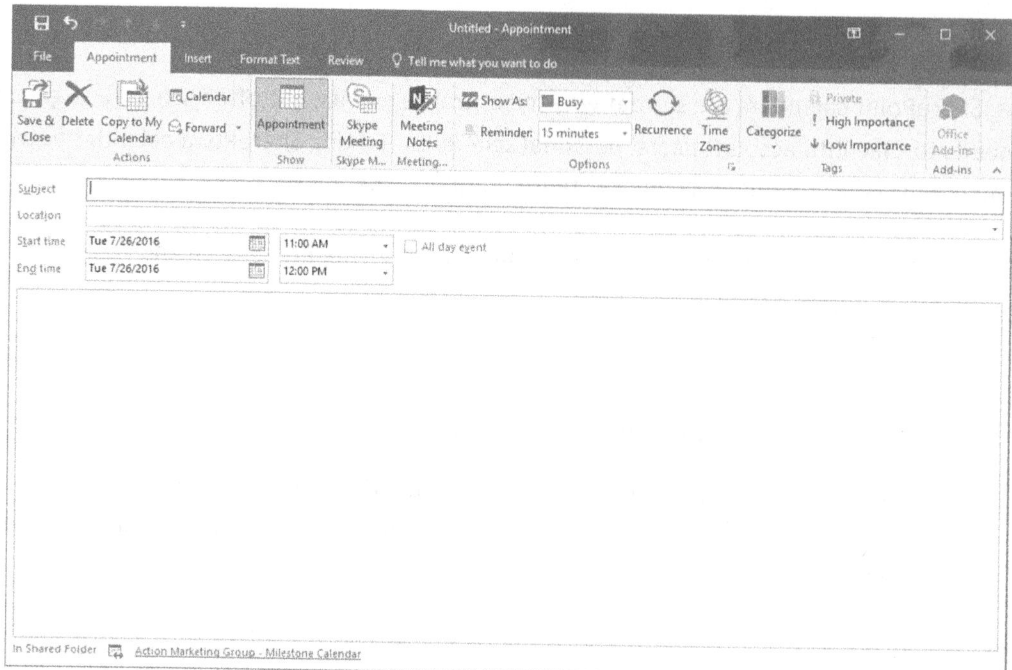

Figure 2: The Appointment Dialog Box.

4. Fill in the fields and click Save & Close. The event changes will appear on the SharePoint calendar.

Task: Remove a Library App from Outlook

Purpose: Once you no longer need a connection to a SharePoint app, you can remove it from Outlook with ease. This disconnects Outlook from SharePoint for the specified app.

Example: The Action Marketing Group coordinator no longer needs a connection to the Trade Show library and will remove it.

Steps:

1. In Outlook, navigate to the view and folder pane containing the SharePoint resource you want to remove (in this case, a document library found in the Mail view).
2. Right click the name of the resource. The context menu will appear.

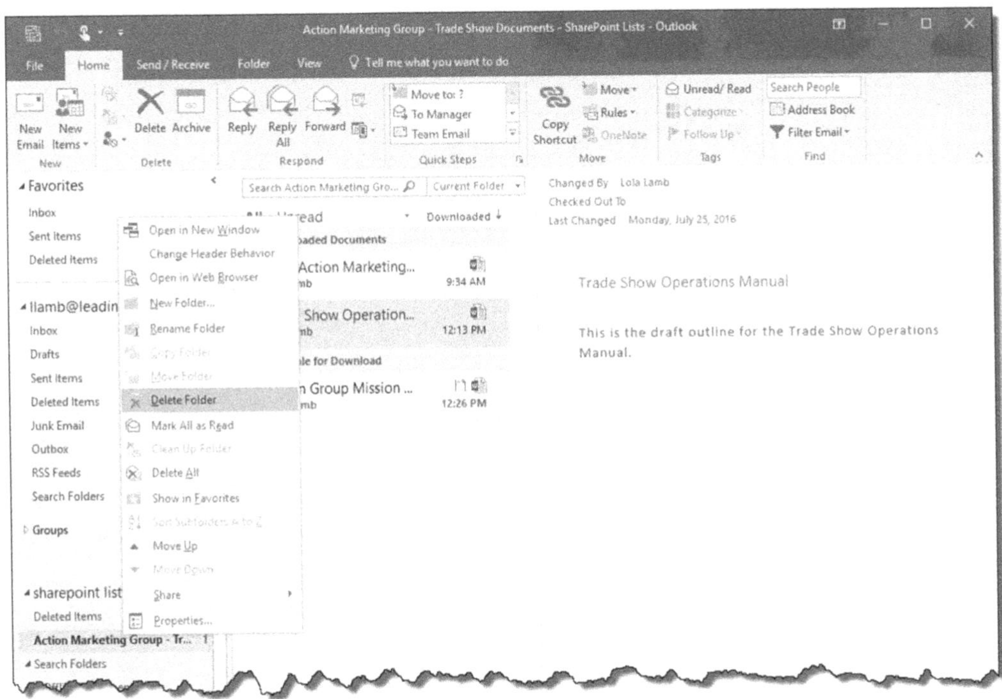

Figure 1: The Context Menu in Outlook

3. Select the Delete Folder option. A confirmation dialog box will open.

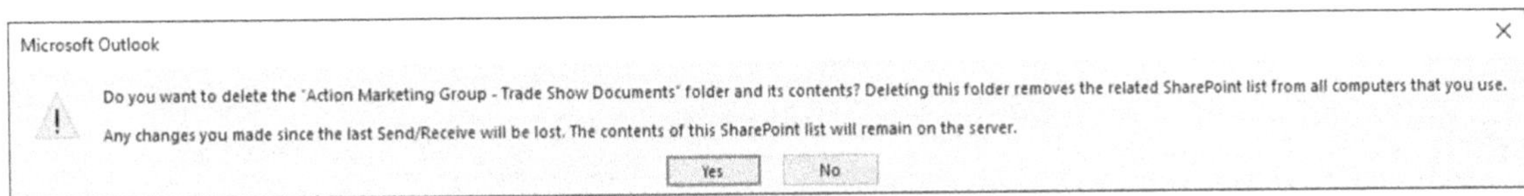

Figure 2: The Delete Confirmation Dialog Box

4. Click Yes. The resource will be removed from Outlook. It will still exist on the SharePoint server, but as a user, you will not be able to connect to the resource through Outlook until you create the link again.

Task: Share SharePoint Content with a Sharing Message

Purpose: You can invite others to view a SharePoint resource by sending a Sharing Message. The message will show up in their Outlook inbox, making it easy for others to connect with your SharePoint resource.

Example: The Action Marketing Group manager needs to share a link to the new Trade Show Manual so other group members can easily access it.

Steps:

1. Start Internet Explorer and type the URL for your organization's SharePoint server. The Start page will open.
2. Navigate to the document library where the document you want to share is found. The library's page will open.
3. Find the document you wish to share and click the ellipsis control next to the document's title to open the document's menu.

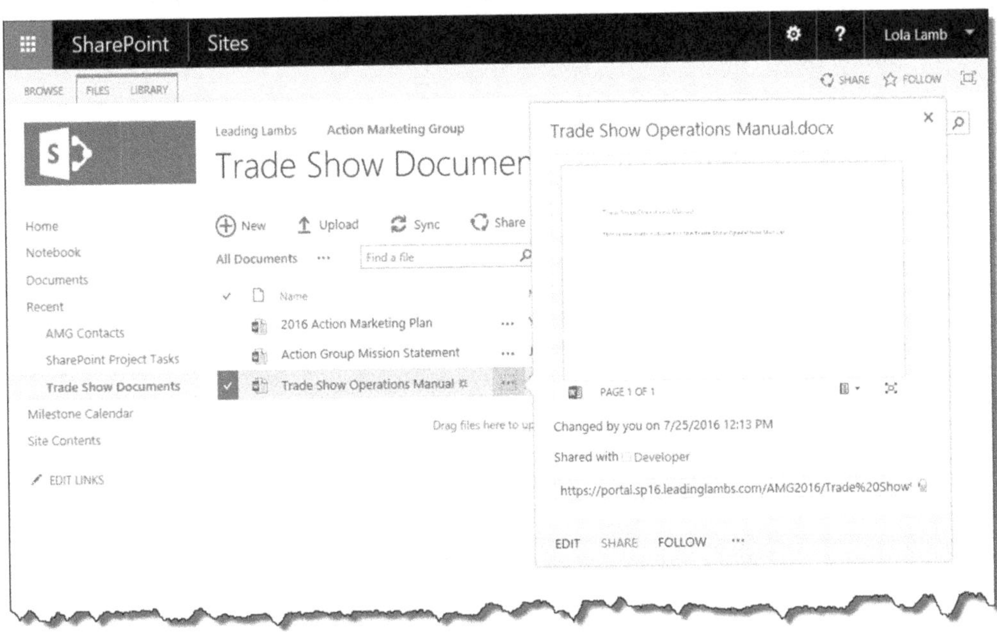

Figure 1: The Document Menu

4. At the bottom of the document menu, click Share. The Share dialog box will open.

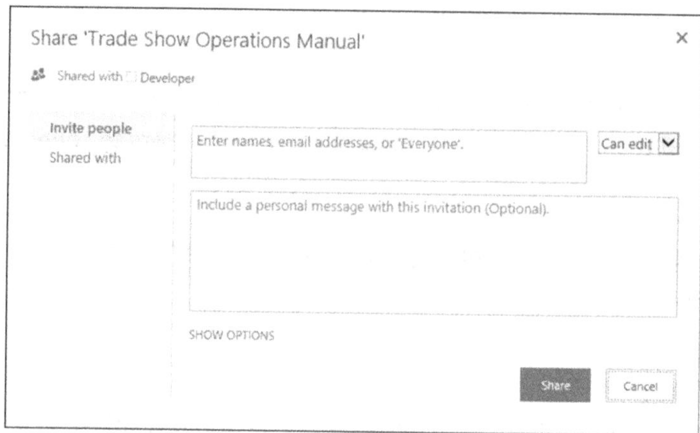

Figure 2: The Share Dialog Box

5. In the Invite people tab, type the names or email addresses of the people you wish to share the document with.

6. People you share with are by default given editing privileges. You can change this permission to view-only by clicking the **Can edit** drop-down box and selecting **Can view**. You can also choose to include a personal message that will be sent to everyone.

7. Click **Share** to send your Sharing Message. The Sharing Message will now appear as an email in your invitees' inboxes.

Conduct Surveys

When you need to quickly gather data or opinions from a group, a fast way to accomplish this is to use a SharePoint survey. Surveys, which are specialized SharePoint tracking lists, are easy to make, easy to distribute, and easy to read.

In this section, you'll learn how to:

- Create a Survey: The basics of creating a survey.
- Preview Your Survey: Once a survey is created, testing it is a good idea.
- Enable Survey Branching: Branching is used when a user's answer to a survey question will influence which questions are asked later in the survey. Branching is a vital component of effective survey design.
- Send a Survey Link: Like a document library or other SharePoint resource, it's often useful to send out a notice of a survey so users will be aware of it for participation.
- View Survey Results: Once a survey is completed, you can view the results in a comparative graphical form, or view the answers given by individual respondents.
- Compile Survey Results: When a survey with many questions and/or many respondents is completed, just viewing the results might not be enough. You may need to do some serious data tabulation and number crunching.

Task: Create a Survey

Purpose: When you need to quickly gather data or opinions from a group, a fast way to accomplish this is to use a SharePoint survey. Surveys, which are really specialized tracking lists, are easy to make, easy to distribute, and easy to read—complete with built-in analysis of the results.

Example: The Action Marketing Group human resource manager would like to survey employees about the new corporate leave policy.

Steps:

1. Start Internet Explorer and type the URL for your organization's SharePoint server. The Start page will open. If you want your new survey located as a subsite of another site, navigate to that site.
2. Click the **Settings** menu gear icon, then click **Add an App**. The Your Apps page will appear.
3. Scroll down and click the **Survey** icon. The Adding Survey dialog box will appear.
4. Click **Advanced Options**. The new Survey page will appear.
5. In the Name field enter a title for the new survey. This will appear in any list of surveys in SharePoint. Especially if you have multiple surveys, it's best to keep the title specific and descriptive.
6. In the Description field enter a summary of the survey.
7. In the Survey Options section, select the appropriate options. There are two options to select: you can choose whether you want user names to be displayed with each survey result, and if you want to allow users to submit multiple responses when filling out the survey.
8. Click **Next**. The New Question page will open.

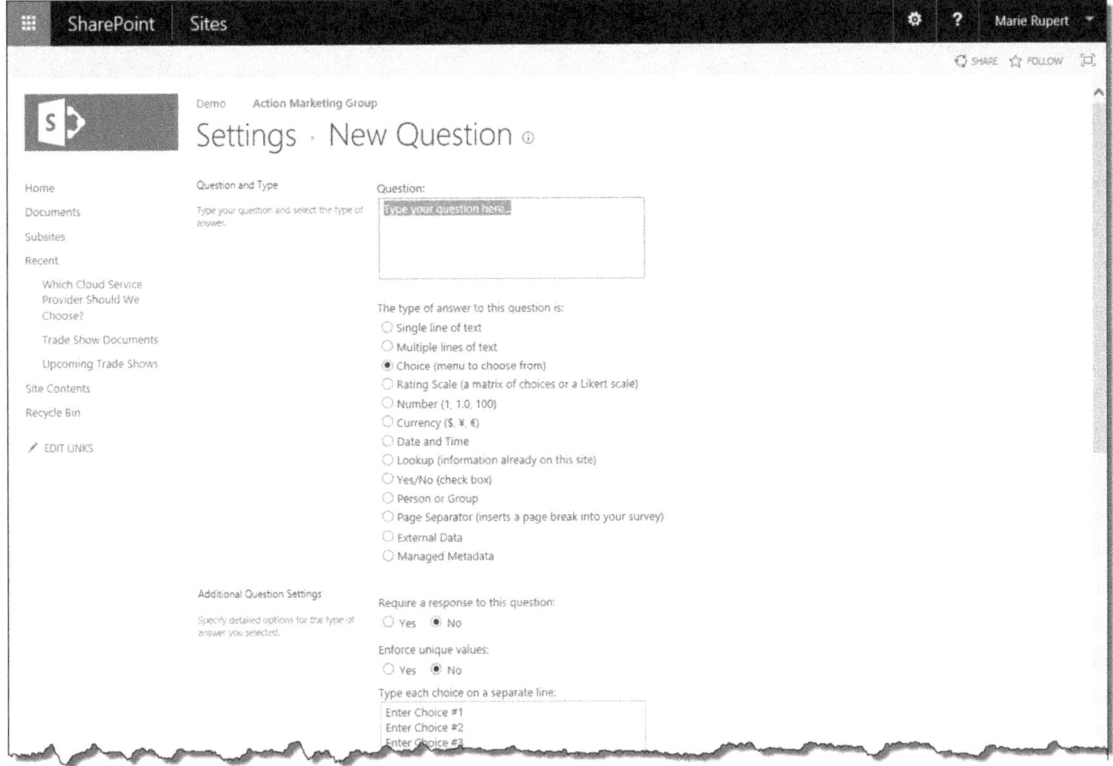

Figure 1: The New Question Page

9. In the Question field, enter text for which you want to solicit user feedback.
10. Select a type of answer. Based on your selection, the fields in the Additional Question Settings section will change.
11. In the Additional Question Settings section, fill in the appropriate fields.
12. To add another question, click **Next Question** and repeat steps 9-11.
13. When you are finished adding questions, click **Finish**. The Survey Settings page will appear.

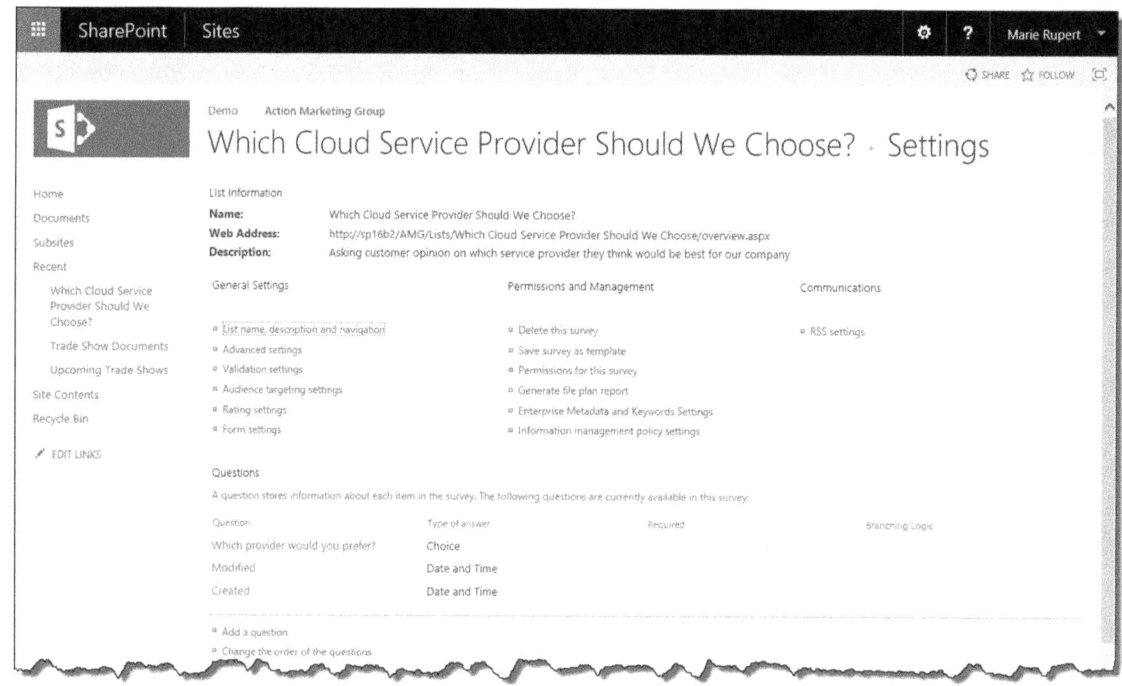

Figure 2: The Survey Settings Page

Task: Preview Your Survey

Purpose: SharePoint allows for the ability to test a survey before making it live. This allows you to make sure that the survey works as intended before asking a larger group of people to fill it out. This helps to ensure that it works as you intend it – particularly if you've implemented complex survey branching.

Example: The Action Marketing Group human resource manager wants to test the policy survey before sending it out for everyone to fill out.

Steps:

1. Start Internet Explorer and type the URL for your organization's SharePoint server. The Start Page will open.
2. Navigate to the survey in which you are interested. The Survey Overview page will open.

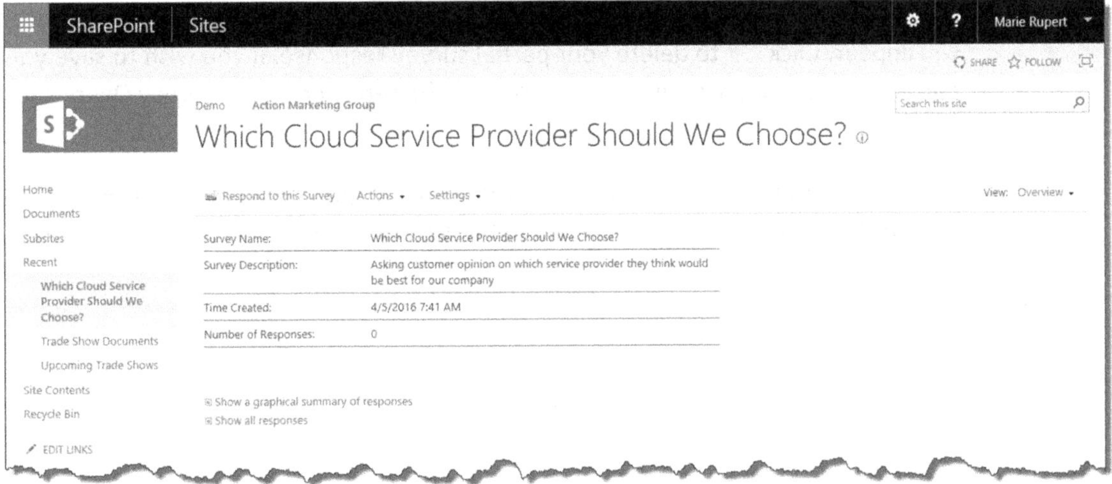

Figure 1: The Survey Overview Page

3. Click the **Respond to this Survey** link. The first survey question page will open.

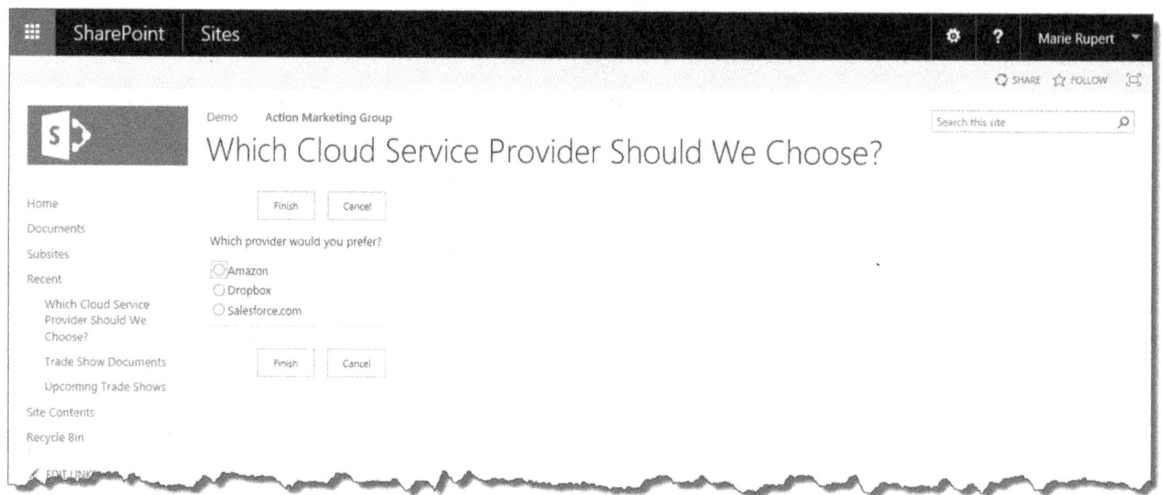

Figure 2: The First Survey Question

4. Review the survey as a test to verify correctness. Click the **Next** button to move to the next question. If all is in order, click the **Cancel** button. A confirmation dialog box will appear. Click **OK** to delete your partial survey response. If you wish to save your partial survey response, click **Cancel**. You will be returned to the Survey Overview page.

5. To actually respond to the survey, answer all of the questions and click the **Finish** button. The answers will be recorded in the survey results.

Task: Enable Survey Branching

Purpose: When a survey is being created, not every question will be applicable to every respondent. For instance, if you want to poll users about their favorite candidate, and you've already asked their political party preference, you would want to narrow their choices to those candidates who are actually in that party. When a question asked depends on the answer of a previous question, this is known as branching. Keep in mind that branching depends on the order of the questions. You can only branch "forward" to subsequent questions; you cannot branch "backward" to previous questions.

Example: The survey for the copy vendors needs to be expanded, and the next question in the survey depends on the answer to the first.

Steps:

1. Start Internet Explorer and type the URL for your organization's SharePoint server. The Start page will open
2. Navigate to the survey in which you'd like to enable branching. The Survey Overview page will appear.
3. Click the arrow next to **Settings** to open the drop-down menu, then select **Survey Settings**. The Survey Settings page will appear.

Note: For survey branching to work, there must be more than two questions in the survey, or branching cannot be set up.

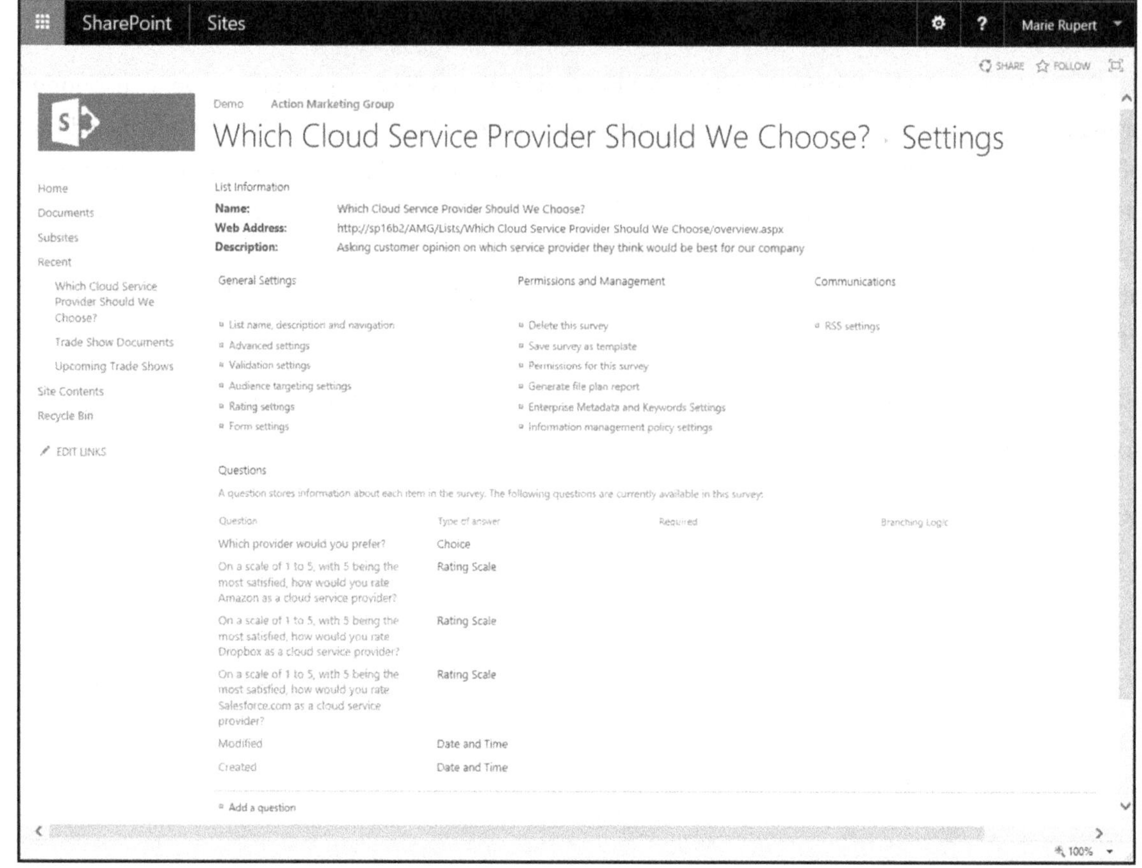

Figure 1: The Survey Settings Page

4. In the Questions section, click the link for the question with the answers that create a branch in the survey. The Edit Question page will open.

5. In the Branching Logic section, for each of the possible choices, select the question that will next appear from their respective **Jump To** drop-down menus. Selecting **No Branching** will direct the user to the next question in the order listed in the survey Settings' Questions section.

Note: Selecting the last question will only allow branching to a Content Type, if available. Remember that branching depends on the order of questions. If you cannot select the questions you wish to branch to, try changing the order of your questions. To do this, navigate to the Survey Settings page. At the bottom of the page, click the **Change the order of the questions** link. Then select the desired order from the drop-down menus next to each item, and click **OK** to save your changes.

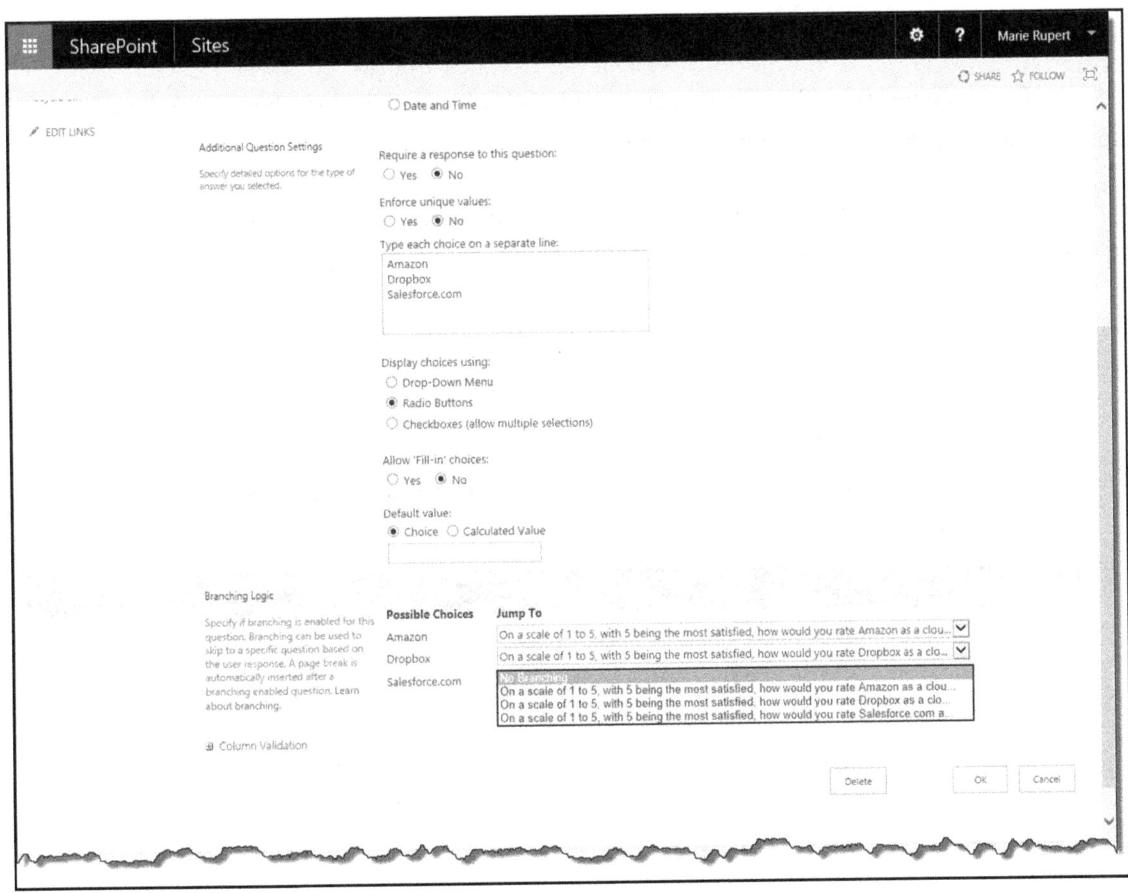

Figure 2: The Branching Logic Section on the Edit Question Page

6. When you're finished, click OK. The Survey Settings page will open and the survey will be ready for use.

Task: Send a Survey Link

Purpose: Once you've created a survey, you need to let your users know where it is so they can respond to it. That requires sending out a link.

Example: Now that the survey is completed, the team members need to be notified of its existence and encouraged to participate.

Steps:

1. Start Internet Explorer and type the URL for your organization's SharePoint server. The Start Page will open.
2. Navigate to the survey in which you are interested. The Survey Overview page will open.

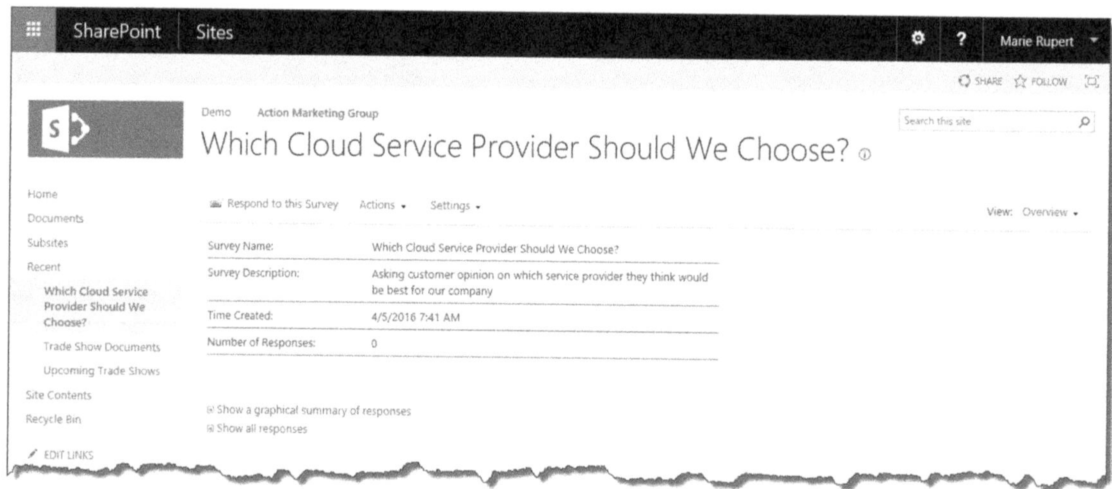

Figure 1: The Survey Overview Page

3. In the Address bar of your browser, select the entire address. The shortcut Ctrl + A is useful for this.
4. Use the shortcut Ctrl + C to copy the URL, or right-click the highlighted URL, and then select Copy.
5. Open a new message window in Microsoft Outlook.
6. Use the shortcut Ctrl + V to paste the URL into the body of the message, or right-click in the body of the message, and then select Paste. The URL will appear.
7. Complete the message and press Send. The survey link will be distributed.

8. To create a direct link to the first question of the survey is only a few extra steps. After you have pasted the URL into the body of the email message, take a look at the URL. You'll see that the URL ends with /overview.aspx.

9. Delete overview and in its place type newform. The ending of your URL will now read /newform.aspx. What this does is create a new survey response that starts on the first question of your survey, instead of sending the people you invite to the Survey Overview page.

10. Complete the message and press Send. The direct survey link will be distributed.

Task: View Survey Results

Purpose: SharePoint has the ability to graph the survey responses. Once a survey is completed by one or more respondents, you can view the results in a comparative graphical form, or view the answers given by individual respondents.

Steps:

1. Start Internet Explorer and type the URL for your organization's SharePoint server. The Start Page will open.
2. Navigate to the survey in which you are interested. The Survey Overview page will open.
3. To view a graphical summary, click the **Show a graphical summary of responses** link; or in the upper-right corner, click the **View** drop-down menu and select the **Graphical Summary** option. The Graphical Summary page will open.

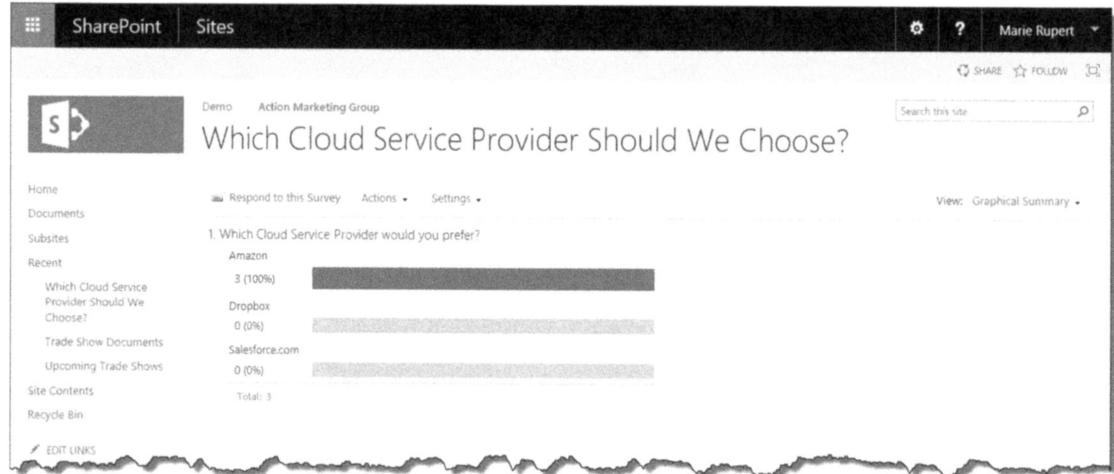

Figure 1: The Graphical Summary Page

4. To return to the Survey Overview page, click the **View** menu and select the **Overview** option. The Survey Overview page will open.
5. To view all responses to the survey, click the **Show all responses** link, or click the **View** drop-down menu and select the **All Responses** option. The All Responses page will open.

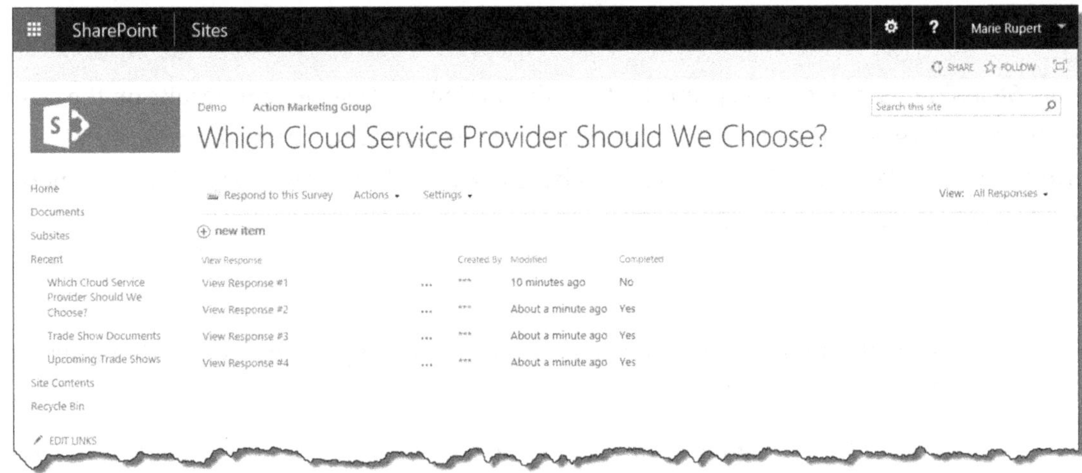

Figure 2: The All Responses Page

6. Click any **View Response** link. The View Response page will open.

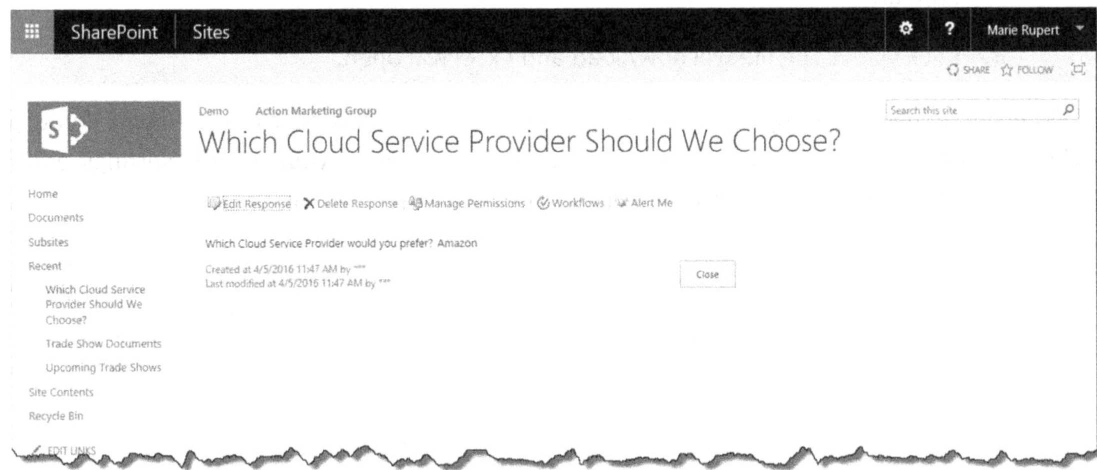

Figure 3: The View Response Page

7. When finished, click **Close**. You can now compile the survey, as demonstrated in the "Compile Survey Results" task.

Task: Compile Survey Results

Purpose: SharePoint surveys can capture a lot of information, and viewing the results on the screen is great for a quick review. However, sometimes it will be necessary to look at the details and perform the kind of data analysis that is only available in Excel. Thankfully, SharePoint can export the results of a survey into an Excel spreadsheet.

Steps:

1. Start Internet Explorer and type the URL for your organization's SharePoint server. The Start page will open.
2. Navigate to the survey in which you are interested. The Survey Overview page will open.
3. Click the arrow next to **Actions** to open the drop-down menu and select the **Export to Spreadsheet** option. The File Download message box for your browser will appear.
4. Click **Open**. The file will download and Excel will open.

Note: If a warning dialog box appears identifying a potential security concern, click **Enable** if you were the one who initiated the export from SharePoint. Depending on your security settings, another dialog box may appear. Click **Yes** to proceed.

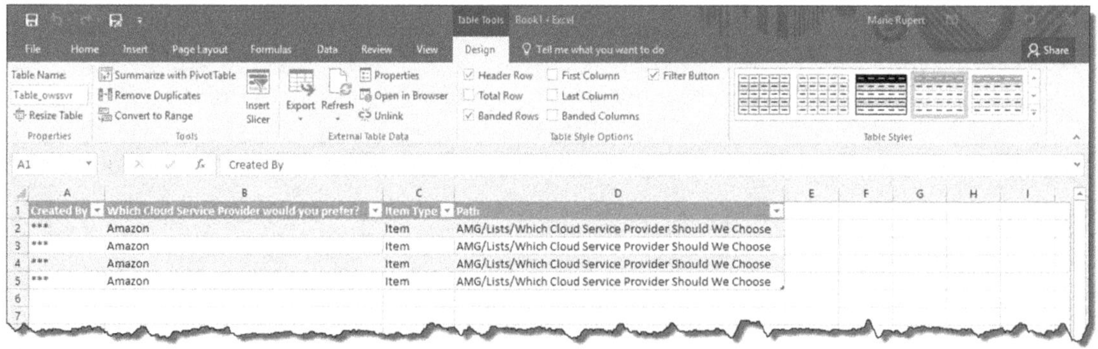

Figure 1: The Survey in Excel

5. The survey responses will appear in the spreadsheet. You can now edit the spreadsheet as you normally would, using the table tools.

Getting Social with SharePoint

One of the more compelling features of SharePoint is its capability to create personal sites for users. These sites give users a place to express themselves more creatively, share interests and hobbies, and generally make the work environment a more pleasant place.

Other social tools within SharePoint include the capability to create and edit your own blog and wiki pages. Content throughout a SharePoint site can be tagged so other users can find it faster.

In this section, you'll learn how to:

- Configure a User Profile: Create profiles for users to give users a place to express themselves.
- Edit a Personal Site's Links: The first thing a user should do is edit their personal site with links to content.
- Add an App to a Personal Site: You can add apps to your personal site.
- Edit an App in a Personal Site: You can edit any app within a personal site as you would any other app.
- Remove an App from a Personal Site: You can remove apps you've created on your personal site.
- Create a Blog Entry in SharePoint: How to write a blog post in SharePoint.
- Register a Blog in Word: Connecting a blog site to Microsoft Word so blog entries can be published from Word.
- Write a Blog Entry with Word: How to post entries to a SharePoint blog from Word.
- Post a Newsfeed Entry: A new feature in SharePoint 2016 is the Newsfeed, a component of a personal or other site that acts as a microblogging tool.
- Reply to a Newsfeed Entry: Once Newsfeed entries are posted, you can quickly reply to them, just as you would with any other microblogging tool.
- Tag SharePoint Content: One of the great new features of SharePoint is the capability to tag any SharePoint page you find as a favorite, thus allowing you to find it again.
- Tag External Content: Another nifty feature of SharePoint is the capability to tag any Internet page.
- Create a Wiki Home Page: One of the more interesting features of SharePoint is the ability to create a wiki page as your site's home page.

- **Edit a Wiki Home Page**: If you decide to use a wiki page in your SharePoint site, either as a home page or for some other utility, editing it is a very straightforward process.

Task: Configure a User Profile

Purpose: One of the more compelling features of SharePoint is its capability to create profiles for users. These profiles give users a place to express themselves more creatively, share interests and hobbies, and generally make the work environment a more personal place.

Example: The human resources manager at the Action Marketing Group team members wants to enhance their user profile.

Steps:

1. Start Internet Explorer and type the URL for your organization's SharePoint server. The Start page will open.
2. In the upper-right corner of any SharePoint page click the menu with your user name and select the **About Me** option. Your personal site will appear.

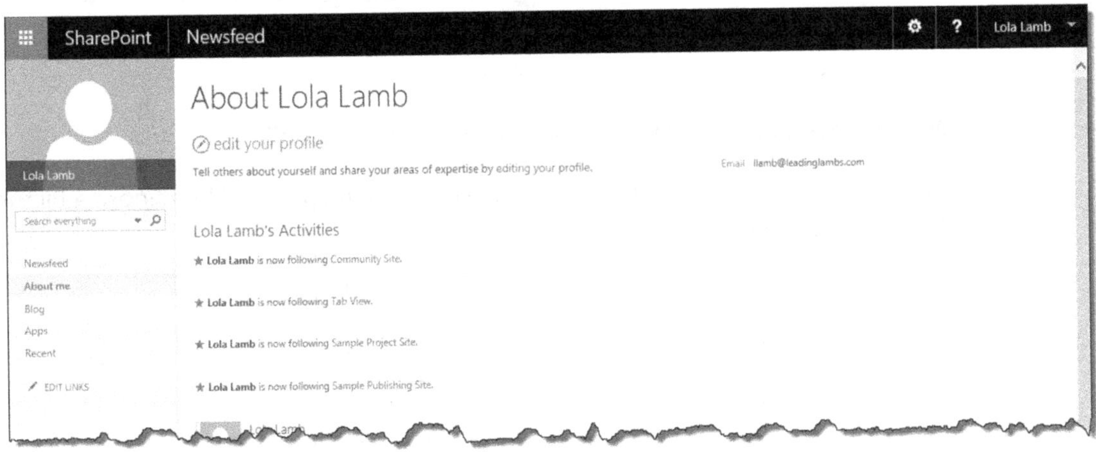

Figure 1: A Personal Site

3. Click the **edit** your profile link. The Edit Details page for your user account will be displayed.

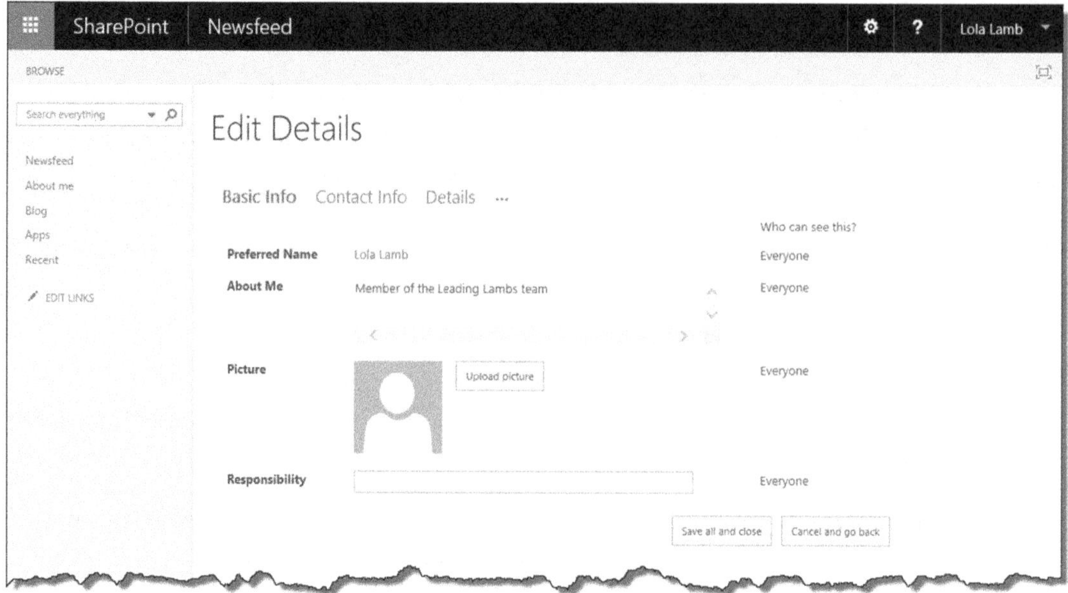

Figure 2: The Edit Details Page

4. Within the About Me field, add a description about yourself.
5. Click the **Upload picture** button to add a picture to the profile. The Choose a Picture dialog box will open.

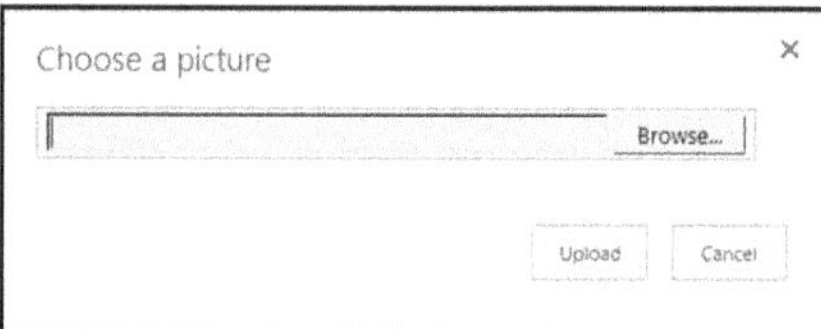

Figure 3: The Choose a Picture Dialog Box

6. Click the **Browse** button. The Choose File to Upload dialog will open.
7. Navigate to the image file you want to use and select it.
8. Click **Open**. The file path to the image will appear in the Choose a Picture dialog.
9. Click **Upload**. The image will appear in the Picture section.

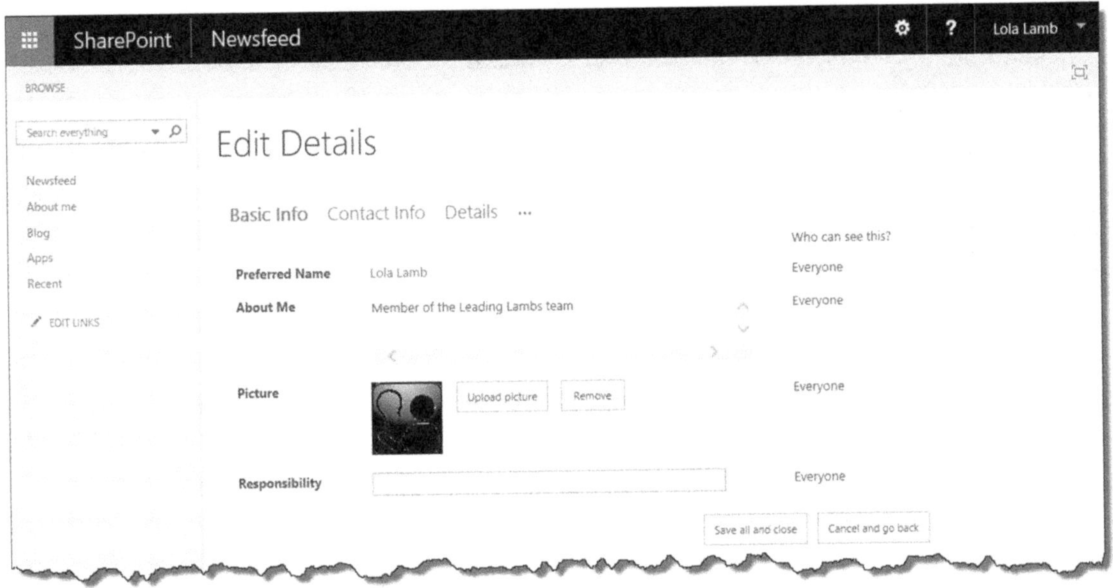

Figure 4: The Edit Details Page in Progress

10. In the Ask Me About field, enter information such as the topics that you're knowledgeable about or an expert on.
11. At the top of the Edit Details page, click the **Contact Information** link. Enter relevant information in that section.
12. At the top of the Edit Details page, click the **Details** link. Enter relevant information in that section.
13. When you're finished, click the **Save all and close** button. A Profile Changes dialog box will appear.

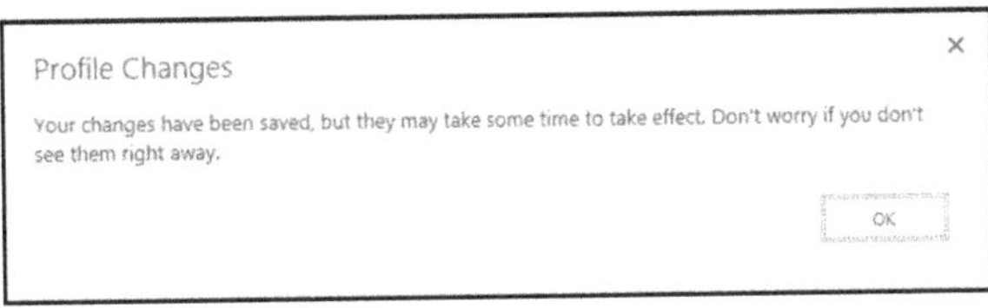

Figure 5: The Profile Changes Message Box

14. Click **OK**. Your personal site will appear with the new profile information.

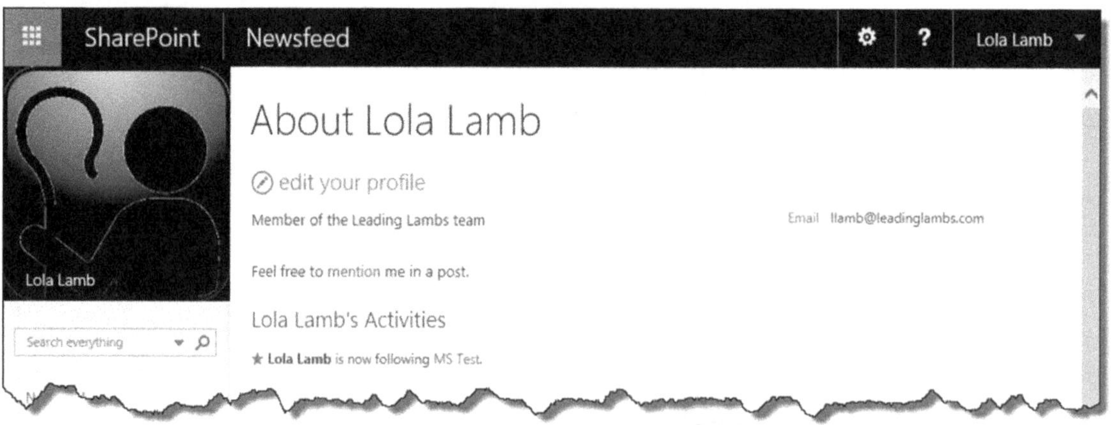

Figure 6: The Updated Profile in a Personal Site

Task: Edit a Personal Site's Links

Purpose: A personal site is more than just a place where colleagues can find out more about you; it's also a place where you can start working, using apps and links to launch the tools you need throughout the day. SharePoint allows you to maintain links that are important to you.

Example: The Action Marketing Group human resources manager has a link to the Society of Human Resource Managers (SHRM) that she wants to keep handy for when she needs to learn more about human resources issues that may impact the organization.

Steps:

1. Start Internet Explorer and type the URL for your organization's SharePoint server. The Start page will open.
2. In the upper-right corner of any SharePoint page, click the menu with your user name and select the **About Me** option. Your personal site will appear.

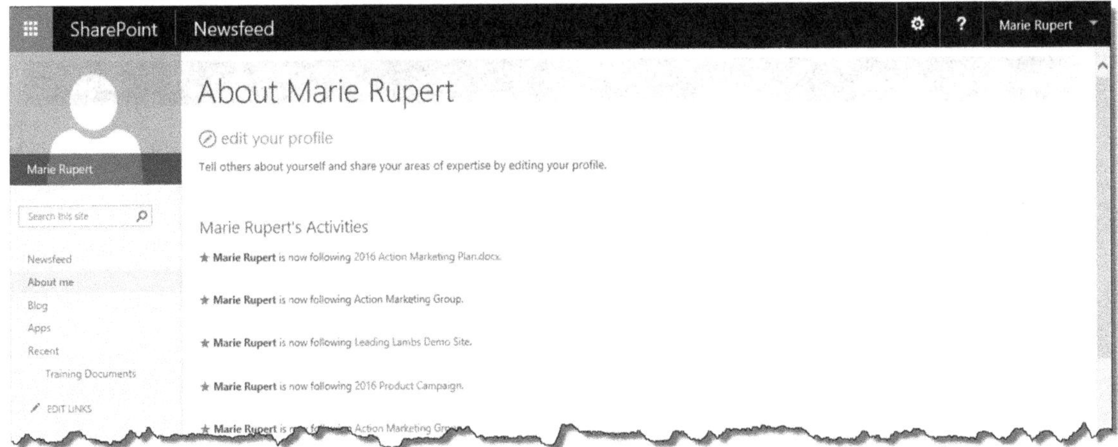

Figure 1: A Personal Site

3. In the Quick Launch on the left side, click the **Edit Links** link. The Edit Link tools will be displayed.

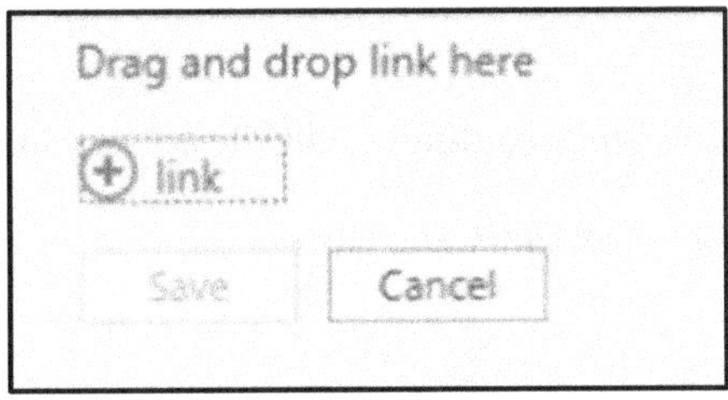

Figure 2: The Edit Link Tools

4. Click the **+ link** link. The Add a Link dialog box will open.

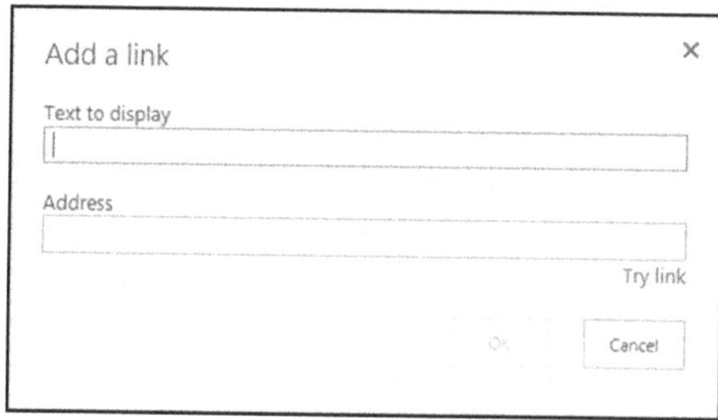

Figure 3: The Add a Link Dialog Box

5. In the Text to display field, type the text for the link.
6. In the Address field, type the URL for the page or site to which you want to link.
7. Click OK. The link will be added to the side navigation bar.
8. Click Save. The Edit Link tools will close and the new link will be added to the Quick Launch.

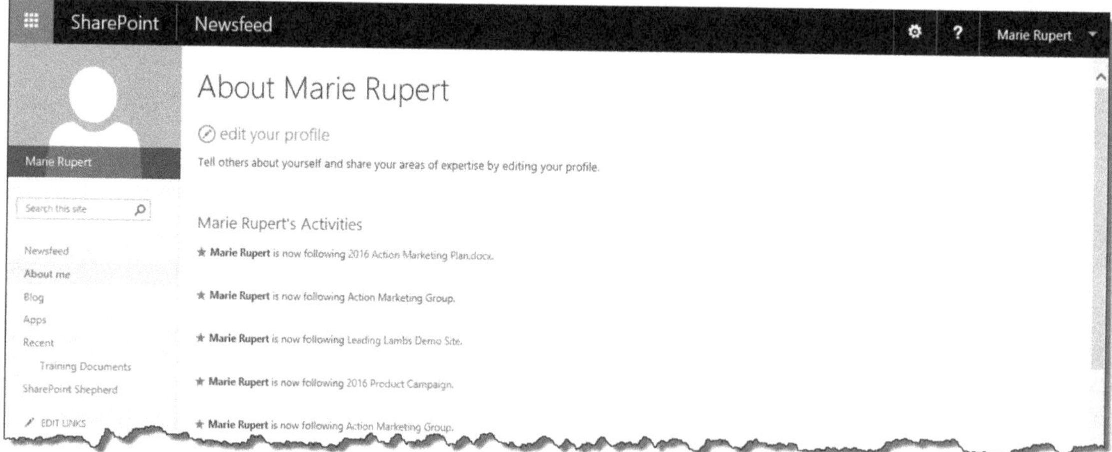

Figure 4: The Updated Links

9. In the Quick Launch, click the Edit Links link to remove a link. The Edit Link tools will be displayed.
10. Next to the link you want to delete, click the Close link. The link will be removed.
11. Click Save. The Edit Link tools will close.

Task: Add an App to Your Personal Site

Purpose: Your personal space is a place where you can get work done much like a desk in the office. Also, like a desk in the office, you can add new things – like organizers – to make it quicker and more efficient to do your job. You can add new apps to your personal site just like in other SharePoint sites.

Example: The Action Marketing Group receptionist would like to add a tag cloud to their Personal Site.

Steps:

1. Start Internet Explorer and type the URL for your organization's SharePoint server. The Start page will open.
2. In the upper-right corner of any SharePoint page click the menu with your user name and select the **About Me** option. Your personal site will appear.
3. In the Quick Launch, click the **Apps** link. The Site Contents page will open.

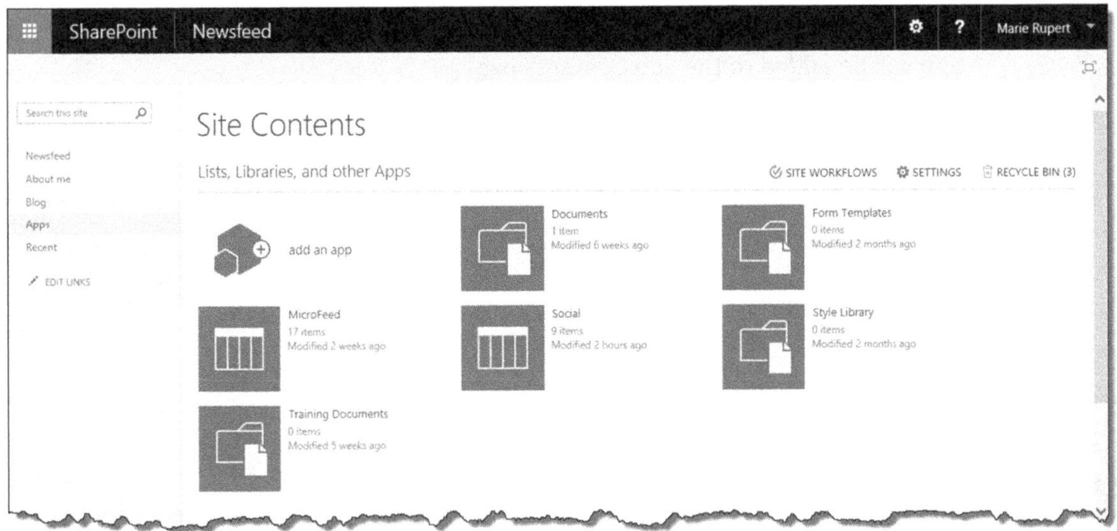

Figure 1: The Site Contents Page

4. Click **add an app**. The Your Apps page will open.

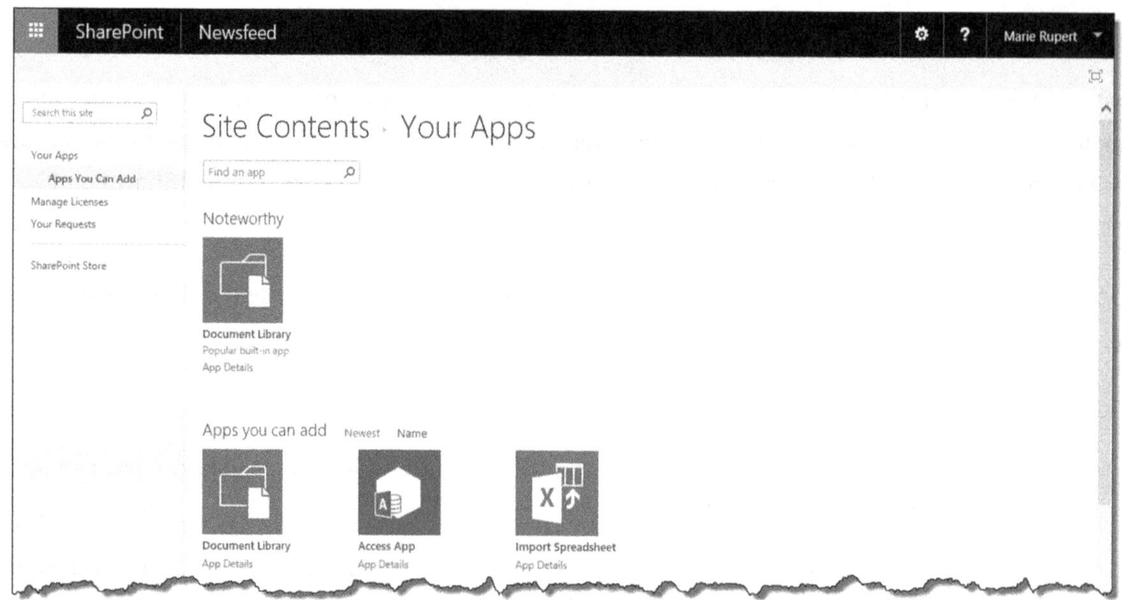

Figure 2: The Your Apps Page

5. Click the app that you want to add. Enter a name for your app, then click **Create**. The app will be added to the Site Contents page.

Task: Edit an App in a Personal Site

Purpose: The apps in your personal site are like other applications anywhere in SharePoint. You can change the settings by going to the app's Settings page.

Example: The Action Marketing Group team member would like to change the name of an app.

Steps:

1. Start Internet Explorer and type the URL for your organization's SharePoint server. The Start page will open.
2. In the upper-right corner of any SharePoint page click the menu with your user name and select the **About Me** option. Your personal site will appear.
3. In the Quick Launch, click the **Apps** link. The Site Contents page will open.
4. Select an app's menu icon and click the **ellipsis** control. The app's menu will appear.
5. Click the **Settings** option. The app's Settings page will open.

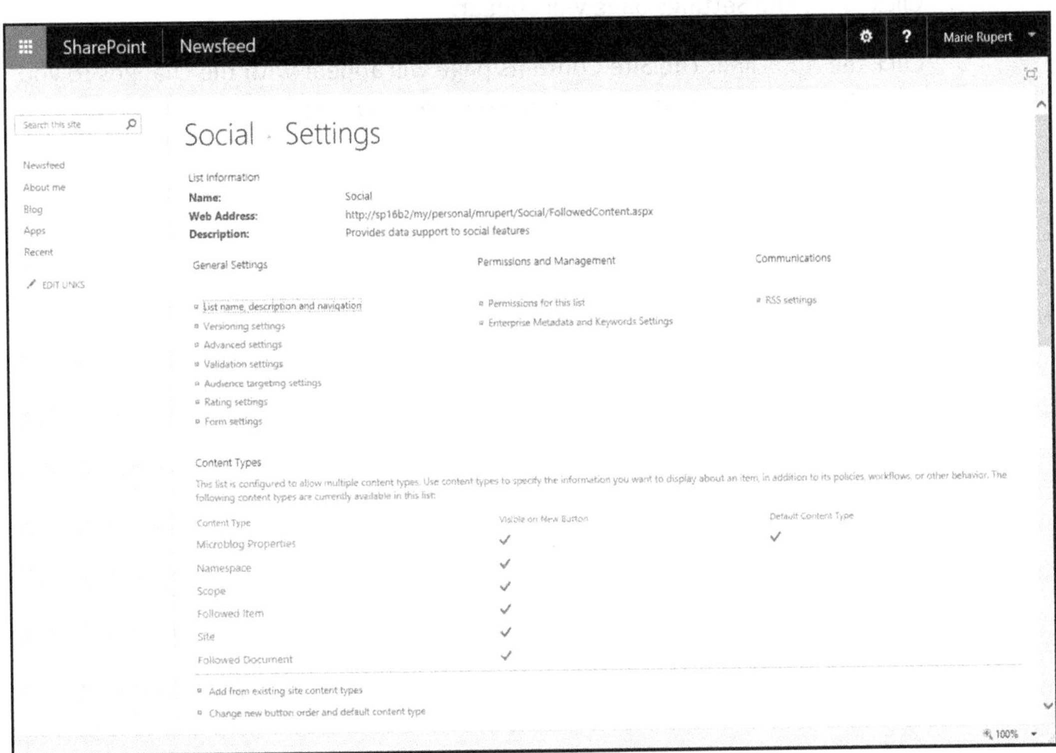

Figure 1: The App's Settings Page

6. Under General Settings, click the **List name, description and navigation** link. The General Settings page will open.

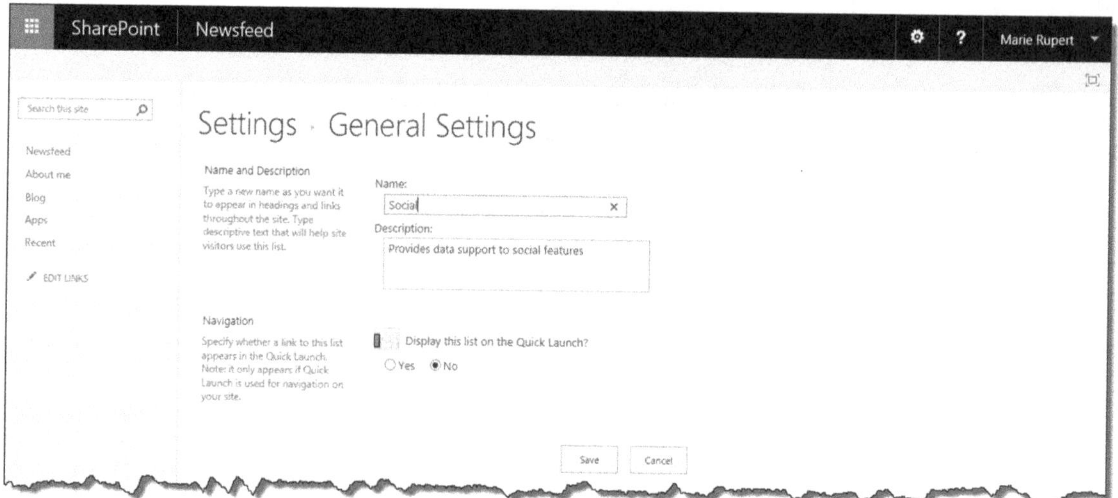

Figure 2: The General Settings Page

7. In the Name field, change the name of the app.
8. Click **Save**. The Settings page will appear.
9. Click the **Apps** link. The Site Contents page will appear with the changes to your app. Click the **About Me** link to return to your personal site.

Task: Remove an App from a Personal Site

Purpose: Like any site, you may add an app to your personal site, only to realize later that you no longer need it. Safely deleting an app is quick and easy.

Example: The operations manager at the Action Marketing Group was using a list to track the effectiveness of a new training program that has now been discontinued. She wants to remove the app to prevent cluttering her personal site.

Steps:

1. Start Internet Explorer and type the URL for your organization's SharePoint server. The Start page will open.
2. In the upper-right corner of any SharePoint page click the menu with your user name and select the **About Me** option. Your personal site will appear.
3. In the Quick Launch, click the **Apps** link. The Site Contents page will open.
4. Select an app's menu icon and click the **ellipsis** control. The app's menu will appear.
5. Click the **Remove** option. A confirmation dialog box will appear.

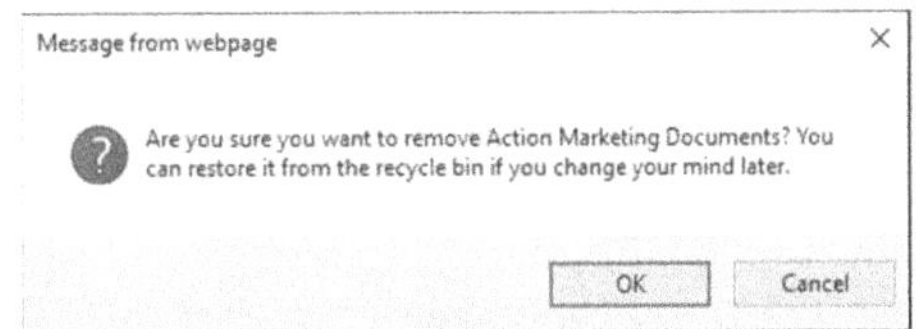

Figure 1: The Message from Webpage Dialog Box

Exception: You can only remove apps that you have previously added to your personal site, as some apps are required.

6. Click **OK**. The app will be removed from your personal site.

Task: Create a Blog Entry in SharePoint

Purpose: One of the fastest growing aspects of the Internet is the web log, or "blog". Blogs serve as a daily (or other interval) diary of your activities, whether business or personal. SharePoint includes a blog management system to get you started on a blog right away.

Example: The Action Marketing Group office manager wants to add an entry to her blog.

Steps:

1. Start Internet Explorer and type the URL for your organization's SharePoint server. The Start page will open.
2. In the upper-right corner of any SharePoint page click the menu with your user name and select the **About Me** option. Your Personal Site will appear.

Note: If the blog you want create an entry for isn't in your Personal Site, navigate to the blog and resume at step 4.

3. In the Quick Launch, click the **Blog** link. The Blog home page will open.

Figure 1: The Blog Home Page

4. In the Blog tools section click the **Create a post** link. The new Blog entry page will open.

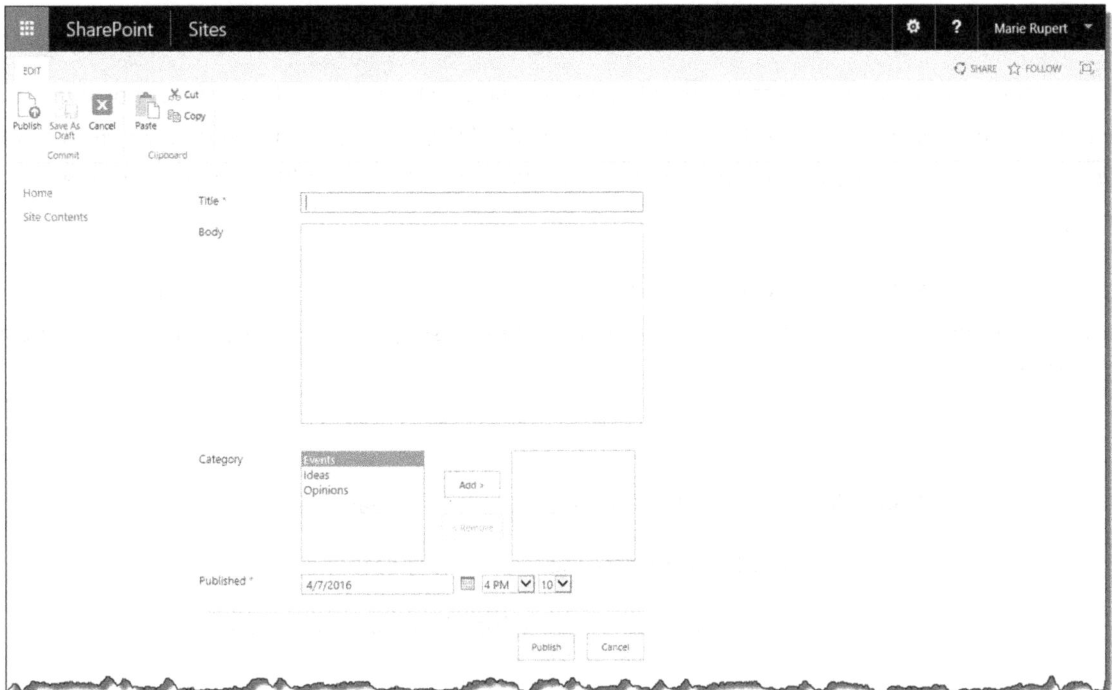

Figure 2: The New Blog Entry Page

5. Enter information and content into the appropriate fields.
6. Click **Publish**. The new blog entry will appear on the Blog home page.

Task: Register a Blog in Word

Purpose: SharePoint allows you to create blog entries directly from the web interface, however, most office workers are more comfortable writing in Word than they are writing long works in a web page. Word can be connected to SharePoint so that you can author your blog posts in Word and directly post them.

Example: The Action Marketing Group human resources clerk will be posting to the corporate blog and wants to route content to others for comment before posting and so will be using Word to post to the blog.

Steps:

1. In Word, click the **File** tab. The File screen will appear.
2. Click the **New** tab. The templates screen will appear.
3. Click the **Blog post** template. The Blog Post dialog box will open.

Figure 1: The Blog Post Dialog Box

4. Click **Create**. If you have never used the template before, it will be downloaded. Then the Register a Blog Account dialog box will open

Figure 2: The Register a Blog Account Dialog Box

5. Click Register Now. A New Blog Account dialog box will appear.

Note: If you've already registered a blog and need to register another you can look in the ribbon for a Manage Accounts button and click it. Once the Blog Accounts dialog box comes up, you can click the New button and follow the rest of the steps here.

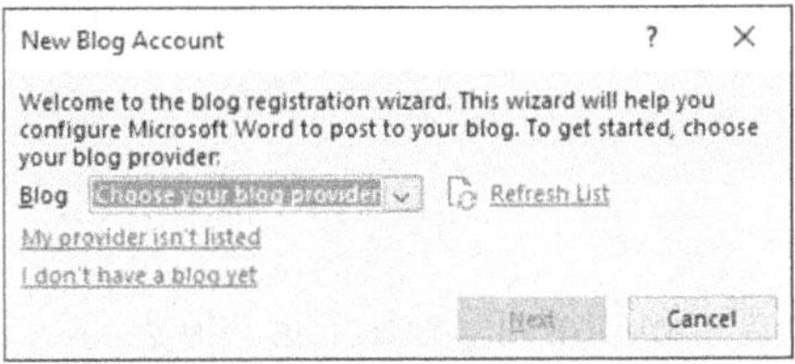

Figure 3: The New Blog Account Dialog Box

6. In the Blog drop-down control, select the SharePoint blog option, then click Next. The New SharePoint Blog Account dialog box will appear.

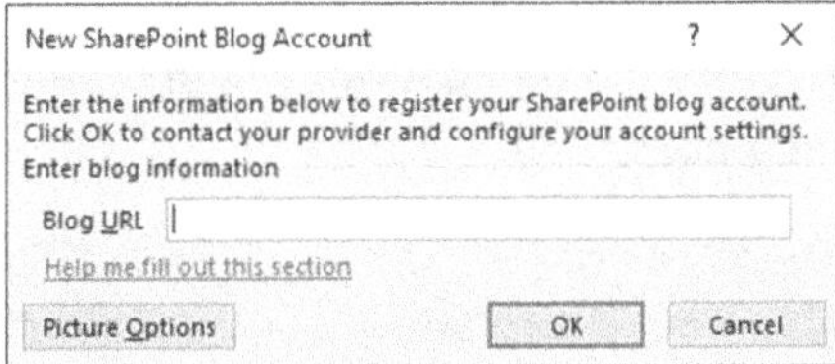

Figure 4: The New SharePoint Blog Account Dialog Box

7. In the Blog URL field, enter the URL for your SharePoint blog and click OK. A confirmation dialog box will open.

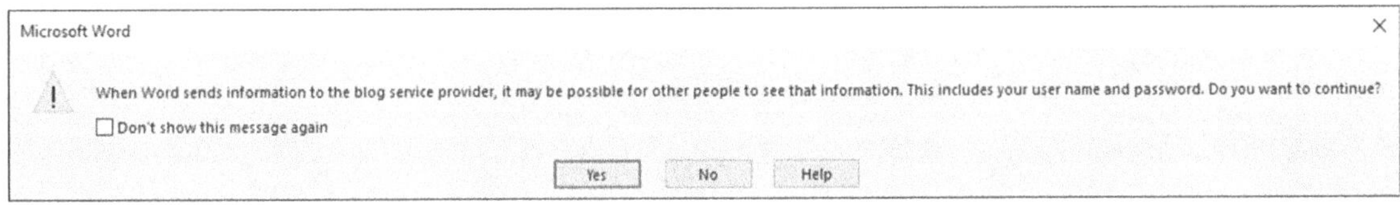

Figure 5: The Confirmation Dialog Box

8. Click Yes. A notification dialog box will open. (Sometimes the notification box appears twice; click Yes again.)

9. Click OK. The New SharePoint Blog Account dialog box will close and Microsoft Word will be ready to create a new blog post.

Task: Write a Blog Entry with Word

Purpose: One of the standard templates in Word is a blog post template which can be used to create blog posts in SharePoint – once SharePoint has been registered as a blog provider.

Example: The Action Marketing Group human resource clerk wants to post a new blog post about the company picnic using Word.

Steps:

1. In Microsoft Word, click the **File** tab. The File screen will appear.

Note: You can also start Microsoft Word. Word will open with the templates screen. Go to step 3.

2. Click the **New** tab. The templates screen will appear.
3. Click the **Blog Post** template. The Blog Post dialog box will open.
4. Click the **Create** button. A Blog Post tab will open and Microsoft Word will be ready to create a new blog post.

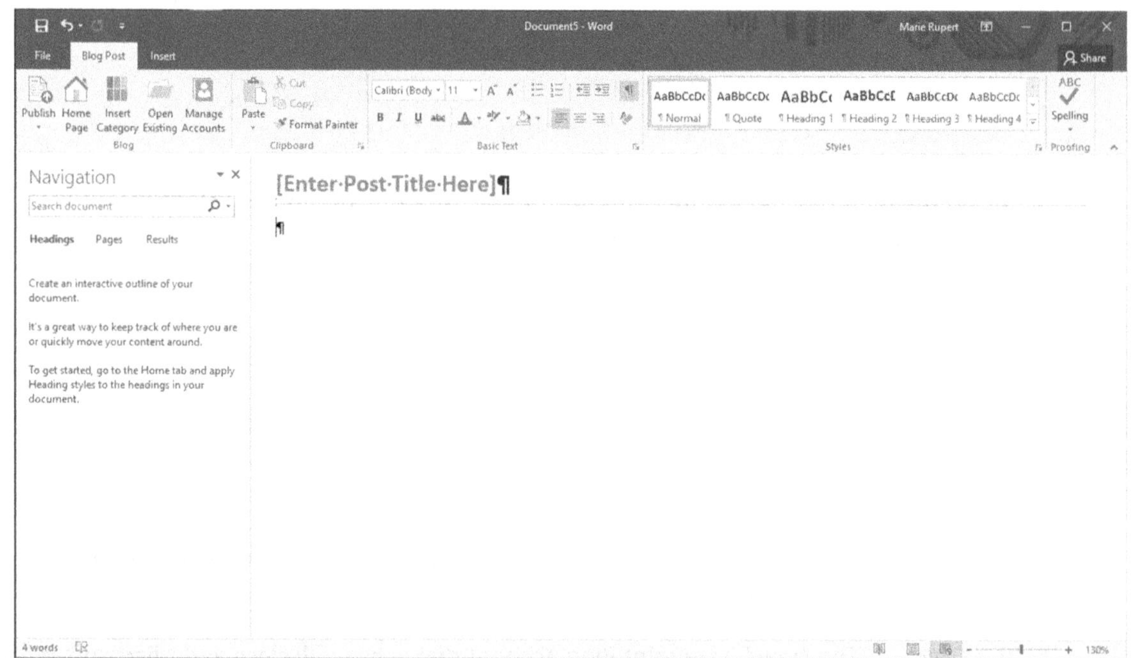

Figure 1: The Blog Post Page in Word

5. Create a blog entry, including a title and content.
6. In the Blog Post ribbon, click the **Publish** button. A confirmation dialog box will open.

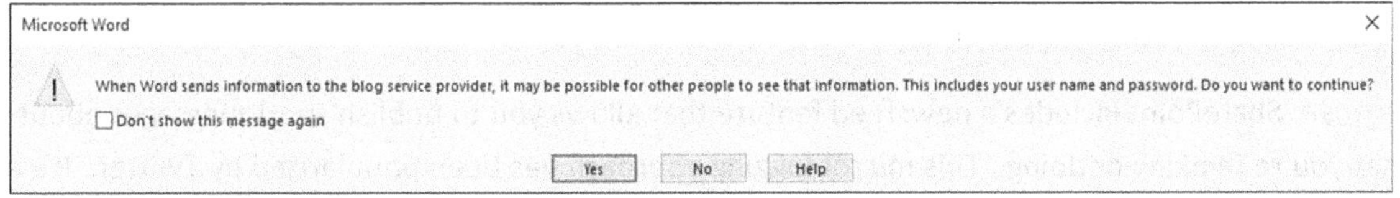

Figure 2: The Notification Dialog Box

7. Click Yes. The entry will be posted to your blog.

Task: Post a Newsfeed Entry

Purpose: SharePoint includes a newsfeed feature that allows you to publish short messages about what you're thinking or doing. This microblogging approach has been popularized by Twitter. It's a way that your colleagues can see what's going on in your world and in your head.

Example: Action Marketing Group's IT team had some leftover pizza from a lunch and learn. The IT manager wants to let everyone know that they can have the remaining pizza in the break room.

Steps:

1. Start Internet Explorer and type the URL for your organization's SharePoint server. The Start page will open.
2. In the Suite Bar of any SharePoint page, click the **App Launcher**, then select the **Newsfeed** icon from the menu. The Newsfeed page will open.

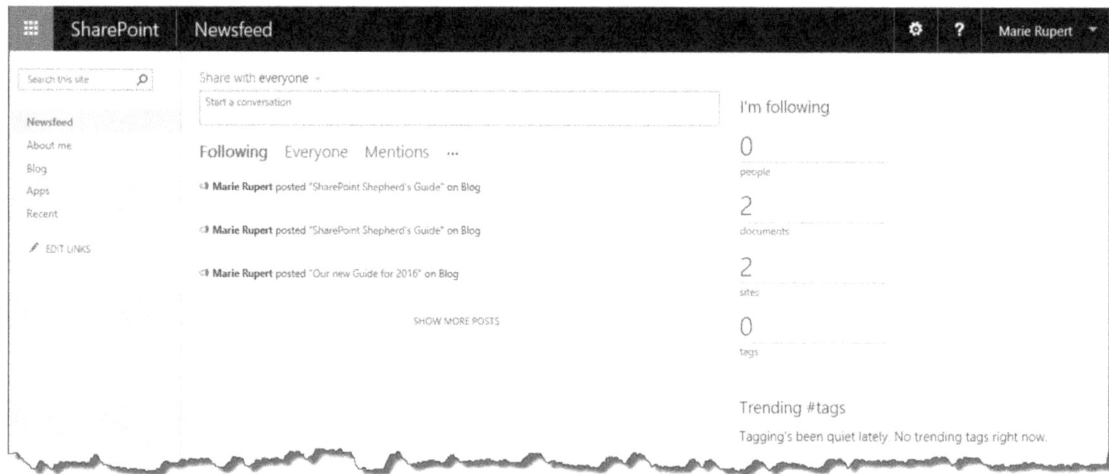

Figure 1: The Newsfeed Page

3. Click the Start a conversation field. The field will appear in Edit mode.
4. Type a brief message and click the **Post** button. The entry will appear in the newsfeed.

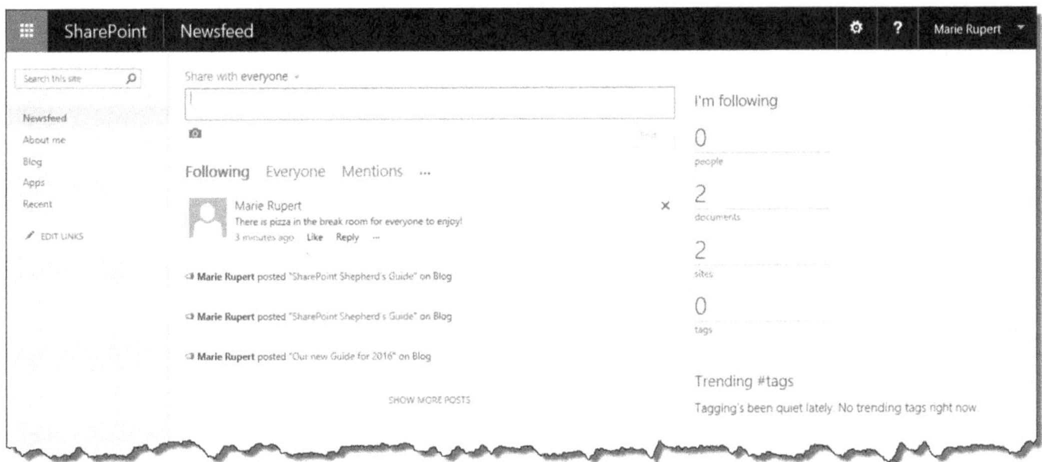

Figure 2: The New Newsfeed Entry

Task: Reply To a Newsfeed Entry

Purpose: In a world of short updates via microblogging it can sometimes be difficult to maintain the continuity of the conversation. Rather than having to search a newsfeed for posts by a person to regenerate a conversation, everyone can reply to posts. This keeps a conversation together and makes it easy to review everyone's thoughts.

Example: The safety officer at the Action Marketing Group wants to reply about a door that was propped open.

Steps:

1. Start Internet Explorer and type the URL for your organization's SharePoint server. The Start page will open.
2. In the Suite Bar, click the **App Launcher**, then select the **Newsfeed** icon. The Newsfeed page will open.
3. Click the **Reply** link for the newsfeed entry to which you want to reply. An entry field will appear in Edit mode.
4. Type a brief message and click the **Post** button. The reply will appear in the newsfeed.

Figure 1: The Newsfeed Entry With Reply

Task: Tag SharePoint Content

Purpose: Finding content across the information resources of the organization can be difficult. Finding content again that you once found can be even harder. SharePoint allows you to tag content so that you can browse through your tags later and find more easily the information you're looking for.

Example: The Action Marketing Group's new manufacturing intern wants to tag interesting company history information for him to read on break.

Steps:

1. Start Internet Explorer and type the URL for your organization's SharePoint server. Navigate to any page on the SharePoint site.
2. When you find a page that interests you, in the upper right, click the **Follow** link. The page will be tagged.
3. To manage tags for a page, click the **Page**, **Library**, or **List** tab to open the page's ribbon.
4. Click the **Tags & Notes** icon for a tagged page. The Tag dialog box will open.

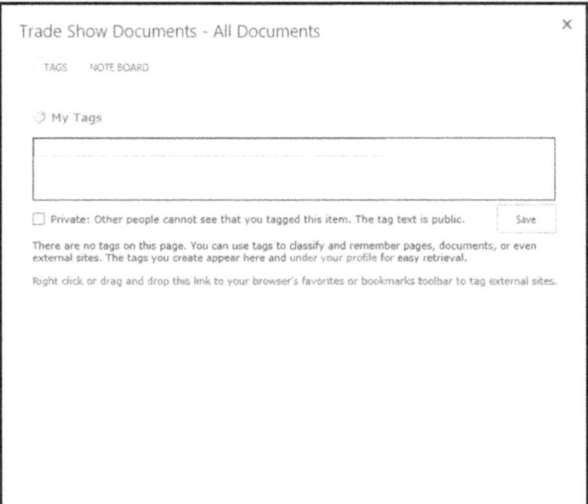

Figure 1: The Tag Dialog Box

5. In the My Tags field, add tags, separated by commas or semicolons. As you type, suggested keywords may appear. Click appropriate tags to add them to the field.
6. Click **Save**. The page will be tagged with the new tags.
7. Click the **Note Board** tab. The Note Board page will appear.
8. In the main field, add notes about the page.

9. Click Post. The notes will be assigned to this page.

10. Click the Close control in the top right corner. The Tag dialog box will close.

Task: Tag External Content

Purpose: Tagging content in SharePoint is an important start to allowing you to organize information that you want to find again; however, not everything that you care about will be on SharePoint. SharePoint allows you to tag content which isn't on your server.

Example: The Action Group team production intern has found an important regulatory guideline that he wants to tag for finding later.

Steps:

1. Start Internet Explorer and type the URL for your organization's SharePoint server. The Start page will open.
2. Click the Page tab to open the Page ribbon.
3. Click the Tags & Notes icon. The Tag dialog box will open.
4. Right-click the Right click or drag and drop this link to your browser's favorites or bookmarks toolbar to tag external sites link. The context menu will appear.
5. Select the Add to favorites option. The Add a Favorite dialog box will open.

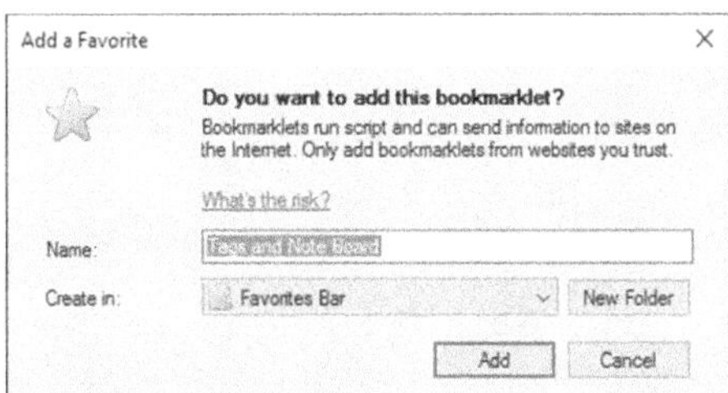

Figure 1: The Add a Favorite Dialog Box

6. In the Create in field, select the Favorites Bar option, then click Add. The favorite will appear in the browser's Favorites Bar.

Note: An Overwrite dialog box may appear if the favorite already exists.

7. Navigate to any page of interest. This can be any Internet page.
8. Click the Favorites icon, which looks like a star. Then select the Favorites Bar option.
9. From the drop down menu, select the Tags & Note Board favorite. The Tags & Note Board page will appear in a separate window.
10. Add tags, separated by commas or semicolons, to the My Tags field. As you type, suggested keywords may appear. Click appropriate keywords to add them to the field.

Note: Click in the extreme upper left corner of the box for tags to get started and expect a slight delay before you'll see typing or suggestions.

11. Click Save. The page will be tagged with the new tags.
12. If you would like to add a note, click the Note Board tab. The Note Board page will appear.
13. Add notes about the page in the main field.
14. Click Post. The notes will be assigned to this page.
15. Close the window displaying the Tags and Note Board page and continue your Internet session.

Task: Create a Wiki Home Page

Purpose: One of the most interesting features in SharePoint is the capability to create a wiki page and have it become your site's home page.

Example: The Action Marketing Group will try a wiki page as its public site's home page to increase the ease of content generation from the team.

Steps:

1. Start Internet Explorer and type the URL for your organization's SharePoint server. The Start page will open.
2. Navigate to the team site. The team site's home page will open.
3. Click the **Settings** menu gear icon and select **Site settings**. The Site Settings page will open.
4. In the Site Actions section, click the **Manage site features** link. The Site Features page will open.

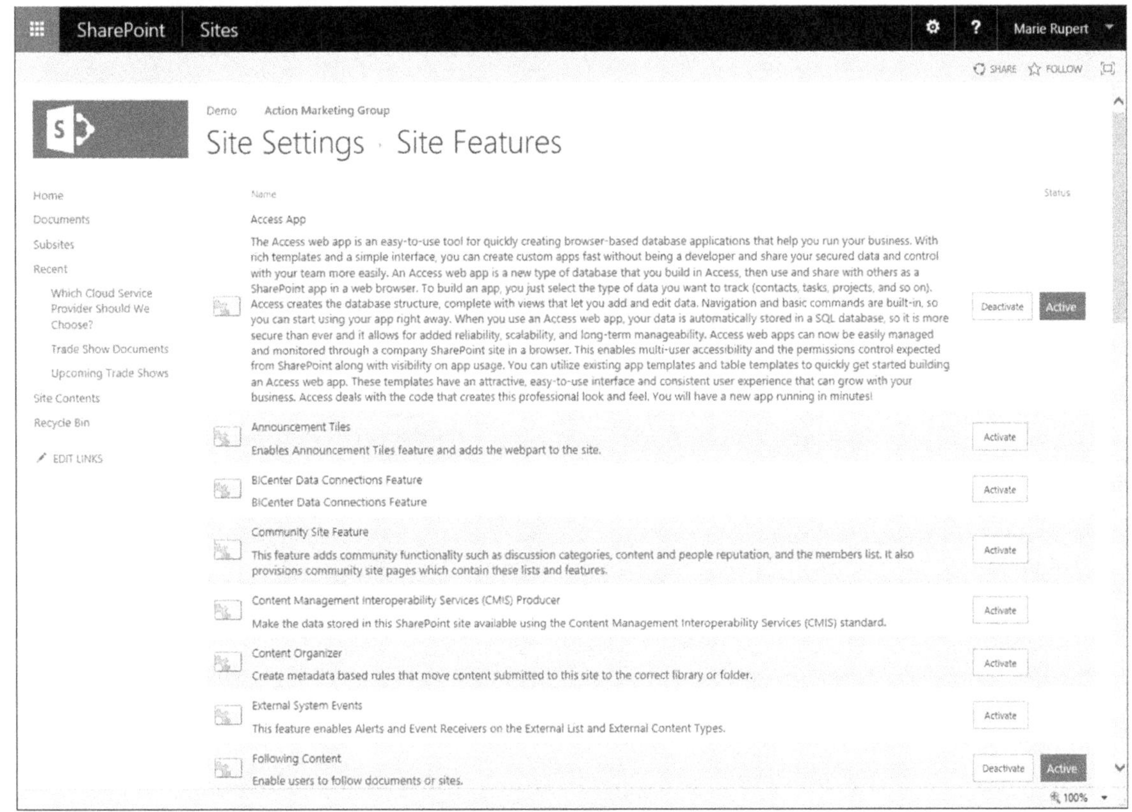

Figure 1: The Features Page

5. Find the Wiki Page Home Page feature, then click the **Activate** button. The feature will become active.

Note: If you want to return to the original home page, simply **Deactivate** the Wiki Page Home Page feature in the Site Features page.

Task: Edit a Wiki Home Page

Purpose: Editing a page in SharePoint is a simple process whether you want to add apps or simply modify the text.

Example: The Action Marketing Group's research team wants to record some best practices for research in the Wiki.

Steps:

1. Start Internet Explorer and navigate to the page you want to edit. The home page will open.
2. Click the **Page** tab. The Page ribbon will appear.
3. Click the **Edit Page** button. The Format Text ribbon will be displayed.

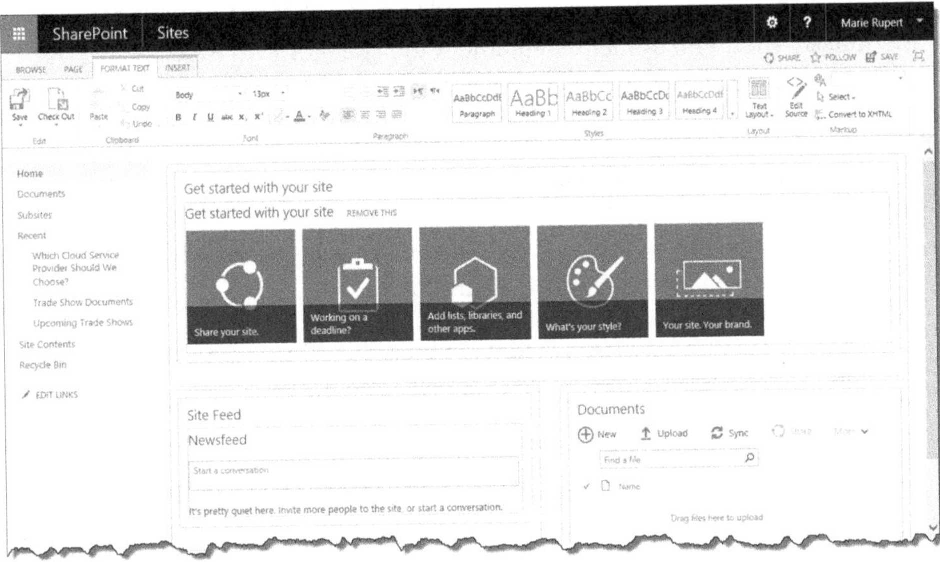

Figure 1: The Format Text Ribbon on the Wiki Home Page in Edit Mode

Note: If your page looks different, you may not be trying to edit a Wiki page. It may be a web part page or a publishing page.

4. Edit the page as needed.
5. When finished, in the Format Text ribbon, click the **Save** button. The changes will immediately be saved and published, without the need for a formal approval process.

Publish Web Content: Site Authors

SharePoint primarily deals with two kinds of sites. The first type is the collaborative site, which has been discussed through much of this manual. The second type, which will be addressed in this section, is the publishing site. A publishing site contains content intended not to be created, but rather shared as is. It can be your team's web presence, or a collection of documents and tools for fellow users to read and use.

In this section, you'll learn how to:

- Create a Site for Published Content: The basics of creating a publishing site.
- Create a Content Page: Once a publishing site is created, users can start creating the content for the site.
- Edit Page Content: Any time you need to make changes on your pages, you can quickly enter edit mode to implement the changes with ease.
- Spell Check Page Content: One of the handier tools in the page content editor is the spell checker. It might seem obvious, but web editor spell checkers are not as robust as one would think... until now.
- Add an Image to a Content Page: Images are sometimes the best thing about a web page. Add your images easily in SharePoint.
- Add Publishing Approvers: Within a publishing site, all pages must be approved for publication every time they are changed or added to the site. This is known as a workflow.
- Submit Page for Publishing Approval: Since publishing sites are more static and represent you or your business, you should not just create the site on your own and publish it as is.
- Approve Content for Publication: If you are designated as a content approver, here's how to edit and formally approve the document.
- Change Page Schedule Expiration Date: Sometimes, you will have a page that only needs to be up for a limited amount of time, such as for a sale or contest.
- Manually Start a Workflow for Publication: At any time, a site administrator can tag a page for improvement using the workflow process.
- Create a Custom Permission Level: Whenever you create a site, you may need to grant permission levels for users that don't match existing types of permissions. In SharePoint, you can create a brand-new permission level to meet your needs.

Task: Create a Site for Published Content

Purpose: SharePoint primarily deals with two kinds of sites. The first type is the collaborative site, which has been discussed through much of this book. Collaborative sites are many-to-many conversations which evolve content. The second type, which has not been as fully addressed, is the publishing site. A publishing site contains content to be shared "as is," and not worked on collaboratively. Publishing sites are also structured in that every piece of data has a place. Finally, publishing sites are one-to-many in that few people write content and many consume it.

Example: The Action Marketing Group Intranet administrator needs to create a new department site.

Steps:

1. Start Internet Explorer and type the URL for your organization's SharePoint server. The Start page will open. If you want your publishing site located as a subsite to another site, navigate to that site.
2. Click the **Settings** menu and click the **Site Contents** option. The Site Contents page will appear.
3. In the Subsites section, click the **new subsite** link. The New SharePoint Site page will open.
4. In the Title field, type a title for the publishing site. The title of your site should be descriptive and can be up to about 50 letters before becoming intrusive.
5. In the Description field, type a description for your site. The description is like a subtitle that will be displayed on some of the pages. It should further clarify the title so that anyone can understand the site's purpose.
6. In the URL Name field, type a short, descriptive name for your group. This will become part of the full website address for your new publishing site. Some features don't work with long URLs, so keeping the name in the URL short but descriptive is recommended.
7. In the Select a template section, click the **Publishing** tab. The Publishing templates will appear.

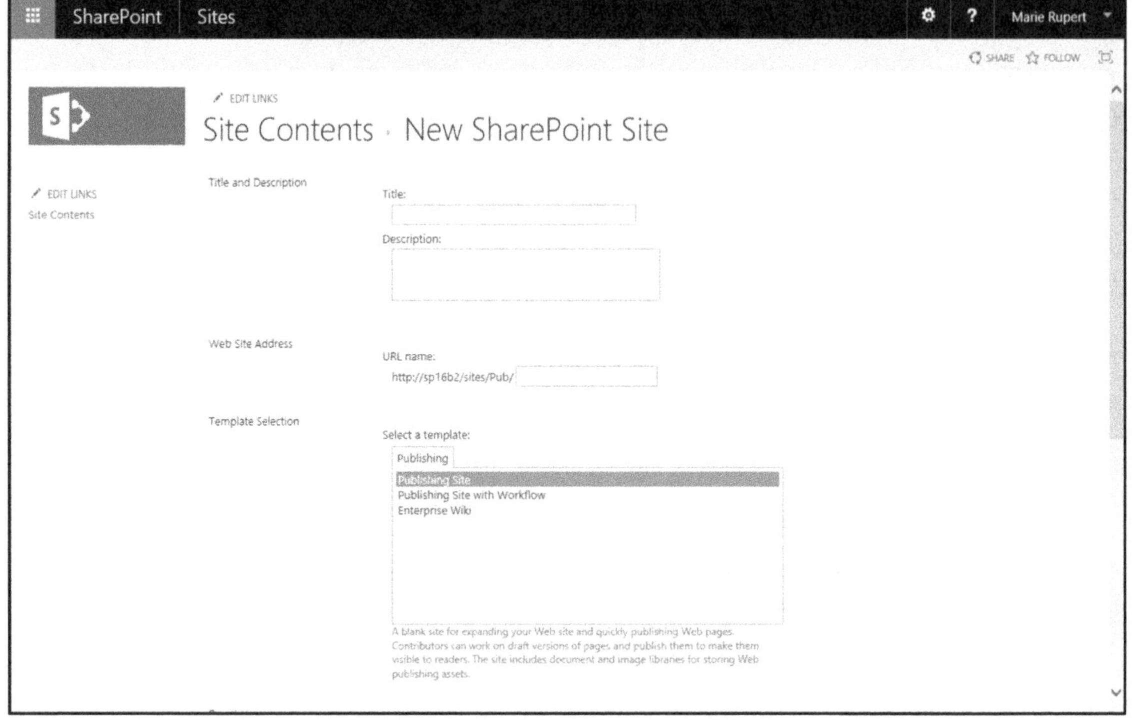

Figure 1: The New SharePoint Site Page

8. Select **Publishing Site** as the template.

Note: If the Publishing tab is not available, a SharePoint administrator may need to activate the SharePoint Server Publishing Infrastructure site collection features.

9. In the User Permissions field, select the **Use same permissions as parent site** option. You can change to unique permissions later as shown in "Assign Users to a Group."

10. In the Use the top link bar from the parent site field, select the **Yes** option.

11. Click **Create**. The "Working on it..." screen will briefly appear, followed by the new Publishing Site page.

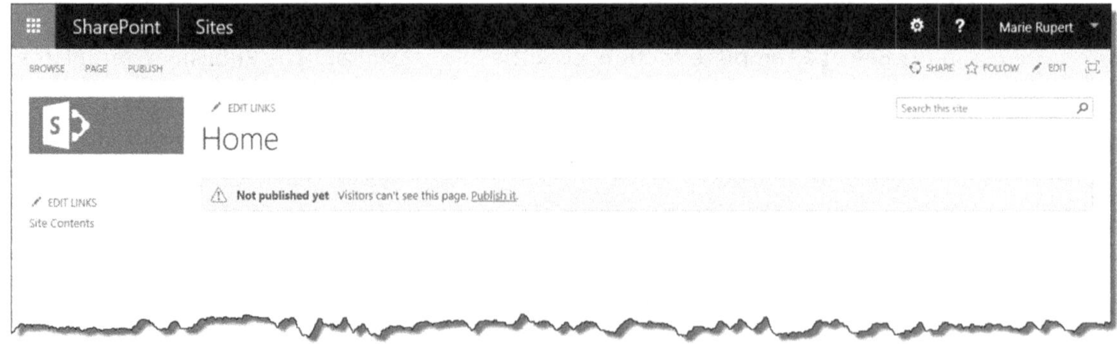

Figure 2: The New Publishing Site Home Page

Exception: If the desired publishing site template is not listed, you do not have specific permission to access that site template, or the site collection's publishing features have not been activated. Check the permissions settings to ensure you have the appropriate access rights for creating publishing sites, or contact your SharePoint administrator regarding the site collection publishing features.

Task: Create a Content Page

Purpose: At the core SharePoint is a web platform and content management system. Creating content, whether you're in a wiki or publishing site, is easy. You can create additional content pages and then add the content and apply metadata to the page.

Example: The new Action Marketing Group's Internet manager needs to create a new page for an upcoming promotion.

Steps:

1. Start Internet Explorer and type the URL for your organization's SharePoint server. The Start page will open.
2. Navigate to the publishing site. The publishing site's home page will open.
3. Click the **Settings** menu and select **Add a Page**. The Add a page dialog box will open.

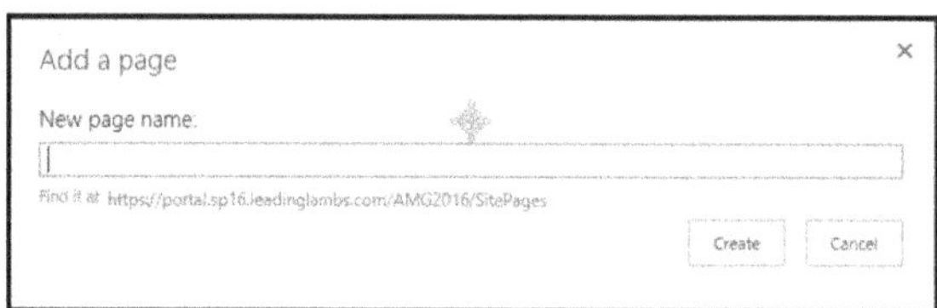

Figure 1: The Add a Page Dialog Box

4. In the New page name field, enter a name for the new page. This is used as the listing for this page throughout SharePoint.
5. Click **Create**. The new page will open in Edit Mode, with the Format Text ribbon open.

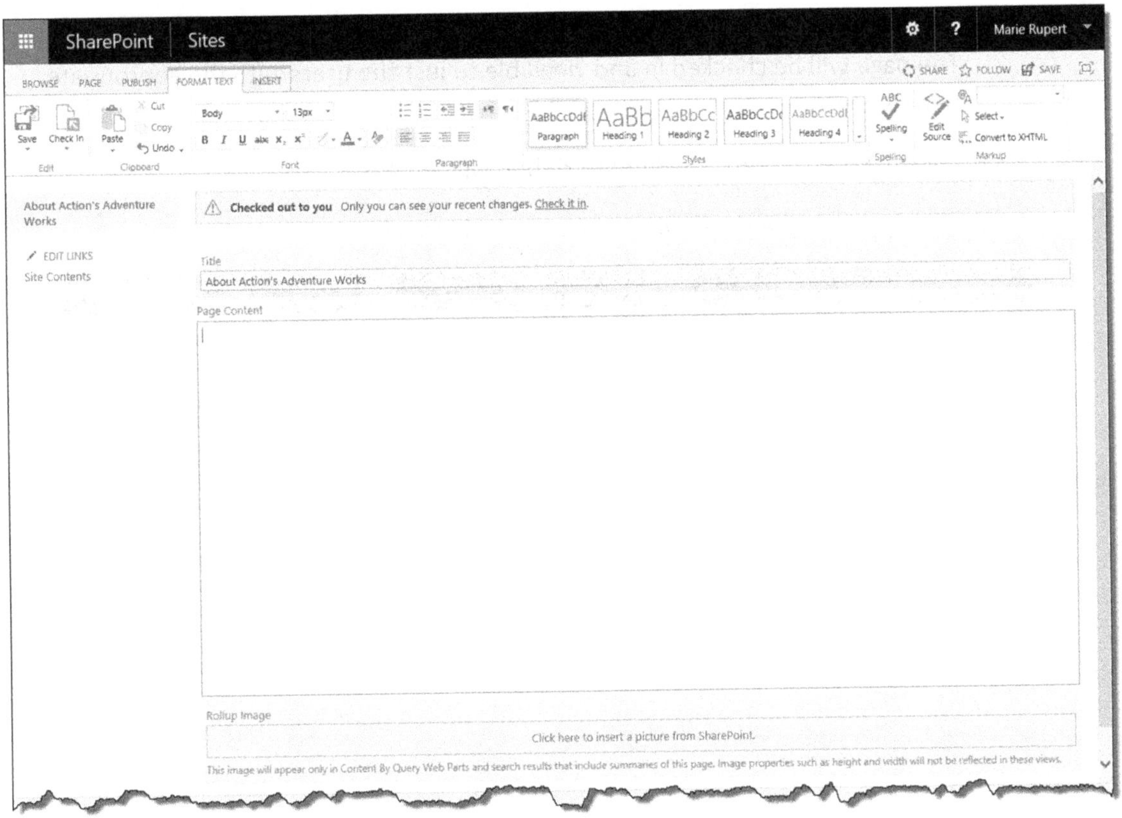

Figure 2: The New Page with the Format Text Ribbon

6. Click the **Page** tab. The Page ribbon will appear.
7. Click the **Page Layout** button. A list of possible layouts for the page will appear.
8. Select the layout option you want to use. The layout of the page will be adjusted.
9. Enter the content on the page, using the available tools to format the text.
10. Click the **Check In** button. The Check In dialog box will appear.

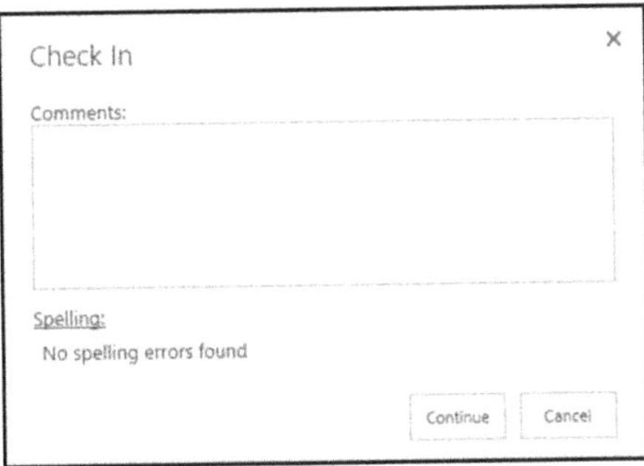

Figure 3: The Check In Dialog Box

11. Enter any comments you might have for this version of the page and click **Continue**. The page will be checked in and viewable to just the users with the appropriate permission.

12. Click the **Publish** tab. The Publish ribbon will appear.

13. Click **Publish**. The page will now be viewable to all users.

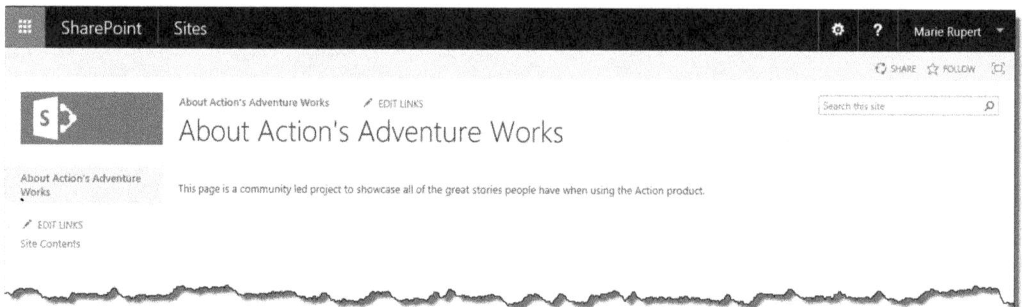

Figure 4: The Published Page

Task: Edit Page Content

Purpose: The authoring experience in SharePoint extends to editing content. You can quickly edit a page from the browser.

Example: The human resource manager at the Action Marketing Group needs to update the recognized holidays for the new year.

Steps:

1. Start Internet Explorer and navigate to the page you want to edit. The page will open.
2. Click the **Settings** menu gear icon, and then the **Edit Page** option. The page will open in Edit Mode and the Format Text ribbon will appear.

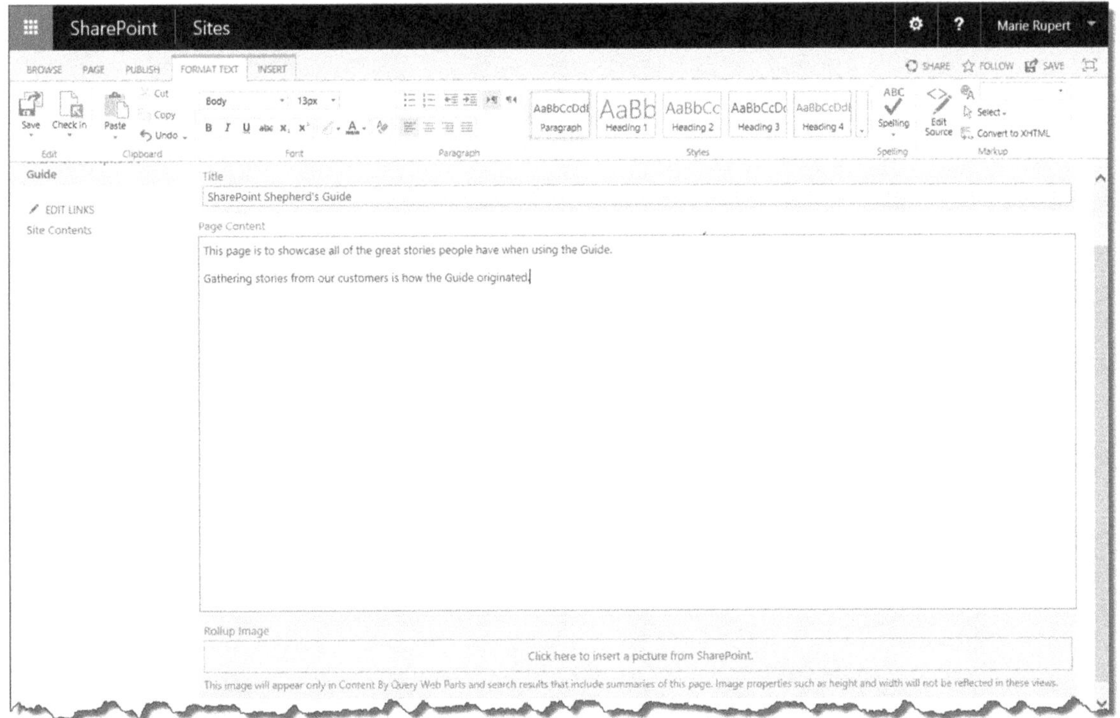

Figure 1: The Page in Edit Mode

3. Edit the page's content as needed.
4. When finished, click the **Check In** button. The Check In dialog box will appear.
5. Enter any comments you might have for this version of the page and click **Continue**. The page will be checked in and viewable to just the users with the appropriate permission.

6. Click the **Publish** tab. The Publish ribbon will appear.
7. Click **Publish**. The page will be now viewable to all users.

Task: Spell Check Page Content

Purpose: SharePoint has integrated spell checking. Like the spell checking in Microsoft Word, it helps to ensure that the words are all spelled correctly, even if they may occasionally not be the right meaning.

Example: The Action Marketing Group intranet manager checks the spelling of the About us page before publishing.

Steps:

1. Start Internet Explorer and navigate to the page you want to edit. The page will open.
2. Click the **Settings** menu, and then the **Edit Page** option. The page will open in Edit Mode and the Format Text ribbon will appear.
3. Edit the page content as needed.
4. In the Format Text ribbon, click the **Spelling** icon. The Spell Check dialog box will appear, notifying you of any spelling errors.

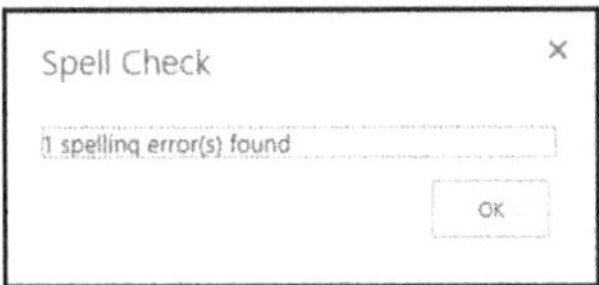

Figure 1: The Spell Check Dialog Box

5. Click **OK**. The Spell Check dialog box will close, and the spelling errors will be highlighted on the page with a red squiggly underline.

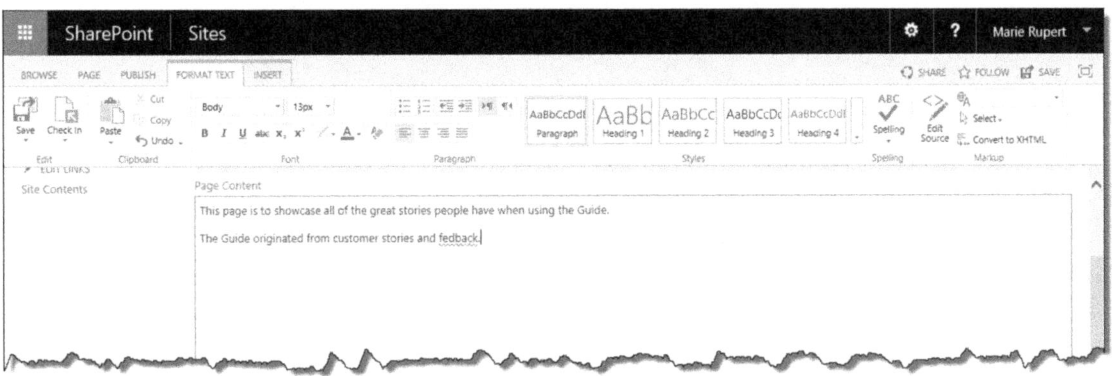

Figure 2: The Highlighted Spelling Errors on the Page

6. Click on each error to see suggested spellings. You can select a suggested word or choose to ignore the error.

7. When the errors are corrected, click the **Check In** button. The Check In dialog box will appear.
8. Enter any comments you might have for this version of the page and click **Continue**. The page will be checked in and viewable to all users with the appropriate permission.
9. Click the **Publish** tab. The Publish ribbon will appear.
10. Click **Publish**. The page will be now viewable to all users.

Task: Add an Image to a Content Page

Purpose: Reading large blocks of text can be exhausting. Adding images helps to make your pages more interesting. SharePoint supports both inline images as well as images that are a part of the structured data of a publishing page.

Example: The plant manager at the Action Marketing Group has a new plant photo showing the new line that he wants to add to the facility page to showcase the new line.

Steps:

1. Start Internet Explorer and navigate to the SharePoint page you want to edit. The page will open.
2. Click the **Settings** menu gear icon, and then the **Edit Page** option. The page will open in Edit Mode and the Format Text Ribbon will appear.
3. Click the **Insert** tab. The Insert ribbon will appear.

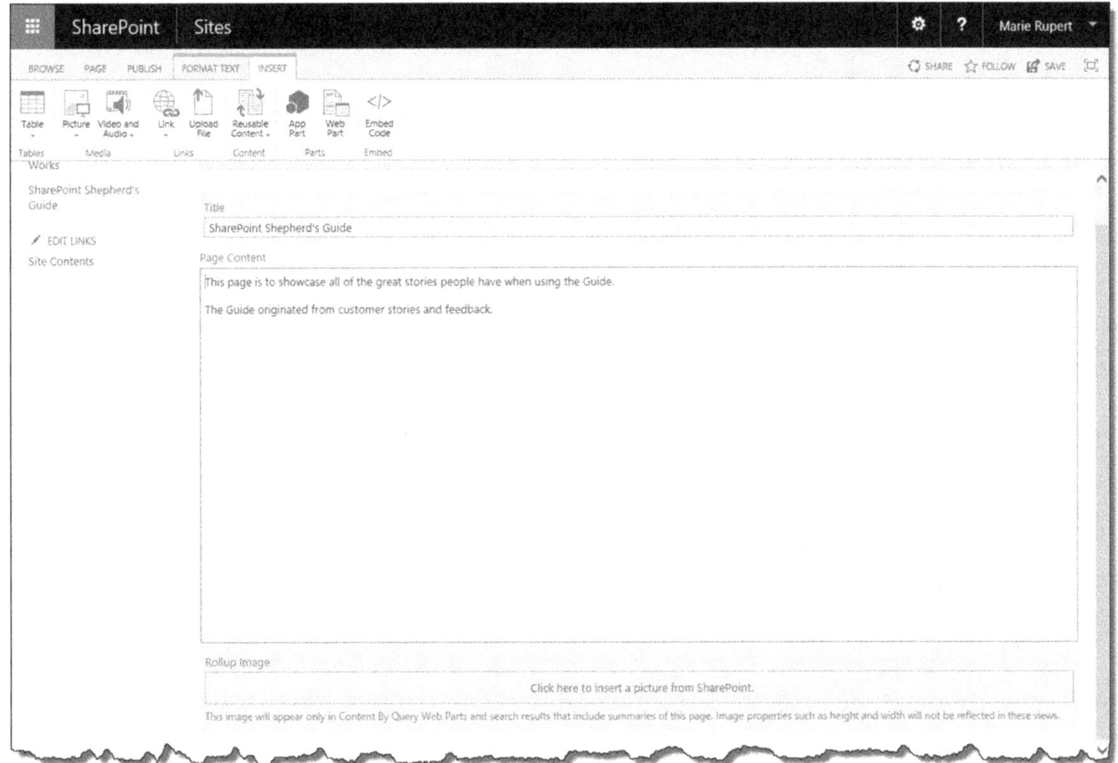

Figure 1: The Insert Ribbon

4. Click the **Picture** button. The Picture menu will appear.
5. Click the **From Computer** button. The Upload Image dialog box will appear.

6. Click **Browse**. The Choose File to Upload dialog box will appear.

7. Select a file and click **Open**. The file and its file path will appear in the Choose a file field.

8. In the Destination Library field, select the **Site Collection Images** option.

9. Click **OK**. The Site Collection Images dialog box will appear.

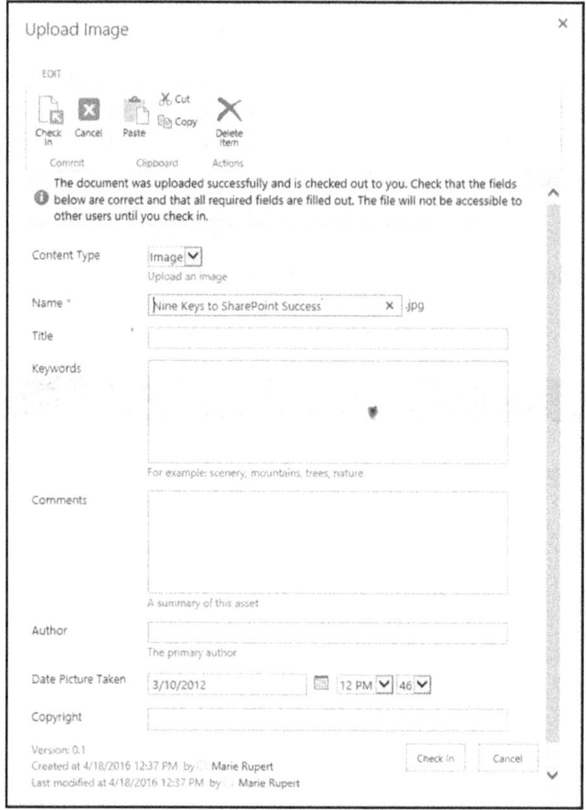

Figure 2: The Site Collection Images Dialog Box

10. Add any pertinent information and click **Check in**. The Site Collection Images dialog box will close and the image will appear in the Page Content field at the insertion point.

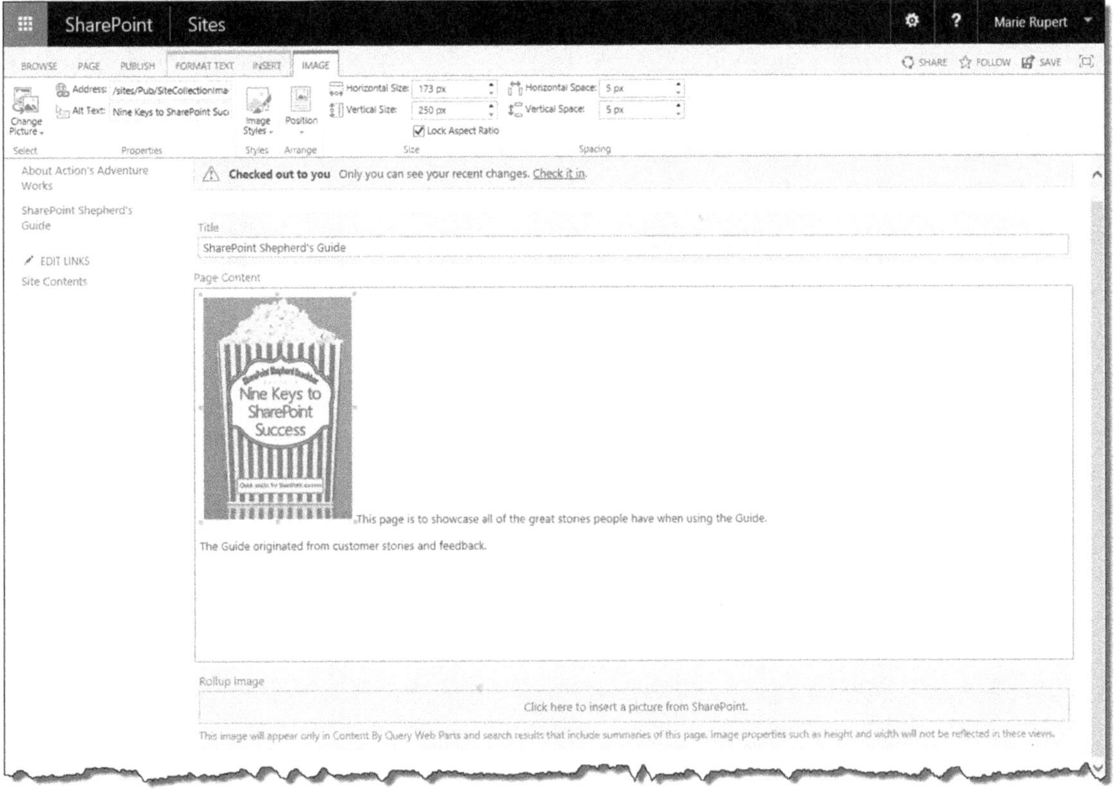

Figure 3: The Inserted Image

11. Click the arrow under the **Position** button to open the drop-down menu, and in the Float section, select **Right**. The image will shift to the right side of the page with the text wrapping around it.
12. Click the **Format Text** tab to open the Format Text ribbon, and then select the **Check In** button. The Check In dialog box will appear.
13. Enter any comments you might have for this version of the page and click **Continue**. The page will be checked in and viewable to all users with the appropriate permission.
14. Click the **Publish** tab. The Publish ribbon will appear.
15. Click **Publish**. The page will be now viewable to all users.

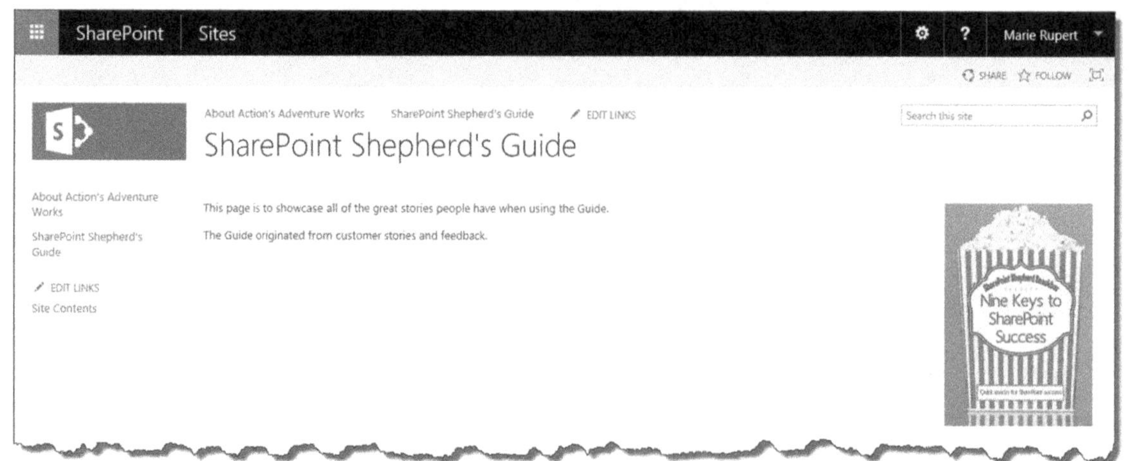

Figure 4: The Updated Page with Inserted Image

Task: Add Publishing Approvers

Purpose: SharePoint allows for numerous publishing models, including direct publishing and workflow-based approval. The default approval workflow will ask for the SharePoint Approvers group to approve pages. You can control who is in this Approvers group. Alternatively, you can create a custom workflow with SharePoint Designer.

Example: The Action Marketing Group has hired a compliance officer responsible for ensuring regulatory compliance that needs to review all of the pages published to the Internet website.

Steps:

1. Start Internet Explorer and type the URL for your organization's SharePoint server. The Start page will open.
2. Navigate to the publishing site. The publishing site's home page will open.
3. Click the **Settings** menu gear icon and select **Site settings**. The Site Settings page will open.

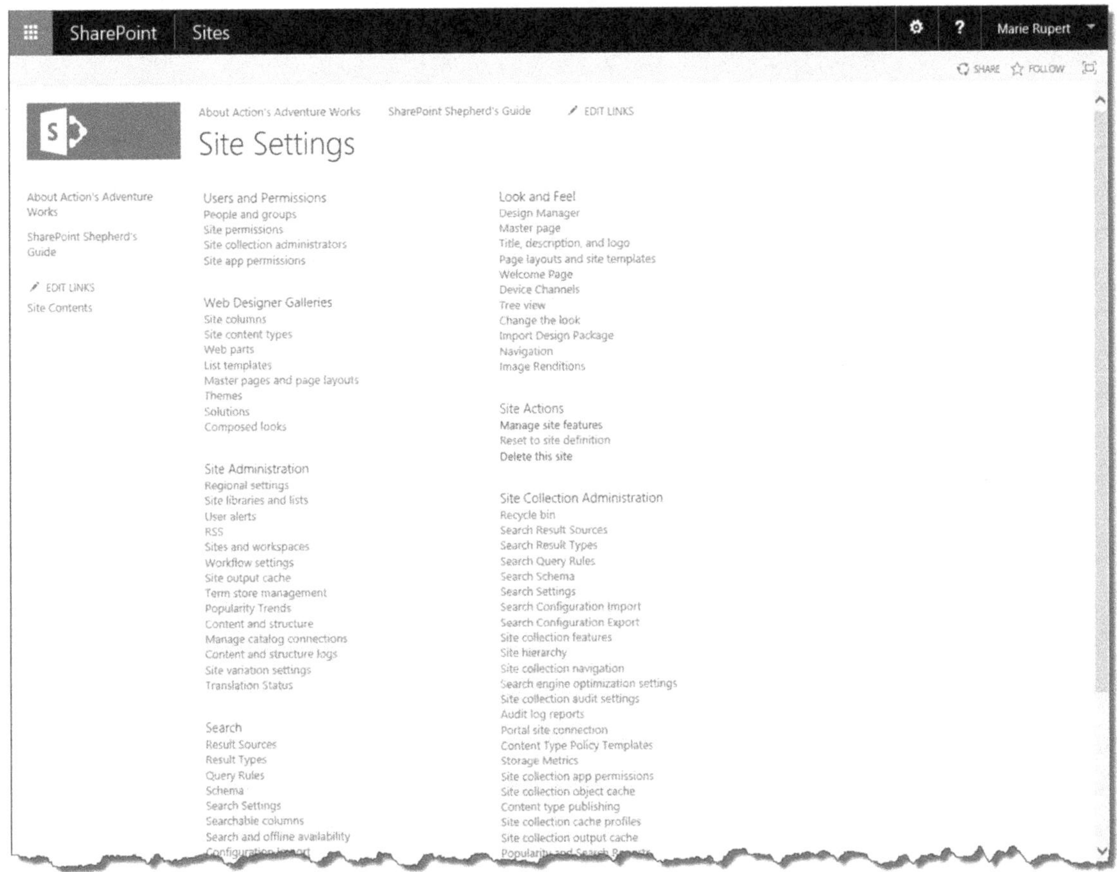

Figure 1: The Site Settings Page

4. In the Users and Permissions section click the **Site permissions** link. The Permissions page will open.

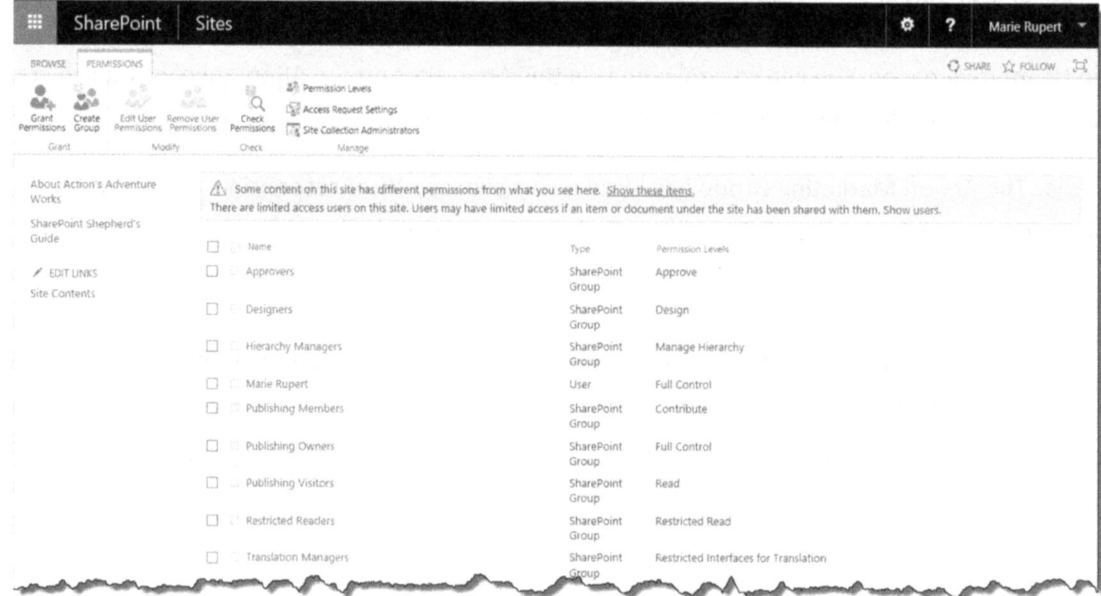

Figure 2: The Permissions Ribbon on the Permissions Page

5. Click the **Approvers** group link. The page for the Approvers group will appear.
6. Click the **New** link. The Share dialog box will open.
7. In the Add people to the Approvers group field, type in the name of a user. If the user is part of the authenticated network, their name will be underlined, which means they are authorized. If a user is not recognized, a red squiggly line will appear. You will need to correct the user name.
8. Add additional names as needed.
9. Click **Share**. The Share dialog box will close and the user(s) will appear in the Approvers group's page.

Task: Submit Page for Publishing Approval

Purpose: SharePoint's models for publishing allows the site administrator to decide that pages must run through an approval workflow. If your administrator requires an approval workflow, here's how you start that process.

Example: The Action Product Line home page is ready to be formally published, but must first be submitted for approval.

Steps:

1. Start Internet Explorer and navigate to the page you want to edit. The page will open.
2. Click the **Settings** menu gear icon, then the **Edit page** option. The page will open in Edit Mode and the Format Text ribbon will appear.
3. Edit the page content as needed.
4. When finished, click the **Check In** button. The Check In dialog box will appear.

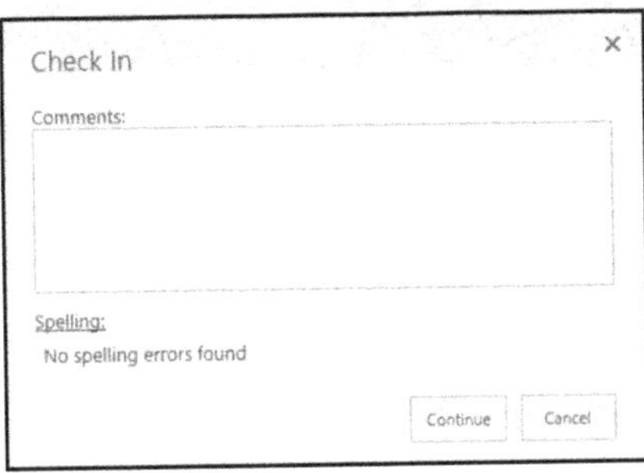

Figure 1: The Check In Dialog Box

5. Enter any comments you might have for this version of the page and click **Continue**. The page will be checked in.
6. Click the **Publish** tab to open the Publish ribbon, then click the **Submit** button. The Start "Approval" workflow default page will open.

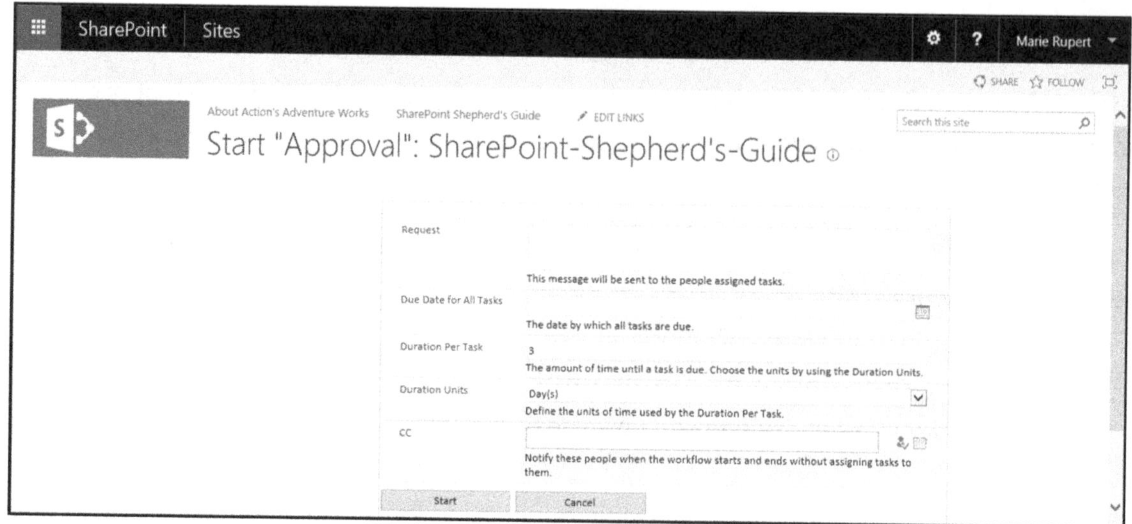

Figure 2: Start Page Approval Page

7. Fill in the necessary information in the fields and click Start. After a brief processing time, the page will be submitted to the approval workflow.

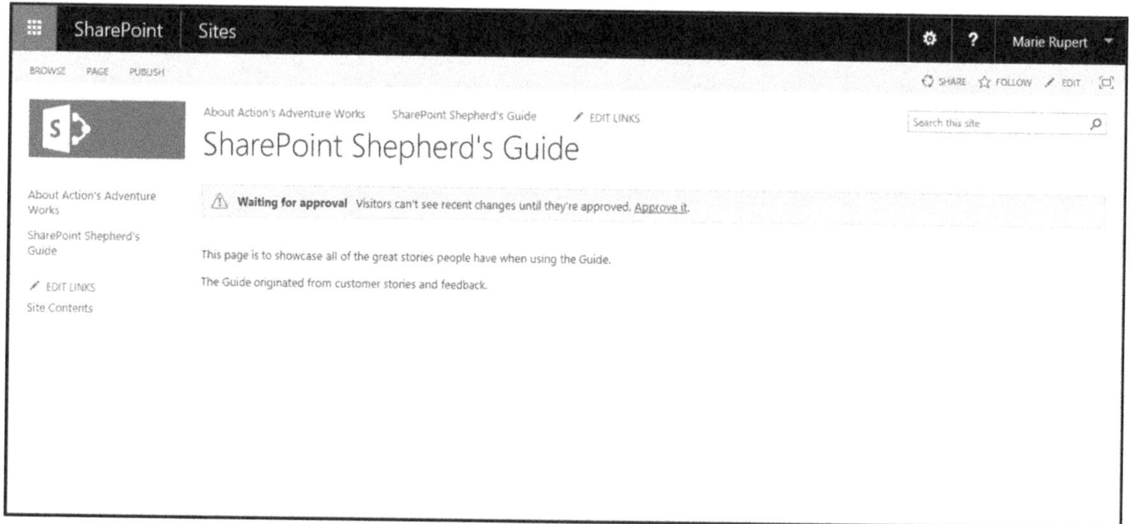

Figure 3: The Page Awaiting Approval

Task: Approve Content for Publication

Purpose: When publishing approval workflows are enabled and you are in the approvers group you'll receive emails to indicate that your approval is necessary on a page. Once you have reviewed the content on the page, you need to complete your approval of the content for publishing.

Example: The Action Product Line home page has been submitted for approval and will need to be approved for publication.

Steps:

1. Start Internet Explorer and type the URL for your organization's SharePoint server. The Start page will open.
2. Navigate to the page to be approved. The page will open.
3. Click the **Publish** tab. The Publish ribbon will appear.
4. Click the **Approve** button. The Approve dialog box will appear, with a place to comment on the approval.

Figure 1: The Approve Dialog Box

5. Enter any comments about the approval and click **Continue**. The approval task page will appear.

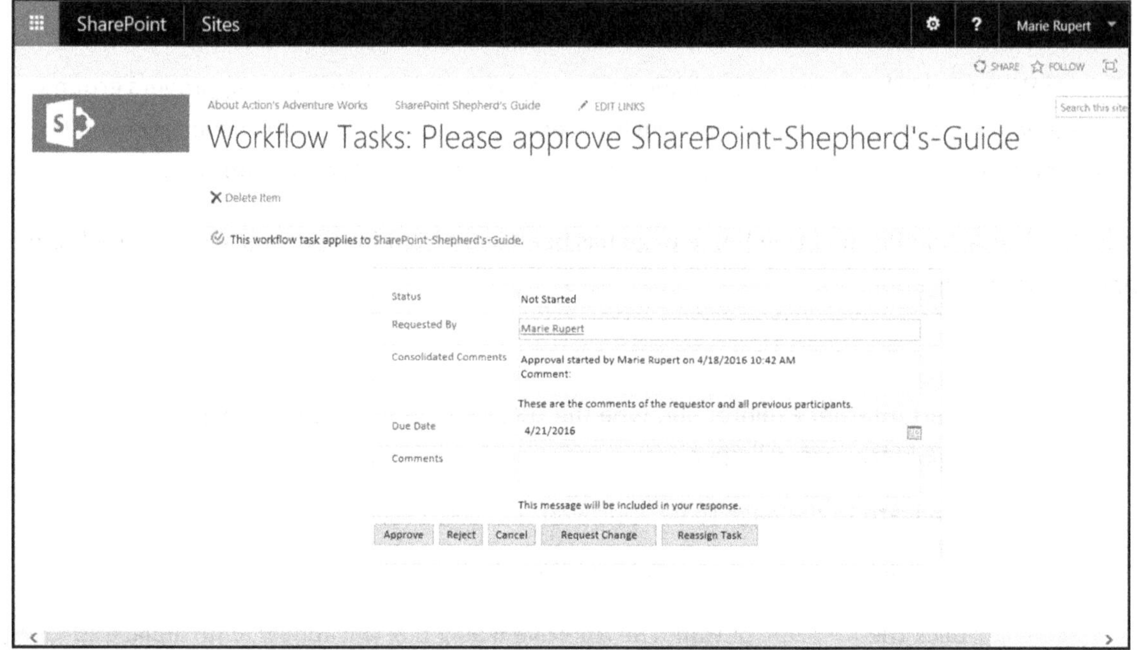

Figure 2: The Approval Task

6. If the page is satisfactory, enter any pertinent information in the fields and click the Approve button. After a brief period of processing, the task will be approved and the page published.

Exception: If the Approve button is disabled, you may be trying to approve your own changes or you do not have specific permission to change content within this particular workflow. In addition, the Publishing features for the site may not be activated. Have another authorized user approve your changes, or check the permissions settings to ensure you have the appropriate access rights. Contact the SharePoint administrator to make sure the Publishing features for the site are activated.

Task: Change Page Schedule or Expiration Date

Purpose: SharePoint allows you to define the date and time that pages become available and when they become unavailable. This is useful when you need to have a page for a promotion disappear – or when you need to have a special offer show up at some point in the future.

Example: The Action Marketing Group has a contest page that only needs to run for three months, so it will be scheduled to expire.

Steps:

1. Start Internet Explorer and type the URL for your organization's SharePoint server. The Start page will open.
2. Navigate to the publishing site. The publishing site's home page will open.
3. Navigate to the page you want to schedule. The page will open.
4. Click the **Settings** menu gear icon and then the **Edit page** option. The page will open in Edit Mode and the Format Text ribbon will appear.
5. In the ribbon click the **Publish** tab. The Publish ribbon will appear.
6. Click the **Schedule** button. The Schedule Page dialog box will appear.

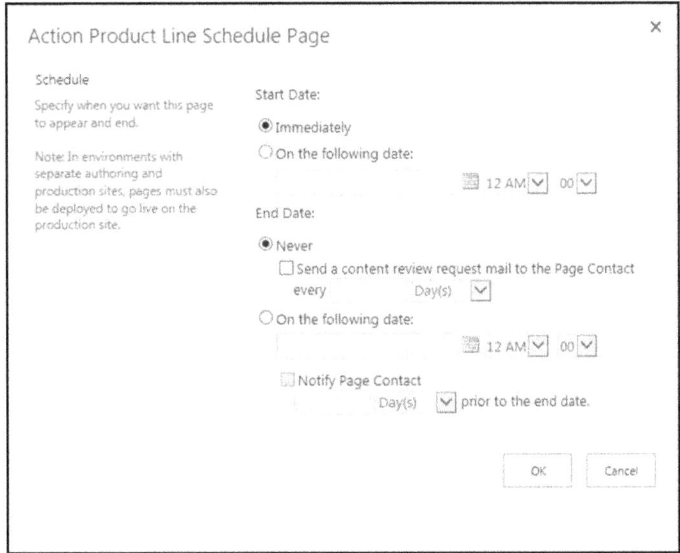

Figure 1: The Schedule Page Dialog Box

7. Set the Start and End Dates for the desired start and expiration dates for the page.
8. Click **OK**. The Schedule Page dialog box will close and the page will need to be submitted for approval.

Note: Upon approval by the designated person, the page will sit in a Scheduled status (i.e., the Content Approval field will indicate Scheduled), rather than Approved, until the scheduled start date. This is to ensure only Approved pages are visible to readers. Once the expiration date occurs, the page is put back in Draft status for the same reason.

Exception: If the **Schedule** button is disabled, you may be trying to approve your own changes or you do not have specific permission to change content within this particular workflow. It may be that the item scheduling feature is not enabled in this library. Have another authorized user approve your changes, or check the permissions settings to ensure you have the appropriate access rights. If permissions are not the issue, contact the SharePoint administrator to have item scheduling enabled for the library.

Task: Manually Start a Workflow for Publication

Purpose: Even in scenarios where a content author would normally be able to approve content, there may be times when they want to get approval from others. SharePoint allows content creators to manually start an approval workflow.

Example: The Action Product Line page is being updated to make some product claims that should be validated by the legal department. The content manager wants to send the page for legal review.

Steps:

1. Start Internet Explorer and type the URL for your organization's SharePoint server. The Start page will open.
2. Navigate to the publishing site. The publishing site's home page will open.
3. Navigate to the page that needs a workflow started.
4. If the editing tools are not available, click the **Settings** menu gear icon and select **Edit page**. The Page ribbon will be displayed.
5. Click the **Check In** button to check the document back in and enter check in comments.
6. Click the **Publish** tab. The Publish ribbon will appear.
7. Click the **Start a Workflow** button. The Workflows page will open.

Note: Workflows for sites must be set up by the system administrator or someone with design rights. If you do not have any workflows available, contact the administrator and discuss what workflow templates you would like to have activated.

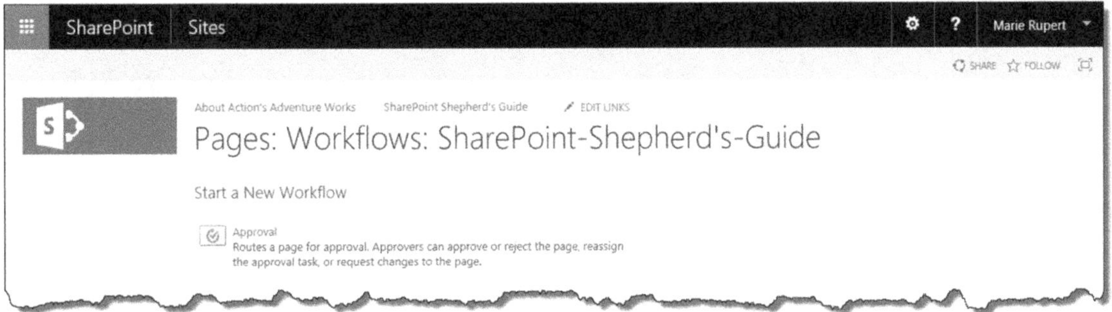

Figure 1: The Workflows Page

8. Click the **Approval** template link. The Start "Approval" page will open.
9. Fill in the pertinent information. Pay particular attention to the Due Date and Duration fields.

10. Type in the name of any users you want to follow along in the approval process in the CC field and click on the Check Names icon. If the user is part of the authenticated network, their name will be underlined, which means they are authorized. If a user is not recognized, a red squiggly line will appear. You will need to correct the user name.
11. Click Start. The workflow will be started and the page will move to Waiting for Approval status.

Exception: If the page does not change to Waiting for Approval status, it may need to be refreshed, so the cache for the page and the page's status will be in sync. Use the shortcut Ctrl+F5 in your browser to update the status of the page.

Task: Create a Custom Permission Level

Purpose: SharePoint's permission system is based on a set of atomic permissions which are grouped into permission levels like design, edit, contribute, and read. These are great when you want to assign a set of permissions that match what's in the predefined level to a group. However, when you need something that's slightly more granular, you can create your own permission level to match your exact needs. See Appendix E for more information on the atomic permissions and the out of the box permission levels.

Example: By default, the Contribute permission level has the ability to delete versions. The Action Marketing Group's compliance department wants to prevent users from doing this to ease their investigations.

Steps:

1. Start Internet Explorer and type the URL for your organization's SharePoint server. The Start page will open.

2. Navigate to the site that needs a new permission level.

Note: For sites that inherit permissions from the parent, navigate to the parent site.

3. Select the **Settings** menu gear icon and select **Site Settings**. The Site Settings page will open.

4. In the Users and Permissions section, click the **Site permissions** link. The Permissions page will open.

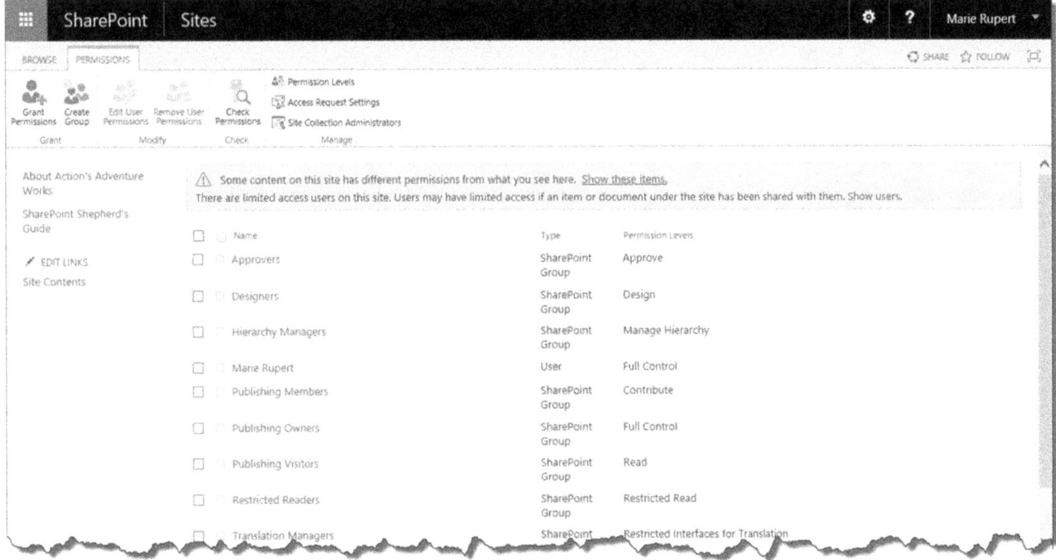

Figure 1: The Permission Ribbon Open on the Permissions Page

5. In the Permissions ribbon, click the **Permission Levels** button. The Permission Levels page will open.

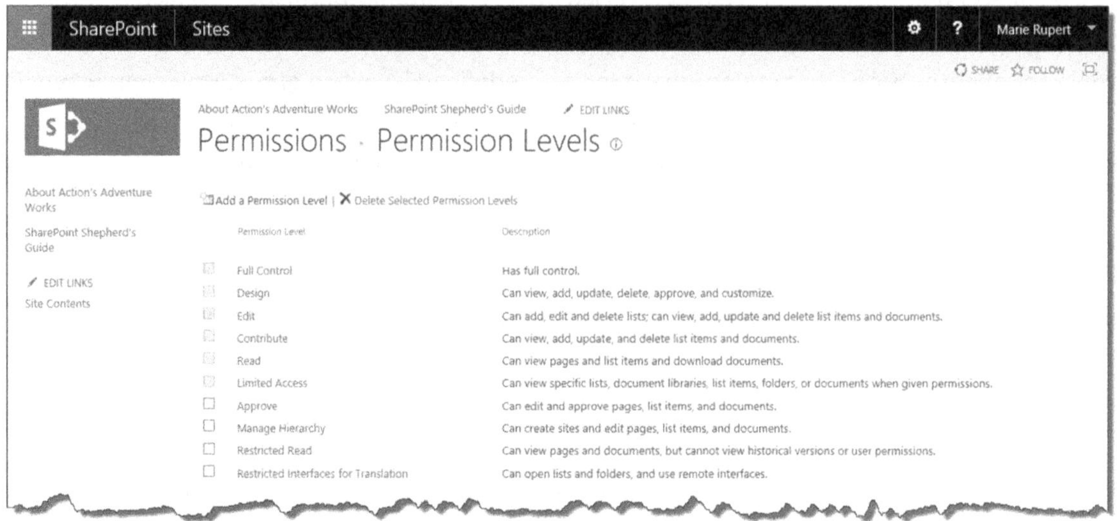

Figure 2: The Permission Levels Page

6. Click the **Add a Permission Level** link. The Add a Permission Level page will appear.

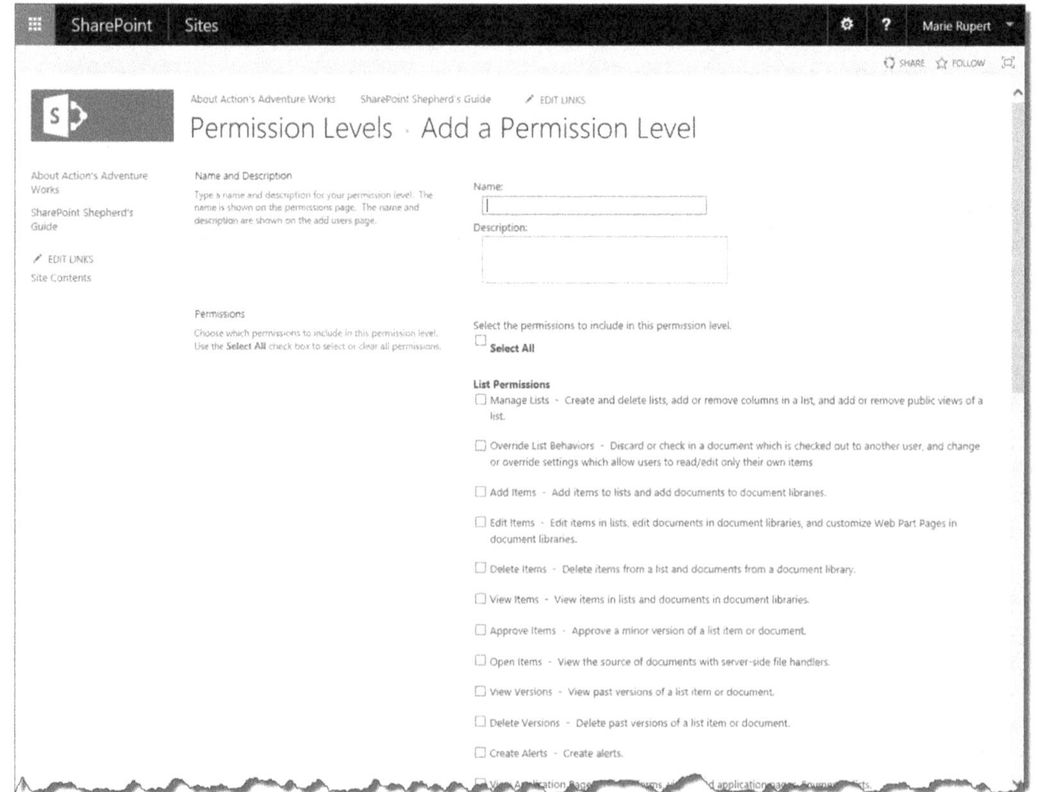

Figure 3: The Add a Permission Level Page

7. Add a Name and Description for the new permission level.
8. Select the permission options that you want to allow for this permission level by clicking on the checkboxes next to their names.
9. Click Create. The new permission level will be created. You can now add users to this group so they can make updates to your site based on the permissions you set.

Publish Web Content: Site Owners

Site owners have more responsibilities and more capabilities than SharePoint site authors. Owners can create whole sites, and modify existing sites at a deeper level.

In this section, you'll learn how to:

- Change a Site Theme: As the owner of a site, you have the ability to make broad changes to the look and feel of your site.
- Change a Site Logo: When SharePoint builds a site from a template, it includes many placeholders, such as images and logos, to mark the general feel of a site.
- Change a Site Master Page: SharePoint site templates include a number of master page settings, which define the basic layout options for the site.
- Add Cascading Style Sheets: If you don't prefer what SharePoint has to offer in terms of style libraries, you can attach your own CSS document to customize the site.
- Organize Pages in a Web Site: As you edit a website, you may discover that you will need to re-organize your site to create a better flow of information and traffic.
- Allow Users to Create Different Subsites: SharePoint will, by default, limit the number of templates that a user can access when creating a subsite.
- Create a Subsite: If you have the appropriate permissions, you can create a new subsite fairly easily in SharePoint.
- Customize Publishing Site Navigation: To make things very clear to site visitors, you need to make sure your navigation tools are laid out properly.
- Add the Content Query Web Part: All SharePoint Sites come with a number of tools to assist users, such as the Content Query Web Part.
- Add the Summary Links Web Part: Another useful Web Part is the Summary Links Web Part, which lets you manually add links to articles and pages on your site, as well as to other sites.
- Export a Web Part: Export your Web Part for use on another page.
- Import a Web Part: Many SharePoint developers have created customized Web Parts that can be easily plugged in to an existing SharePoint site.

Task: Change a Site Theme

Purpose: SharePoint has the capability to change the colors, fonts, and feel of the site through the use of themes. In addition to the out of the box themes provided with the product, you can download and install new themes to allow you to quickly customize the look and feel of the site.

Example: The Action Marketing Group is looking for something to differentiate its confidential site. The systems administrator will change the site's theme to set it apart from other sites.

Steps:

1. Start Internet Explorer and type the URL for your organization's SharePoint server. The Start page will open.
2. Navigate to the site. The site's home page will open.
3. Click the **Settings** menu gear icon and select **Site Settings**. The Site Settings page will open.

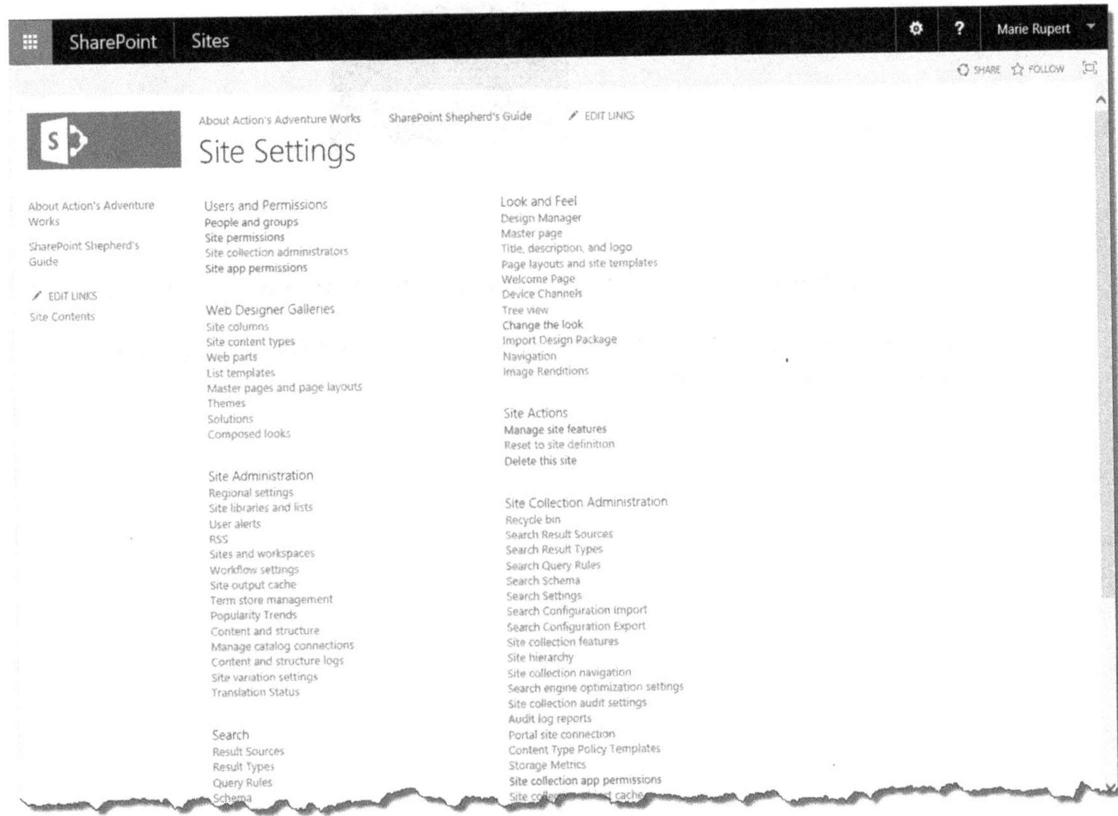

Figure 1: The Site Settings Page

4. In the Look and Feel section, click the **Change the look** link. The Change the look page will open.

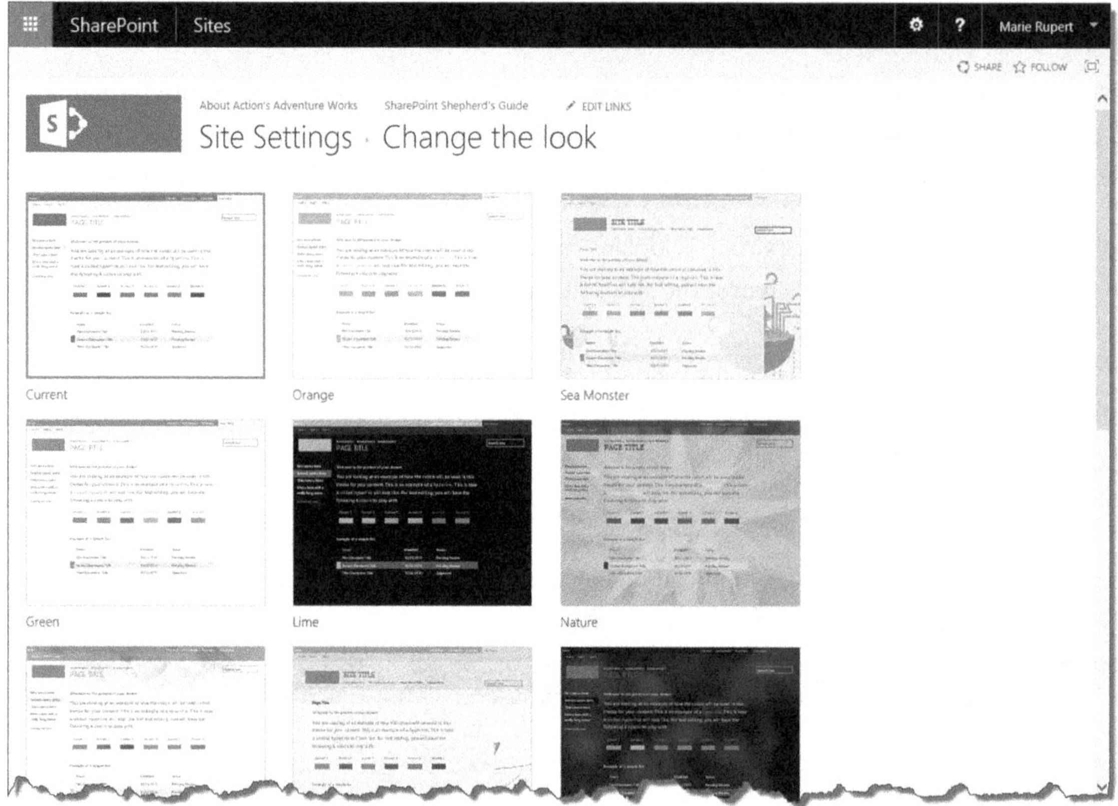

Figure 2: The Site Theme Page

5. Click any of the listed themes. The preview will change to reflect the theme's look.

6. When you have decided on a theme, click Try it out. The Preview page will open, with the new theme applied.

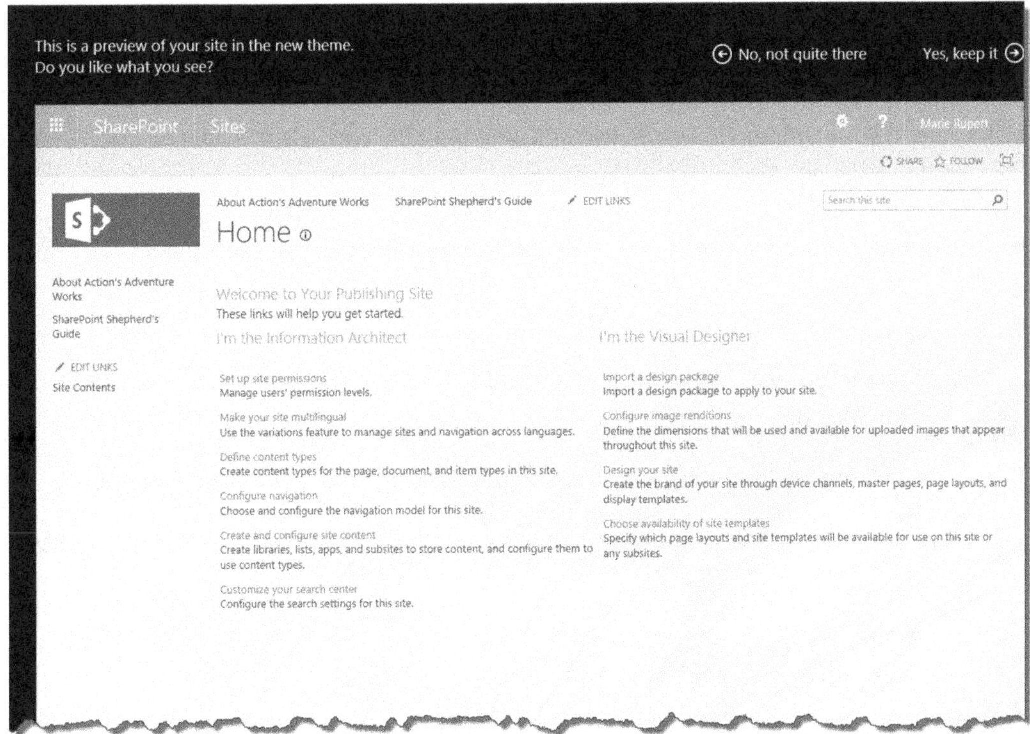

Figure 3: The Preview of the Home Page

7. If you like the theme, click **Yes, keep it**. The Site Settings page will appear with the new theme applied.

Task: Change a Site Logo

Purpose: SharePoint provides a clean professional look – however, SharePoint has a default site logo which won't match you company's brand. By replacing the site logo, it's possible to quickly make a SharePoint site look like it belongs to the organization.

Example: The Action Marketing Group logo will need to be added to the site's pages.

Steps:

1. Start Internet Explorer and type the URL for your organization's SharePoint server. The Start page will open.
2. Navigate to the publishing site. The publishing site's home page will open.
3. Click the **Settings** menu gear icon and select **Site Settings**. The Site Settings page will open.
4. In the Look and Feel section click the **Title, description, and logo** link. The Title, Description, and Logo page will open.

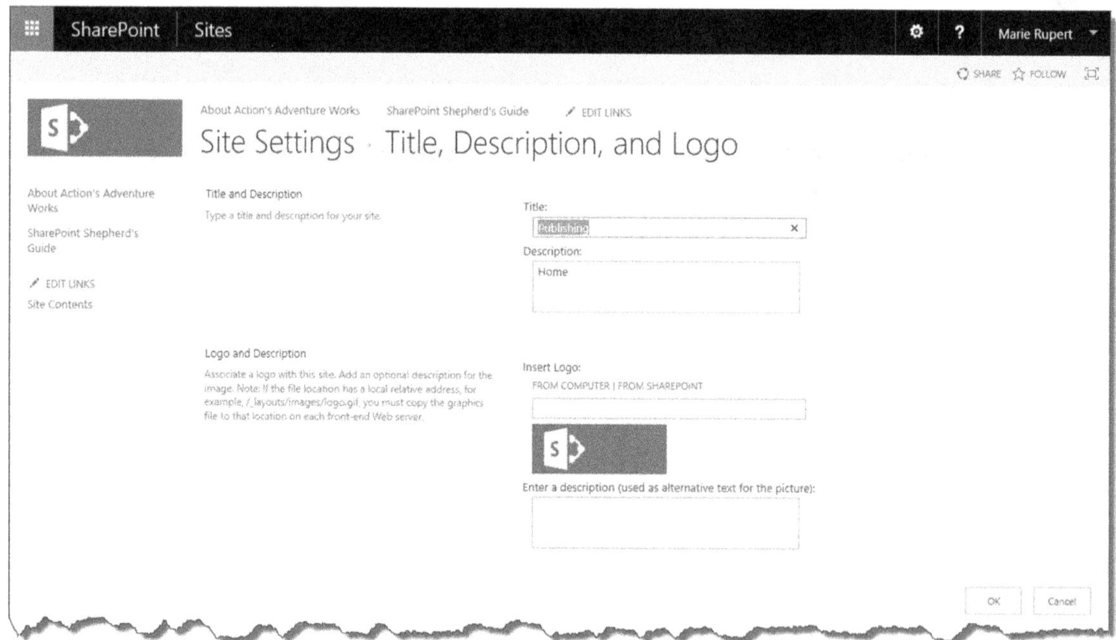

Figure 1: The Title, Description, and Logo Page

5. In the Logo and Description section, click the **From Computer** link. The Add a Document dialog box will open.
6. Click **Browse**. The Choose File to Upload dialog box will open.
7. Navigate to the file you want to use as a logo and select it.

8. Click **Open**. The file's path will appear in the Choose a file field.
9. Click **OK**. The image will appear in the Title, Description, and Logo page.
10. Click **OK**. The Site Settings page will open, with the new logo applied.

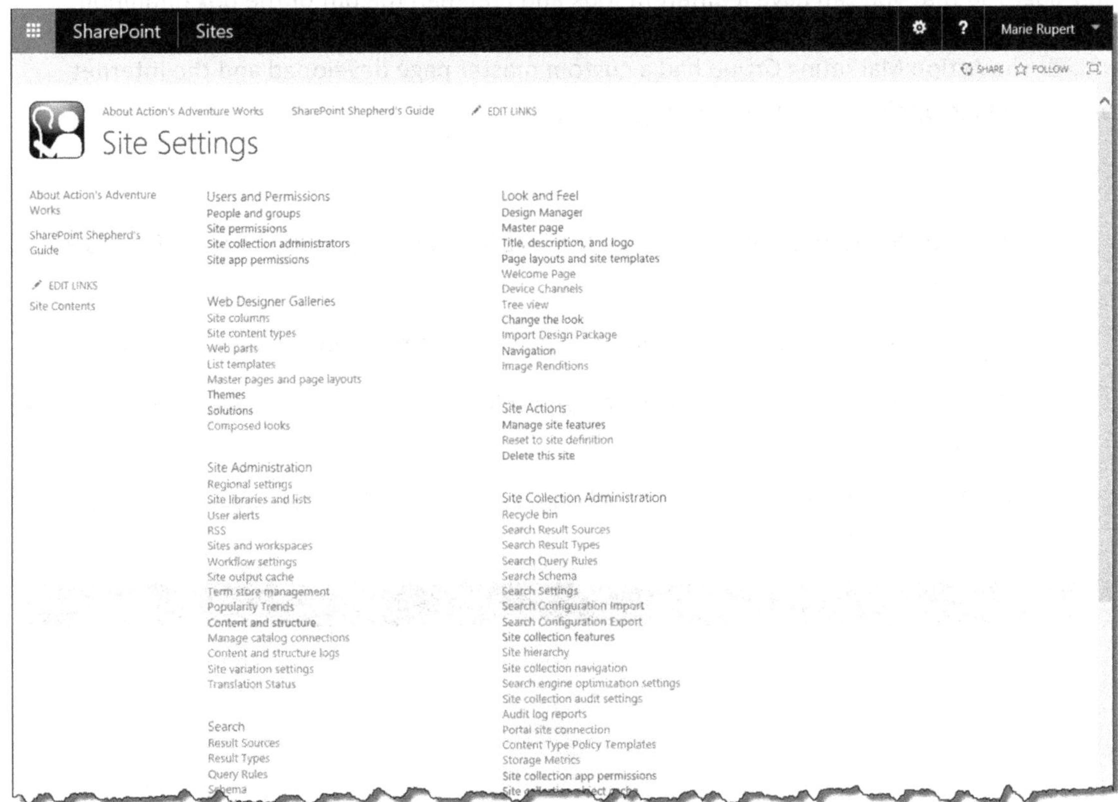

Figure 2: The New Logo Applied to the Site Settings Page

Task: Change a Site Master Page

Purpose: SharePoint master pages control the overall containers on the page, which ultimately control the basic structure of the page – and therefore the site. SharePoint allows you to change master pages so that you can have a different look and feel than the out of the box definition.

Example: The Action Marketing Group had a custom master page developed and the Internet manager wants to apply it to an internal staging site.

Steps:

1. Start Internet Explorer and type the URL for your organization's SharePoint server. The Start page will open.
2. Navigate to the publishing site. The publishing site's home page will open.
3. Click the **Settings** menu gear icon and select **Site Settings**. The Site Settings page will open.
4. In the Look and Feel section, click the **Master page** link. The Site Master Page Settings page will open.

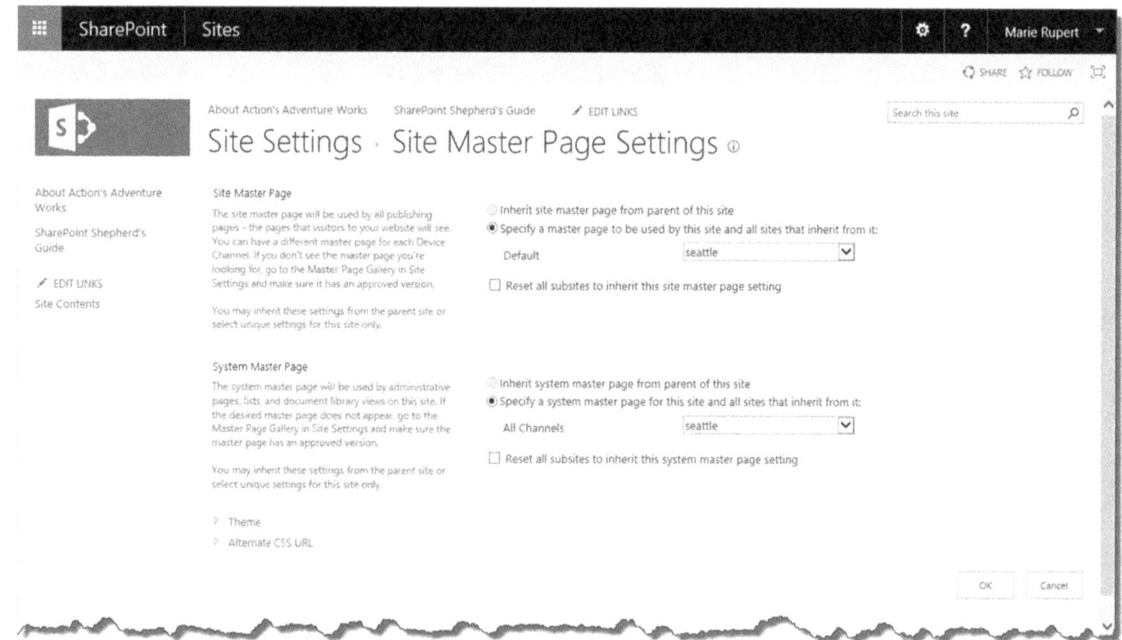

Figure 1: The Site Master Page Settings Page

5. In the Site Master Page section, confirm the **Specify a master page to be used by the site and all sites that inherit from it** option is selected.
6. In the drop down control, select the option you would like (for instance, **oslo**).

7. Click **OK**. The Site Settings page will open and the new master page will be applied.

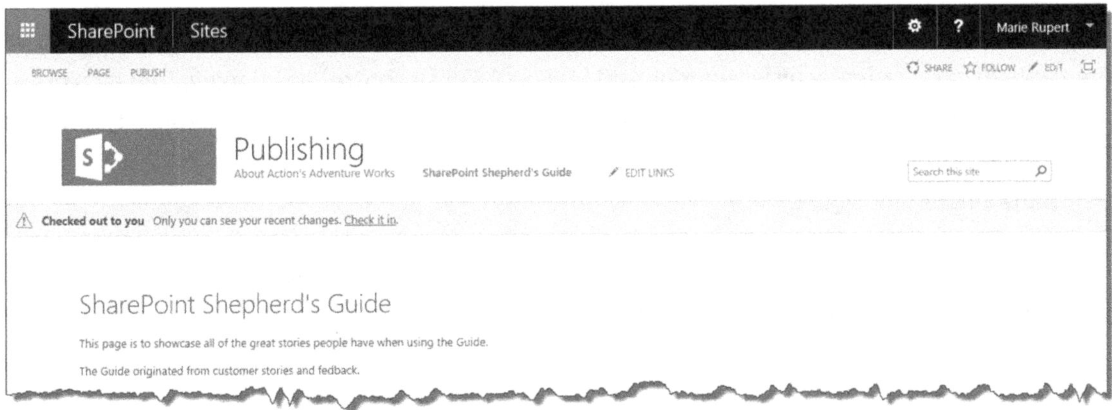

Figure 2: The New Master Page Setting Applied to the Home Page

Task: Add Cascading Style Sheets

Purpose: On the web, much of the styling is handled through Cascading Style Sheets (CSS). With CSS, it is possible to get a radically different look and feel, as CSS can control positioning, fonts, colors, backgrounds, padding, etc. CSS works by a "last one wins" approach; SharePoint defines the standard CSS displayed on a site, but also allows you to add your own CSS at the end of the list so you can override any SharePoint styling.

Example: The Action Marketing Group created a new CSS which they'll use for internal collaboration sites instead of creating a whole new master page.

Steps:

1. Start Internet Explorer and type the URL for your organization's SharePoint server. The Start page will open.
2. Navigate to the publishing site. The publishing site's home page will open.

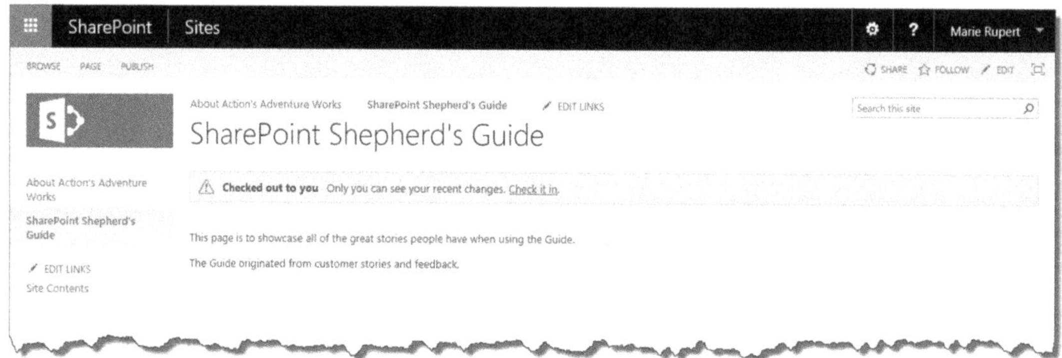

Figure 1: The Publishing Site's Home Page

3. Click the Settings menu gear icon and select Site Settings. The Site Settings page will open.
4. In the Look and Feel section, click the Master page link. The Site Master Page Settings page will open.
5. Click the Alternate CSS URL section heading to expand the section.

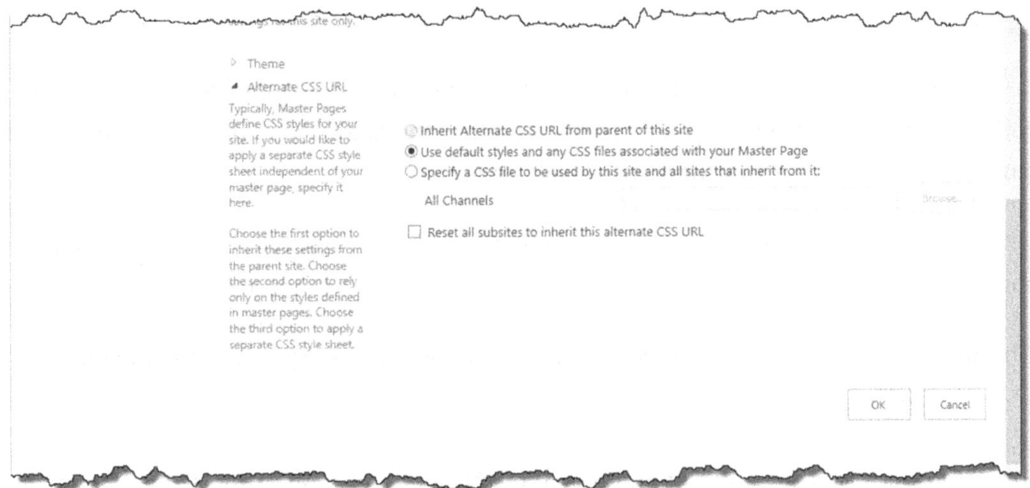

Figure 2: The Alternate CSS URL Section Expanded

6. Click the **Specify a CSS file to be used by this site and all sites that inherit from it** option.
7. Add the URL for the CSS file you would like to use, or click the **Browse** button to open the Select an Asset window.
8. Select the CSS file you would like to use, then click **Insert**. The Select an Asset window will close and the URL will appear in the field.
9. Click **OK**. The Site Settings page will open with the new CSS applied.

Task: Organize Pages in a Web Site

Purpose: Organizations change all the time. Websites should be living and changing over time. SharePoint makes it easy to move pages in a site, whether the goal is to match an organizational change or to accommodate a website's structural change.

Example: The Action Marketing Group is creating a subsite for corporate information and wants to move the pages for contact us, about us, privacy statement, etc., into the new subsite.

Note: This procedure will only work for sites which have the publishing features enabled.

Steps:

1. Start Internet Explorer and type the URL for your organization's SharePoint server. The Start page will open.
2. Navigate to the publishing site. The publishing site's home page will open.
3. Click the Settings menu gear icon and select the Site Settings option.
4. In the Site Administration section, click the Content and Structure link. The Site Content and Structure page will open.

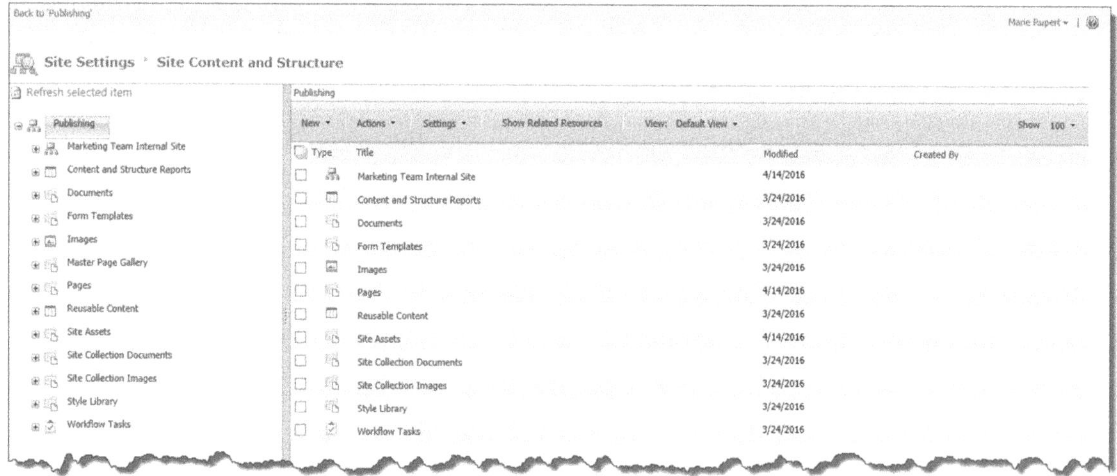

Figure 1: The Site Content and Structure Page

5. In the navigation pane, click the Pages folder. The contents will be displayed in the contents pane.
6. Select the checkboxes for the files you would like to move to select them.
7. Click on the arrow next to Actions to open the drop-down menu, then click the Move option. The Move dialog box will appear.

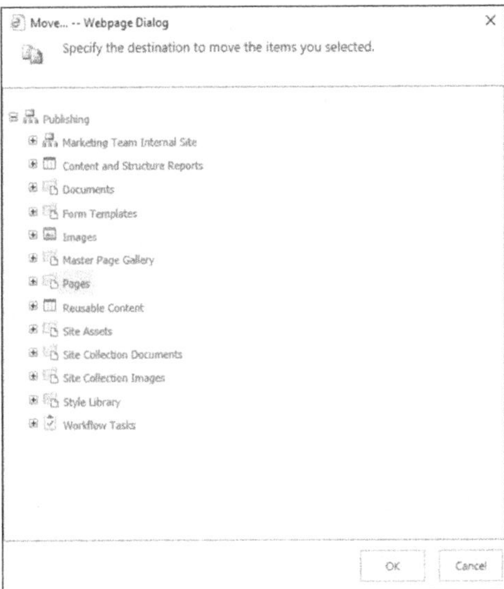

Figure 2: The Move Dialog Box

8. Click the folder for the subsite to which you want to move the files.
9. Click OK. The Move dialog box will close and the files will be moved to the new folder.

Task: Allow Users to Create Different Subsites

Purpose: SharePoint offers a dizzying array of site templates. These templates can be daunting for content managers trying to create a structure for their content. The default behavior for publishing sites is to limit the sites that are available to be used for subsite creation to reduce confusion and to encourage the right uses for the subsites. However, you can change which templates are available.

Example: The Action Marketing Group would like to allow content owners to create sites based off of its custom product template.

Steps:

1. Start Internet Explorer and type the URL for your organization's SharePoint server. The Start page will open.
2. Navigate to the publishing site. The publishing site's home page will open.
3. Click the **Settings** menu gear icon and select **Site Settings**. The Site Settings page will open.
4. In the Look and Feel section, click the **Page layouts and site templates** link. The Page Layout and Site Template Settings page will open.

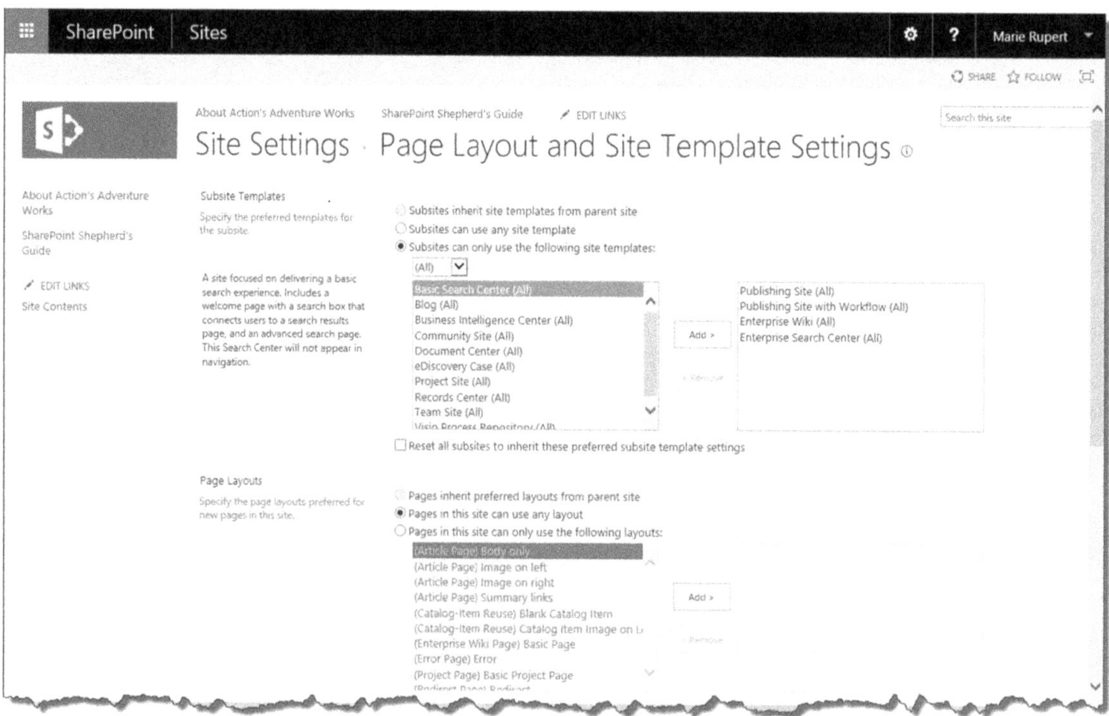

Figure 1: The Page Layout and Site Template Settings Page

5. In the Subsite Templates section, select the templates you want to be available and click **Add**.
6. Click **OK**. The Site Settings page will open and the selected templates will be available to users when they create a subsite.

Task: Create a Subsite

Purpose: If you have the appropriate permissions, you can create a new subsite fairly easily in SharePoint. You might create a subsite to gather a collection of content into a single area, or when you want to provide some separation from the existing content.

Example: The Action Marketing Group will add a basic search subsite to its public site.

Steps:

1. Start Internet Explorer and type the URL for your organization's SharePoint server. The Start page will open.
2. Click the **Settings** menu gear icon and select **Site Contents**. The Site Contents page will open.
3. Click the **new subsite** link. The New SharePoint Site page will open.

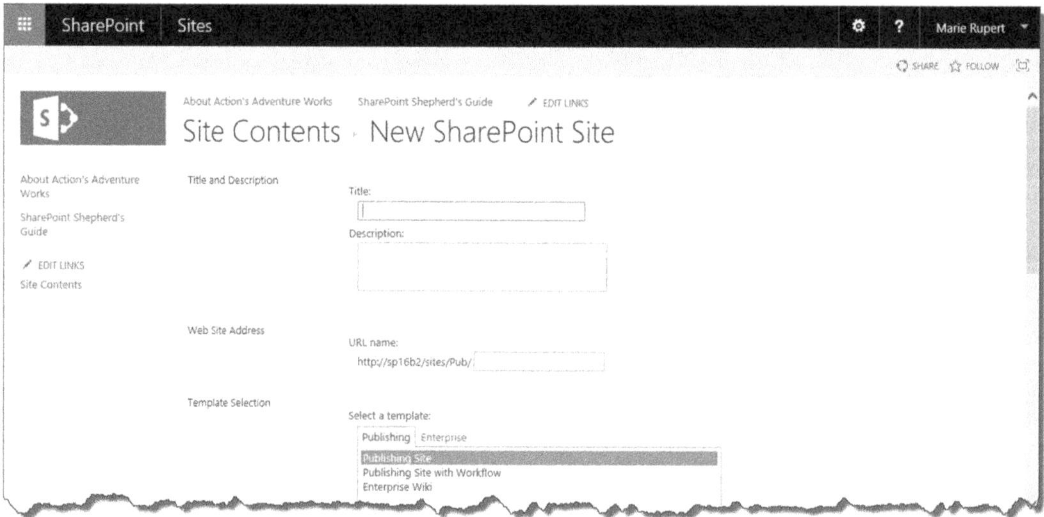

Figure 1: The New SharePoint Site Page

4. In the Title field type a title for your subsite. The title of your subsite should be descriptive and can be up to about 50 letters before becoming intrusive.
5. In the Description field type a description for your subsite. The description is like a subtitle that will be displayed on some of the pages. It should further clarify the title so that anyone can understand the subsite's purpose.
6. In the URL Name field, type a short, descriptive name for your subsite. This will become part of the full website address for your new subsite.

7. In the Template Selection section, select the template you wish to use for your new subsite. You may need to select a different tab in order to find your desired template.

8. In the User Permissions section, select the **Use same permissions as parent site** option. You can change to unique permissions later as shown in the task "Assign Users to a Group."

9. In the Use the top link bar from the parent site field, select the **Yes** option.

10. Click **Create**. The "Working on It" screen will briefly appear, followed by the new subsite's home page.

Task: Customize Publishing Site Navigation

Purpose: Navigation is an important component to any web site. In addition to supporting automatic creation of links for global (top navigation) and local (Quick Launch) navigation, SharePoint allows you to manually change the navigation.

Example: The Action Marketing Group intranet manager needs to add a link to a non-SharePoint resource to their publishing site navigation.

Steps:

1. Start Internet Explorer and type the URL for your organization's SharePoint server. The Start page will open.
2. Navigate to the publishing site. The publishing site's home page will open.
3. Click the **Settings** menu gear icon and select **Site Settings**. The Site Settings page will open.
4. In the Look and Feel section, click the **Navigation** link. The Navigation Settings page will open.

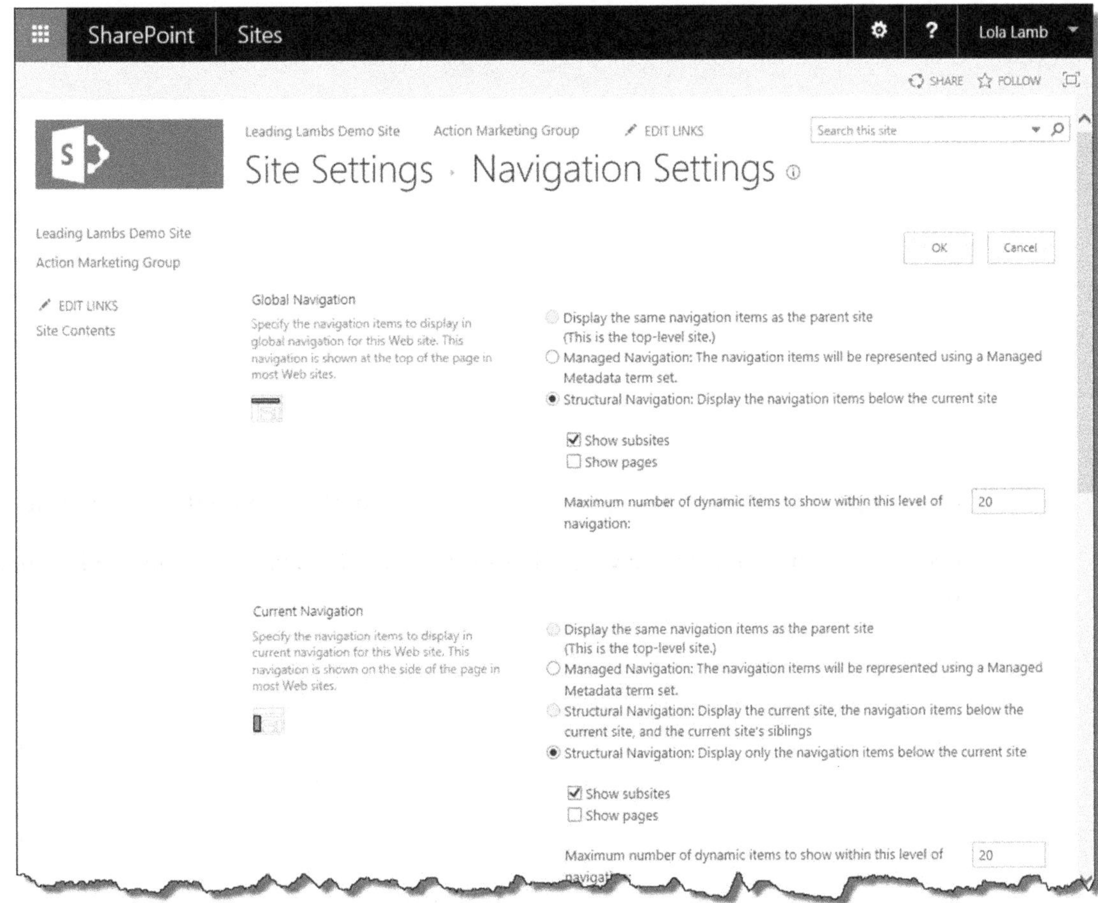

Figure 1: The Navigation Settings Page

5. In the Structural Navigation: Sorting section, select the **Sort manually** option.

Note: Structural Navigation must be enabled to change these options.

6. In the Structural Navigation: Editing and Sorting section, select the **Current Navigation** folder then click **Add Link**. The Navigation Link dialog box will open.

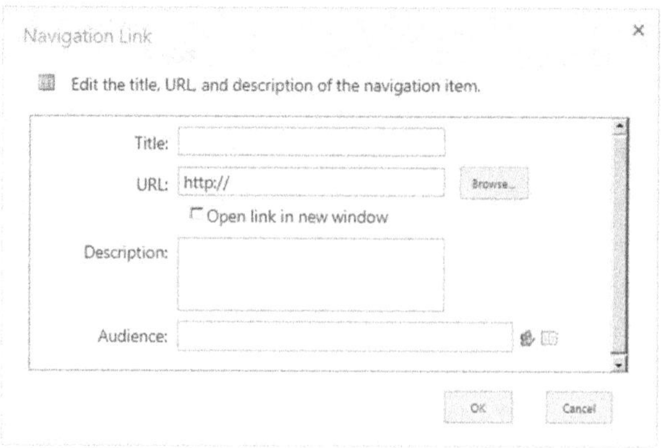

Figure 2: The Navigation Link Dialog Box

7. Add the pertinent information, using the **Browse...** button to find the correct URL.

8. Click **OK**. The new link will be visible in the Structural Navigation: Editing and Sorting section.

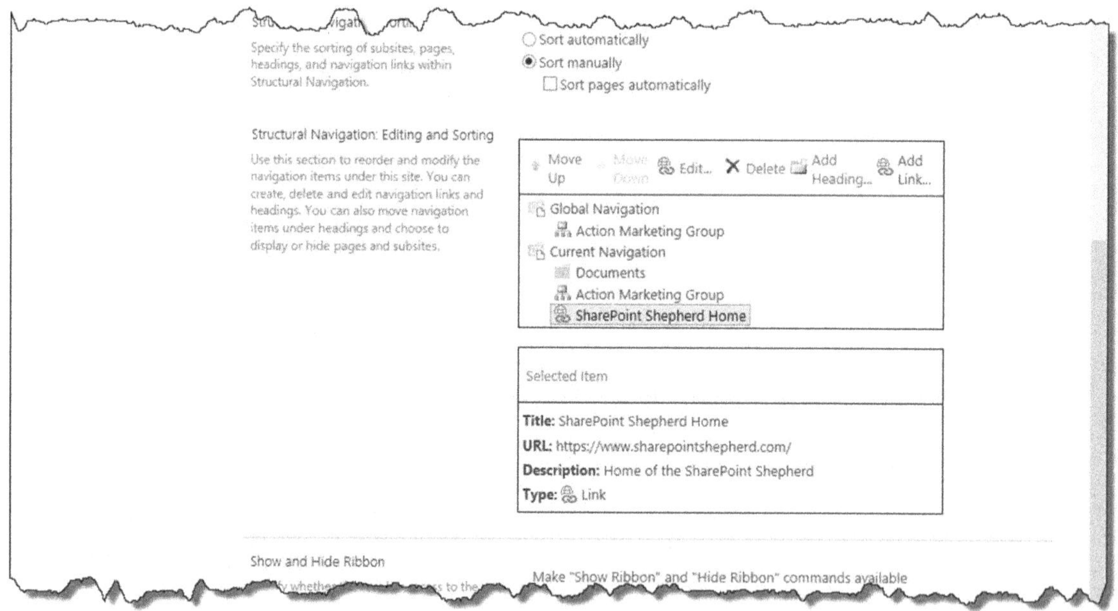

Figure 3: The New Navigation Link

9. Click the new link to select it, then click **Move Up** or **Move Down** until the navigation item is listed in the order you desire.

10. Click **OK**. The Site Settings page will open and the new link will be visible in the site's navigation menu.

Task: Add the Content Query Web Part

Purpose: One of the web parts that is used most frequently in rolling up content and displaying it on the intranet home page is the Content Query Web Part. If you want to accomplish more advanced customization, visit the "Customizing the Content Query Web Part in SharePoint" white paper at http://msdn.microsoft.com/en-us/library/ff380147.aspx.

Example: The Action Marketing Group site will add a Content Query Web Part to their intranet home page.

Steps:

1. Start Internet Explorer and type the URL for your organization's SharePoint server. The Start page will open.
2. Navigate to the site where you want to add the Content Query Web Part.
3. Click the Page tab to open the Page ribbon, and select the Edit button. The page will open in Edit Mode.

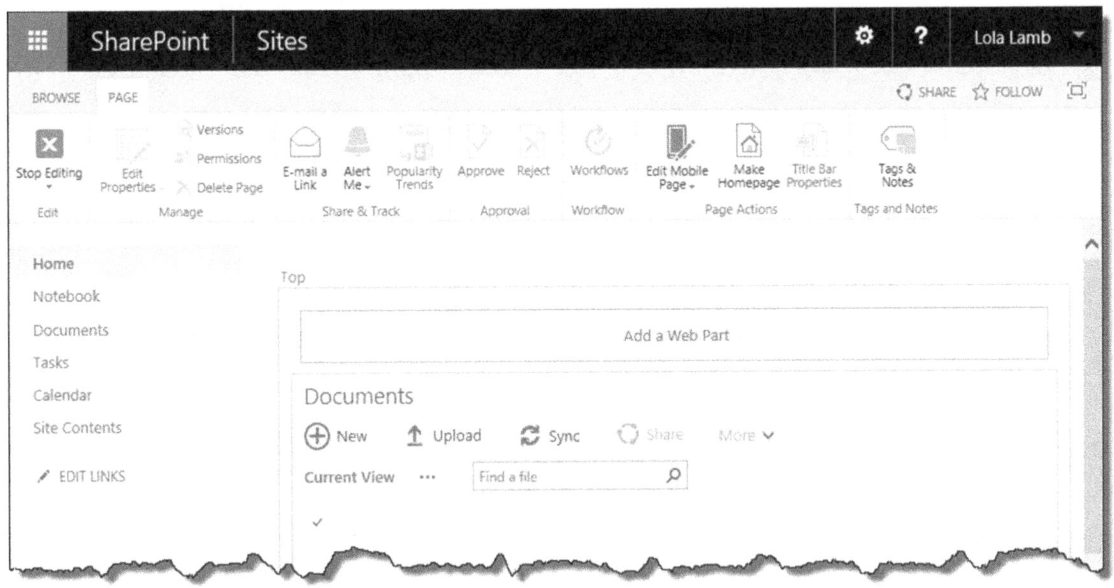

Figure 1: The Page Ribbon and Page in Edit Mode

4. Select a zone and click Add a Web Part. The Add Web Parts header will open.
5. In the Categories column, select the Content Rollup folder. In the Parts column, select Content Query. The web part will be selected and additional information will be displayed in the About the part column.

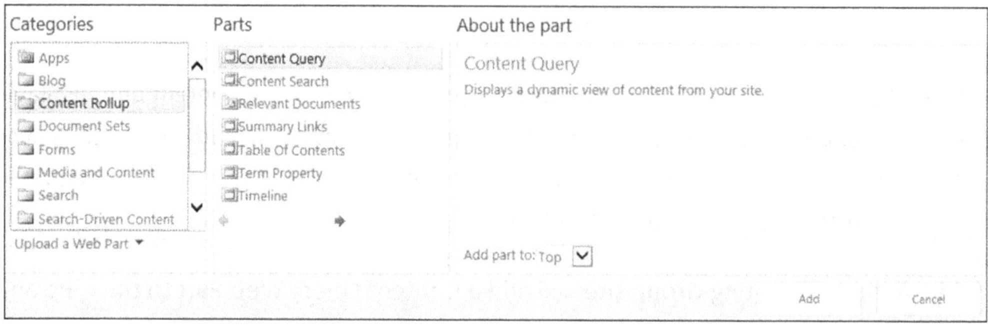

Figure 2: The Add Web Parts Header with Content Query Selected

6. Click Add. The Add Web Parts header will close and the new web part will appear in the selected zone.
7. Click the open the tool pane link. The tool pane for the Content Query Web Part will appear.

Figure 3: The Content Query Web Part Tool Pane

8. Click the Query section header to expand the section, then click the Show items from the following site and all subsites option.
9. In the adjacent URL field, enter the URL for the site, or click Browse... to select from a list of sites, and click OK. The URL will appear in the URL field.
10. Continue to fill out the remainder of the Content Query tool pane as desired.
11. Click OK. The Content Query Web Part Tool Pane will close and the new web part will be visible on the page.

Note: Follow the site approval steps to save and publish the modified page.

Task: Add the Summary Links Web Part

Purpose: SharePoint also includes a Summary Links Web Part which allows you to add links to a page in a structured way. The value of using this web part is that, when pages are moved, the moves will be reflected in the web part (in most cases). The Summary Links Web Part gives you a way to include links across the site and have them displayed in a consistent way.

Example: The Action Marketing Group will add a Summary Links Web Part to its project site home page.

Steps:

1. Start Internet Explorer and type the URL for your organization's SharePoint server. The Start page will open.
2. Navigate to the site to which you'd like to add the Summary Links Web Part.
3. Click the Page tab to open the Page ribbon, then click the Edit Page button. The page will open in Edit Mode.

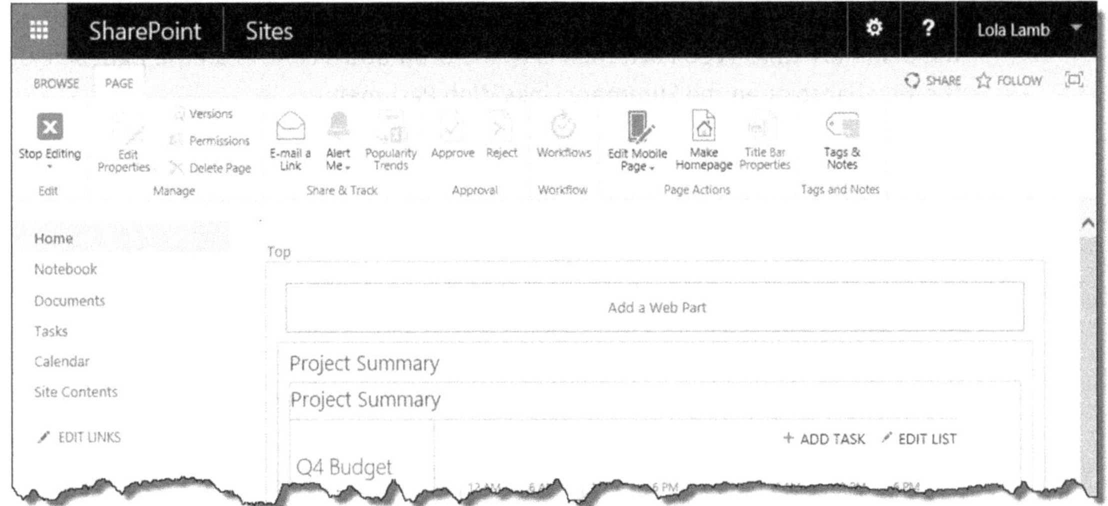

Figure 1: Project Site in Edit Mode

4. Select a zone and click Add a Web Part. The Add Web Parts header will open.
5. In the Categories column, click the Content Rollup folder. In the Parts column, click Summary Links. The web part will be selected and additional information will be displayed in the About the Part column.
6. Click Add. The Add Web Parts header will close and the Summary Links Web Part will appear in the selected zone.

7. To choose how summary links are displayed, click the Configure Styles and Layout link. The Configure Styles and Layout dialog box will open.

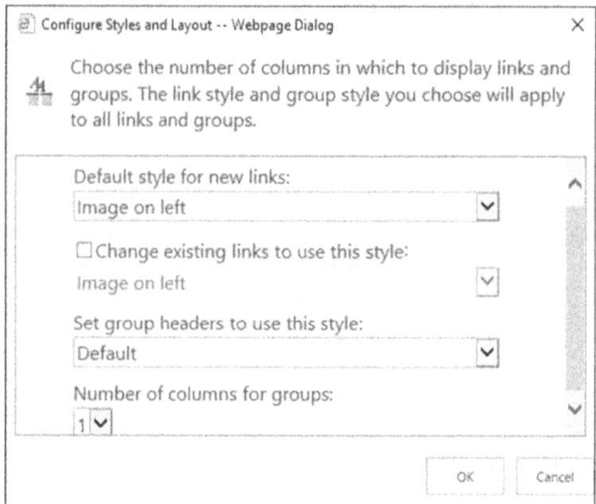

Figure 2: Configure Styles and Layout Dialog Box

8. When you are finished with the configuration, click OK to save your changes and close the dialog box.

9. For appearance, layout, and advanced customization options, hover over the title for the Summary Links Web Part, then click the drop-down control on the right side of the title bar to open the Summary Links Web Part menu.

Figure 3: Summary Links Web Part Menu

10. Click Edit Web Part. The Summary Link Web Part Tool Pane will open.

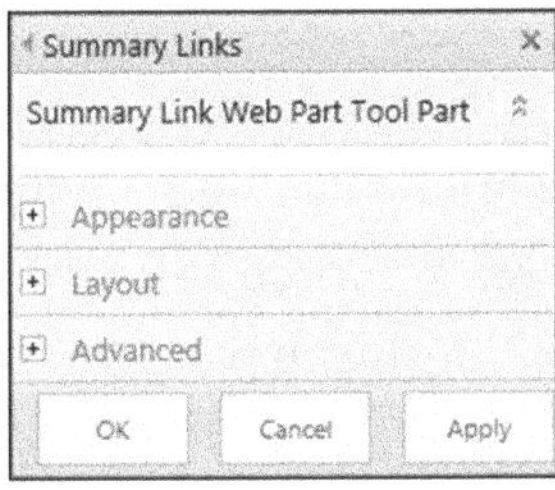

Figure 4: The Summary Links Web Part Tool Pane

11. Use the expand controls for each section to customize your Summary Links Web Part. When you are finished configuring your Summary Links Web Part, click **Apply**. The Tool Pane will close and your changes will be applied.
12. To add a new summary link, at the top of the Summary Links Web Part click **New Link**. The New Link dialog box will open.

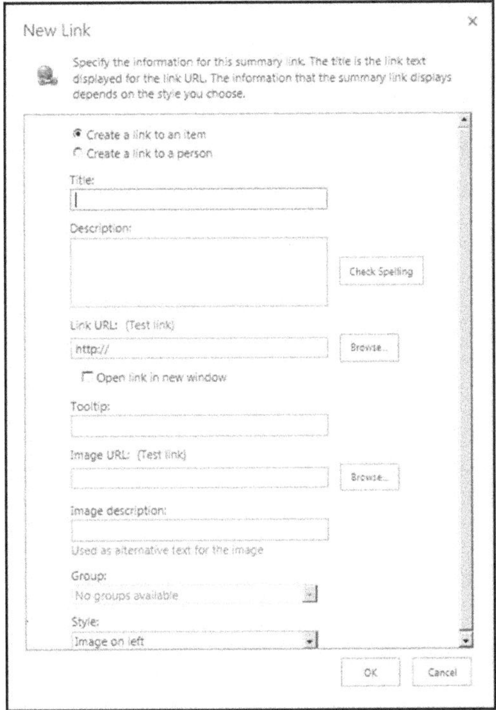

Figure 5: The New Link Dialog Box

13. Add the pertinent information about the link. You can add as much or as little information as needed.
14. Click **OK**. The new summary link will be added to the web part.

Task: Export a Web Part

Purpose: Customizing a web part the way you want takes time and if you want the web part to appear the same way in multiple web sites it may be easier to export the web part and import it than making the settings over and over again. Most web parts can be exported – however, some web parts cannot be exported.

Example: The Action Marketing Group intranet manager has configured a Content Query Web Part and wants to use it on multiple product sites. He'll export it so that he can import it into other sites.

Steps:

1. Start Internet Explorer and type the URL for your organization's SharePoint server. The Start page will open.
2. Navigate to the site from which you want to export the web part.
3. Click the **Page** tab and select the **Edit Page** button. The Page ribbon will appear and the page will open in Edit Mode.
4. Hover over the title for the web part that you want to export, then click the drop-down control on the right side of the title bar to open the Web Part Menu.

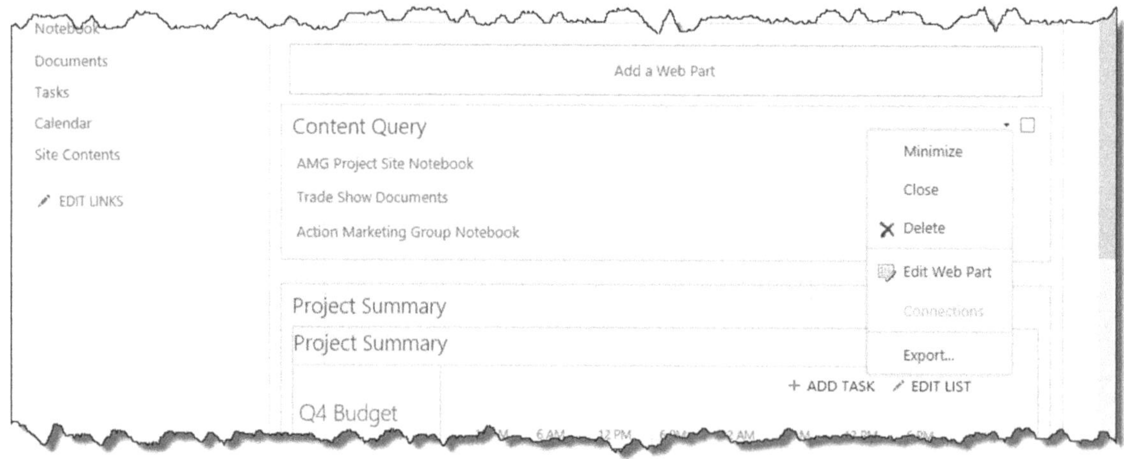

Figure 1: The Content Query Web Part Menu

5. Click the **Export...** option. The File Download dialog box will open.
6. Click **Save**. The Save As dialog box will open.
7. Name and navigate to the folder in which you want to save the Web Part, clicking **Save**. The web part will be saved.

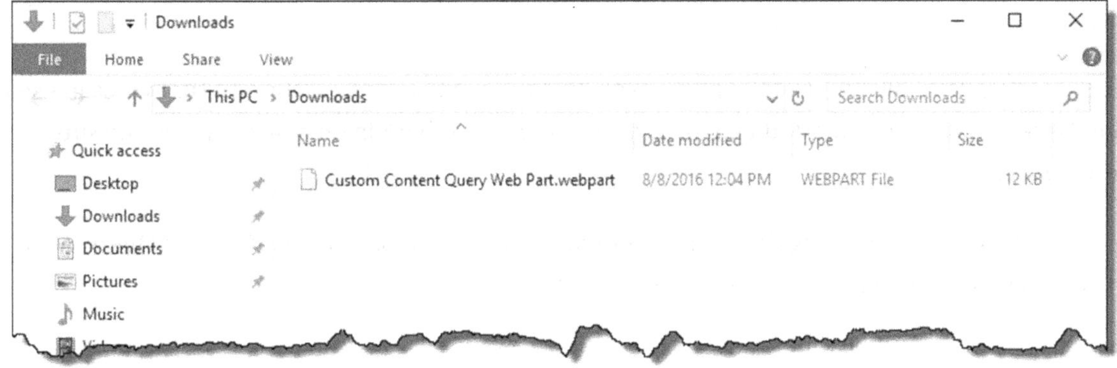

Figure 2: The Downloaded Web Part

Task: Import a Web Part

Purpose: SharePoint allows you to export a web part to save the configuration so that you can use it again. Once you have an exported web part, you can import it back in on a new page in the site where you want it.

Example: The Action Marketing Group intranet manager wants to import the Content Query Web Part she's already configured to each of the product sites.

Steps:

1. Start Internet Explorer and type the URL for your organization's SharePoint server. The Start page will open.
2. Navigate to the site to which you'd like to import the web part.
3. Click the Page tab and select the Edit Page button. The Page ribbon will appear and the page will open in Edit Mode.
4. Select a zone and click Add a Web Part. The Add Web Parts header will open.
5. In the Categories column, click the Upload a Web Part control. The control will expand to an upload field.

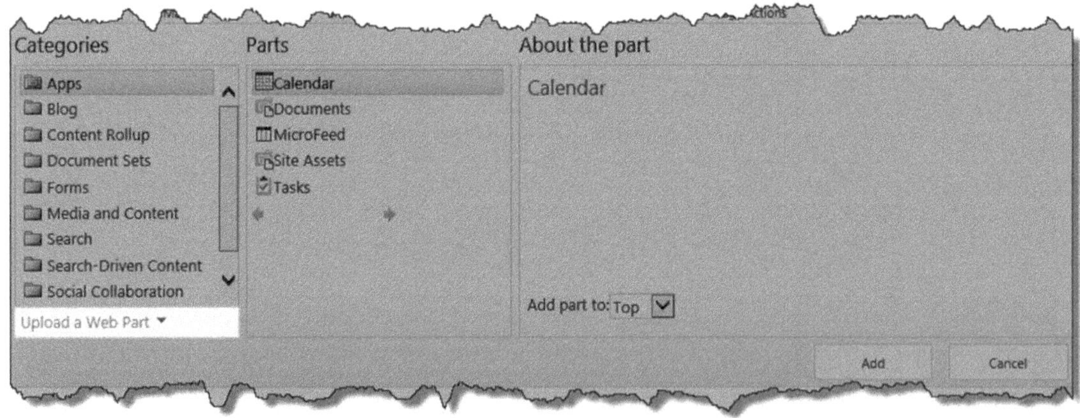

Figure 1: The Upload a Web Part Control

6. Click Browse. The Choose File to Upload dialog box will open.
7. Navigate to the web part you want to upload and click Open. The file path and name of the folder will appear in the field.
8. Click Upload. The web part will be uploaded.

Note: Sometimes it is necessary to click Add a Web Part again to get the Add Web Parts Header to reappear after an upload.

9. In the Categories column, click the **Imported Web Parts** folder. The imported web part will appear in the Parts column. The web part will be automatically selected, and in the About the part column, additional information about the web part will be displayed.

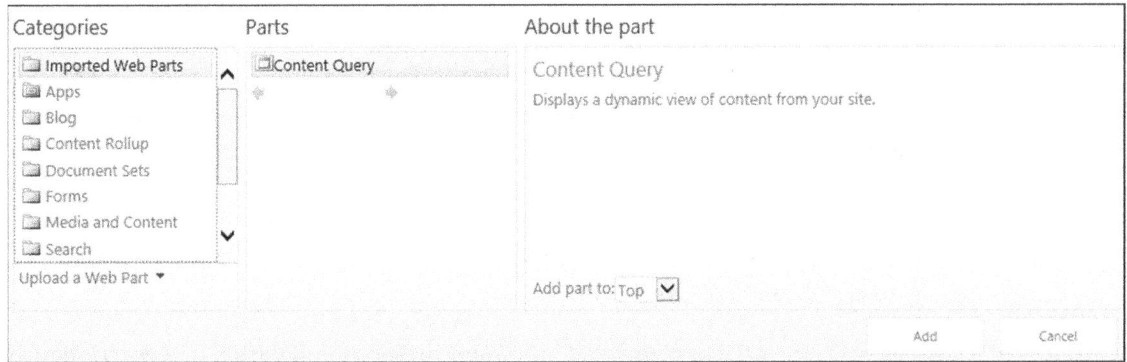

Figure 2: The Add Web Parts Header with Imported Web Parts Folder

10. Click **Add**. The Add Web Parts header will close and the imported web part will appear in the selected zone.

Publish Web Content: Site Collection Owners

Site Collection Owners will have the ability to manage entire collections of sites, which gives them the responsibility to maintain consistency in style as well as site collection efficiency.

In this section, you'll learn how to:

- Enable Output Cache: To counter the time it takes to query a database, and to effectively speed up the time it takes for pages to be served, Site Collection Owners can implement caching.
- Configure Site Collection Default Cache Profiles: Once output caching is implemented on a site, the Site Collection Owner can specify which profiles will apply to which kinds of site visitors.
- Configure Output Cache Profiles: SharePoint provides you with a few preconfigured output cache profiles to apply to your site. Each of these profiles can be tweaked to match your exact needs.
- Add an Output Cache Profile: Sometimes a Site Collection Owner might need to create a new output cache from scratch.
- Override the Configured Output Cache Profile: You can set SharePoint to allow site administrators and designers to configure cache settings for individual pages.
- Configure the Object Cache: Object caching is another way to improve page rendering in SharePoint.
- Flush Object Caches: If you have made significant changes to the cache settings on your site or you suspect that the cache is invalid, it might be a good idea to purge the object and disk-based caches for your server.
- Enable and Configure Cross-List Query Cache: The cross-list query caching improves query performance, but only if the content of your lists or libraries is relatively unchanging.
- Upload and Activate a Sandbox Solution: Sandbox solutions are designed for situations where the developer of a solution isn't trusted by the central administration or the solution pertains only to a single site collection.
- Deactivate a Sandbox Solution: Sandbox solutions can use up a certain number of server resources and thus need to be managed accordingly.

Task: Enable Output Cache

Purpose: Whenever a user requests a page from a website, the request has to go through a variety of steps before the page is actually transmitted back to the user's browser. In the case of SharePoint pages, a big piece of time can be taken up by the process of checking the content database. To counter this, and to effectively speed up the time pages are served, Site Collection Owners can implement caching. This allows SharePoint to keep rendered and partially rendered copies of the page on the local server disk which can be served up much quicker to the users.

Example: The Action Marketing Group site is performing slowly to the customers and the intranet manager wants to quickly increase performance by implementing output caching.

Steps:

1. Start Internet Explorer and type the URL for your organization's SharePoint server. The Start page will open.
2. Navigate to the publishing site. The publishing site's home page will open.
3. Click the **Settings** menu gear icon and select **Site Settings**. The Site Settings page will open.
4. In the Site Collection Administration section, click the **Site collection output cache** link. The Output Cache Settings page will open.

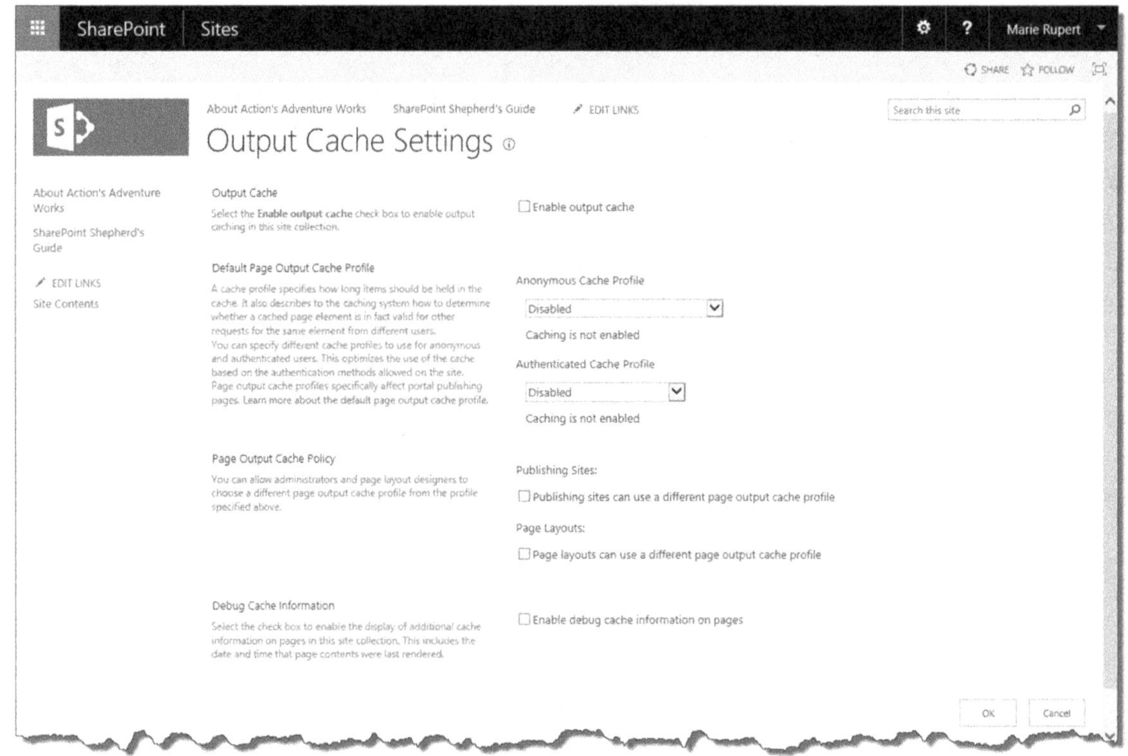

Figure 1: The Output Cache Settings Page

5. In the Output Cache section, select the **Enable output cache** checkbox.
6. Click **OK**. The Site Settings page will open.

Note: To disable the output cache, repeat these steps and de-select the **Enable output cache** checkbox.

Task: Configure Site Collection Default Cache Profiles

Purpose: Implementing caching on a site is good – but leveraging the right cache profile for each type of user is important to manage the consumption of disk space and performance.

Example: The Action Marketing Group site is not performing optimally even after caching was enabled. The Intranet manager is seeking a better performing set of settings.

Steps:

1. Start Internet Explorer and type the URL for your organization's SharePoint server. The Start page will open.
2. Navigate to the publishing site. The publishing site's home page will open.
3. Click the **Settings** menu gear icon and select **Site Settings**. The Site Settings page will open.
4. In the Site Collection Administration section, click the **Site collection output cache** link. The Output Cache Settings page will open.

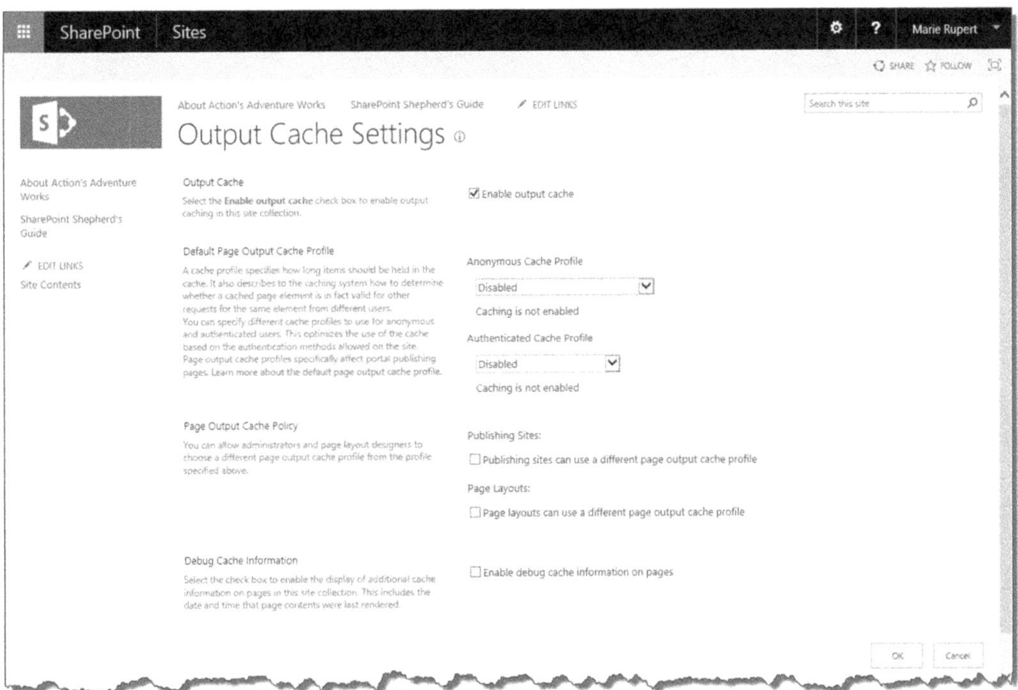

Figure 1: The Output Cache Settings Page

5. In the Default Page Output Cache Profile section, set the Anonymous Cache Profile field to the **Public Internet (Purely Anonymous)** option. The site will be optimized

for public Internet-facing sites or areas that are meant to serve the same content to all users.

6. In the Default Page Output Cache Profile section, set the Authenticated Cache Profile field to the **Extranet (Published Site)** option. The site will be optimized for a public extranet site with the following characteristics: authoring does not take place on the tier, only major versions of pages are deployed to the tier, and users cannot customize web parts on a page in the tier.

7. Click **OK**. The Site Settings page will open.

Task: Configure Output Cache Profiles

Purpose: SharePoint provides you with a few preconfigured output cache profiles to apply to your site. However, the unique needs of your site may require that you implement specific tweaks to these settings.

Example: The Action Marketing Group site cache setting for anonymous users needs its cache duration increased from 180 seconds to 360 seconds.

Steps:

1. Start Internet Explorer and type the URL for your organization's SharePoint server. The Start page will open.
2. Navigate to the publishing site. The publishing site's home page will open.
3. Click the **Settings** menu gear icon and select **Site Settings**. The Site Settings page will open.
4. In the Site Collection Administration section, click the **Site collection cache profiles** link. The Cache Profiles page will open.

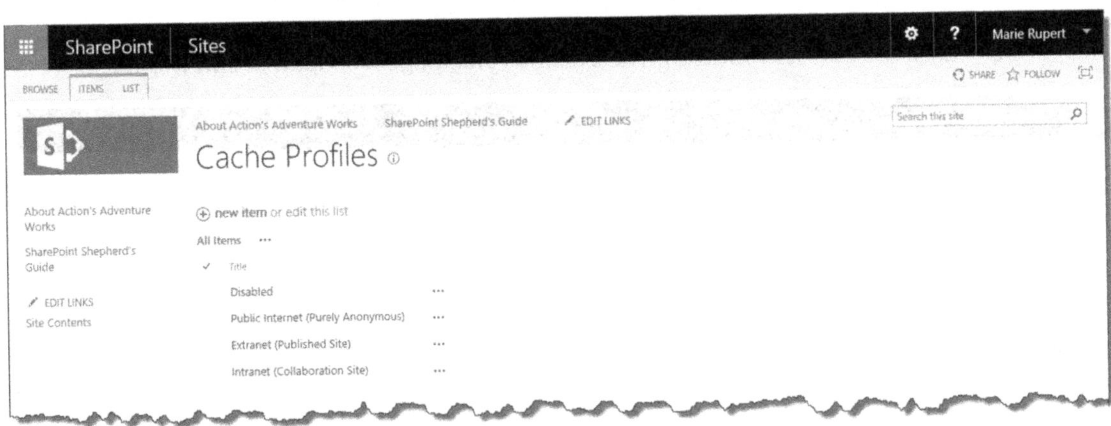

Figure 1: The Cache Profiles Page

5. Click the **Public Internet (Purely Anonymous)** link. The Public Internet (Purely Anonymous) Cache Profile page will open.

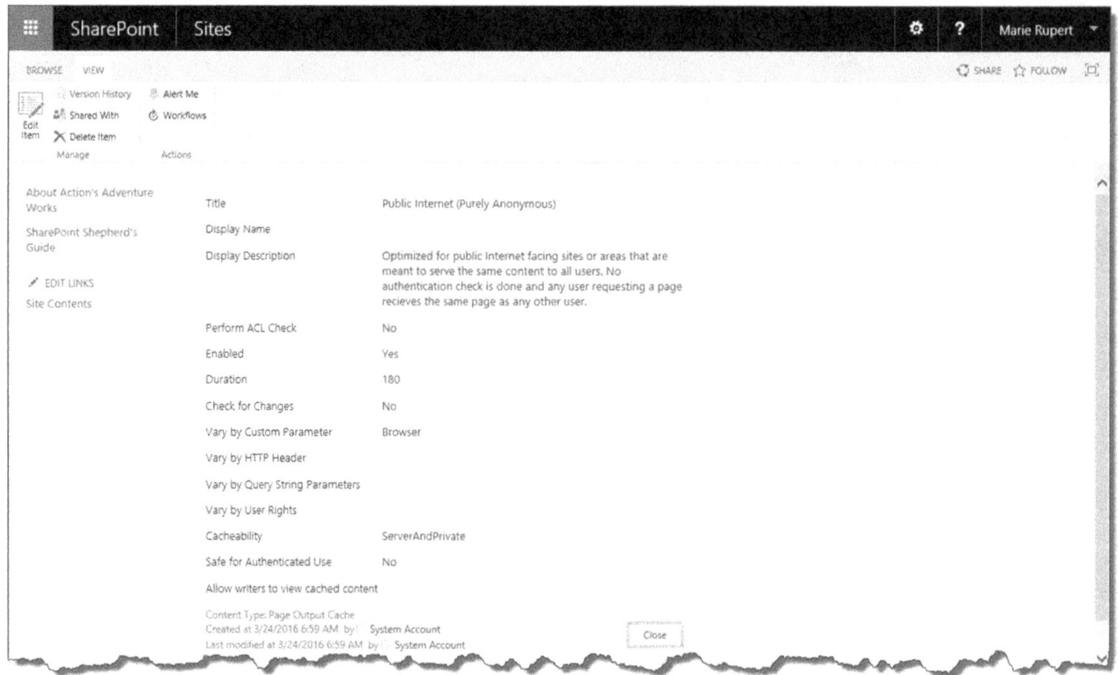

Figure 2: The Public Internet (Purely Anonymous) Cache Profile Page

6. Click the **Edit Item** button. The Cache Profile page will open in Edit Mode.

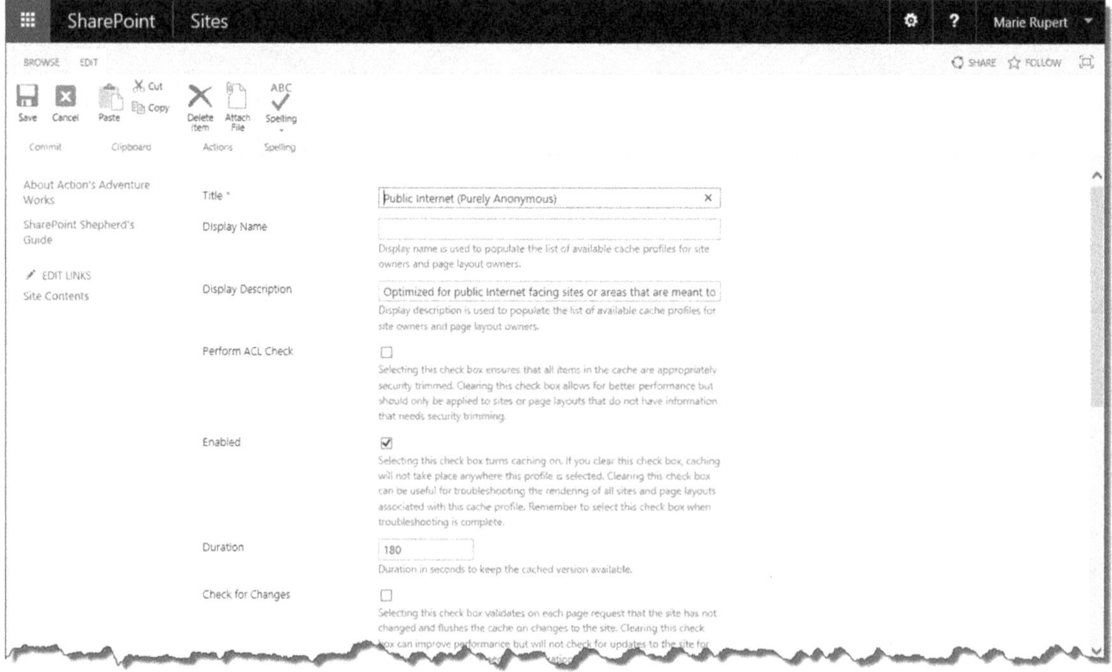

Figure 3: The Cache Profile Page in Edit Mode

7. Make the changes necessary to customize the profile. For instance, change the Duration field to 360.
8. Click Save. The Cache Profile page will return to View Mode.

Task: Add an Output Cache Profile

Purpose: SharePoint provides you with a few preconfigured output cache profiles to apply to your site. Sometimes, however, a Site Collection Owner might need to create a new output cache from scratch.

Example: The Action Marketing Group site needs a cache setting for site developers to optimize the performance for these users.

Steps:

1. Start Internet Explorer and type the URL for your organization's SharePoint server. The Start page will open.
2. Navigate to the publishing site. The publishing site's home page will open.
3. Click the Settings menu gear icon and select Site Settings. The Site Settings page will open.
4. In the Site Collection Administration section, click the Site collection cache profiles link. The Cache Profiles page will open.
5. Click the new item link. The New Cache Profile page will open.

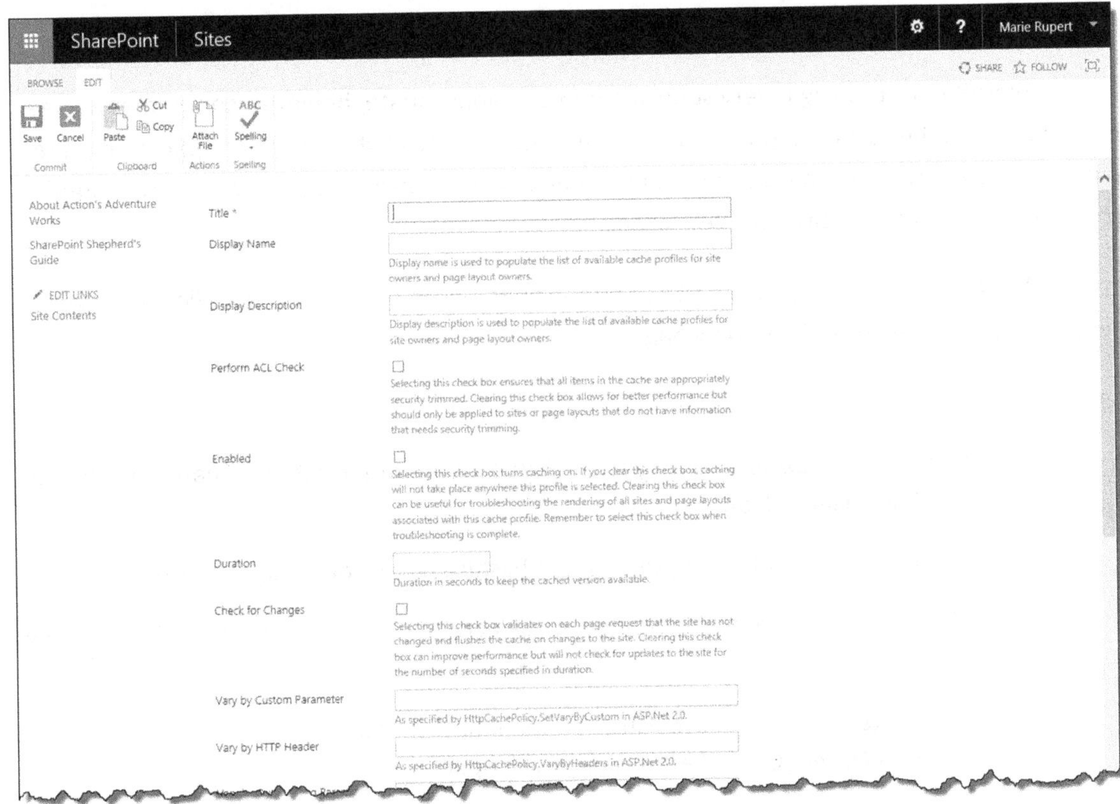

Figure 1: The New Cache Profile Page

6. Fill out the fields in the New Cache Profile page as needed.
7. Click **Save**. The New Cache Profile page will close and the new cache profile will be added to Cache Profiles Page.

Exception: If these settings are not available, the Publishing Infrastructure site collection feature and the Publishing site feature may not be active.

Task: Override the Configured Output Cache Profile

Purpose: SharePoint's caching is very sophisticated and appropriate, however, sometimes a page may not be able to be cached appropriately due to a special circumstance or third party software. Allowing the page owner to change the caching of an individual page allows you to work around specific issues with a single page or a few pages.

Example: The Action Marketing Group site cache settings will be set by the Site Collection owner to allow cache settings to be configured by page.

Steps:

1. Start Internet Explorer and type the URL for your organization's SharePoint server. The Start page will open.
2. Navigate to the publishing site. The publishing site's home page will open.
3. Click the **Settings** menu gear icon and select **Site Settings**. The Site Settings page will open.
4. In the Site Collection Administration section, click the **Site collection output cache** link. The Output Cache Settings page will open.

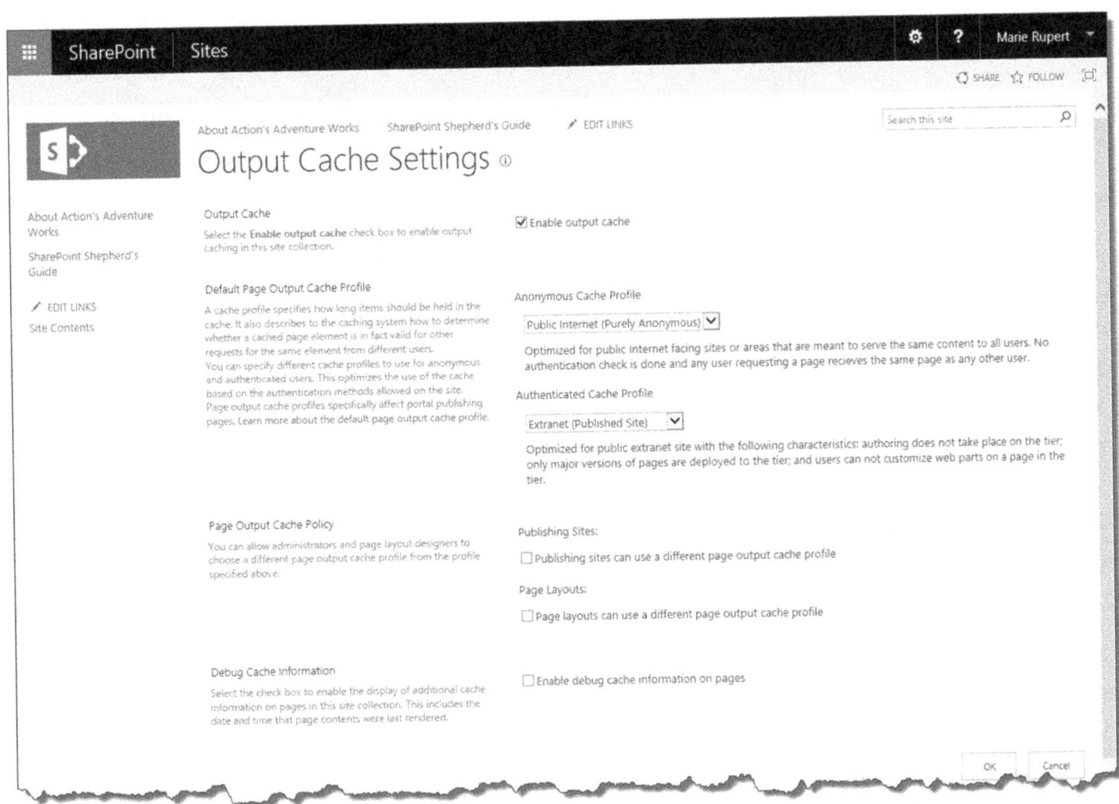

Figure 1: The Output Cache Settings Page

5. In the Page Output Cache Policy section, click the **Page layouts can use a different page output cache profile** checkbox.
6. Click **OK**. The Output Cache Settings page will close and the Site Settings page will appear.

Task: Configure the Object Cache

Purpose: SharePoint offers numerous ways to accomplish caching to improve performance including object caching. Object caching uses memory to reduce the frequency SharePoint has to go back to SQL server reducing load and improving responsiveness to the users.

Example: The Action Marketing Group wants to take better advantage of the SharePoint object cache.

Steps:

1. Start Internet Explorer and type the URL for your organization's SharePoint server. The Start page will open.
2. Navigate to the publishing site. The publishing site's home page will open.
3. Click the **Settings** menu gear icon and select **Site Settings**. The Site Settings page will open.
4. In the Site Collection Administration section, click the **Site collection object cache** link. The Object cache settings page will open.

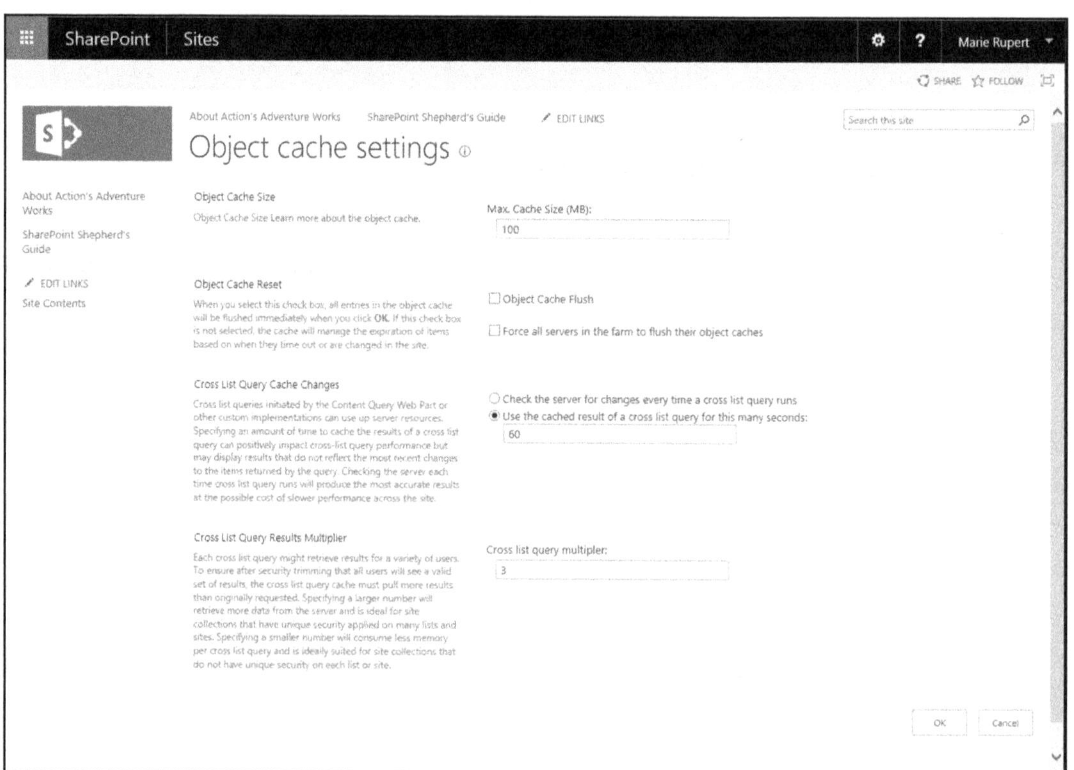

Figure 1: The Object Cache Settings Page

5. In the Object Cache Size section, set the Max. Cache Size (MB) field to the desired value.
6. Click **OK**. The Object cache settings page will close and the Site Settings page will appear.

Task: Flush Object Caches

Purpose: When configured SharePoint caches objects. Sometimes these caches can become corrupt. If you suspect that the cache is invalid, you can reset, or flush, the cache to ensure that you're getting current results. SharePoint enables you to do this for one server, or all servers in the SharePoint server farm.

Example: The Action Marketing Group Site Collection owner will flush the disk-based and object caches for the individual Action Group public site's server.

Steps:

1. Start Internet Explorer and type the URL for your organization's SharePoint server. The Start page will open.
2. Navigate to the publishing site. The publishing site's home page will open.
3. Click the **Settings** menu gear icon and select **Site Settings**. The Site Settings page will open.
4. In the Site Collection Administration section, click the **Site collection object cache** link. The Object Cache Settings page will open.

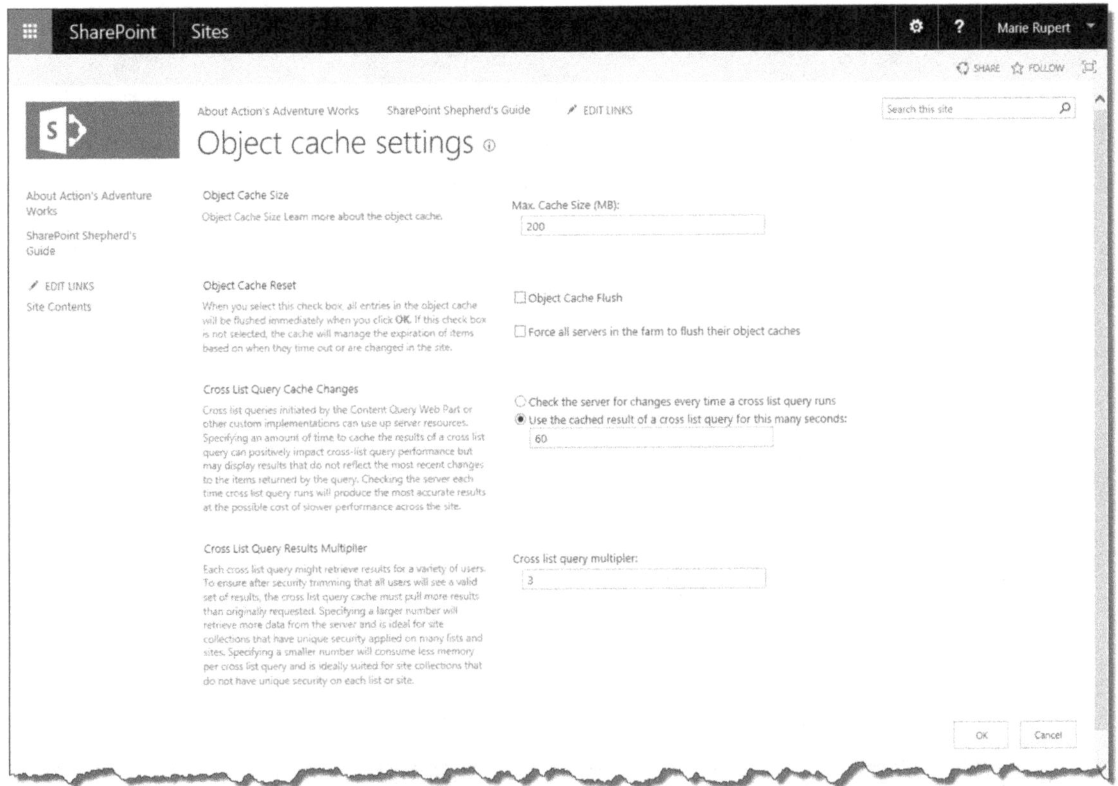

Figure 1: The Output Cache Settings Page

5. In the Object Cache Reset section, click the **Object Cache Flush** checkbox.

6. Click **OK**. The caches for the server will immediately be flushed and the Site Settings page will open.

Task: Enable and Configure Cross-List Query Cache

Purpose: Cross-list queries are expensive for SharePoint to execute. Most cross-list queries involve a list that rarely changes. By caching that list, it's possible to improve SharePoint performance. SharePoint allows you to configure how aggressively the secondary lists will be cached.

Example: The Action Marketing Group Site Collection Owner will set the query cache option to a longer cache because the site's content does not change often.

Steps:

1. Start Internet Explorer and type the URL for your organization's SharePoint server. The Start page will open.
2. Navigate to the publishing site. The publishing site's home page will open.
3. Click the **Settings** menu gear icon and select **Site Settings**. The Site Settings page will open.
4. In the Site Collection Administration section, click the **Site collection object cache** link. The Object cache settings page will open.

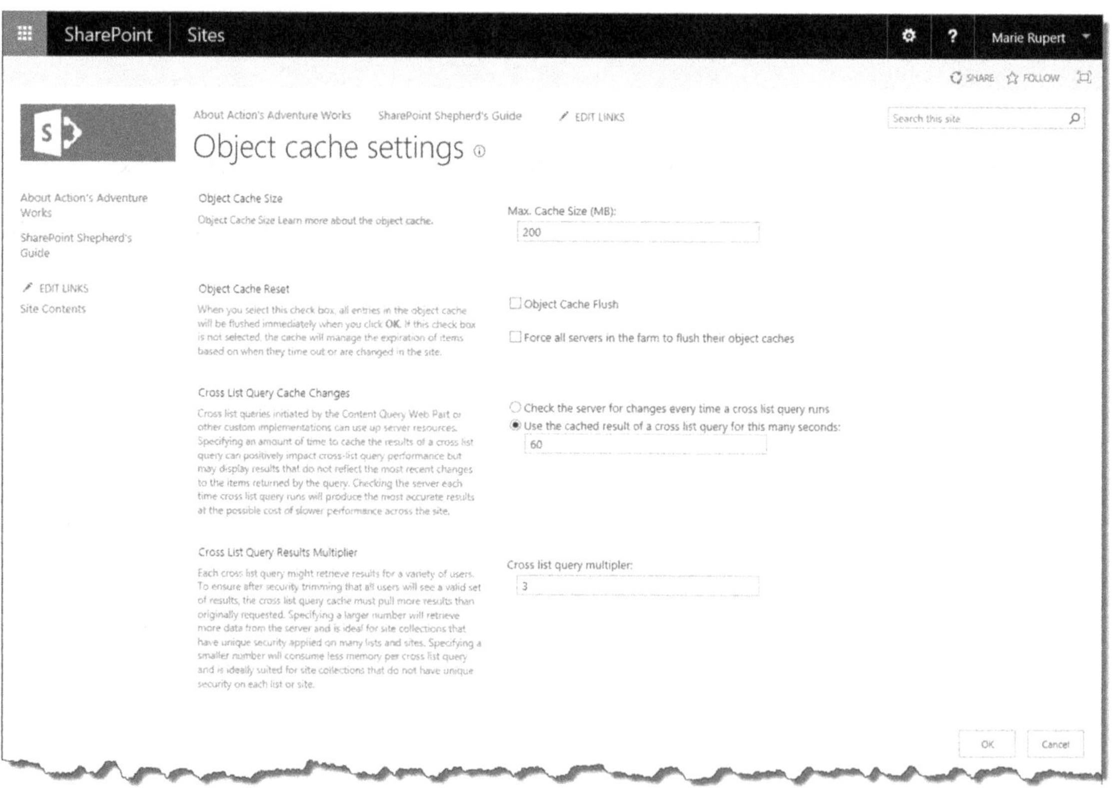

Figure 1: The Object Cache Settings Page

5. In the Cross List Query Cache Changes section, click the **Check the server for changes every time a cross list query runs** option if your content changes often. Otherwise, click the **Use the cached result of a cross list query for this many seconds:** option.

6. Click **OK**. The Object cache settings page will close and the Site Settings page will appear.

Task: Upload and Activate a Sandbox Solution

Purpose: SharePoint 2010 introduced a concept of Sandboxed solutions – sometimes called user solutions. These solutions are able to be uploaded and activated by site collection administrators and can be templates for lists and libraries to create – including data – or they can include code that will be run in a special "sandbox" so that it can't impact other users on the farm.

Example: The Action Marketing Group test site before implementing it in a production environment.

Steps:

1. Start Internet Explorer and type the URL for your organization's SharePoint server. The Start page will open.
2. Navigate to the site where the solution will be used. The site's home page will open.
3. Click the **Settings** menu and select **Site Settings**. The Site Settings page will open.
4. In the Web Designer Galleries section click the **Solutions** link. The Solutions page will open.

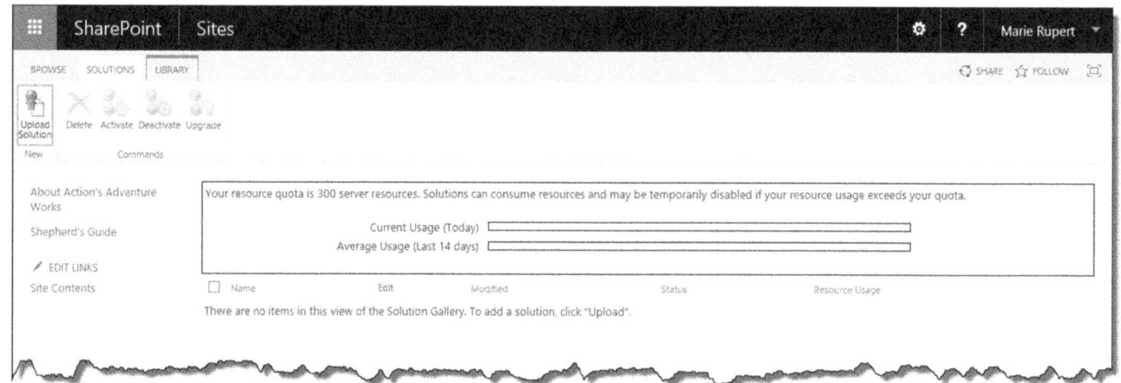

Figure 1: The Solutions Page

5. Click the **Solutions** tab. The Solutions ribbon will appear.
6. Click the **Upload Solution** button. The Add a document dialog box will appear.

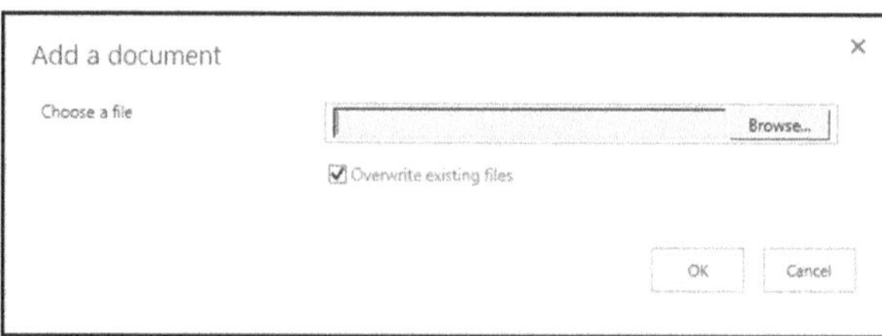

Figure 2: The Add a Document Dialog Box

7. Click Browse.... The Choose File to Upload dialog box will open.
8. Navigate to the sandbox solution file you want to use and click Open. The file will appear in the Name field.
9. Click OK. The new template will be uploaded and appear in the Solutions gallery.
10. Click the solution item to select it. A confirmation dialog box will open.
11. Click the Activate button. The solution will be activated.

Task: Deactivate a Sandbox Solution

Purpose: SharePoint Sandbox solutions enable functionality and when they contain code can consume resources. By deactivating a solution, you can remove templates that you no longer want users to use and you can stop code from consuming resources.

Example: The Action Marketing Group has decided that the third party web part they were evaluating won't work and the intranet manager will deactivate it.

Steps:

1. Start Internet Explorer and type the URL for your organization's SharePoint server. The Start page will open.
2. Navigate to the main site from which the new sandbox site will be deactivated. The site's home page will open.
3. Click the Settings menu gear icon and select Site Settings. The Site Settings page will open.
4. In the Web Designer Galleries section, click the Solutions link. The Solutions page will open.
5. Click the solution item to select it.

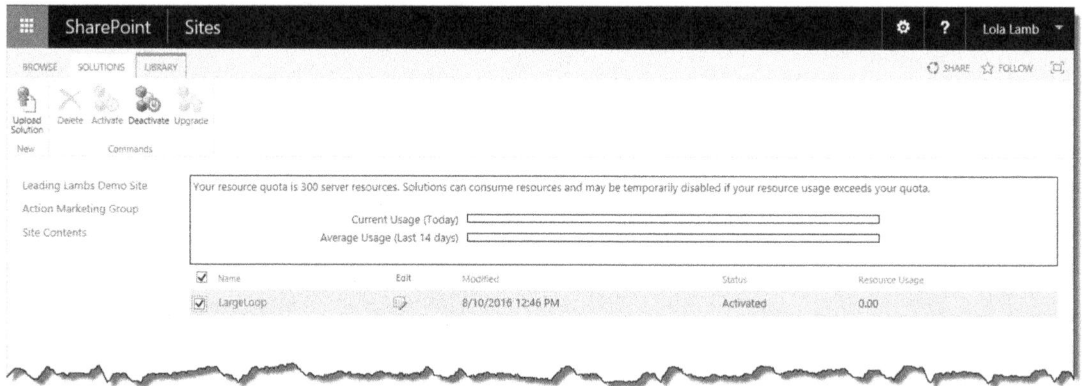

Figure 1: Selecting a Solution Item

6. Click the Deactivate button. After confirming the action, the sandbox solution will be deactivated.

Appendix A: Site Definitions

Purpose: There are many different kinds of sites that can be created in SharePoint. You have seen some in action throughout the tasks in this book. In this Appendix, all of the site definitions will be reviewed and displayed, to make your choices easier when it's time to create your own site.

The site definitions that can be available on the New SharePoint Site page are:

- Collaboration Sites
    - Team Site
    - Blog
    - Project Site
    - Community Site
- Enterprise Sites
    - Document Center
    - Records Center
    - Business Intelligence Center
    - Enterprise Search Center
    - Basic Search Center
    - Visio Process Repository
- Publishing Sites
    - Publishing Site
    - Publishing Site with Workflow
    - Enterprise Wiki

Collaboration Sites

The four sites in this category all have the same basic purpose: to allow you and your co-workers to share and collaborate on documents to get work done more efficiently.

Team Site

A team site is a site for teams to quickly organize, author, and share information. It provides a document library, and lists for managing announcements, calendar items, tasks, and discussions.

The Team Site template creates default instances of these lists and libraries:

- Documents Library

- Notebook Library
- Site Assets
- Site Pages
- Microfeed

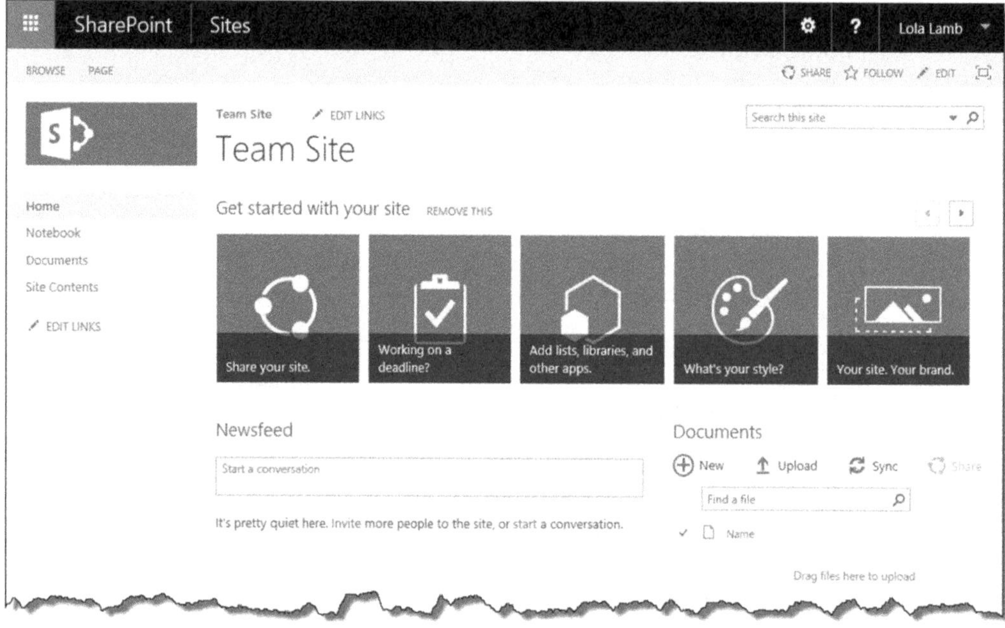

Figure 1: Team Site

Blog Site

This is a site for a person or team to post ideas, observations, and expertise on which site visitors can comment.

The lists and libraries created in a Blog Site template are:

- Photo Library
- Categories
- Comments
- Links
- Posts
- Alerts

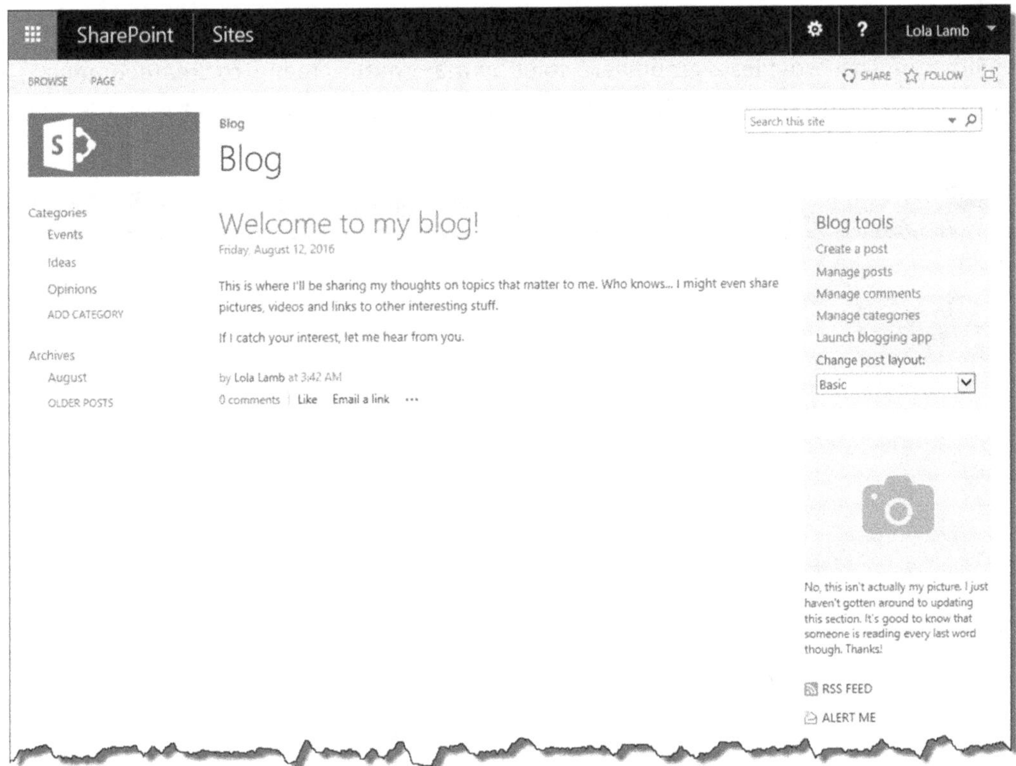

Figure 2: Blog Site

Project Site

A Project Site template provides a groupware solution that enables teams to create, organize, and share information quickly and easily. It includes a Calendar, Task List, and the other basic lists included in the Team Site.

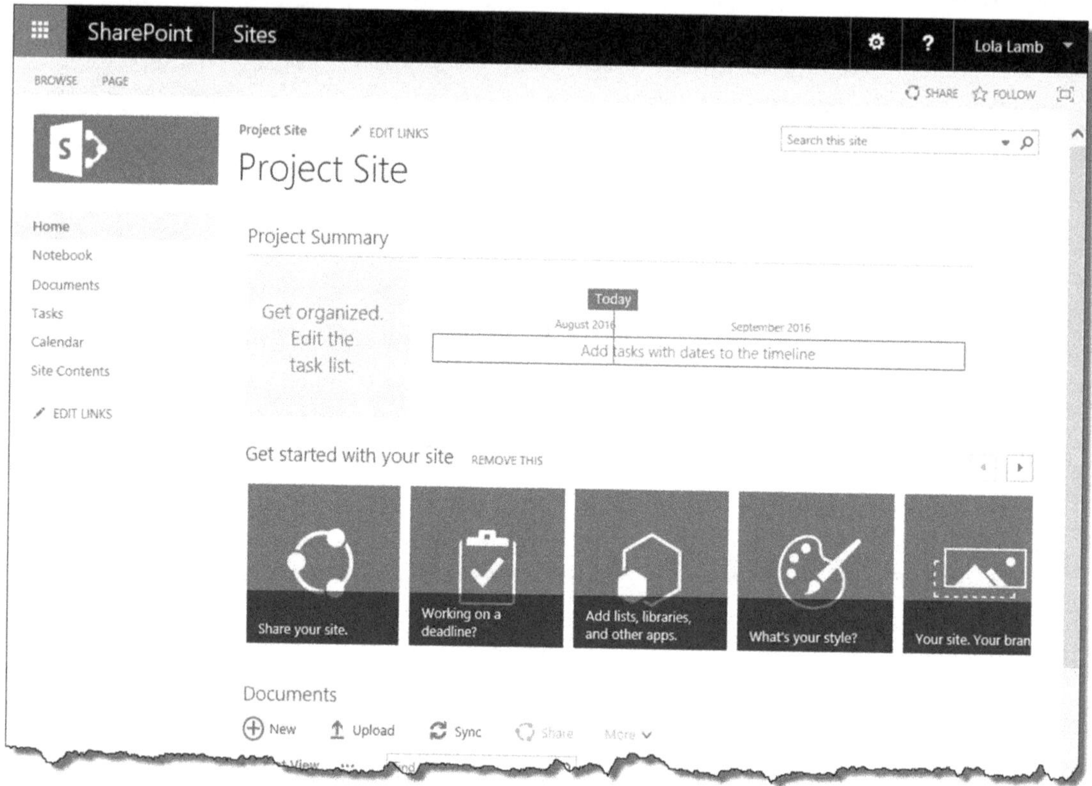

Figure 3: Project Site

Community Site

A community site is a site for colleagues to work together and discuss relevant topics. It provides several lists geared to creating a collaborative environment. The Community site includes these lists:

- Categories
- Members
- Discussion
- Badges
- Reputation

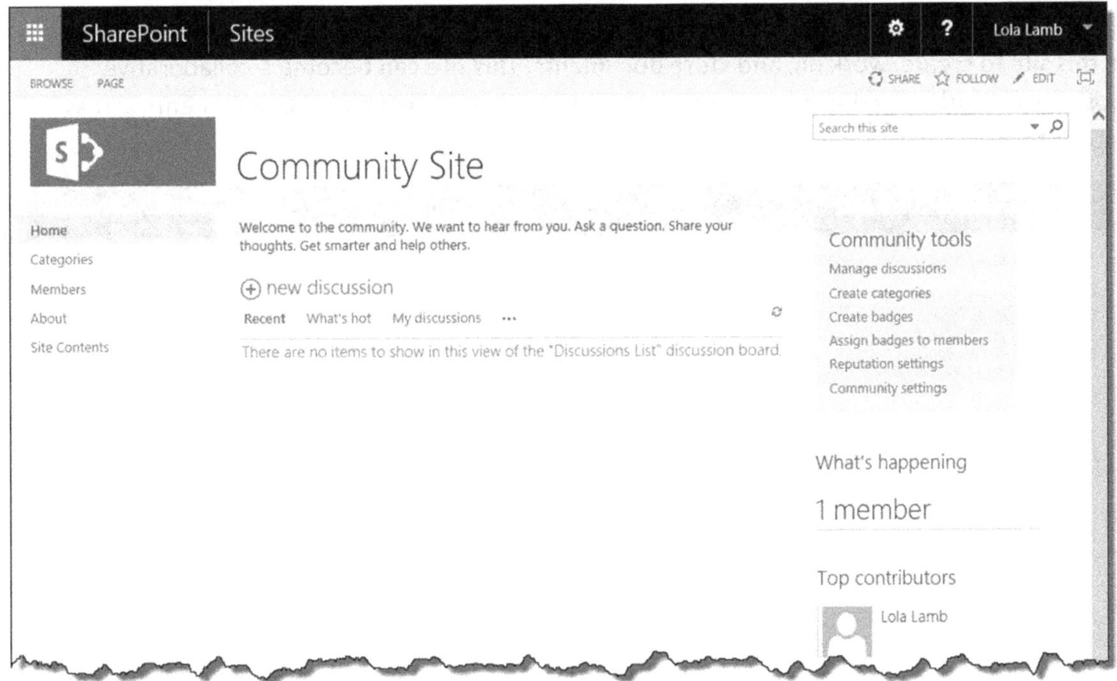

Figure 4: Community Site

Enterprise Sites

These sites contain powerful tools to help you manage your business processes no matter what size business you work in.

Document Center

Use this site to create, work on, and store documents. This site can become a collaborative repository for authoring documents within a team, or a knowledge base for documents across multiple teams.

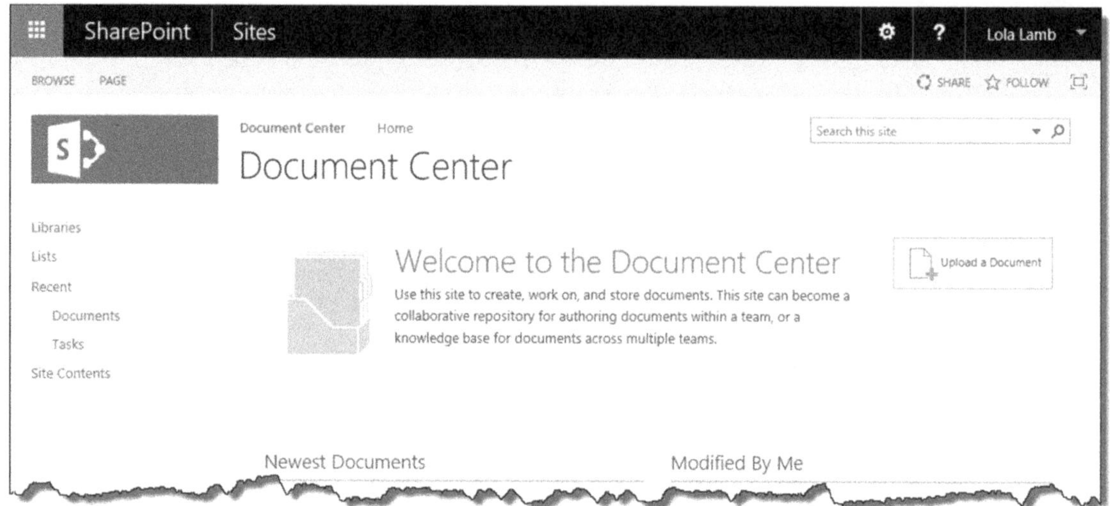

Figure 5: Document Center

Records Center

This template creates a site designed for records management. Records managers can configure the routing table to direct incoming files to specific locations. The site prevents records from being modified after they are added to the repository.

The records center creates a number of libraries and lists when it is started:

- Libraries
    - Hold Reports
    - Missing Properties
    - Records Pending Submission
    - Unclassified Records
- Lists
    - Holds
    - Records Routing
    - Records Center
    - Submitted E-Mail Records
    - Tasks

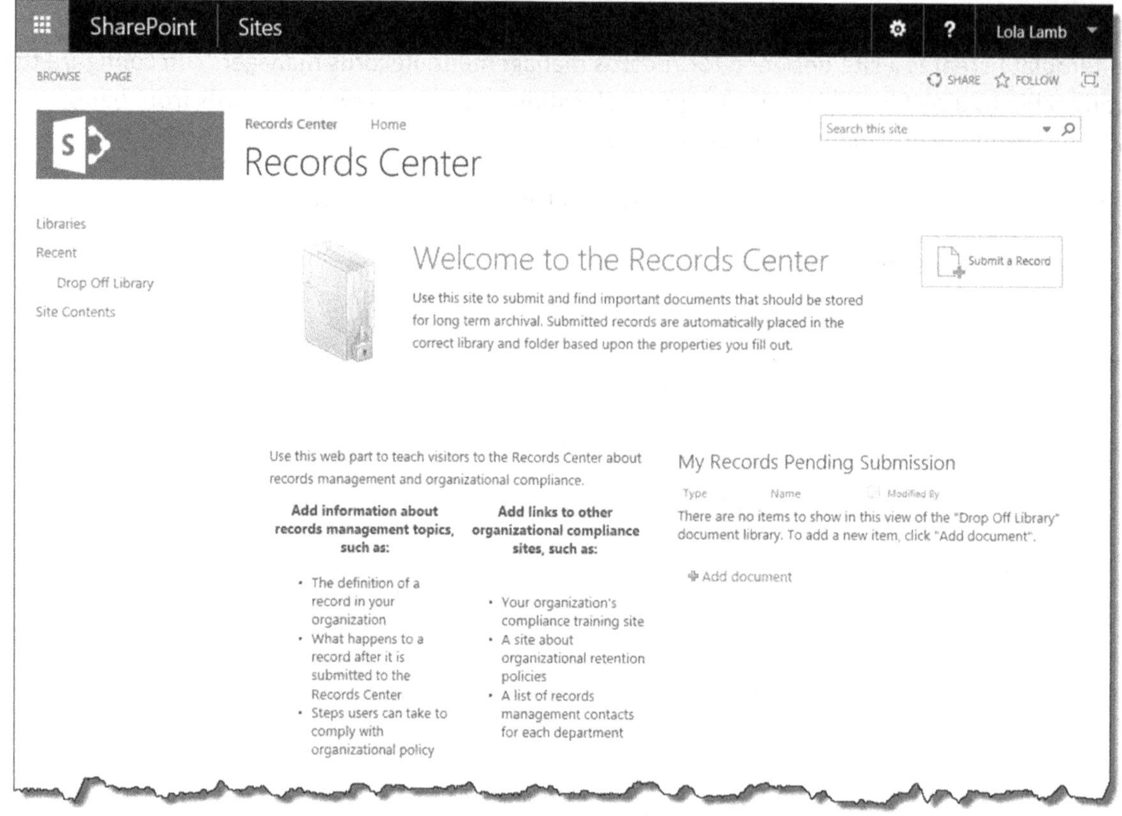

Figure 6: Records Center

Business Intelligence Center

The Business Intelligence Center site helps you organize that data in a useful way and present that data as meaningful information. It uses business intelligence tools such as scorecards, dashboards, data connections, status lists, and status indicators to convey the information you need.

Enterprise Search Center

The Enterprise Search Center is a SharePoint search that includes several components, each responsible for a specific search task.

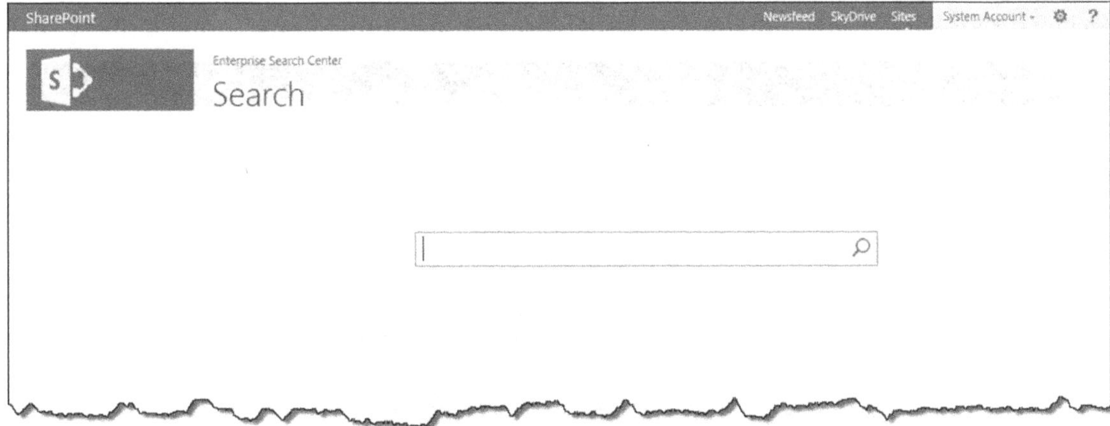

Figure 7: Enterprise Search Center

Basic Search Center

This site is for delivering a custom search experience. The site includes pages for search results and advanced searches.

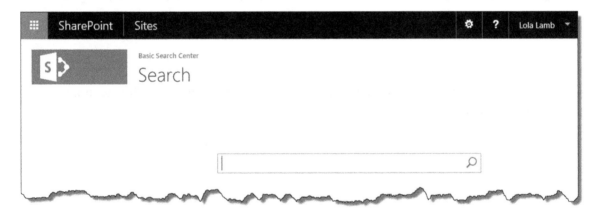

Figure 8: Basic Search Center

Visio Process Repository

This is a site for teams to quickly view, share, and store Visio process diagrams. It provides a versioned document library for storing process diagrams, and lists for managing announcements, tasks, and review discussions.

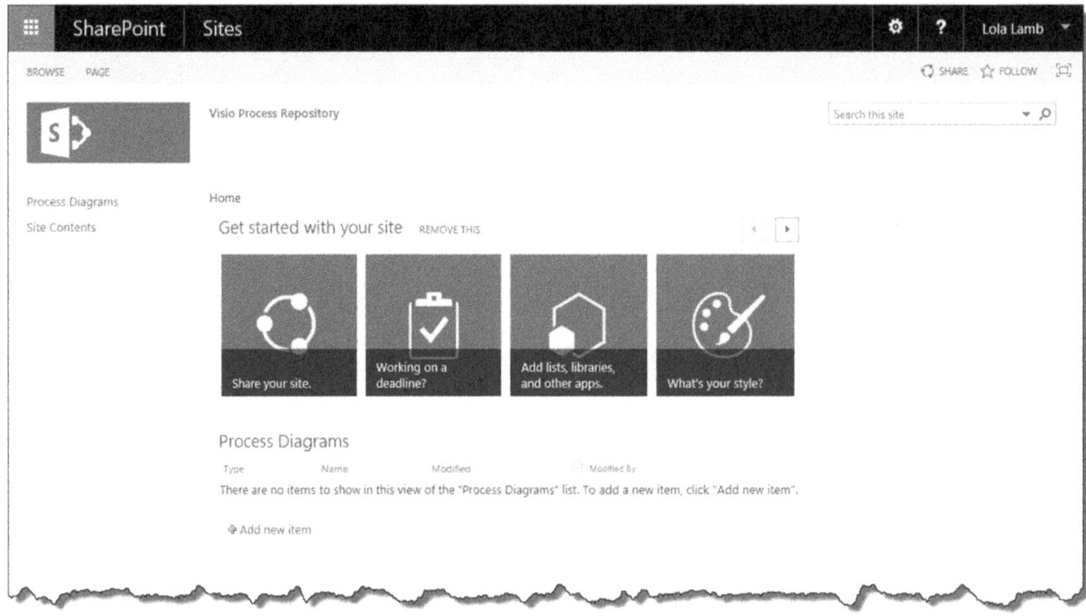

Figure 9: Visio Process Repository

Publishing Sites

The three sites in this category are for publishing custom web or wiki pages, with or without a workflow process in place.

Publishing Site

This is a blank site for expanding your website and quickly publishing web pages. Contributors can work on draft versions of pages and publish them to make them visible to readers. The site includes document and image libraries for storing web publishing assets.

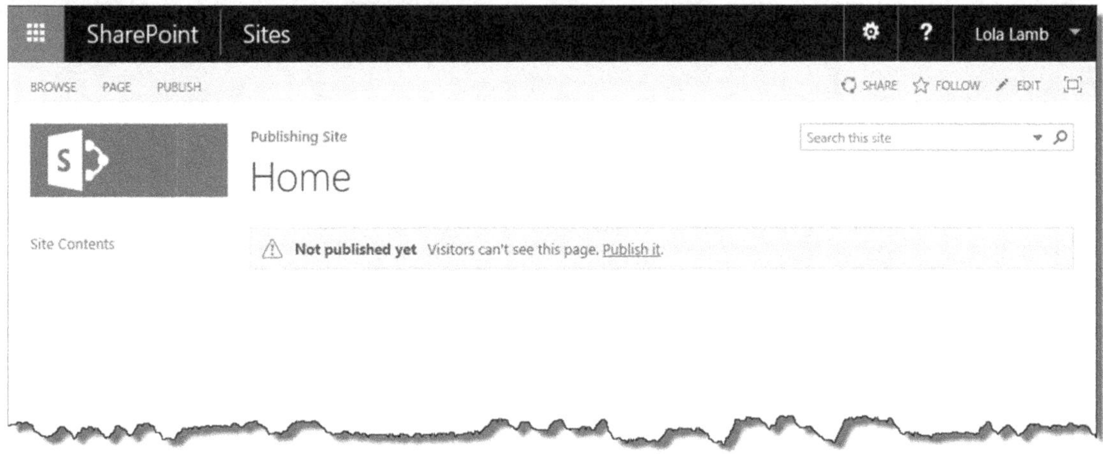

Figure 10: Publishing Site

Publishing Site with Workflow

This is a site for publishing web pages on a schedule by using approval workflows. It includes document and image libraries for storing web publishing assets. By default, only sites with this template can be created under this site.

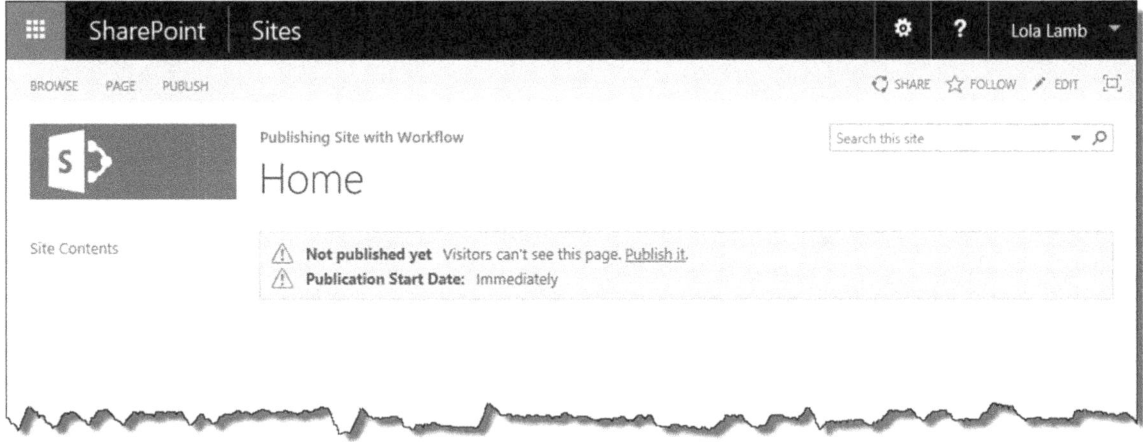

Figure 11: Publishing Site with Workflow

Enterprise Wiki

An Enterprise Wiki is a publishing site for sharing and updating large volumes of information across an enterprise.

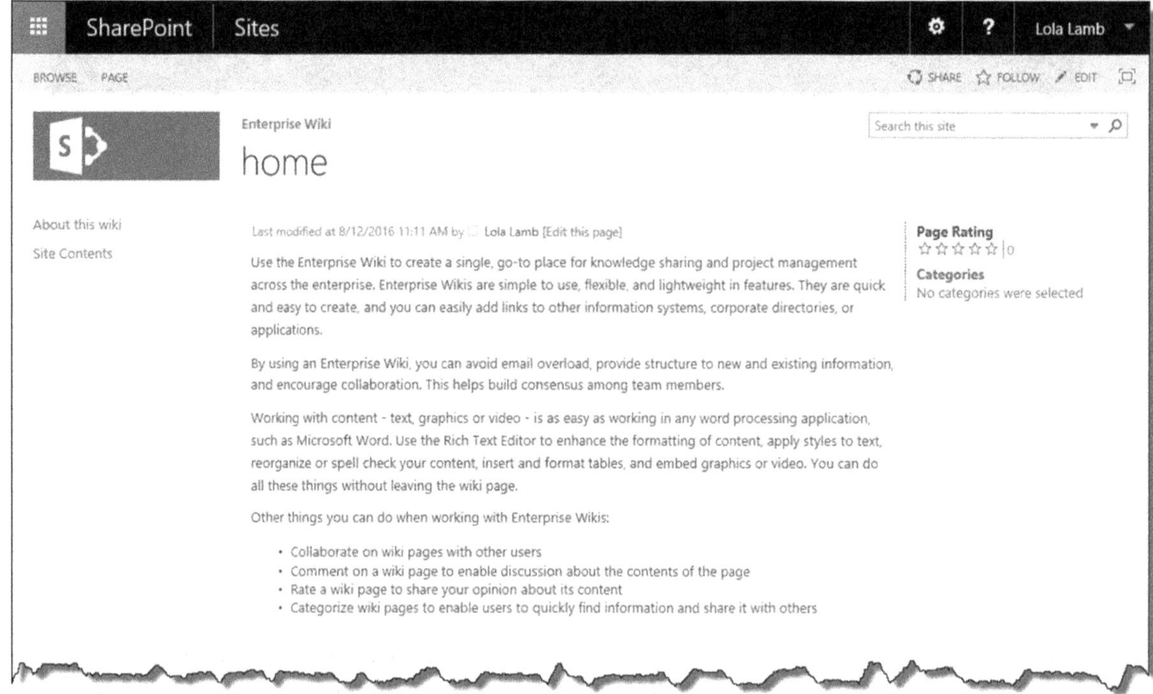

Figure 12: Enterprise Wiki

Appendix B: App Definitions

Purpose: Libraries, lists, discussion boards... in SharePoint 2016, they're all some sort of app. In this Appendix, all of the apps will be reviewed and displayed, to make your choices easier when it's time to create your own list.

Libraries

Libraries are essentially lists that have one and only one file associated with each item.

Asset Library

A library for managing and sharing digital assets, such as audio, video, and other rich media files.

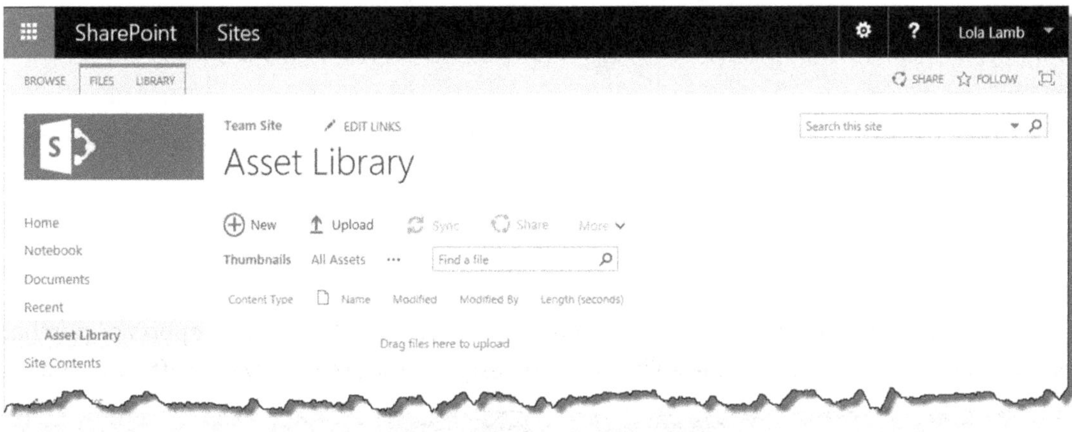

Figure 1: Asset Library

Data Connection Library

Create a Data Connection Library to make it easy to share files that contain information about external data connections.

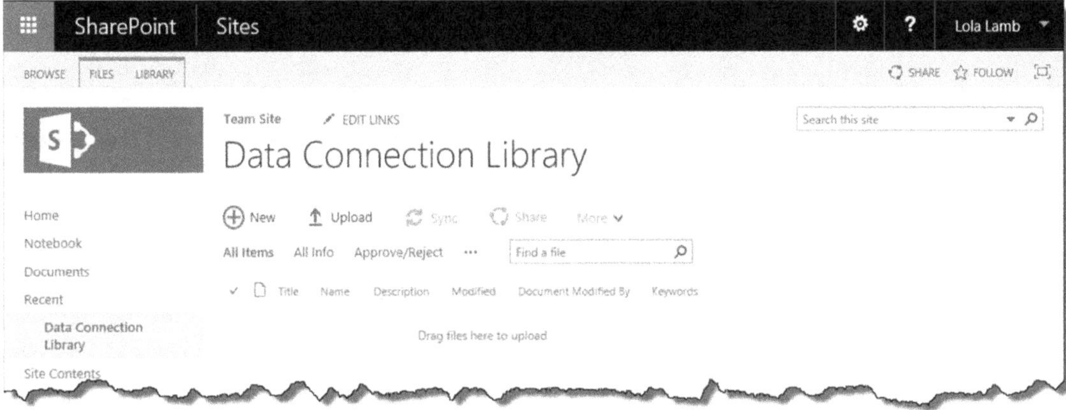

Figure 2: Data Connection Library

Document Library

Create a document library when you have a collection of documents or other files that you want to share. Document libraries support features such as folders, versioning, and check out.

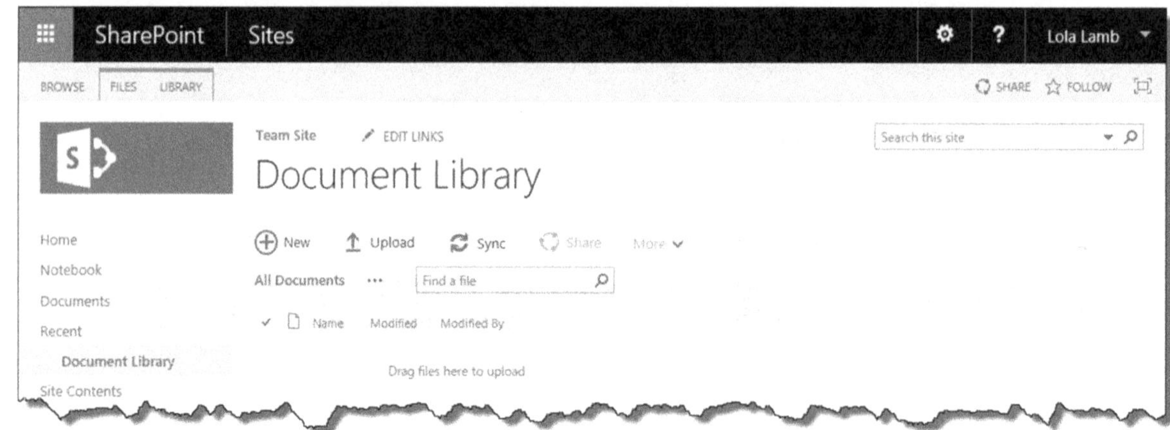

Figure 3: Document Library

Form Library

Create a form library when you have XML-based business forms, such as status reports or purchase orders, that you want to manage. These libraries are designed for use with Microsoft Office InfoPath.

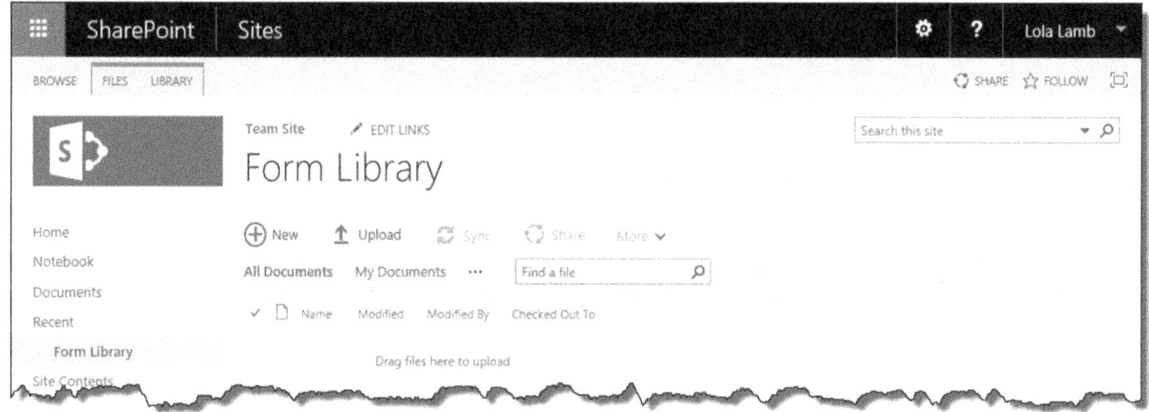

Figure 4: Form Library

Picture Library

Create a picture library when you have pictures you want to share. Picture libraries provide special features for managing and displaying pictures, such as thumbnails, download options, and a slide show.

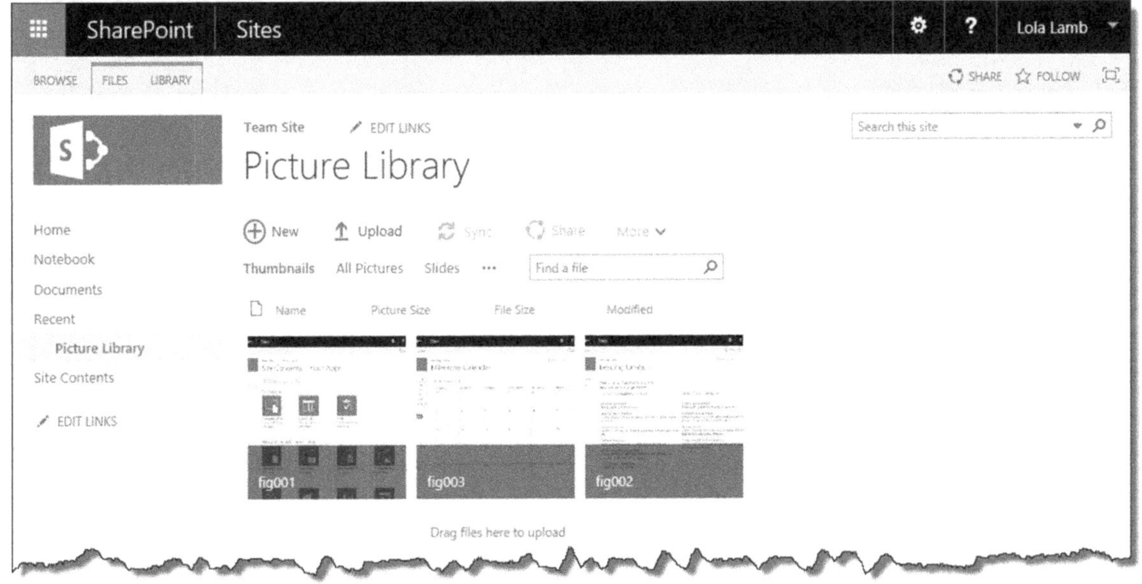

Figure 5: Picture Library

Report Library

A library designed to manage and share SQL reports.

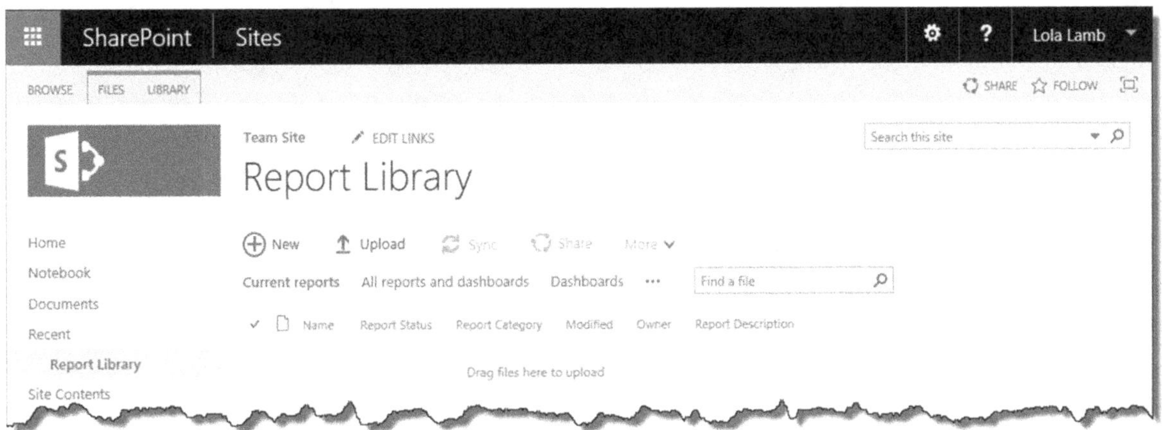

Figure 6: Report Library

Wiki Page Library

Create a wiki page library when you want to have an interconnected collection of wiki pages. Wiki page libraries support pictures, tables, hyperlinks, and wiki linking.

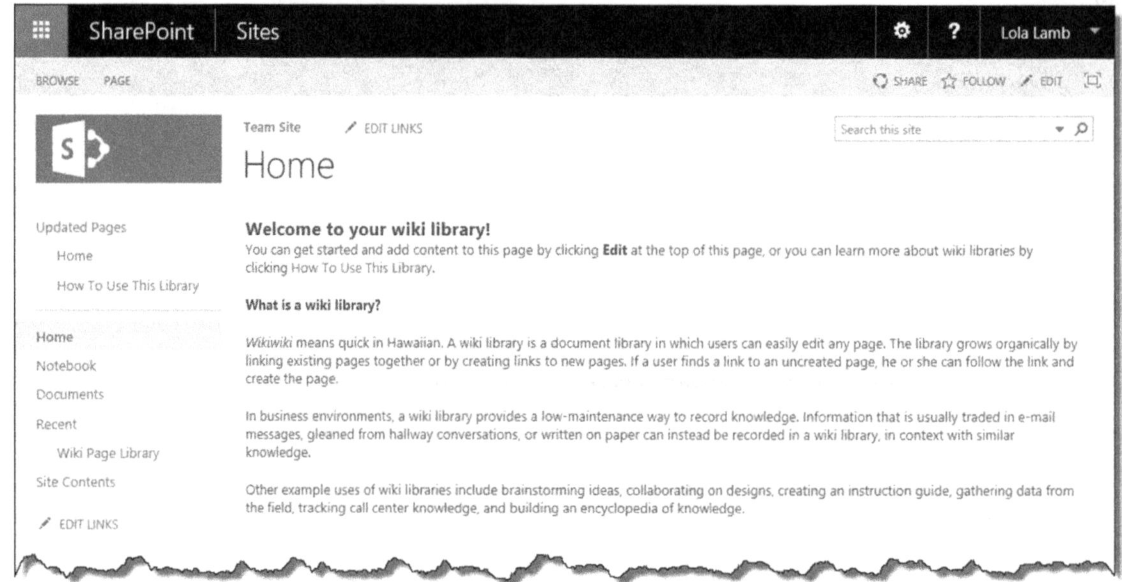

Figure 7: Wiki Page Library

Lists

Lists in this collection are designed to be used as tools to connect with your co-workers.

Access App

An app for creating web-based databases with Microsoft Access.

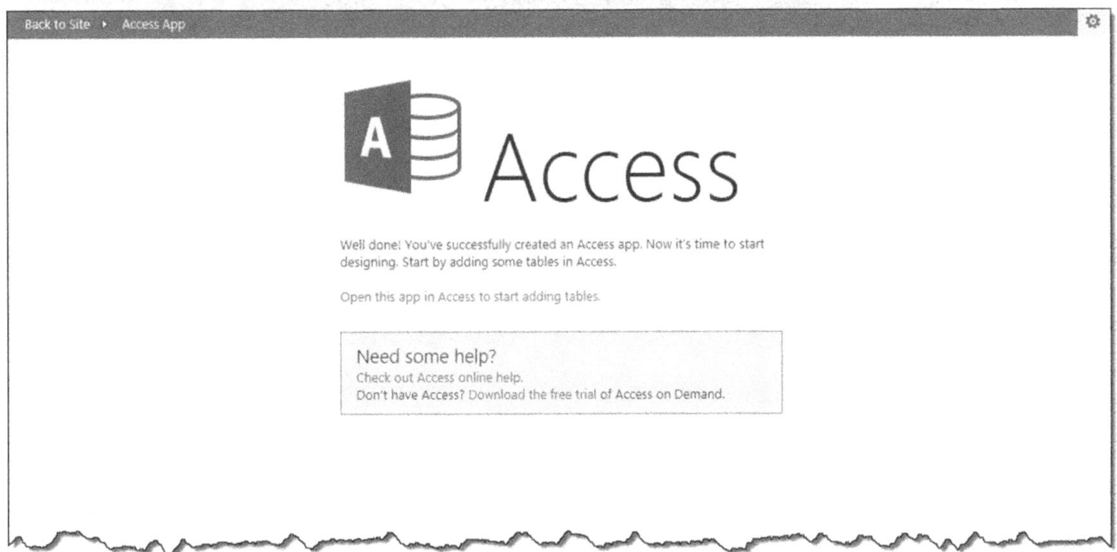

Figure 8: Access App Welcome Page

Announcements

Create an announcements list when you want a place to share news, status, and other short bits of information.

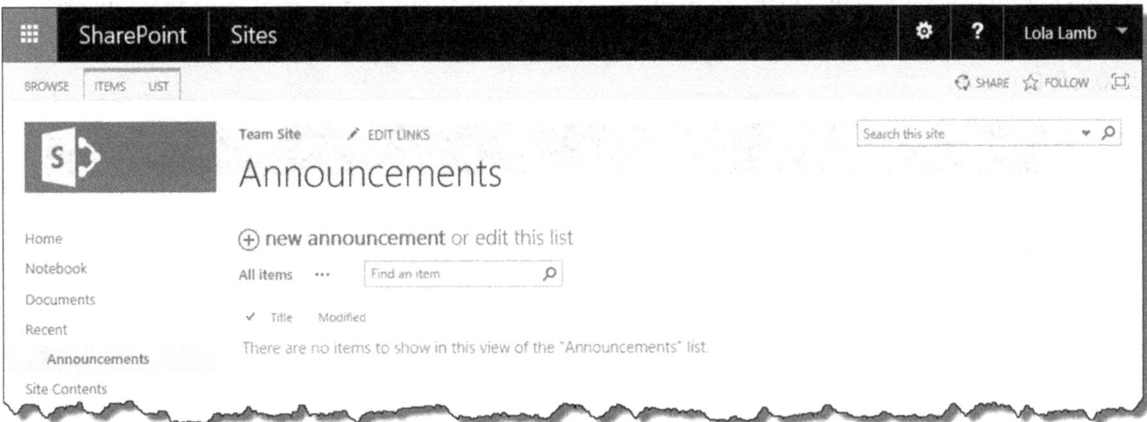

Figure 9: Announcements

Calendar

Create a calendar list when you want a calendar-based view of upcoming meetings, deadlines, and other important events. You can share information between your calendar list and Windows SharePoint Services-compatible events programs.

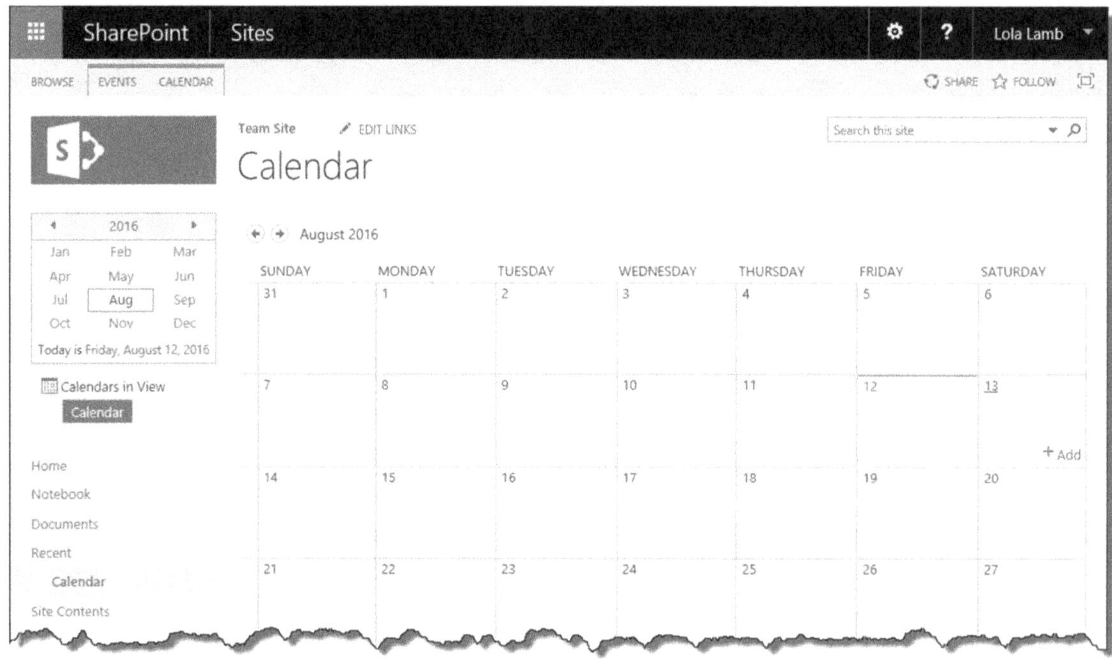

Figure 10: Calendar

Contacts

Create a contacts list when you want to manage information about people that your team works with, such as customers or partners. You can share information between your contacts list and Microsoft Outlook.

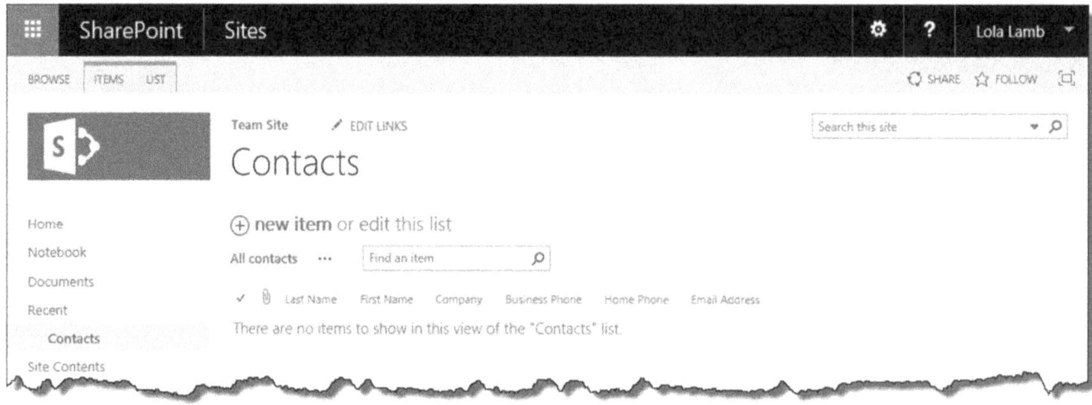

Figure 11: Contacts

Custom List

Create a custom list when you want to specify your own columns. The list opens as a web page and lets you add or edit items one at a time. Your title field must be a single line of text, but it can be renamed. You can also add all of the columns that you want, as shown in the task "Create a List."

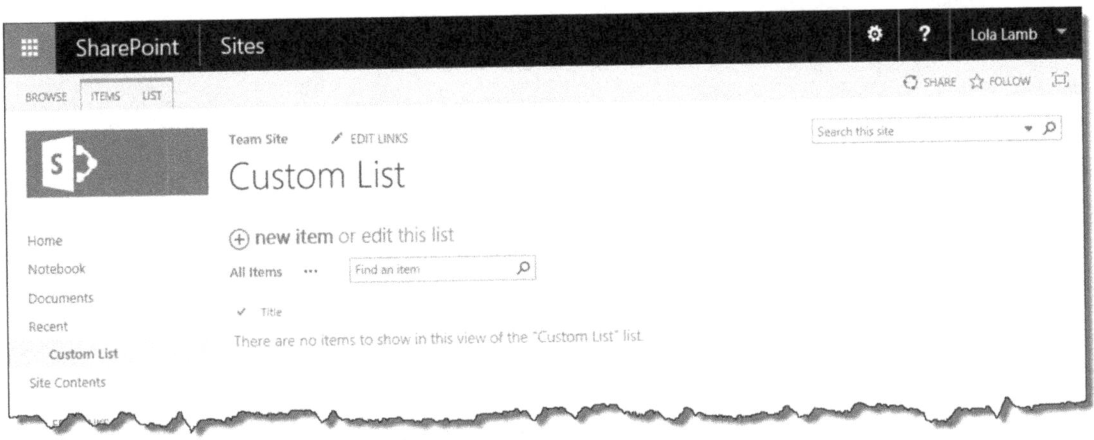

Figure 12: Custom List

Custom List in Datasheet View

Create a custom list when you want to specify your own columns, just like a regular custom list. In this case, the list opens in a spreadsheet-like environment for convenient data entry, editing, and formatting. It requires Microsoft Access and a browser with ActiveX control support.

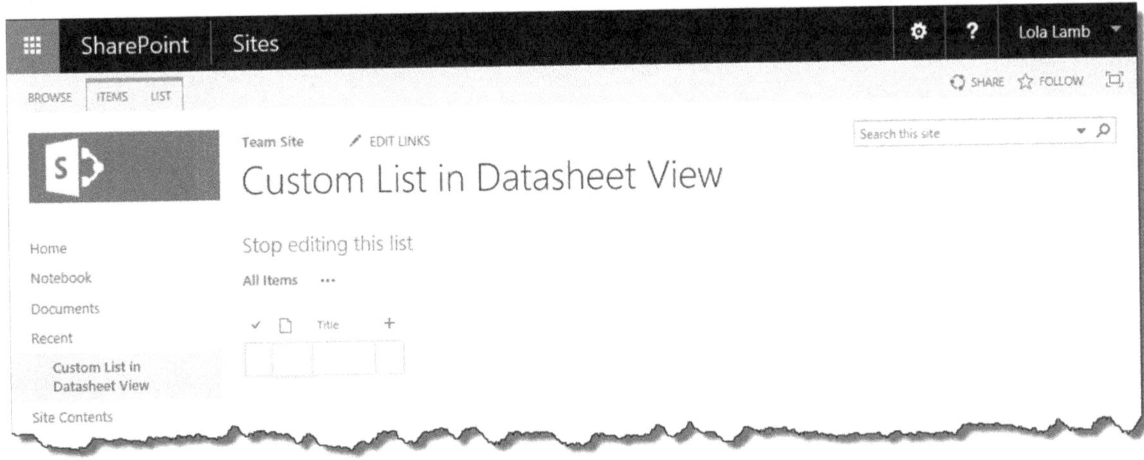

Figure 13: Custom List in Datasheet View

Discussion Board

Create a discussion board when you want to provide a place for newsgroup-style discussions. Discussion boards provide features for managing discussion threads and ensuring that only approved posts appear.

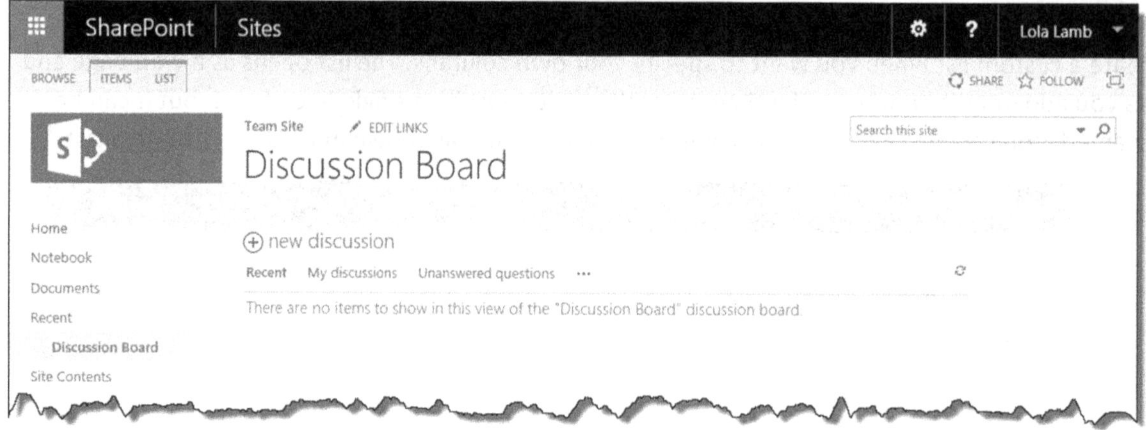

Figure 14: Discussion Board

External List

Create an external list to read and write data with the familiarity of a SharePoint list.

Import Spreadsheet

Import a spreadsheet when you want to create a list that has the same columns and content as an existing spreadsheet. Importing a spreadsheet requires Microsoft Excel.

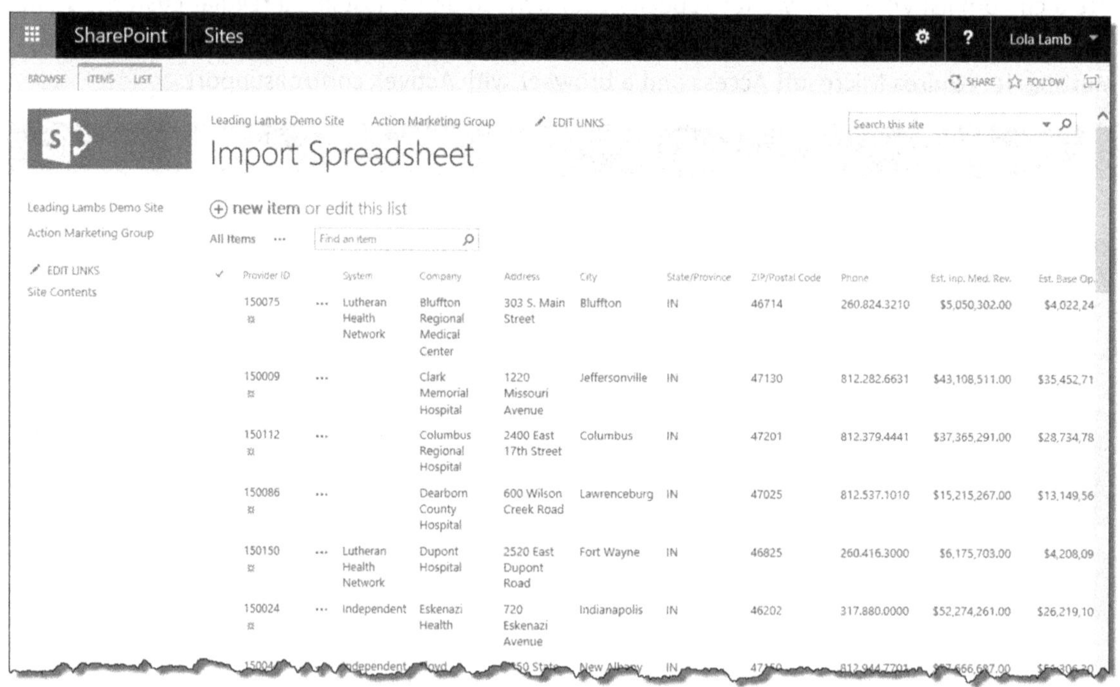

Figure 15: Import Spreadsheet

Issue Tracking

Create an issue tracking list when you want to manage a set of issues or problems. You can assign, prioritize, and follow the progress of issues from start to finish. Another key feature is that you can relate issues to one another, which makes it easier to create logical progressions of work to be done.

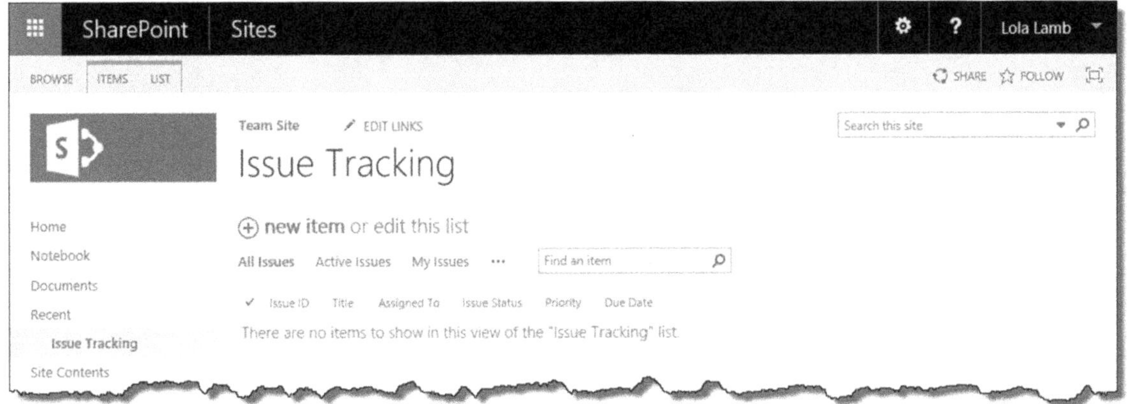

Figure 16: Issue Tracking

Links

Create a links list when you have a set of links that you want to share. This is an especially helpful list for the most commonly used links in your site or site collection or other resources.

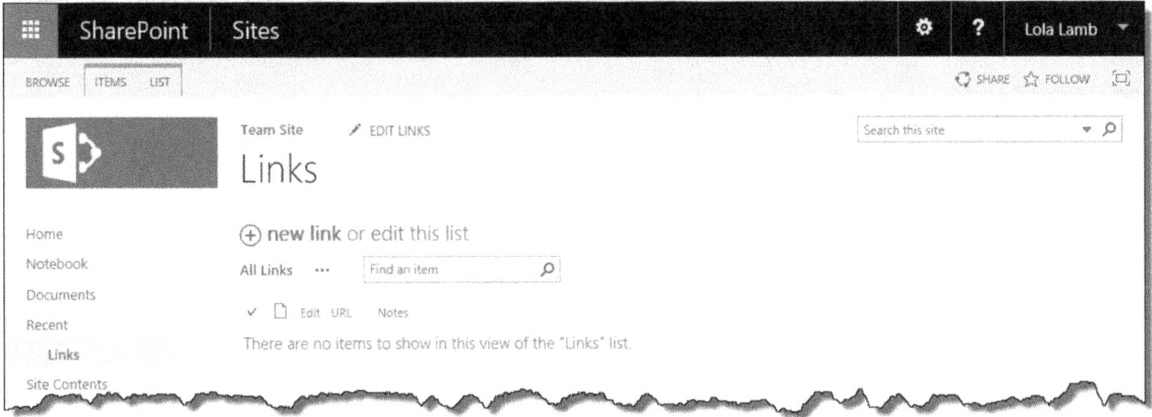

Figure 17: Links

Promoted Links

Create a promoted links list when you have links to web pages or other resources that you want to share. This list can also the source for the tile icons web part view similar to the Welcome Page when a new site is created.

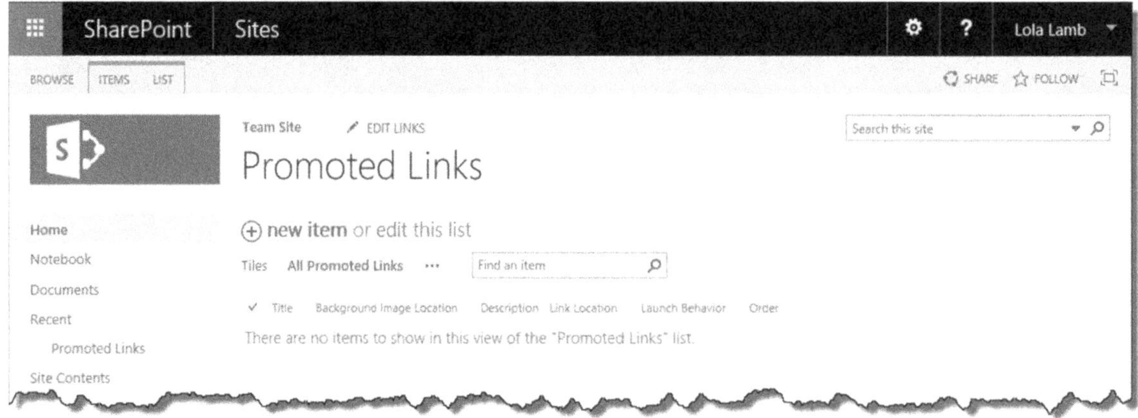

Figure 18: Promoted Links

Survey

A list for conducting and managing surveys for team members.

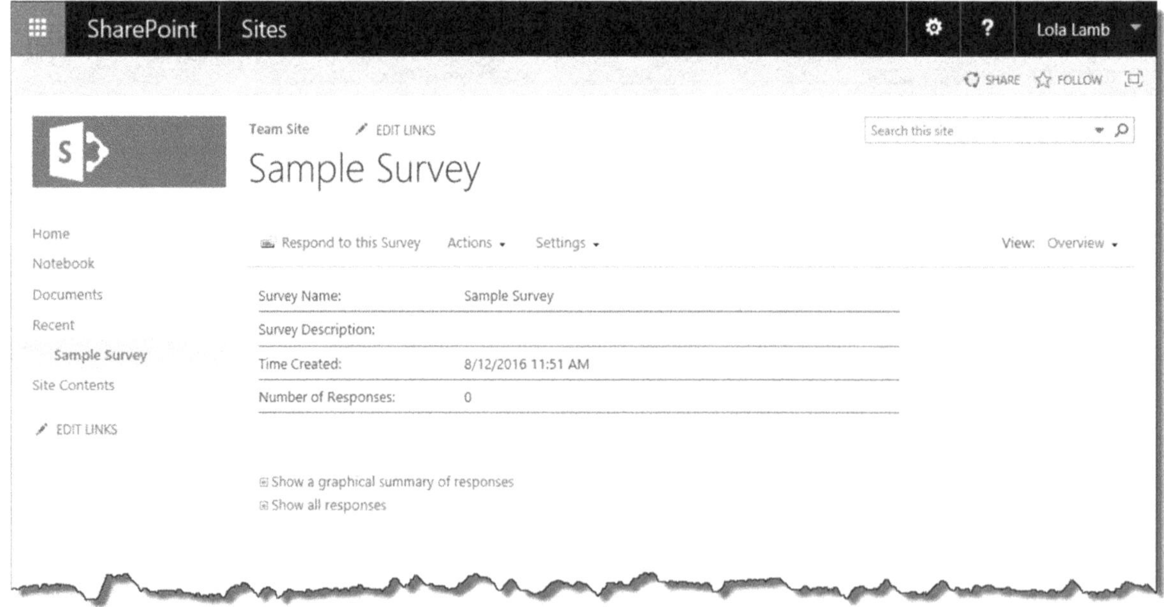

Figure 19: Survey

Tasks

Create a tasks list when you want to track a group of work items that you or your team needs to complete.

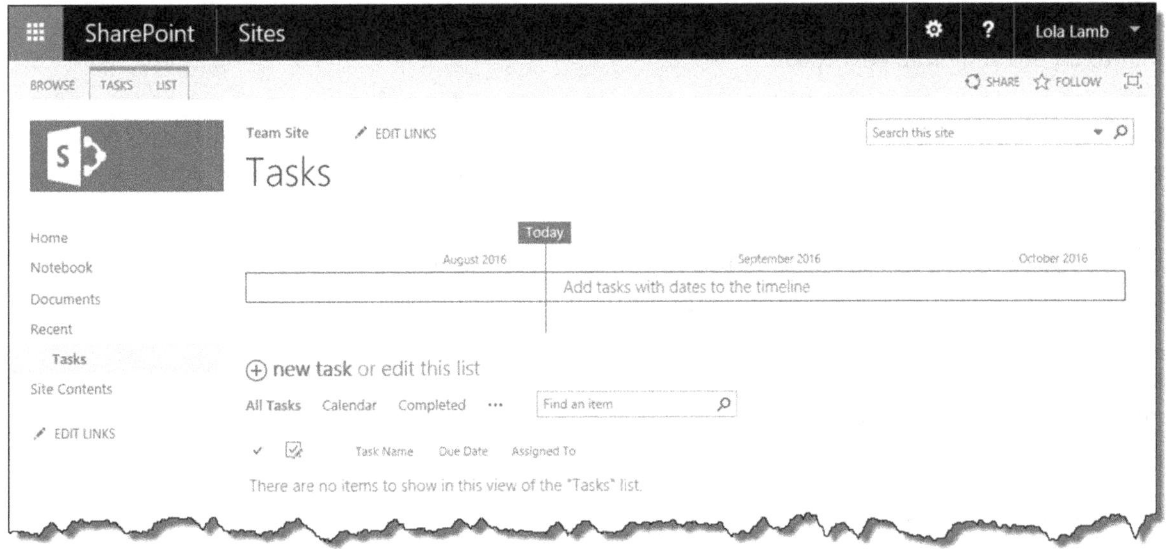

Figure 20: Tasks

Appendix C: Web Parts

Purpose: When you create a Web Parts page, you can easily insert content from almost any list made available in SharePoint. There are also some specialized content web parts. In this Appendix, the most common web parts will be reviewed and displayed, to make your choices easier when it's time to create your web parts page.

Apps

Not only can whole pages be created for an app, but some app functionality can be inserted within a section of a page.

Calendar

The Calendar app can track dates on a web page.

Documents

List documents on a web page.

MicroFeed

Display alerts and messages from other users.

Site Assets

List components and tools on your site.

Tasks

List the things that need to be done.

Blog

Web Parts for adding blogging capabilities to a page.

Blog Archives

Provides quick links to older blog posts.

Blog Notifications

Provides quick links to register for blog posts notifications using Alerts or RSS feed.

Blog Tools

Provides blog owners and administrators with quick links to common settings pages and content lists for managing a blog site.

Business Data

Connect to your data easily with these Web Parts.

Business Data Actions

Displays a list of actions from Business Data Connectivity.

Business Data Connectivity Filter

Filters the contents of Web Parts using a list of values from the Business Data Connectivity.

Business Data Item
Displays one item from a data source in Business Data Connectivity.

Business Data Item Builder
Creates a Business Data item from parameters in the query string and provides it to other Web Parts.

Business Data List
Displays a list of items from a data source in Business Data Connectivity.

Business Data List Related List
Displays a list of items related to one or more parent items from a data source in Business Data Connectivity.

Excel Web Access
Use the Excel Web Access Web Part to interact with an Excel workbook as a Web page.

Indicator Details
Displays the details of a single Status Indicator. Status Indicators display an important measure for an organization and may be obtained from other data sources including SharePoint lists, Excel workbooks, and SQL Server 2005 Analysis Services KPIs.

Status List
Shows a list of Status Indicators. Status Indicators display important measures for your organization, and show how your organization is performing with respect to your goals.

Visio Web Access
Enables viewing and refreshing of Visio Web Drawings.

Community
Introduce collaborative features to any web page.

About this Community
This Web Part displays the community description and other properties, like established date. This Web Part will work on Community Sites or any other site that has Community Features turned on.

Join
Provides the ability for non-members of a community site to join the community. The button hides itself if the user is already a member. This Web Part will work on Community Sites or any other site that has Community Features turned on.

My Membership
Displays reputation and membership information for the current visitor of a community site. This Web Part will work on Community Sites or any other site that has Community Features turned on.

Tools

Provides community owners and administrators with quick links to common settings pages and content lists for managing a community site. This Web Part will work on Community Sites or any other site that has Community Features turned on.

What's Happening

Displays the number of members, topics and replies within a community site. This Web Part will work on Community sites or any other site that has Community Features turned on.

Content Rollup

Web Parts in this category can aggregate content from a variety of sources.

Categories

Displays categories from the Site Directory.

Content Query

Displays a dynamic view of content from your site.

Content Search

Content Search Web Part will allow you to show items that are results of a search query you specify. When you add it to the page, this Web Part will show recently modified items from the current site. You can change this setting to show items from another site or list by editing the Web Part and changing its search criteria. As new content is discovered by search, this Web Part will display an updated list of items each time the page is viewed. Depending on the search configuration, there may be a delay between when the content is modified and when it appears.

Project Summary

Displays information about a project in an easy to read overview.

Relevant Documents

Displays documents that are relevant to the current user.

RSS Viewer

Displays an RSS feed

Site Aggregator

Displays sites of your choice.

Sites in Category

Displays sites from the Site Directory within a specific category.

Summary Links

Allows authors to create links that can be grouped and styled.

Table of Contents

Displays the navigation hierarchy of your site.

Term Property

Displays the specified property of a Term.

Timeline

Use this timeline to show a high level view of data from another Web Part or tasks list.

WSRP Viewer

Displays portlets from Web sites using WSRP 1.1.

XML Viewer

Transforms XML data using XSL and shows the results.

Document Sets

Manage document sets in your SharePoint site.

Document Set Contents

Displays the contents of the Document Set.

Document Set Properties

Displays the properties of the Document Set.

Filters

Add filter controls to your SharePoint pages.

Apply Filters Button

Add this button to a page so users can decide when to apply their filter choices. Otherwise, each filter is applied when its value is changed.

Choice Filter

Filters the contents of Web Parts using a list of values entered by the page author.

Current User Filter

Filters the contents of Web Parts by using properties of the current user.

Date Filter

Filters the contents of Web Parts by allowing users to enter or pick a date.

Page Field Filter

Filters the contents of Web Parts using information about the current page.

Query String (URL) Filter

Filters the contents of Web Parts using values passed via the query string.

SharePoint List Filter

Filters the contents of Web Parts by using a list of values.

SQL Server Analysis Services Filter

Filters the contents of Web Parts using a list of values from SQL Server Analysis Services cubes.

Text Filter

Filters the contents of Web Parts by allowing users to enter a text value.

Forms

Web Parts in this category build Web page forms for users.

HTML Form

Connects simple form controls to other Web Parts.

InfoPath Form

Use this Web Part to display an InfoPath browser-enabled form.

Media and Content

Web Parts in this category display a variety of multimedia content.

Content Editor

Allows authors to enter rich text content.

Get Started With Your Site

This Web Part displays a set of tiles with common SharePoint actions.

Image Viewer

Displays a specified image.

Media

Use to embed media clips (video and audio) in a Web page.

Page Viewer

Displays another Web page on this Web page. The other Web page is presented in an IFrame.

Picture Library Slideshow

Use to display a slideshow of images and photos from a picture library.

Script Editor

This Web Part displays a set of tiles with common SharePoint actions.

Silverlight

A Web Part to display a Silverlight application.

Search

Web Parts that help determine search results.

Refinement

This Web Part helps the users to refine search results.

Search Box

Displays a search box that allows users to search for information.

Search Navigation

This Web Part helps the users to navigate among search verticals.

Search Results

Displays the search results and the properties associated with them.

Taxonomy Refinement Panel

This Web Part helps the user to refine search results on term set data. To use this Web Part, you must also have a Search Data Provider Web Part on this page and use Managed Navigation.

Search-Driven Content

Web Parts that produce content lists based on content type.

Catalog-Item Reuse

Use this Web Part to reuse or republish the content of an item from a catalog.

Items Matching a Tag

This Web Part will show items that are tagged with a term.

Pages

This Web Part will show any items that are derived from the Pages content type.

Pictures

This Web Part will show any items that are derived from the Picture or Image content type.

Popular Items

This Web Part will show items that have been recently viewed by many users.

Recently Changed Items

This Web Part will show items that have been modified recently. This can help site users track the latest activity on a site or a library.

Recommended Items

This Web Part will show content recommendations based on usage patterns for the current page.

Videos

This Web Part will show any items that are derived from the Video content type. It will sort items by number of views.

Web Pages

This Web Part will show any items that are derived from the Page content type.

Wiki Pages

This Web Part will show any items that are derived from the Wiki Page content type.

Social Collaboration

Web Parts in this category enable user to engage in collaborative and social activities.

Contact Details

Displays details about a contact for this page or site.

Note Board

Enable users to leave short, publicly-viewable notes about this page.

Organization Browser

This Web Part displays each person in the reporting chain in an interactive view optimized for browsing organization charts.

Site Feed

Site Feed contains microblogging conversations on a group site.

Site Users

Use the Site Users Web Part to see a list of the site users and their online status.

Tag Cloud

Displays the most popular subjects being tagged inside your organization.

User Tasks

Displays tasks that are assigned to the current user.

Appendix D: Views

Purpose: When you create a new view of an app in SharePoint, you are given a choice of six default views. In this Appendix, these views (with the exception of the SharePoint Designer view) will be reviewed and displayed, to make your choices easier when it's time to customize the way you look at a list.

Standard

View data on a web page. This view displays a standard data grid type view of the data, as seen on most web pages and sites.

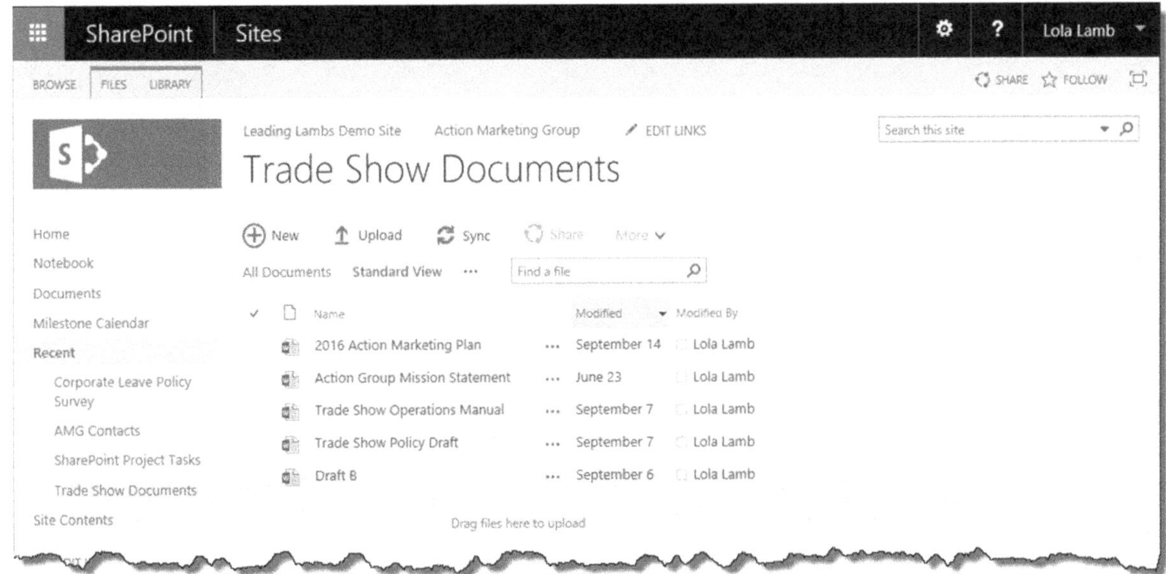

Figure 1: Standard View

Calendar

View data as a daily, weekly, or monthly calendar.

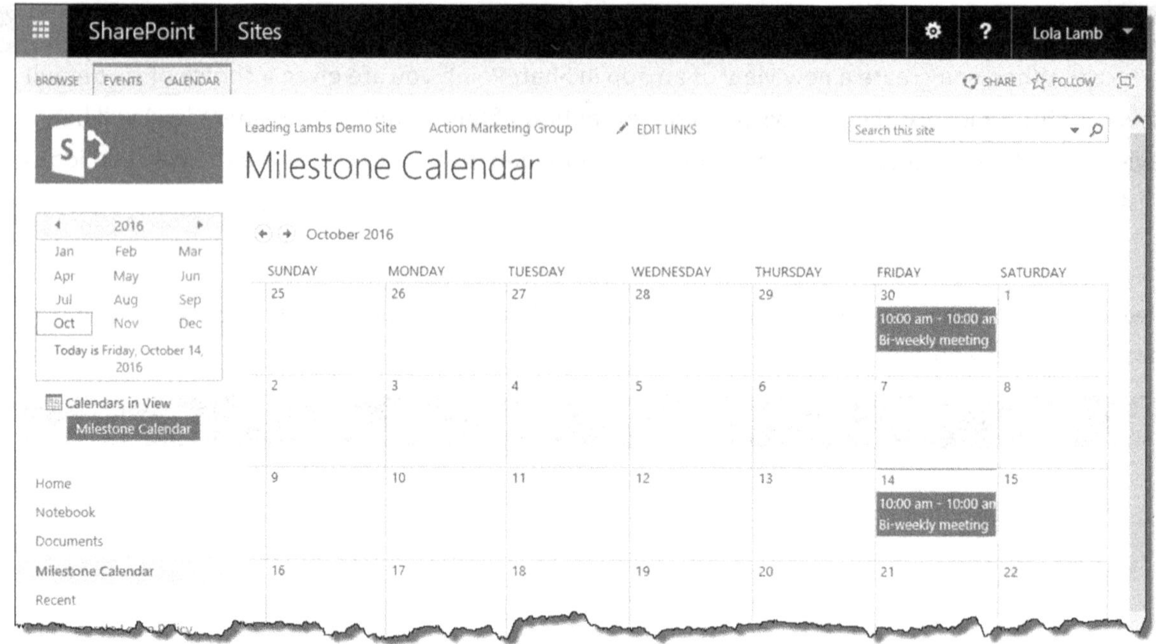

Figure 2: Calendar View

Gantt

View list items in a Gantt chart to see a graphical representation of the items related over time.

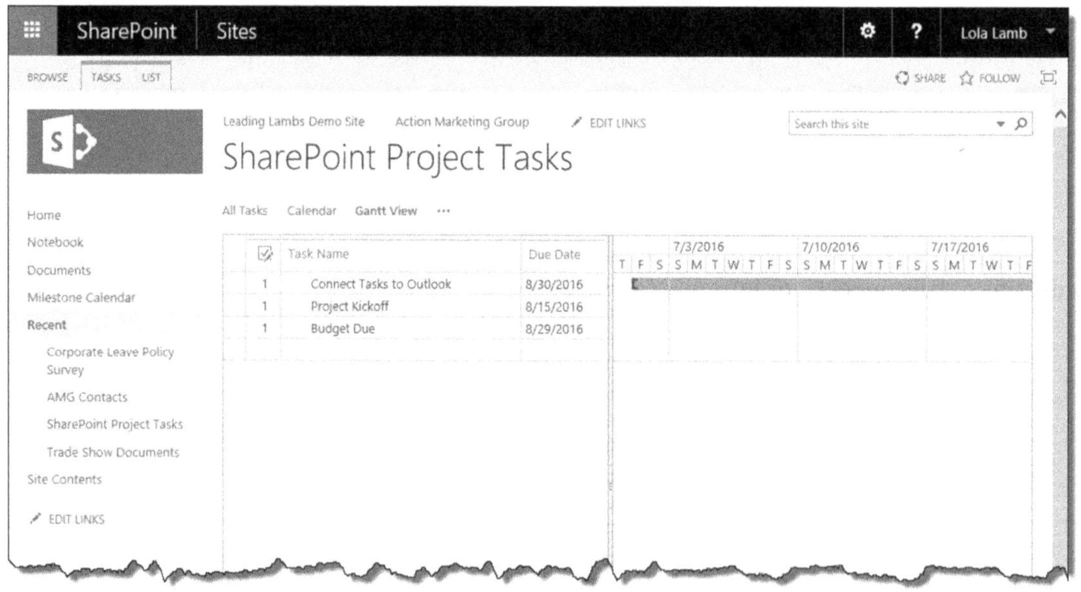

Figure 3: Gantt View

Datasheet

View data in an editable spreadsheet format that is convenient for bulk editing and quick customization. This view requires the use of an ActiveX-capable browser and Microsoft Access.

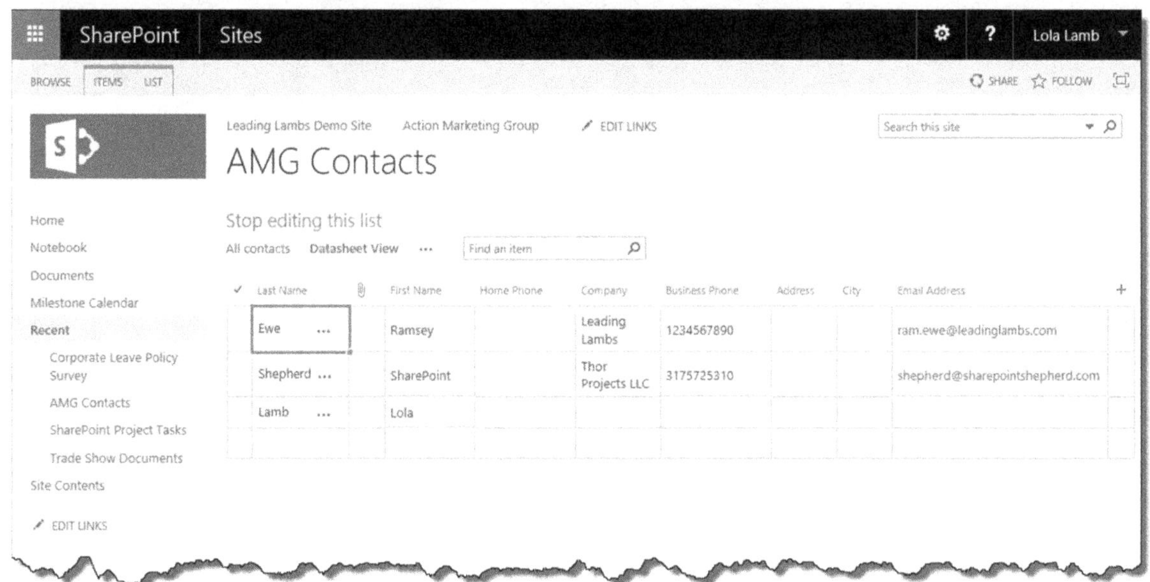

Figure 4: Datasheet View

Access

Start Microsoft Office Access to create forms and reports that are based on this list.

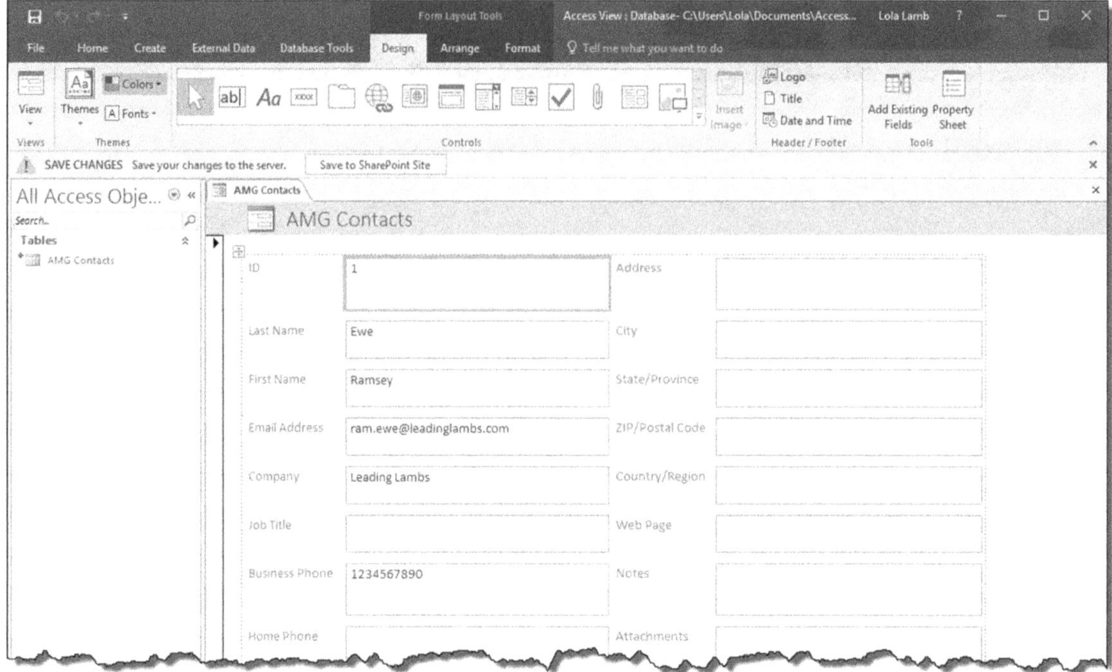

Figure 5: Access View

Appendix E: Permissions in SharePoint

Purpose: To keep documents secure in SharePoint, there are a number of permission levels that can be assigned to individual users or user groups. You can also manage permissions for a user or group at the site level, at the individual list item level, and everywhere in between within SharePoint. In this Appendix, the definitions of the various default permission levels in SharePoint are listed.

> Note: SharePoint administrators can define additional permission levels, so there may be other permission levels defined for your organization's sites.

Permission Levels

	Name in browser	Description	* Visitors (Restricted Read)	* Members (Contribute)	* Owners (Full Control)	Designers (Design)	Approvers (Approve)	Hierarchy Managers (Manage Hierarchy)
Create	Add Items	Add items to lists and add documents to document libraries.		✓	✓	✓	✓	✓
Read	Browse Directories	Enumerate files and folders in a Web site using SharePoint Designer and WebDAV interfaces.		✓	✓	✓	✓	✓
Read	Enumerate Permissions	Enumerate permissions on the Web site, list, folder, document, or list item.			✓			✓
Read	Open	Allow users to open a Web site, list, or folder to access items inside that container.	✓	✓	✓	✓	✓	✓
Read	Open Items	View the source of documents	✓	✓	✓	✓	✓	✓

		with server-side file handlers.						
	View Application Pages	View forms, views, and application pages. Enumerate lists.		✓	✓	✓	✓	✓
	View Items	View items in lists and documents in document libraries.	✓	✓	✓	✓	✓	✓
	View Pages	View pages in a Web site.	✓	✓	✓	✓	✓	✓
	View Versions	View past versions of a list item or document.		✓	✓	✓	✓	✓
Update	Approve Items	Approve a minor version of a list item or document.			✓	✓	✓	
	Edit Items	Edit items in lists, edit documents in document libraries, and customize Web Part Pages in document libraries.		✓	✓	✓	✓	✓
	Override List Behaviors	Discard or check in a document which is checked out to another user, and change or override settings which allow users to read/edit only their own items			✓	✓	✓	✓
Delete	Delete Items	Delete items from a list and documents from		✓	✓	✓	✓	✓

		a document library.						
	Delete Versions	Delete past versions of a list item or document.		✓	✓	✓	✓	✓
Email	Create Alerts	Create alerts.		✓	✓	✓	✓	✓
	Manage Alerts	Manage alerts for all users of the Web site.			✓			✓
Personalize	Edit Personal User Information	Allows a user to change his or her own user information, such as adding a picture.		✓	✓	✓	✓	✓
	Manage Personal Views	Create, change, and delete personal views of lists.		✓	✓	✓	✓	✓
	Add/Remove Personal Web Parts	Add or remove personal Web Parts on a Web Part Page.		✓	✓	✓	✓	✓
	Update Personal Web Parts	Update Web Parts to display personalized information.		✓	✓	✓	✓	✓
Program	Use Remote Interfaces	Use SOAP, WebDAV, the Client Object Model, or SharePoint Designer interfaces to access the Web site.		✓	✓	✓	✓	✓
	Use Client Integration Features	Use features which launch client applications. Without this		✓	✓	✓	✓	✓

		permission, users will have to work on documents locally and upload their changes.						
Security	Create Groups	Create a group of users that can be used anywhere within the site collection.			✓			
	Manage Permissions	Create and change permission levels on the Web site and assign permissions to users and groups.			✓			✓
Structure	Create Subsites	Create subsites such as team sites, Meeting Workspace sites, and Document Workspace sites.			✓			✓
	Manage Lists	Create and delete lists, add or remove columns in a list, and add or remove public views of a list.			✓	✓		✓

	Manage Web Site	Grant the ability to perform all administration tasks for the Web site as well as manage content.			✓			✓
	Add and Customize Pages	Add, change, or delete HTML pages or Web Part Pages, and edit the Web site using a Microsoft SharePoint Foundation-compatible editor.			✓	✓		✓
Style	Apply Themes and Borders	Apply a theme or borders to the entire Web site.			✓	✓		
	Apply Style Sheets	Apply a style sheet (.CSS file) to the Web site.			✓	✓		
Misc.	Browse User Information	View information about users of the Web site.		✓	✓	✓	✓	✓
	View Web Analytics Data	View reports on Web site usage.			✓			✓

Get access to more helpful resources, quick reference materials, and SharePoint tips and tricks. Sign up at tinyurl.com/followtheshepherd.

Appendix F: Exploring the SharePoint Interface

Purpose: SharePoint 2016 emulates many of the interface features found in Office 2016 and Office 365 applications, especially in regards to the App Launcher and Library controls. While many of the interface controls are self-explanatory, a quick visual primer on the various interface tools and controls should prove helpful.

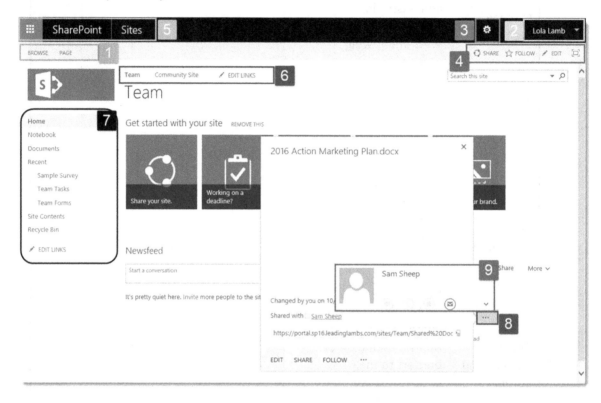

Figure 1: SharePoint Interface Elements

1 The Ribbon

These links are actually tabs for different sets of controls that are relevant to where you are. When you click one of the links, the appropriate set of controls will appear. If you want the ribbon to go away, click Browse.

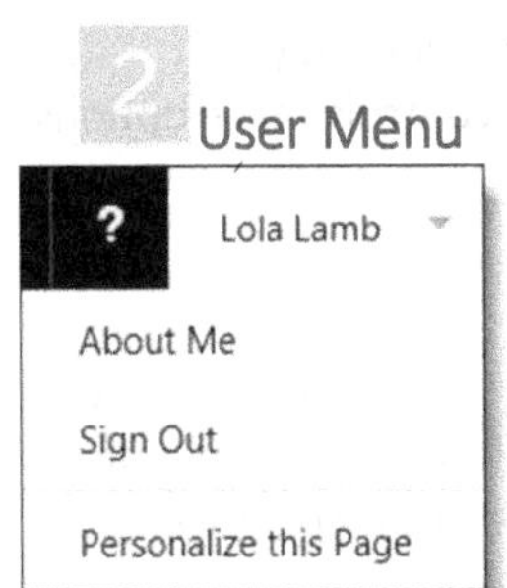

This menu contains navigation and action that pertains to you. You can use About Me to navigate to your personal My Site. Sign Out signs you out of SharePoint, and Personalize this Page allows you to change your personal view of a page.

The settings menu is the primary place to take action on the site and the current page. You can change the site settings, add an app, a page, or review the site contents. Additionally, most other action settings will appear in this menu or lead you to pages which allow you to control the site.

4 Quick Access Toolbar

In the Quick Access Toolbar, you'll find actions that you can perform in the context of where you're at – these same actions are on the ribbon, but here you can access them in one click. The common actions are:

Share the site with someone inside the organization – or externally if allowed.

Add this site, library, etc., to your newsfeed so you will see updates automatically.

Synchronize the files in this site or library to your computer using OneDrive for Business.

Edit the contents of this page including changing web and app parts.

Focus on content by minimizing the navigation and chrome in the display to allow more space for the content.

5 Suite Bar

The Suite Bar allows you to navigate between the various applications in your organization – or on Office 365. Your IT systems administrator controls these options.

6 Top Navigation Bar

The top navigation bar is "big picture" navigation in your site or set of sites. Like highways they move you between different large areas in your SharePoint space. You, or your site administrator, control these options.

7 Quick Launch

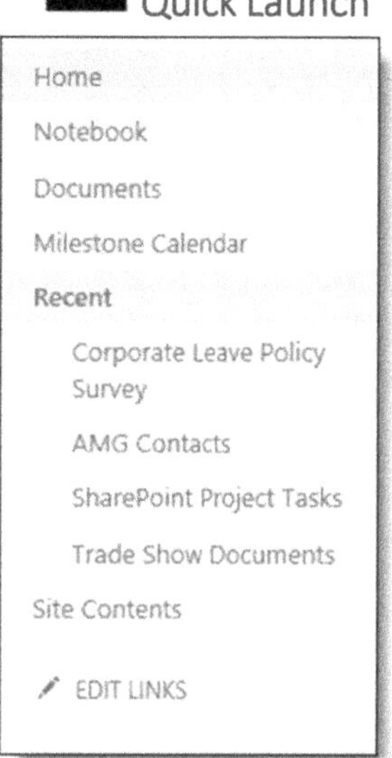

Local navigation is handled in the Quick Launch area. This may include links that you add to the area manually as well as recent links. This is where you navigate to the site, list, or library containing the precise content you are looking for.

8 Ellipsis Control

These three dots indicate that there is more information available that has been "hidden" for brevity. In SharePoint, whenever you see the three dots of an ellipsis, you can click it to get more items or more information about the current item. On a document, the ellipsis will lead you to a hover panel with more information and a preview of the document.

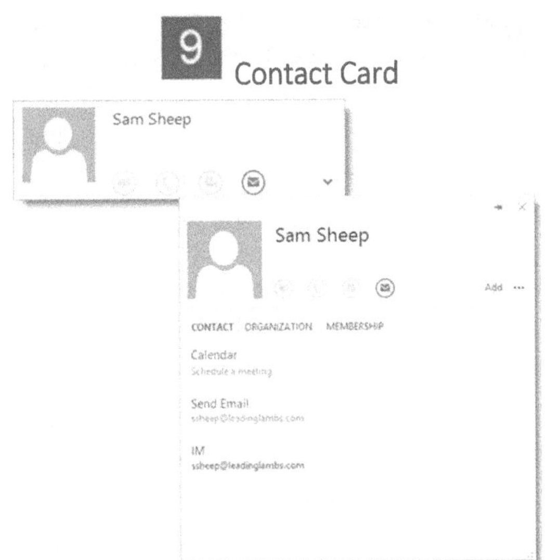

Hovering over any name will cause a preview of the contact card for that person to appear. If you and the other person are logged into Skype for Business, you'll get presence information and an opportunity to contact them via email, chat, or phone. Clicking the drop down arrow opens the whole contact card.

Get access to more helpful resources, quick reference materials, and SharePoint tips and tricks. Sign up at tinyurl.com/followtheshepherd.

Appendix G: List Columns and Fields

Purpose: Columns are one of the most powerful tools in SharePoint. It can make column creation confusing and intimidating; when used improperly, columns can make your libraries and lists a mess. However, your choice of column could be the pillars that hold up the structure of your site. In this Appendix, we'll go over column types, their corresponding fields, and how they are best used.

The first option you must decide on is whether to use a List or a Site column. A good guideline to follow is by asking, will I need access to this sort of data in a different list or library? Put another way, will I need to create this column more than once to give me the same type of information? If the answer is yes, try looking into your existing site columns. Site columns can keep your data consistent and organized across your site, and SharePoint comes with many standard site columns out of the box, such as Office Address, Job Title, and even Birthday columns – and that's just for Calendars and Contact lists. However, if there is a set of information that is specific to one list or library, such as invoice numbers or sales tracking status, a list column will work just as well.

Fields by Column Type

When creating a column, most column types have very different fields that need to be filled out. While some fields have the same name in different columns, but have different uses in context. There are only a few fields that are shared across all (or almost all) column types, so we will go through those first. Those fields are:

Column name: This field acts as a name for your column. This is what will appear on your list or library view. It should be simple and specific – while you can usually rename your column, you cannot have two columns with the same name.

The type of information in this column is: Of course, you must select what information this particular column will hold. This is probably the most important choice, so the factors will be detailed below.

Description: This field is for a brief description of the information stored in this column. This description is not visible unless you are creating a new item or editing an item's properties. It is useful to specify what information should be put in that particular column, especially if you think it could be confused with another column.

Require that this column contains information: As simple as this field is (either Yes or No), there is a reason this option is disabled by default. Clicking "Yes" for this option forces anyone creating a new item to have information for this column. In any instances where information may be missing or unavailable, it will force users to fill in potentially incorrect information to allow creation of the item.

Add to default view: This option is checked by default, meaning the column will appear in the default view of the list. This option can be changed at any time.

Each column type will be listed below with detailed information on the applicable fields that appear.

Single line of text

This column is good for short descriptions, titles, and information of less than 255 characters. The additional fields to fill out are:

> Enforce unique values: This means that no two entries in this column may contain the same information. This option requires that you index its contents.
> Maximum number of characters: The default maximum will always be 255. SharePoint will not allow a higher number than this, but you can make this number lower if so desired.
> Default value: This setting is used when new entries are created to automatically display specified text or a calculated value. When someone creates a new entry, they can either leave it as the default value, or fill in the field with text of their choice.

Multiple lines of text

This column is good for notes, comments, and other places where there may be a great deal of text to be entered. You typically cannot sort or filter by this column type. The additional fields to fill out are:

> Allow unlimited length in document libraries: This option only appears when adding this column in a document library. The default is No.
> Number of lines for editing: This specifies the number of lines that are visible for editing. The default value is 6; this means that, after 6 lines of editing have been reached, a scrollbar will appear, but you can still add more text.
> Specify the type of text to allow: This setting allows enhanced rich text by default, which lets you both format text (italics, bold, etc.) as well as include hyperlinks, pictures, or tables. You can, however, disable text formatting for this column by selecting the Plain text option.
> Append changes to existing text: This feature will store all changes to the field, and will display a list of those changes on the Edit or View fields. This can be great if you need to see past changes to this field, and functions sort of like versioning. However, this feature also stores blank changes, which means that it will consider every change to any field in the item as a change to this field, which can result in a lot "blanks" in the entry history. It also creates a "View Entries..." link on your list view instead of displaying the most recent entry in the field. The default option is No. You can change this at any time as long as versioning is enabled.

Choice (menu to choose from)

This column is good for single-level predefined values, including statuses, states, and conditions. Great for grouping. The additional fields to fill out are:

> Enforce unique values: This means that no two entries in this column may contain the same information. This option requires that you index its contents.

Type each choice on a separate line: This field specifies the actual choices available when creating a new entry. Each line indicates a separate choice, so press Enter to create a new line.

Display choices using: You have the option to display choices using a drop-down menu (a box that expands to display choices), radio buttons, or checkboxes. The default is Drop-Down menu, which is best if you have a long list of choices but only want people to choose one. Radio buttons are good for choosing one of a short list of choices. Checkboxes are the only option that allows you to select multiple choices.

Allow 'Fill-in' choices: This allows you to choose whether 'Fill-in' choices are enabled. Think of it like the 'write-in' line on a ballot, or 'Other' line in a survey. By clicking Yes, you allow the option to type in a new choice instead of selecting from the list you made above. The default is No, which is good if you prefer people only use the choices you specify.

Default value: This setting is used when new entries are created to automatically select a specific choice or display a calculated value. When someone creates a new entry, they can use the default value, or make another choice if they need to.

Number (1, 1.0, 100)

This column is good for numeric data, including counts and values. It's great when you need to sort data numerically. This column supports minimum and maximum values, as well as integers and floating point numbers. The additions fields to fill out are:

Enforce unique values: This means that no two entries in this column may contain the same information. This option requires that you index its contents.

You can specify a minimum and maximum allowed value: Use the Min: field to specify a minimum value allowed, and use the Max: field to specify a maximum value allowed. For example, if this column is to be used for percentages, you can specify the minimum to be 0, and the maximum to be 100.

Number of decimal places: This gives you an option to allow or restrict the number of decimal places for any numbers in this column. (Think of it as significant figures.) Automatic is the default, and will not restrict the number of decimal places in a number. However, you can choose to only allow whole numbers by choosing 0, or allow up to 5 decimal places.

Default value: This setting is used when new entries are created, to automatically set a value or allow people to input a different value if they need. For example, if this column is to contain a percent value for task progress, you could set the default value as 0, to indicate a new task. You can also choose to use a calculated value.

Show as percentage: Check this box if you wish to display the value of this column as a percentage.

Currency ($, ¥, €)

Used for currency values. Defaults the formatting to look good for your country's currency. The additional fields to fill out are:

Enforce unique values: This means that no two entries in this column may contain the same information. This option requires that you index its contents.

You can specify a minimum and maximum allowed value: Use the Min: field to specify a minimum value allowed, and use the Max: field to specify a maximum value allowed. For example, you could set the minimum at 0, which will only allow positive currency values such as profit, or set the maximum at 0 to indicate negative currency values such as expenses.

Number of decimal places: This gives you an option to allow or restrict the number of decimal places for any numbers in this column. (Think of it as significant figures.) Automatic is the default, and will not restrict the number of decimal places in a number. However, you can choose to only allow whole numbers by choosing 0, or more specific currency values by choosing 2. (You can choose to allow up to 5 decimal places.)

Default value: This setting is used when new entries are created to automatically set a value, or allow people to input a different value if they need. You can also choose to use a calculated value.

Currency format: Select which currency you wish to use, which will ensure all values in the column are based on the same currency. The drop-down box includes over 100 countries, so you can choose most local formats.

Date and Time

Good for date and time values, including values that are date only. The additional fields to fill out are:

Enforce unique values: This means that no two entries in this column may contain the same information. This option requires that you index its contents.

Date and Time Format: You can choose whether to include both the date and the time, or just the date.

Display format: This setting allows you to decide whether to use Standard or Friendly format. Standard is your basic date and time format. Friendly will display more friendly terms, such as "A few minutes ago", "Tomorrow", or "2 weeks ago". Friendly format is a user-friendly way to display when items were last modified, or when a task is coming due. Standard date format, on the other hand, is better when you need to be specific and consistent.

Default value: This setting is used when new entries are created to automatically set a date or calculated value, or allow people to set their own date if they need to. The default option for this setting is (None). However, you can choose "Today's Date", to automatically set the value to the date an item is created, or specify another date to be used.

Lookup (information already on this site)

Good for connecting this list to other data in SharePoint. This references the values in another list, or target list. When you view a list item's Lookup column, there will be a link that you can click to view that data. The additional fields to fill out are:

> Enforce unique values: **This means that no two entries in this column may contain the same information. This option requires that you index its contents.**
> Get information from: **Select the target list from which to get information. This can be a list, document library, or discussion board. You cannot select a subsite, wiki, or blog. (Essentially, you need to select an app that already has columns.)**
> In this column: **Select which column you will get information from within the target list. The drop-down box will only allow you to select appropriate columns in the target list. Check "Allow multiple values" to allow people who are editing or creating entries to select multiple values, which will be separated by semicolons within columns. If your lookup column is in a document library, you can also select "Allow unlimited length in document libraries" to remove the 255-character restriction in the lookup field. This can be handy if you allow multiple selections, but may cause issues with client Office products, which will still have issues with fields longer than 255 characters.**
> Add a column to show each of these additional fields: **This option will create new columns based on the additional fields you select. Again, these columns are based off of the target list. For example, if you select "Job Title" and "Company" as columns to add, then select Bob Jones in your lookup field, the new columns will display Bob Jones' job title, as well as the company Bob Jones works at.**
> Relationship: **A lookup column establishes a relationship between list items in this list and related items in the target list. When items in the target list are deleted, it can disrupt lookup columns. Selecting "Enforce relationship behavior" allows you to specify what behavior item deletion causes. "Restrict delete" will prevent deletion of an item in the target list if there are related items in this list. "Cascade delete" means, if an item in the target list is deleted, then all related items in this list will also be deleted.**

Yes/No (check box)

Good for checkboxes, true/false, and yes/no type data. The additional field to fill out is:

> Default Value: **The default value in this type of column is Yes – however, a person can choose No if they so choose.**

Person or Group

Good for assignment of the item to a person or group for management, or to indicate the last user to use the system. Will be validated to your network or optionally to a specific group of people. The additional fields to fill out are:

Enforce unique values: This means that no two entries in this column may contain the same information. This option requires that you index its contents.

Allow multiple selections: This options lets you choose whether people are allowed to select multiple values.

Allow selection of: This setting specifies whether you can select both People and Groups, or just People.

Choose from: Specify which groups of people can be chosen. By default, all users can be selected. However, you can restrict the selection to specific groups on your SharePoint site if you so desire.

Show field: Select from the drop-down menu how selected people or groups are displayed. You can choose just Name, Name with details, or various other options to display the selected person.

Hyperlink or Picture

A special field that includes both the hyperlink (location) and description for either a link or a picture. The additional field to fill out is:

Format URL as: This allows you to select whether to format the URL as a Hyperlink or as a Picture.

Calculated (calculation based on other columns)

The value is calculated from other columns and static information in the item. Calculated fields are great for transforming different fields. The additional fields to fill out are:

Formula: This box is where you type the formula for your calculation. To use the data from other columns, find the column you wish to use in the "Insert Column" box, then click the Add to formula link to add it to the formula.

The data type returned from this formula is: Specify what type of data will be displayed after the formula is run. By default, single line of text is selected. However, you can also select number, currency, date and time, or yes/no.

Task Outcome

A special choice field variant that allows the results of the field to be used as a part of a workflow. The additional fields to fill out are:

Enforce unique values: This means that no two entries in this column may contain the same information. This option requires that you index its contents.

Type each choice on a separate line: This field specifies what choices are displayed when a list item is created or edited.

Default value: This setting is used when a new item is created to automatically select a specific choice or display a calculated value. When someone creates a new entry, they can choose the default value, or select another value if they need to.

External Data

SharePoint has the ability to access data stored in other systems in your enterprise. If this has been set up, you can connect your list data to your master list. The additional fields to fill out are:

External Content Type: In this field, select the External Content Type Picker (list icon on the right) to select the appropriate item from the list of external content types.
Select the Field to be shown on this column: From the drop-down menu, select the field to display on this column. You can choose to display or not display the actions menu, or whether to link or not link this column to the Default Action of the External Content Type.
Add a column to show each of these additional fields: Select which fields in the external data to create additional columns for. If your list will rely heavily on the external data, you can also choose "Select All" to create columns for all fields.

Managed Metadata

A hierarchical collection. The additional fields to fill out are:

Enforce unique values: This means that no two entries in this column may contain the same information. This option requires that you index its contents.
Allow multiple values: Enabling this setting allows this column to have more than one value.
Display Value: You can decide whether to display the single value of the term, such as *City*, or the full hierarchical path to the term, such as *Location, Continent, Country/Region, City*.
Term Set Settings: This allows you to choose between a managed term set, or a custom term set. Enter one or more terms, separated by semicolons, and select Find (the binoculars icon) to filter the options to only include those which contain the desired values. After finding the term set that contains the list of values to display options for this column, click on a term to select the first level of the hierarchy to show in the column. All levels below the term you select will be seen when users choose a value.
Allow 'Fill-in choices: Enabling this option will allow users to add values to the term set. Only open term sets will allow fill-in choices. Choose No if you do not want users to add their own values.
Default value: This setting is used when a new item is created. Select a default value for this column from the term set that you have selected. People can choose the default value, or select another value if they need to.

Index

CPSIA information can be obtained
at www.ICGtesting.com
Printed in the USA
BVHW080818121118
532890BV00008B/333/P

9 780982 419823